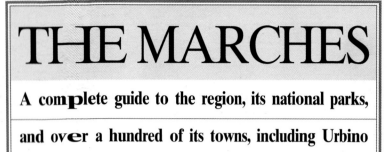

◆ The Heritage Guide ◆

THE MARCHES

A complete guide to the region, its national parks,

and over a hundred of its towns, including Urbino

Touring Club of Italy

Touring Club of Italy

President and Chairman: *Giancarlo Lunati*

Chief executive officer: *Armando Peres*

Managing Directors: *Marco Ausenda* and *Radames Trotta*

Editorial Director: *Michele D'Innella*

Managing Editor: *Anna Ferrari-Bravo*

Senior Editor: *Cinzia Rando*

General Consultant: *Gianni Bagioli*

Jacket Layout: *Federica Neeff*

Map Design: *Cartographic Division - Touring Club of Italy*

General Consultant: *Gianni Bagioli*

Contributors to the production of this guide:

Uomini e Terre s.r.l., *Marco Lissoni* and *Carlo Unnia* (chapters 2-8, inset p. 100); *Giorgio Mangani* (Regional Identity); *Fabio Mariano* (The cities and their art, chapter 1, intro. chapter 2, inset p. 58, Places of worship and pilgrimage); *Nazarena Croci* (The Marche: a visitor's guide, intro. chapter 8, insets pp. 145, 158, The Middle Ages on the coast); *Marta Paraventi* (intro. chapter 6, insets pp. 31, 36, 53, 79, 89, 92, 98, 108, 113, 129, 131, "Other places of interest" except for hotels and restaurants section); *Grazia Calegari* (intro. chapters 3-5, insets pp. 66, 102); *Giulio Angelucci* (intro. chapter 7, Fermo, inset p. 138, Non-religious sites and events).

Translators: *David Lowry* (pp. 2-118); *Andrew Ellis* (pp. 119-end)

Copyeditor: *Andrew Ellis*

Drawings: *Giorgio Pomella*

Plans of monuments: *Studio Pennati*

Route maps: *Graffito s.r.l.*

Layout: *Studio Tragni*

Production: *Giovanni Schiona, Vittorio Sironi*

Filmsetting: *Emmegi Multimedia - Milan*

Printing and binding: *G. Canale & C. - Borgaro Torinese (Turin)*

www.touringclub.it

© 1999 Touring Editore s.r.l. - Milan

Code L1K

ISBN 88-365-1467-7

Printed in July 1999

Foreword

The main appeal of the Marches region of Italy lies, for many people, in its enchanting landscape; others would say that its most distinguishing feature is its wealth of beautiful historic towns and cities. The two opinions do not contradict one another: part of what makes these towns so interesting and so beautiful is their setting amongst boundless rolling hills sloping gently down to the sea.

This harmonious blend of history, art and landscape was the inspiration for this guide, part of "The Heritage Guide" series.

The region is blessed with great natural beauty: the golden, translucent world of the Frasassi caves, the Sibillini mountains, the Conero and its Mediterranean scrubland, the beaches of Gabicce, Senigallia, Sirolo and San Benedetto del Tronto. It is no less rich in history, for this is the land of condottieri, of popes and of artists, famed for the "ideal city" of Urbino, the fortified towns of San Leo and Gradara, Rossini's Pesaro, the Sphaeristerium in Macerata, the historic squares in Ascoli Piceno and Fermo, and for the craft work done in Fabriano.

22 detailed itineraries, accompanied by 45 maps and plans and a selection full of practical information will help visitors appreciate the wealth of culture, art, crafts, food and scenery the area has to offer.

The Marches are, then, a highly varied and almost unlimited

The Ducal Palace, Urbino

storehouse of opportunities for the tourist: the region is in some ways one big "museum", and boasts a natural beauty that offers excellent seaside vacationing along its 180 km of coastline, plus winter sports and other outdoor pursuits in its rugged hills and mountains. To say nothing of its folklore, of its poetical, theatrical and musical traditions.

Contents

Introduction to the Marche
Historical and cultural outline of the region

Chapters and itineraries
Detailed profiles of the places to visit

1 Ancona and the Conero promontory

2 Around Ancona

3 Pesaro and its surroundings

4 Urbino and environs

Tourist information and indexes

Excursions in the Marche Region and Index of Maps and Plans

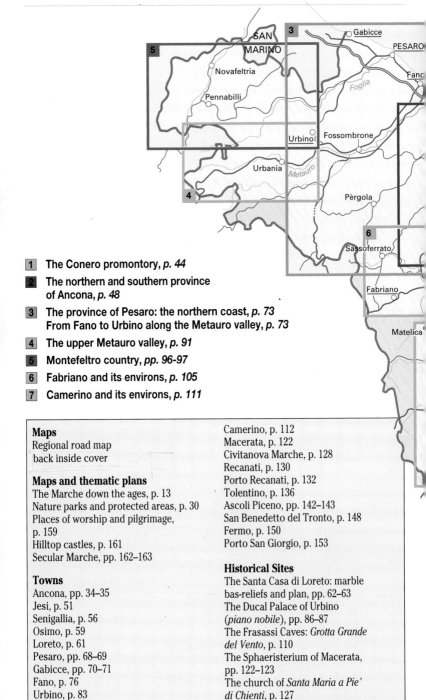

1. The Conero promontory, *p. 44*
2. The northern and southern province of Ancona, *p. 48*
3. The province of Pesaro: the northern coast, *p. 73*
   From Fano to Urbino along the Metauro valley, *p. 73*
4. The upper Metauro valley, *p. 91*
5. Montefeltro country, *pp. 96-97*
6. Fabriano and its environs, *p. 105*
7. Camerino and its environs, *p. 111*

The regional map below indicates the various areas, and the separate maps for each drive through the region.
The numbered list provides the heading of each driving tour, with its relative page number. The cities underlined in red have their own street map.

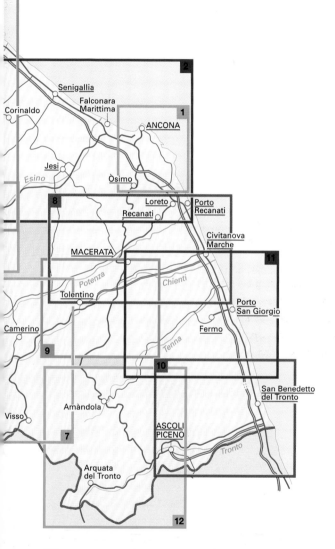

How to Use this Guidebook

Although this central Italian region is known in English as «The Marches», it is also referred to in this guidebook as «the Marche region», to familiarize visitors with its Italian name: Le Marche.

The color blue is used to indicate the most interesting monuments, museums, streets and squares in the city itineraries, and the places worth staying at in the out-of-town excursions.

The altitude (elevation) above sea level of the cities, towns and villages is given in meters, together with the most up-to-date population figures available (pop.).

An asterisk (*) denotes something of special interest; double asterisks (**) mean that the place described is of outstanding interest.

Towns and monuments not shown in blue but nevertheless of great touristic importance are given in **bold type**.

Other towns, monuments and artworks deserving attention are shown in *italics*.

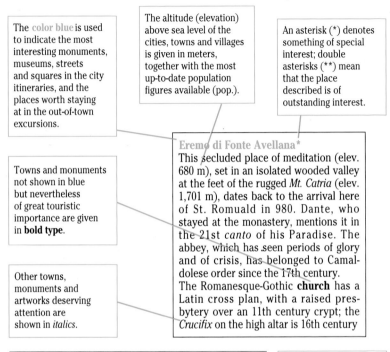

Eremo di Fonte Avellana*

This secluded place of meditation (elev. 680 m), set in an isolated wooded valley at the feet of the rugged *Mt. Catria* (elev. 1,701 m), dates back to the arrival here of St. Romuald in 980. Dante, who stayed at the monastery, mentions it in the 21st *canto* of his Paradise. The abbey, which has seen periods of glory and of crisis, has belonged to Camaldolese order since the 17th century.
The Romanesque-Gothic **church** has a Latin cross plan, with a raised presbytery over an 11th century crypt; the *Crucifix* on the high altar is 16th century

The street maps are divided up into grids with letters and numbers so that places can be located using the **coordinates** referred to in brackets in the descriptions. E.g. *San Pietro Martire* (A2), *Santa Maria inter Vineas* (A-B2)

In the case of particularly complex walking tours, the suggested route is shown in blue on the **street maps**.

If the monument is off the map the closest reference is given.

Monuments are **classified according to importance** in the following way:

 monuments of outstanding artistic interest

 monuments of great interest (black)

monuments of interest (dark brown)

 other buildings (light brown)

For a complete list of symbols used on the street maps see p. 10

6.2 Camerino and environs

The **maps** accompanying each excursion trace the suggested route in color, with places of interest along the way highlighted in **bold type**. The starting and finishing points are marked with a triangular and a square flag respectively (in some cases the two are combined). For a complete list of symbols used on these maps see p. 10.

The Church of Loreto

The **floor plans** of some of the more complex monuments are designed to facilitate the visit. Any reference letters or numbers are explained in the legend accompanying the plan or given in brackets in the description.

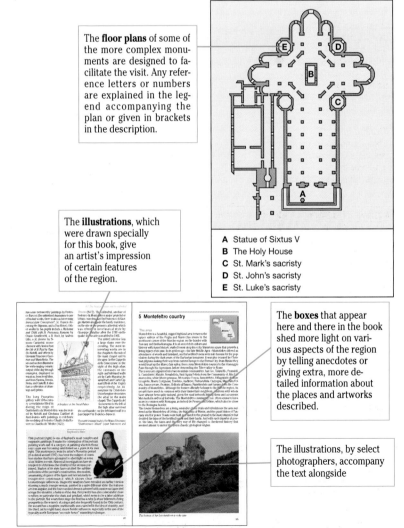

A Statue of Sixtus V
B The Holy House
C St. Mark's sacristy
D St. John's sacristy
E St. Luke's sacristy

The **illustrations**, which were drawn specially for this book, give an artist's impression of certain features of the region.

The **boxes** that appear here and there in the book shed more light on various aspects of the region by telling anecdotes or giving extra, more detailed information about the places and artworks described.

The illustrations, by select photographers, accompany the text alongside

How to use this guide

Information for Travelers

Hotels are listed with their official star ratings. **Restaurants** are rated according to quality using the traditional silverware symbols (on a scale of one to five).

There are brief descriptions of **other places of interest**, including tourist amenities, places of entertainment and recreation, local festivals, craft shops selling typical products found throughout the region, and useful phone numbers.

Visiting arrangements and opening times given for **museums** and **cultural institutions** are correct at the time of going to press, however some subsequent changes may have been made to hours or schedules.

Osimo

Page 58 ✉ 60027 ☎ 071

i *Ufficio Informazioni turistiche.* Piazza Boccolino, tel. 7249247, 7249282.

🏨🍴 Hotels, restaurants, and campsites

★★★ *La Fonte.* Via Fonte Magna 33, tel. 714767, fax 7133547. 36 rooms. Air conditioning (A2, **a**).

🍴 *Cantinetta del Conero.* At Osimo station. Tel. 7108651. Closed Sat; holidays vary. Air conditioning, parking. Marchigian cuisine, specialty fish.

☕ Cafés and pastry shops

Caffè del Corso. Piazza Gallo 2, tel. 714707. Also well-furnished wine cellar.

🏛 Museums and national monuments

Biblioteca comunale e Archivio storico comunale. Via Campana, tel. 714621.

☐ Visitors should be aware that museums, monuments and archaeological sites are usually closed on 1 January, at Easter, on 25 April, 1 May, the first Sunday in June, 15 August and 25 December. Note also that visiting hours for churches are not given unless they differ from the normal opening times (usually 8am–noon and 4pm–7 pm).

Key to symbols used in the maps and street plans

Main throughfare		Monuments of outstanding interest
Main road		Monuments of particular interest
Other roads		Other monuments to visit
Street with steps		Churches
Street under construction	△	Public offices
Pedestrian zone	☐ ●	Hotels & Restaurants listed
Railway and station	⚑ ⚐	Youth hostels / Campsites
Cableway, funicular, chair lift	✚	Public gardens / Hospitas

Key to symbols used in sightseeing tours

➡ Sightseeing tour		Urban area
Motorway		Parks and nature reserve
Motorway under construction		State border
Main road	🏛	Villas
Other roads	⌂ ⌂	Churches / Castles
ANCONA Main towns of the itinerary	∴	Ruins
○ **Genga** Nearby place	◖ ◗	Caves / Shelters
○ Pollenza Other place to visit	✈	Airport

Regional Identity

Geographical features

The Marche region, a rectangle measuring 9,693 km^2, or 3.2% of Italy's total surface area, lies between the Marecchia and Tronto rivers (its northern and southern borders) and to the east of the Apennine mountains, which form the backdrop to what is essentially a highland region (31% mountains and 69% hills). The Montefeltro, Mt. Catria, Mt. San Vicino, Mt. Pennino, and Mt. Sibillini chains running from north to south flatten out into the Apennine foothills, which in turn give rise to a system of parallel river valleys sloping eastward down to the Adriatic Sea. The narrow 180-km coastal plain is interrupted to the north of Pesaro by the San Bartolo hill and to the south of Ancona by the cliffs of Mt. Conero (572 m), features that modify an otherwise straight section of coast. IS-TAT figures for 1994 put the number of residents in the region at 1,441,031.

The landscape around the Sibillini

So much for the standard geography book and travel guide description of the Marche region. What, though, of its underlying character? It is hardly surprising that what was in many ways a scientifically legitimate attempt to define the individual character of a geographical area as a natural region was codified in the early 20th century by Ettore Ricci, an exponent of a "regionalist" movement that delved into the Marche's historical and cultural background to explain a unity which had been institutionalized just a few decades earlier when the region became part of the Kingdom of Italy. Positivism and evolutionism were at their height in those years (1870–1910), a period that witnessed one of the most decisive attempts to organize culture in a way that would give this former papal state a more distinct identity and impress upon it a sense of its own historical development. It is almost impossible to detect any such widespread, consciously felt need for regional identity before this time, at least among the ruling classes.

The Picenes and Romanization

Our knowledge of the ancient *Piceni*, or Picenes, is probably also influenced by late 19th–century study methods. The Picene population lived in villages scattered throughout the present-day Marche region (from Novilara near Pesaro to Ancona, Fabriano, Monte Roberto, Pitino near San Severino Marche, Tolentino, Belmonte, Piceno and Ripatransone), and in part of neighboring Abruzzo. They buried their dead, used war chariots, spoke a language that shows similarities with the Indo-European linguistic family, and had links with the Etruscans (7th–6th century BC) and the ancient Greeks (from the mid-6th century BC) through the mediation of Numana. Their name, which later gave rise to *Picenum* (the area south of Ancona), may derive from *picus*, or woodpecker, a totemic bird sacred to Mars. The etymology of the word has, however, also been associated with amber (*pix, picis*) often found in

11

Piceno tombs, and even to the Illyrian word *pik*, suggesting that this people originally came from across the Adriatic. In the 4th century BC relations with the Greek world intensified with the foundation of the Siracusan colony of Ancona, while the invasion of the Senonian Gauls further north probably altered the anthropological make-up of the area and brought about a major cultural disruption. The creation of a dividing line at Senigallia (*Sena Gallica*) split the region into an area of Gallic tradition to the north and a Picene area to the south, a division that can still be seen in the linguistic differences. When the Picene confederation formed an alliance with Rome in 299 BC, the original Picene people had probably intermingled with the Gauls to the north and with other Italic peoples in the center and south such as the Sabines, who may have reproduced the Etruscan model of city federation. Scholars have more recently used the term *picentes* to refer to these peoples. The insurrection against Rome in 269 BC was unsuccessful but resulted in the transfer of a section of the *picentes* population to an area of the Gulf of Salerno later called *Ager picentinus* and in a mingling of Roman colonizers with local populations in the newly established cities (*Castrum Novum* and *Firmum* in 264 BC, *Pisaurum* and *Potentia* in 184 BC and *Auximum* in 157 BC).

The Trajan Arch in Ancona

This marked the beginning of relations between the region and Rome which lasted for several centuries.

An almost ungovernable region

Christianity reached the region mostly through the port of Ancona. The area north of the city, along the coast in particular, came under the Byzantine influence of the maritime Pentapolis (the five cities of Rimini, Pesaro, Fano, Senigallia and Ancona), before it was given by Pepin the Short and Charlemagne to the popes; Longobard domination persisted in the south.

The complex developments of the period up to the 13th century eventually brought greater stability. A number of towns came under the control of imperial representatives while others fought for their municipal independence. Ancona fought off Frederick I Barbarossa in 1167 and Christian of Mainz in 1173; in 1155 Urbino passed from Barbarossa to Montefeltro control. Meanwhile, the smaller towns began to extend their territories at the expense of their neighbors.

In the 13th–15th centuries a number of families increased their influence as they strove to govern and to subjugate – though not always with lasting success – a substantial part of Marca, as the region was known from the 10th century under the Ottonian imperial dynasty (after the German term *Mark*, meaning a border area). The Malatesta family, from Rimini and Pesaro, reached the height of their power in the years up to 1445 and also governed Ancona briefly (1348–55). The Montefeltro ruled in Urbino from the 12th century to around 1508, when the Della Rovere took control, annexing Pesaro in 1512. Alessandro Sforza, governor of the *Marca d'Ancona* in 1434, established a period of rule in 1445 that lasted until 1500 and kept the territories of Pesaro and Ancona united until about the mid-15th century, when the latter became independent under the direct protection of the pope. In Camerino Gentile da Varano (a public magistrate in 1262) founded a seignory that survived until 1540, apart from a brief interlude (1502–03) in which Cesare Borgia took control.

This failure to construct an autonomous state in an area dominated by seigniorial rule and tyranny, and the struggle for municipal autonomy by the small towns (the root cause of the ungovernable image the region gave of itself, the *Infidelitas*

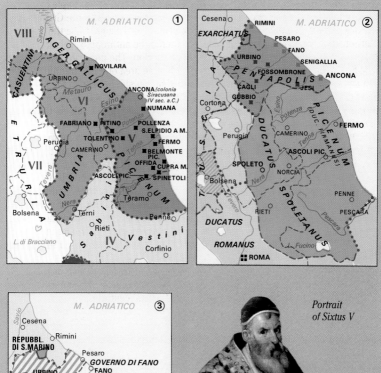

Map 1 — ANTIQUITY

M. ADRIATICO ①

VIII
AGER GALLICUS
Savio
Rimini
CASUENTINI
NOVILARA
URBINO
Metauro
ANCONA *(colonia Siracusana / IV sec. a.C.)*
VI
Esino
NUMANA
E
T
R
U
R
I
A
FABRIANO   FITINO   Potenza   POLLENZA
S.ELPIDIO A M.
TOLENTINO
UMBRIA   V   FERMO
CAMERINO
BELMONTE PIC.
Tevere   VII   OFFIDA   CUPRA M.
ASCOLI PIC.   SPINETOLI
PICENUM
Perugia   Nera   Teramo
Bolsena   Terni
L. di Bracciano   Sabini   Penne
IV   Vestini
Rieti   Corfinio

Map 2 — EARLY MIDDLE AGES

Cesena   RIMINI   M. ADRIATICO ②
EXARCHATUS   PESARO
FANO
URBINO   SENIGALLIA
FOSSOMBRONE   ANCONA
PENTAPOLIS
CAGLI   JESI
Cortona   GUBBIO
DUCATUS   PICENUM   FERMO
Perugia   CAMERINO   (DUC. FIRMANUS)
ASCOLI PIC.
SPOLETO   NORCIA
Bolsena   SPOLETANUS   PENNE
RIETI   PESCARA
DUCATUS
ROMANUS   Fucino
ROMA

Map 3 — THE SITUATION IN 1521

M. ADRIATICO ③
Cesena
Rimini
REPUBBL. DI S.MARINO
Pesaro
GOVERNO DI FANO
URBINO   FANO
DUCATO DI   DUCATO (PICCOLOMINI)
MONTEMARCIANO
DUCATO DI URBINO   Ancona
(DELLA ROVERE)
Gubbio   GOVERNO
Potenza
MATELICA   MACERATA
GOVERNO GENERALE
SIGNORIA
(OTTONI)   CAMERINO   DUCATO   D. MARCA
(VARANO)   Ascoli Piceno
Spoleto
Terni   Teramo

Map 4 — THE NAPOLEONIC ERA (1808-15)

REP. DI S.MARINO   PESARO   ④
URBINO   M ADRIATICO
SENIGALLIA
Metauro   ANCONA
DIPARTIM. D. METAURO   JESI
Musone
Gubbio   FABRIANO   MACERATA
DIPARTIM. D. MUSONE   TOLENTINO
PERUGIA   FERMO
CAMERINO   DIPARTIMENTO DEL TRONTO
Tevere   ASCOLI PICENO
SPOLETO   TERAMO

Portrait of Sixtus V

THE MARCHE

① **ANTIQUITY**

■ Finds from the Picene era

Roman regions in the age of Augustus

② **EARLY MIDDLE AGES**

Bizantine territories

Maritime and "Annonaria" Pentapolises

Longobard territories

③ **THE SITUATION IN 1521**

Territories directly under papal power

Territories under mediated papal power

④ **THE NAPOLEONIC ERA (1808-15)**

13

Marchianorum lamented by the papal administration, which claimed it as its own) prompted the popes to impose a more stable form of government. This became apparent in the *Constitutiones Aegidianae* set up in 1356 by Cardinal Egidio Albornoz, which divided the territory into 75 cities and regions (*maiores, magnae, mediocres, parvae* and *minores*) and into dozens of *castra*. This system subdivided the states and cities into *immediate subiecti* and those which were subjected but through the mediation of the local sovereign, who ruled on the basis of an accord with Rome. The *signori* (the Montefeltro, Della Rovere, Da Varano etc.) held onto their possessions and administered them on behalf of a central authority.

The new administrative arrangement in the 16th century was therefore based on the authority of the governor of the Marca di Ancona in Macerata, who administered justice and nominated the local authorities. Clearly, the vicariate system did not admit of strong central influence and legitimized the widespread power of local dynasties, whose formal feudal role was recognized. But papal influence was anything but evenly spread. To avoid coming under the yoke of nearby cities, some territories requested direct relations with the pope. Such were the cases of the Fano enclave, which at the moment of its submission was granted an autonomous prelate governor, and of the State of Urbino, which, following devolution to the pope in 1631 (upon the death of Francesco Maria II Della Rovere), continued to be administered by a cardinal president, resident in Pesaro. Although the Gallery of Maps in the Vatican Palace in Rome (painted in 1580–83 to celebrate the power of the pope and his Guelph ambitions for Italy) depicts *Picenum, Anconitanus Ager* and *Urbini Ducatus* as places of great Christian stability, pontifical rule over the region was, even during its most influential period, anything but solid, achieving only a limited measure of unity. The former Marca of Ancona was in fact variously subdivided into the State of Urbino, the Governments of Macerata, Ancona, Jesi, Fabriano, San Severino and Loreto, the State of Ascoli, the Government of Matelica and the Department of Montalto. Some 80% of the municipalities in the region were self-governing – the highest proportion in any church state. The absence of a strong economic focus prevented the formation of a true regional capital. The local communities invested what were very modest resources in developing the small towns around which social life revolved. The predominance of farming in the local economy, the unmarketable nature of its produce and the low concentration of capital shifted attention to the purely administrative functions and feudal privilege in the development of the towns in the area.

Federico da Montefeltro and his son Guidobaldo, by Pedro Berruguete

The brief Napoleonic interlude radically altered the region's institutions and legal system. Practical considerations and communication requirements dictated the way the departments were organized; the small local state communities ceased to exist and the once hereditary administrative posts became elective – albeit by a limited suffrage; and the municipalities were brought under strict centralized control. Under the Roman Republic (1798–99) the Department of Metauro brought together the areas of Urbino and Fano and much of the Ancona area (although in 1798 Pesaro became part of the Cisalpine Republic); the Department of Musone (chief town: Macerata) comprised Fabriano,

San Severino Marche, Loreto, Matelica and Civitanova Marche; the Department of Tronto (chief town: Fermo) covered Ascoli Piceno and Camerino, which in 1808 became part of the Musone Department.

The church kept very much to the French system when it regained power after 1816, and the Marche region (first referred to as such in the final protocol of the Congress of Vienna) was divided into four delegations (Ancona, Macerata with Camerino, Urbino and Pesaro, Fermo, and Ascoli Piceno). This gave rise to a provincial hierarchy that was later ratified with the Unification of Italy, which also sanctioned the transfer of Gubbio and its surrounding area to neighboring Umbria.

The city of Fermo in the Marca d'Ancona under the Church State

Building a material and mental identity: tenant farming

The year 1000 saw a reversal in the region's fortunes. Farming returned, and the land was once again tended and tilled, thanks in no small measure to the efforts of the monastic settlements that grew up between the Foglia and Tronto rivers. The proximity of the monasteries – each one a day's walk from the next – made for greater internal mobility. Between the 13th and 15th centuries a host of farming settlements sprang up in the region, their tenant farmers cultivating the land owned by their landlords under the system known as *mezzadria*. This agricultural formula created today's beautiful Marche landscape , one which has been profoundly influenced by the many farmhouses dotting the countryside and by its hill towns (the "hundred walled cities"). It also explains many of the deep-rooted local cultural characteristics: a review of farming practices carried out as recently as the mid-19th century found that three fifths of the population were involved in agricultural activities, and that a total of 83,159 farming families lived in the area. According to the Jacini agrarian survey following the Unification of Italy, each farm owned an average of eight hectares of arable land.

Tenant farming encouraged intensive crop production with often excessive exploitation of the soil. Farmers, who jealously guarded the land they tilled, were in turn kept under close scrutiny by the landlords, who often lived in small nearby towns with revenues from farming activities that seldom allowed them to live in the lap of luxury. Tenant farming heavily influenced the life of the farmers, who worked full time on their farms with their families in an arrangement of mutual assistance that kept any potential social conflicts at bay. And this agricultural system accustomed the ruling classes to earning an income, however modest, which dispensed with the need for huge amounts of capital, though also dampened down any spirit of innovation and enterprise. Rather, it encouraged small-scale social relations within the city walls (local government positions, marriage strategies, theater, religious functions). Both were the result of the order and social organization that prevailed under the papal state, which discouraged trade and industry because of the lack of adequate legislation, and reserved too many state and political careers for the clergy.

The absence of any substantial opportunities to trade the region's farming produce (only in the 18th century did the development of the free port of Ancona open up a significant channel of trade) and an underdeveloped network of major roads did nothing to help generate wealth. As a result, social, economic and cultural life in the region in the 17th and 18th centuries remained largely self-sufficient. Not that it was totally isolated from the outside world, since books did arrive, mainly from Venice. The academies that opened in the 1700s introduced new illuminated ideas, although these did little more than "graze the surface." In the middle of the century, when

15

Genius loci

It could be said that for all his individualistic, stateless sensibility, the poet Giacomo Leopardi (right) left his own special stamp on the Marche landscape. The "wild native town" he both hated and loved, the metaphysical aura in which he shrouded the "solitary hill" in his poem "L'Infinito" that one can dream of losing oneself in, and the poet's own impassioned philosophy gave late 19th-century scholars and literary critics – in their efforts to find an objective explanation for genius through positivist and the theories of the Italian psychiatrist and critic C. Lombroso – an opportunity to discover a profound, almost genetic kinship between the land, nature and climate of the Marche region and the young Recanati-born poet's verse. In the mid-19th century, Recanati and its countryside suddenly found itself on the literary map and soon became one of poetry's "hallowed shrines," as Leopardi's mournful verse began to echo over a land that was in some ways its very inspiration. The land that had spawned Leopardi's metaphysical aspirations was now itself a place of the spirit, visited with almost religious zeal by Giovanni Pascoli, Vincenzo Cardarelli, Alfredo Panzini, Luigi Bartolini, and Paolo Volponi (all of whom had been forced to emigrate to pursue their profession). Through their art and literature they in turn created the legend of a region suffused with an introspective, metaphysical nostalgia tinged with melancholy.

Today's visitors, too, will find it difficult to detach themselves from this sentiment as they roam the Recanati area and gaze down from its ancient palaces onto the cultivated hills that slope gently down to the sea, taking in a landscape which, with the monuments of its towns and cities, form one of Italy's main "literary parks."

economic development was at its height, some resources were channeled into urban redevelopment, with the restoration of palaces and churches (popularizing the typical neoclassical brick style) and of many farmhouses.

It is easy to see how this framework of extreme individualism (albeit one based around the family) and conservative adherence to tradition led to the establishment of ideologies which, in the early 1800s, celebrated the natural hard-working nature of the Marche people, creating an ethos that soon became codified anthropologically into the kind of "social docility" extolled by the pro-Piedmontese ruling class and later by Fascist-Agrarian culture. The compiler of the regional study for the Jacini Survey defines the prevalent condition of farmers as *aurea mediocritas*, a state of relative poverty but not penury that permitted a relatively good standard of living. The socialists and radicals tried to capitalize on the rebellious tendencies of the Italic and Umbro-Sabellic populations, taking advantage of pro-papal insurgence during the Napoleonic repression and frequent failure to report for military service. But the hard-working Marche character, like the gentle rolling hills romanticized in Leopardi's poetry, gained the upper hand and became even more marked during the Fascist period, with the glorification of rural life and provincial culture that came with the *Strapaese* movement.

Modernization halved?

Industrial development in recent decades – which while having much in common with industrialization elsewhere in northern Italy also had characteristics peculiar to itself, as studies by contemporary economists confirm – has led historians tracing the economic development of the Marche region to ascertain industrial activities as early as the 18th century in today's principal areas of specialized industry (furniture in the Pesaro area, mechanical engineering in Jesi and Fabriano, shoes and leather items in the Fermo and Tolentino areas, musical instruments, and – since the 1980s – electronics near Castelfidardo, to name but a few).

Generally speaking, postwar industrial development has reinforced the region's osmotic relationship with agriculture. Confirmation of this comes from the traditional mechanical versatility of the tenant farmer, well used to carrying out a whole range of farming duties, from the widespread presence of mills converted for energy production, and from the capital generated from farming revenues. The pioneers of enterprise in the late 19th and early 20th centuries were aristocrats (such as Count Aurelio Balleani of Jesi, or Francesco Luigi Merli of Ascoli Piceno), petty traders (Silvio Meletti of Ascoli Piceno), technical experts (like Adriano Cecchetti of Civitanova Marche, Giuseppe and Giovanni Benelli of Pesaro), and artisans (Nazareno Gabrielli in Tolentino), but they needed landed property to gain access to credit. After World War II this process affected a much broader section of the Marche population, who used the profits they had accumulated in their family-based economies to start up small-scale craft or industrial enterprises.

Tenant farming in Marche has been likened by Max Weber to the role played by the Protestant Reformation in the development of capitalism in Northern Europe and the Anglo-Saxon world. The strong family ties that came with the tenant farming system permeated economic relations and brought about a selection of functions in the process of modernization, allowing the development only of those aspects that were compatible with the existing social fabric (hence the idea of a modernization halved). The family ethic engendered great social cohesion and a spirit of solidarity, taking the place of the all-too-absent state and defusing potential social conflict. At the same time, however, it led to a certain degree of political immobility favoring economic growth to the detriment of the develop-ment of the region as a whole, which lacks many of the services one would expect to find in such a heavily industrialized area. In 1951 over 40% of the population still lived in scattered dwellings (one of the highest per-centages in Italy), where-as by the 1960s and 1970s most had moved to the coast and the valleys that cut across the region like

Castelfidardo: making piano accordions

the teeth of a comb – the areas, that is, that were best served by recent communica-tion links. Traditional emigration patterns have given way in recent years to an infra-regional mobility, which has profoundly transformed the region: populations are dwindling rapidly, for example, in the mountain areas. Little has been done in the way of improving infrastructures to stop this from happening, by the creation, say, of high-speed road links connecting the valleys with each other, with Rome, and with western central Italy. The Marche economy now finds itself in a new phase of inter-national competition that makes the size of businesses and the quality of public ser-vices more important than ever. Idelly, it should preserve the specific characteris-tics and the wealth of its polycentric history, at the same time guaranteeing the effi-ciency and effectiveness demanded by the globalization of the markets and the more sophisticated civil and cultural demands of its citizens. The descendants of Italy's most highly-respected tenant farmers will undoubtedly find ways of solving these problems, but the success of their undertaking will also depend on their ability to prevent any further disruption to the cultural and environmental equilibrium of the Marche system.

The cities and their art

The region boasts 234 museums, over 200 Romanesque churches, 163 shrines in the 14 dioceses, over 70 historic theaters, 7 parks and 24 archaeological sites, at least 1,000 major monuments, countless artworks and about 100 culturally significant cities. And yet there are still those who will quip: "The Marche region's good fortune lies in the fact that it appears not to exist, that is, it does not appear at all."

How true this is. The region's largely unknown cultural heritage is seldom given the attention it deserves, even though its treasures are among the most complete in Italy, exemplifying with no perceptible interruptions most of the country's historical periods and styles. Not that its finest treasures are all "home grown" – quite the reverse is in fact true. At various periods in its history hundreds of outstanding painters, sculptors and architects – from neighboring regions or from much further afield – have converged on the region, which geographically and politically has always been a place of transit. Even those who did not establish local schools as such planted a fertile seed in those who would become their often worthy imitators. If there is no art or architecture that can be defined as *marchigiana*, it is because the Marche cannot be said to exist as a single historical and social unit, being more accurately described as a set of polycentric local, provincial and in some cases municipal cultures. For this reason it is more apt to speak of art *in* the Marche than art *of* the Marche.

Origins

The first timid signs of civilization date back to the Lower Paleolithic period (stone tools on Mt. Conero, 20–29,000 BC) with more substantial finds of huts from the Neolithic Age (6,000 BC). From the Iron Age there is more extensive documentation of Italic necropolises (over seventy have been found) with lavish offerings associated with burial (Piceno culture) and cremation (proto-Villanovan culture). The Picenes (7th–3rd cent. BC) of mythological Sabine origin left few settlements but lavish burial grounds between the Foglia and Tenna rivers (at Novilara, Numana, Fabriano, Pitino, Belmonte Piceno).

Head of a Picene warrior found at Numana

From the early 4th century BC, the Senonian Gauls settled to the north of the Esino river (splendid gold offerings in Celtic and southern style have been found near Arcevia and Filottrano) and Syracusan exiles colonized Ancona, which became a flourishing trading port (Attic and Lucan ceramics, Apulian vases etc.) and later a manufacturing center (upper Adriatic red and black ceramics).

Roman civilization

Colonization began in 295 BC after the victory of *Sentinum* over the Senonian Gauls, with the foundation of the first Roman settlement (*Sena Gallica*). The arrival of the Romans marked the start of a major process of regional reorganization that saw the founding (or refounding) of many important towns, whose basic *cardo-decumanus* layout survives to this day. From 220 BC an efficient road network opened the region up to development. In particular the *Via Flaminia* and *Via Salaria* and their various offshoots featured some superb feats of Roman engineering (the Furlo tunnel at Acqualagna, Ponte Mallio in Cagli, Ponte Grosso in Cantiano, and city bridges in Ascoli Piceno). Some impressive remains of city walls can be seen in Fano, Osimo, and Ascoli Piceno; the best preserved monumental arches and city gateways are the triumphal *Arco di Traiano* in Ancona, the *Arco d'Augusto* in Fano and the biforate *Porta Gemina* in Ascoli Piceno. The remains of some theaters are clearly visible (*Falerio, Helvia Ricina, Pitinum*, Ascoli Piceno) and also of some amphitheaters (Ancona, *Urbs Salvia, Suasa*). However, little remains of the sacred buildings of the age, the best-preserved being in Ascoli Piceno, in what are now the churches of *San Gregorio* and *San Venanzo* (tetrastyle temples). The most notable surviving work of sculpture is the bronze Cartoceto group (from the Julian-Claudian period), the gable terracottas in Civitalba and Monte Rinaldo (early 2nd cent.), the late ancient and early Christian tombs in Tolentino, Sant'Elpidio a Mare, Fermo, and Osimo. Frescoes are rare (Ancona), but figurative and geometric mosaics are found in Ancona and Matelica. When work currently being carried out to uncover the early Christian floor (ca. 6th cent.) in Pesaro Cathedral is complete, the result will doubtless be spectacular.

The early Middle Ages

The gradual unification of the region – begun by Augustus in the 5th Reign, redefined by Diocletian, and consolidated during the exarchate rule of Ravenna in the two Pentapolises – was put under severe strain by the cruel invasions of the Goths and Longobards (testified to by an interesting necropolis in Castel Trosino), but gathered steam once again with the gift to the pope of the Pentapolitan territories to the north, which was ratified by Pepin the Short (752) and renewed by Charlemagne (774). The valleys were gradually abandoned and new settlements grew up on higher, safer ground, creating the region's typical polycentric network of hill towns. One rare vestige of the late medieval period is the Carolingian ciborium in the church in San Leo (882).

From the Romanesque to the Late Gothic

From the 10th century onward the network of monasteries became more firmly established as existing 6th-century Benedictine settlements were restored and more and more new abbeys and monasteries were built between the Foglia and Tronto rivers. The monks tilled the land and economic and artistic life began to flourish.

The region's greatest architectural legacy is in the solemnly ponderous Romanesque style of architecture (11th–13th centuries), with some of the best works to be found in the whole of Italy. Influences are chiefly Lombard (arched corbel tables, buttresses etc.) although there are also plenty of Byzantine and Ravenna influences, especially the "quincunx" Greek cross plan (*San Vittore alle Chiuse* in Genga, *Santa Croce* in Sassoferrato, the two-story church of *San Claudio al Chienti*, and part of the church of *Santa Maria di Portonovo*). Other important examples of the style are *San Ciriaco* in Ancona, the church and cathedral in San Leo, *San Marco* at Ponzano di Fermo, *San Vincenzo al Furlo* near Acqualagna, *San Lorenzo in Doliolo* at San Severino Marche, and also *Santa Maria Intervineas* and the octagonal baptistery of *San Giovanni* in Ascoli Piceno, and *San Giusto* at San Maroto di Pievebovigliana, an extremely interesting example of a circular plan with spherical calotte. The radiating apse in the church of *Santa Maria a Piè di Chienti*, in Montecosaro, probably a stopping place on the pilgrim route to Jerusalem, is unique in the region and extremely rare for central Italy as a whole. Among the region's best-

The hermitage of Fonte Avellana in the heart of the Apennines near Pesaro

The Adriatic Gothic

Poised between the "romantically" decorative sensibility of the late Gothic age and the dawning of the humanist, classicist vision of the Renaissance, this style took on a significance of its own in the Marche region, in particular in sculpture and architecture. It was influenced by the self-sufficient, "conservative" Venetian culture, spreading from Venice down both sides of the Adriatic through Dalmatia and the Marche, where the best examples are to be found. This little-known phenomenon – part of a figurative tradition that was not so much a belated movement as a reflection of the customs of the stone-cutting corporations working on the Gothic cathedrals – testifies to the persistence of a particular taste among patrons (especially the religious orders) and was supported by the trading links that had been developing between the two shores of the Adriatic for centuries. Fancifully ornate, naturalistic decoration mingles smoothly with the innovation of the classicist canons of construction, creating an independent style that endured until the last quarter of the 15th century, forging what deserves to be described as a "transitional" style.

preserved Romanesque facades are that of *Santa Maria della Piazza* in Ancona (Apulian style, adorned with Byzantine sculptures) and the church in Ascoli Piceno of *SS. Vincenzo e Anastasio* (in the flat-topped Abruzzi style popular until the 16th century). The Benedictine and Cistercian monasteries that flourished between the 13th and 14th centuries of Fonte Avellana, the abbey of *Santa Maria* at Chiaravalle di Fiastra and *Santa Maria in Castagnola* at Chiaravalle are worth a visit; no less interesting are those of the mendicant orders, including two Franciscan complexes in Fermo and Ascoli Piceno (the latter with a large double cloister) and the Augustinian complex in Tolentino. Civil architecture did not develop so extensively in medieval Marche, with the exception of a number of turreted municipal palaces (Fano, Montelupone, Montecassiano etc.) and, more conspicuously, the impressive Palazzo degli Anziani and the facade of the Palazzo del Senato in Ancona, Palazzo del Podestà in Ripatransone and Palazzo Comunale in Fabriano with its characteristic ogival arch over the street. One of the finest civil buildings in Ascoli Piceno is the 13th-century Palazzetto Longobardo. Meanwhile military architecture, a major feature in such a tumultuous age, took the form of countless isolated look-out towers, both in the fortresses (Porto San Giorgio, Priora in Falconara Marittima, Albornoz in Sassoferrato, and Da Varano in Sfercia di Camerino) and the *grancie*, or castle farms of Rancia in Tolentino and of Monte Varmine in Carassai.

The figurative arts in the Middle Ages largely complemented the architecture. In the primitive crypts under the presbyteries – which were raised to a particularly high level in the Marche – rare examples of Romanesque sculpture are found particularly in the capitals (*San Pietro* on Mt. Conero, *Santa Maria di Rambona* in Pollenza), but also in the crossings of the naves (Osimo Cathedral) and in the delicate plutei in San Ciriaco, Ancona and on the pulpit in Fano Cathedral. Major examples of pictorial art from the 13th century are to be found in the church of *San Vittore* in Ascoli Piceno and of *Sant'Agostino* in Fabriano (of Abruzzo and Umbrian influence), and from the following century masterpieces from the Giotto school include the fresco cycles in the churches of *San Nicola* in Tolentino, *San Marco* in Jesi, and *San Francesco* in San Ginesio, and the works of Allegretto Nuzi and the Maestro di Offida in various locations.

The courtly or International Gothic period (14th–15th cent.) glows with the serene humanity of Gentile da Fabriano, whose works have now alas been scattered outside the region, but also with the feverish activity – a heritage Marche has not lost – of the schools of Camerino (Carlo da Camerino and Arcangelo di Cola) and San Severino Marche (Lorenzo e Jacopo Salimbeni, especially the oratory of *San Giovanni Battista* in Urbino). Gentile da Fabriano's pupils Antonio Alberti and the Venetian Jacobello del Fiore also made important contributions to the period. The late Gothic period in Marche lasted well into the 15th century, with the expressionist works of Carlo Crivelli and the Vivarini brothers, late exponents of an Adriatic medieval period on the wane. The style found expression in the work of the Venetian-Dalmatian masters, whose refined sculptural sensibility – seen particularly well in the work of Giorgio da Sebenico (or Giorgio Orsini) in Ancona – produced masterpieces of ornamental marble work: the churches of *Sant'Agostino* and *San Francesco delle Scale*, and the Loggia dei Mercanti. One isolated example of the Tuscan version of "flamboyant" Gothic is Nanni di Bartolo's fine portal (1432) for the church of *San Nicola* in Tolentino.

The Renaissance

The burgeoning of Humanism ushered in a period of splendor in the Marche region, a golden age that also saw the establishment of new seigniories that were keen to be directly involved in the new cultural climate: the Montefeltro in Urbino, the Malatesta in Fano, the Sforza in Pesaro, the Da Varano in Camerino, the Della Rovere in Senigallia to name but a few. The focal points were the courts of Mantua and Milan, but Tuscany was the main source of skilled, "progressive" artists.

Federico da Montefeltro, who was as much a military leader as a cultured patron of the arts, is one of the symbols of the Italian Renaissance.

The Duke's Palace in Urbino – that paradigm of Marche art and architecture – was the self-portrait of his grandeur as a just, pious and liberal prince. It was an image he carefully cultivated (to the point of creating a distinct "Urbino" style) through the selected work of 15th-century Italy's finest artists and architects: Luciano Laurana, Paolo Uccello, Piero della Francesca, Francesco di Giorgio Martini. But he also drew on the talents of highly-refined imitators of the late Gothic, such as painters Pedro Berruguete and Joos van Gent, and numerous decorative stonemasons from the Po Valley, who framed the doors and windows of the "palace that seemed more like a city" (as Baldassare Castiglione termed it), or *non domus sed urbs* as this landmark edifice was described from its earliest days. It was inspired by the leading Renaissance humanist Leon Battista Alberti, and the emblematic model of that ideal city which Piero della Francesca also wished to depict. Francesco di Giorgio Martini went on working for the court after the death of Federico. He was the main adviser in the military reorganization of the duchy, and displayed his engineering skills in the numerous fortifications which had had to be hastily adapted to withstand the new, fearsome power of firearms: for the first time this architecture was considered as an art form

Madonna and Child, one of the works by Carlo Crivelli in the Marche region

in its own right. The fortresses of Sassocorvaro, Cagli, Fossombrone and San Leo – and more notably Mondavio, which survives intact – are major masterpieces of the genre, and made their Malatesta predecessors (Fano, Gradara etc.) look woefully out of date. Palazzo della Signoria in Jesi and the Palazzo del Governo in Ancona are other surviving masterpieces of civil engineering by Martini; military works were continued by his pupil Baccio Pontelli, who produced a wide range of masterpieces: fortresses at Acquaviva Picena, Offida, Senigallia, Jesi and Osimo (the latter two were demolished); civil architecture (Palazzo Bonafede in Monte San Giusto, Palazzo Ducale in Camerino) and

*Madonna and Child in the facade
of the Holy Shrine in Loreto*

religious buildings (the church of *Santa Maria Nuova* in Orciano di Pesaro, and the convent of *Santa Maria delle Grazie* in Senigallia). Pesaro from the time of the Sforza boasts a *loggiato* of mathematical proportions in its Palazzo Ducale and the fortified Rocca Costanza.

When Federico's line died out, Urbino sank into a long period of decline. Bramante and Raphael, lured by the attractions of Rome, were gone, and the city was bereft of its brightest stars. The influence of Bramante lives on in the Palazzo Apostolico in Loreto, part of which, however, was the work of Antonio da Sangallo the Younger. The "never-ending construction site" of Loreto was indeed the other main focus of attention during the Marche Renaissance: a dazzling array of artists, including Sansovino, Luca Signorelli, and Lorenzo Lotto, all worked on the Shrine of the Holy Virgin. Jesi relived the artistic legacy of Francesco di Giorgio Martini in the portals of its noble palaces by acquiring masterpieces of pictorial art from the discomfiting brush of Lorenzo Lotto.

Recanati did likewise, adding to its heritage of works by Giuliano da Maiano.

Ascoli Piceno witnessed a period of intense architectural activity from the early 16th century on. Mostly local stone was used for construction work on the Palazzo dei Capitani, the Loggia and the splendid arcaded square. The town of Fermo was embellished with the two Rosati palaces by Antonio da Sangallo the Younger; Cristoforo Resse di Simone built the new walls in Macerata and Giuliano da Maiano the Loggia dei Mercanti.

Mannerism

Urbino and Pesaro flourished again with the rapid spread of Capitoline classicism, most dazzlingly through the refined hand of brilliant architect and painter Girolamo Genga: his works include the splendid *Imperiale* villa in Pesaro, a masterpiece of out-of-town leisure architecture. The Roman classicist influence established itself firmly with the paintings in Ancona of Pellegrino Tibaldi (who also designed Palazzo Ferretti, a cornerstone of regional architecture) and the Zuccari brothers and those by Pomarancio in Loreto and Jesi, before giving way to the troubled personalities of Andrea Lilli and Andrea Boscoli. But the influence of Venice was as strong as ever, not only through Lorenzo Lotto and his local followers (Ercole Ramazzani, Durante Nobili and the De Magistris), but also in the works Titian was commissioned to paint in Urbino, Ascoli, and Ancona. The minor art forms found original expression in the graceful decorative work of Federico Brandani and the ceramics school of Casteldurante, Pesaro, and Urbino. The century closed – as the Counter-Reformation forged ahead under the towering personality of Pope Sixtus V – with the contemplative and luminescent works of Federico Barocci, one of the finest artists the region has ever produced.

From the Baroque to the end of the 18th century

Throughout the Renaissance the Marche region had remained rooted in its tradition of seigniorial or oligarchic autonomies, shunning regional status in favor of a kind of vassal-like condition of servitude. In the 17th century, with the consolidation of central papal control during the Counter-Reformation and the gradual surrender of all or part of the autonomy enjoyed by the cities, the region acknowledged complete subservience to papal rule.

Recent studies have shown that the Baroque period was not one of particular economic recession, thanks partly to the intense building and artistic activities prompted by the appearance of various independent ecclesiastical congregations, most notably the Oratory of San Filippo Neri, which established no fewer than 26 foundations throughout the region in the 17th and 18th centuries, creating Italy's biggest Oratorian group.

The eclectic architectural and artistic activity this congregation spawned can be seen as the most representative example of Baroque art in the Marche region. It is no coincidence that the most interesting church typologies derive from the swirling designs of Gian Lorenzo Bernini and Francesco Borromini in Rome. These buildings were based on centralized oval or rounded plans: the churches of San Filippo in Macerata, Osimo and Cingoli, all of whose designs are attributed to G. B. Contini; the elliptical church of *Santa Maria in Via* in Camerino (1639) is an important earlier work inspired by Bernini.

All this was happening while the more subdued Sistine classicist current prevailed in the region, especially in the works of Girolamo Rainaldi in Ascoli Piceno and Fano, but also in the church of San Giovanni in Macerata designed for the Jesuits by Rosato Rosati (1610). The same, plain structural style was embellished in Ascoli Piceno by the Bernini-inspired Giuseppe Giosafatti, who simply added decoratively-shaped moldings to Palazzo dell'Arringo (1683), and revealed his talents to the full in the minor masterpiece of Sant'Emidio alle Grotte. Secular Baroque architecture brought fountains to the cities and rationalized the urban expansion of the old towns. The taste for theatrical effects was expertly contrived by Nicolò Sabbatini and Giacomo Torelli, Europe's two undisputed masters of illusion, founders of modern theater and stagecraft (see the Spanish style *Nome di Dio* church in Pesaro). The graceful gallery in Palazzo Pianetti in Jesi, meanwhile, is an isolated example of the Rococo style.

The Baroque facade of the church of Sant'Emidio alle Grotte near Ascoli Piceno

Seventeenth century painting is a catalogue of influences and idioms, since there was no academic center to lead a unified movement. The placid "Caravaggesque fringe" of Giovanni Francesco Guerrieri, seen in a more formal version in the work of Orazio Gentileschi, soon gave way to mainstream Bolognese classicism with Annibale Carracci in Loreto, and spread through the influence of Bolognese painters Guercino, Domenichino, Giovanni Lanfranco, Guido Reni and his follower in Pesaro, Simone Cantarini, who effectively shifted attention away from Rome. The precocious Pieter Paul Rubens, who worked for the Oratorians in Fermo (1608), aroused the curiosity of the Barberini group of clients: Pietro da Cortona, Baciccia. Southerners Mattia Preti, Salvatore Rosa, Sebastiano Conca and Luca Giordano were also attracted to the Marche, as was Verona-born Claudio Ridolfi, who established himself successfully in Corinaldo. The last Venetian masterpiece to appear in the region (in Camerino) was the *Madonna in Glory with St. Philip* by G. B. Tiepolo. Meanwhile some of Marche's own masters were leaving the region (Carlo Maratta, Sassoferrato and the Ghezzi family), abandoning their promising provincial workshops to take up more lucrative offers of work in Rome.

From Neoclassicism to Art Nouveau

Luigi Vanvitelli, who embodied the transition to a functional concept of architecture and Neoclassical town planning derived from late-Baroque patterns of spatial organization and perspective, carried out his earliest experiments in Marche. Sent by Pope Clement XII to redevelop the port of Ancona when it was granted free port status (1732), he shed new light on the ever-changing idiom of the century's architecture through his innovative works (the Lazzaretto, the North Quay, the Arco Clementino, the Lanterna, the church of *Gesù*). The legacy he left behind in Marche (Ancona, Loreto, Macerata, and Recanati), provided valuable lessons for two generations of architects, most notably of all Andrea Vici, his only pupil in the Marche region. Carlo Marchionni, Giuseppe Valadier, Camillo Morigia, Cosimo Morelli and Luigi Poletti also created important works in this period.

The revolution that arrived with Napoleon Bonaparte in 1797 came as a rude awakening. The Restoration had changed everything, in form and in ideas, if not in outward appearance. The emerging middle classes demanded theaters and other public utilities and the cultural developments that followed in the 18th and 19th centuries became a socio-economic phenomenon as theaters large and small sprang up in the region. As their architects argued over auditorium design and acoustics, work was proceeding on other buildings such as food and fish markets, slaughterhouses, hospitals, cemeteries and sphaeristeria, which opened up new thoroughfares in the towns and cities, prompting revolutionary urban expansion projects (Senigallia) and clearance schemes.

The Art Nouveau Villa Ruggeri

One final burst of creative activity came with the *fin-de-siècle* Art Nouveau movement, especially by the sea where, with the construction of the new coastal railroad, the first bathing establishments and the holiday villas began to appear. Two of the most ornate are the Conti villa at Civitanova Marche (1910), and the Ruggeri villa in Pesaro (1904–08).

The 1800s were rather less prolific in terms of painting, and were dominated by the figure of Francesco Podesti, who lived for almost the whole century. Somewhere between Pre-Raphaelitism and Art Nouveau comes Adolfo De Carolis, a friend of Giovanni Pascoli, and Gabriele D'Annunzio's favorite illustrator. His contemporary and fellow Pre-Raphaelite Biagio Biagetti produced a number of prestigious religious works; meanwhile the woodcuts of Bruno Marsili, a pupil of De Carolis, were informed with a transcendental spirituality.

Large Sphere, by Marche sculptor Arnaldo Pomodoro

The 20th century

Osvaldo Licini, an intellectual and inventor of "imaginary figures," stands in a category of his own; the culturally eclectic Anselmo Bucci was similarly independent of the rest. The "1910 generation" brought together Corrado Cagli, Orfeo Tamburi and Sante Monachesi, widely diverging though their styles were. The Marche region has one of Italy's foremost engraving traditions, headed undoubtedly by Luigi Bartolini, who turned this art form into a vehicle for poetic expressionism. Exponents of the medium include Arnaldo Ciarrocchi, Walter Piacesi, Nino Ricci and, more recently, Roberto Stelluti. Valeriano Trubbiani is an internationally acclaimed sculptor and engraver whose passionate creativity extends over a range of materials. Also well known outside Italy are brothers Giò and Arnaldo Pomodoro, and Eliseo Mattiacci. The avant-garde is well represented both in the neo-Mannerism of Bruno D'Arcevia and in Enzo Cucchi's *transavanguardia* movement.

The Marche: a visitor's guide

The very fact that this region is referred to in the plural (in English, too, it is often known as "The Marches") suggests an intriguing variety of cultural identities. Each one is strong enough to have survived the region's checkered history and is still clearly visible today (a recent publicity slogan "Italy in one Region" neatly sums up the idea). The region positively teems with diversity, and the past merges imperceptibly with the present in the eleven valleys that cross it. Marche's cultural legacy is dominated by a number of great personalities, who interpreted the spirit of their native region and left a lasting mark on it: Frederick II and Gentile da Fabriano in the Middle Ages; the Renaissance geniuses Raphael and Bramante; major European composers Gioacchino Rossini, Gaspare Spontini, and G. B. Pergolesi; and the eternal poet, Giacomo Leopardi. Journeying through the region means not only hunting out the "not-to-be-missed" attractions, but also exploring whatever other routes may take the fancy of the traveler who wishes to indulge a personal passion or is just curious to see what lies round the next corner. Small though the region is, it is a microcosm of excellence that appears in the spirit of enterprise that permeates the entire

The Ducal Palace and cathedral of Urbino seen from the Albornoz Fortress

region, in the widespread sense of community, in its wealth of artistic treasures (234 museums, 70 historic theaters, 315 libraries and thousands of churches) combined with a whole host of cultural events ranging from historical re-evocations to major theatrical performances, every bit as prestigious as those laid on in Italy's bigger cities. All this, together with its rural areas, nature parks, its centuries-old craft traditions and its state-of-the-art technologies, means that Marche does indeed have a great deal to offer. Exploring one aspect opens up a whole set of others in a never-ending series of cross-references that reveal the essentially complementary nature of the region's structure: only by understanding the system as a whole can its true identity be perceived.

One approach to the region is through its archaeology (in its 7 archaeological parks and 24 special sites). As for architecture, the most widely occurring style is Romanesque, an idiom still found throughout the region and followed by the Gothic, rare examples of which have miraculously survived. The golden age of the Renaissance lives on in some truly outstanding monuments, but is seen at its most spectacular in the "city-palace" of Urbino and the "palatial square" in Ascoli Piceno. The list of artistic treasures continues down to the great artists of the 20th century. Geographically and culturally the region offers us the unique legacy of an ancient urban system that survives to this day, with its cities, old craft and industrial activities, dialects and legends, its food, and of course the landscape of a region that looks out eastward to the Adriatic and, away over the hills to the west, to the capital city the Marche has so often reached out to and yet so greatly feared, Rome.

A border region. At the origin of differences

Traveling through "the Marches" means crossing several borders. This marchland people has borders in its blood; indeed dissimilarity is a geo-morphological vocation in these parts, and each of the Marche's eleven parallel valleys is a little world unto

The fish market in Fano

itself. The Esino river has kept apart Gauls and Picenes, Byzantines and Longobards, the State of Urbino and the Marche of the popes. It has several different regional capitals: Ancona, the city port that stretches out before the Adriatic and so far removed from the tenant farming Marche further inland; Loreto, the city-shrine and universal place of pilgrimage with the artistic treasure house that surrounds the Santa Casa (Holy House). To say nothing of the capitals that never were; the centers of historically subjugated lands: Fermo and its state; Jesi and its castles; the noble Camerino in splendid decline; Fabriano the capital of the upper Vallesina valley and now an industrial center.

The sub-regional areas need to be seen in relationship to the worlds on which they border. Montefeltro, which lost Gubbio to Umbria, speaks the language of Umbria and Tuscany, and once had extremely close links with Camerino and the Macerata uplands; Piceno is part of a macro-region straddling the Apennines that takes in Umbria, Lazio, and Abruzzo, from which it is separated by the Tronto river, the border between the Marca d'Ancona and the Kingdom of the Two Sicilies until the Unification of Italy (the most stable border in the history of Italy).

The natural borders were never divisive. Rather, they provided an opportunity for contact. Even the Adriatic Sea was a major artery that helped the spread of civilization in Marche, down the coastal strip of the "Venetian Gulf." From the 12th to the 16th century the Serene Republic of Venice exerted a strong pull as a Mediterranean emporium to which raw materials and semi-finished goods (paper, wool, woolen cloth and silk yarn) from the manufacturing centers in the Marche mountains could be sent. They were loaded onto ships in the ports of Ancona and Fano and sold at the fairs in Senigallia, Recanati and Fermo. So the sea brought together the major mercantile ports of the northern Marches (the Pentapolis kept alive through the presence of Byzantium) but it was also a major element of integration for the southern towns with their fishing traditions, "discovered" in the 1700s after centuries of Longobard influence over the coastal settlements.

Moving in time and place

In a region dotted with so many local capitals, imposing inland borders and strong links with valleys on the other side of the Apennines, an efficient road network is clearly of fundamental importance, smoothing out some of the differences as well as forming the backbone of this complex regional organism. By far the quickest way to cross Marche from north to south is the *A14 Bologna–Taranto* expressway, which runs parallel to state road *SS16 Adriatica*. There are fast roads to Rome from Fano (*SS3 Flaminia*, along the route of the old Flaminian Way, which opened up the *ager gallicus* to the Romans, and boasts that great feat of engineering, the Furlo tunnel), from Ancona (SS76 della Val d'Esino), from Civitanova Marche (SS485 Corridonia Maceratese and SS77 Val di Chienti), from Porto d'Ascoli (SS4 Salaria, laid out by the Picenes and improved by the Romans to connect the Adriatic salt coast to the imperial capital; a recently-built tunnel has shortened the route to Umbria: traffic now emerges at Norcia without having to cross the Forca Canapine pass). But it is by getting off the beaten track that visitors can savor a much slower pace of life and feel the influence the past still exerts on the present-day region. Continental and Apennine Marche are best discovered along the roads that run up the valleys through the hills and to the more mountainous interior: the SS258 Marecchia crosses Montefeltro country and descends to Sansepolcro; the 257 Apecchiese from Acqualagna to Città di Castello; the 424 della Val Cesano from Marotta, on the coast, to Cagli; the 361 Septempedana, named after the Roman settlement near San Severino Marche, connects the Adriatic via Osimo to Nocera Umbra; the 210 Fermana Faleriense runs almost the entire length of the Tenna valley, connecting Porto San Giorgio and Amandola; the 433 Val d'Aso runs from Pedaso to Comunanza. There are also some particularly interesting roads connecting the valleys, for example the SS362 Jesina from Jesi to Macerata, from the Chienti valley to the Tronto (SS78 Picena from the abbey church of Fiastra to just outside Ascoli Piceno), and between Muccia and Visso (SS209 Valnerina). No less charming are the short drives from Pesaro to Gabicce Mare, from Visso to Ussita, from Polverina to Fiastra and to Bolognola, from Amandola to Montefortino, and from Ascoli Piceno to Rotella across Mt. Ascensione.

The Milan–Lecce railroad hugs the coast. The hub of Marche's rail system is the station of Ancona (tel. 071 5921). There are good views of the hills on the Ancona-Falconara Marittima–Rome line and along the line connecting Civitanova Marche and Fabriano with Rome; a small railway runs inland from San Benedetto del Tronto up to Ascoli Piceno.

For visitors with less time to spare the region has one airport, the Raffaello Sanzio (tel. 071 28271), at Ancona-Falconara.

The port of Ancona (tel. 071 2074697) takes vacationers across the Mediterranean, to Croatia, Greece, Turkey, Cyprus, and Israel. There is also a hydrofoil service from San Benedetto del Tronto to Croatia (tel. 0735 582542, fax 0735 582893).

Tourist attractions old and new. A region with a hundred towns and a thousand squares

One look at the figures gives a good idea of the importance of town life in Marche: there are 1,000 urban communities, 246 municipal authorities, 750 villages and hamlets, and new coastal and valley settlements. The common origin of the walled towns were the *castra* and the *plebes*, the network of baptismal churches. The system of towns was defined in 1357 by Cardinal Egidio Albornoz and remains to this day. Hence the firmly established, fragmented network of these proudly independent municipal units, each with their own town hall, bishop's palace, the-ater and main square, lined with the palaces of the leading families. The cities were palatial,

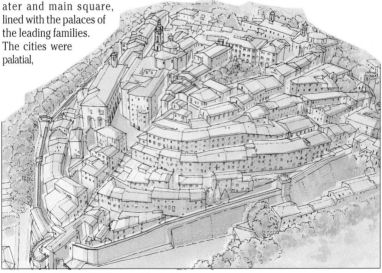

Aerial view of the medieval town of Corinaldo

the squares their elegant salons, like Piazza del Popolo in Ascoli Piceno, set against the backdrop of the travertine-clad church of *San Francesco*, a rare departure from the more commonly found brick. The region's squares never lack in artistic grace, even in the small mountain towns (take Visso, for example) and can be considered a model of the Italian *piazza* in general as a focal point of Italian urban life.

From tenant farming to rural tourism

Marche's sea of hills, broken up by gullies, has been unrelentingly shaped by tenant farming. This system has now largely been replaced by specialized crop farming: orchards in Val d'Aso, vineyards reaching as far as the eye can see in the Esino valley (Verdicchio wine) and on the Piceno hills. The galaxy of farmhouses – self-sufficient microcosms producing woven woolen cloth from sheepswool and linen from the flax grown in the fields – was a world apart that was in a sense the forerunner of

The colors of the Marche countryside near Cossignano

the modern Marche family-run business. The architecture is simple but eye-catching, with the rich, warm colors of its golden brown and pink brick. High up in the hills, in the Montefeltro region and in the mountains around Ascoli, are stone, ashlar or pebble houses, built with fortified towers, or with dovecotes.

Tenant farming in the region, the agricultural implements, looms, spinning wheels, carts and other early farming machinery can be seen in the Farming Culture Museums scattered around the region. Some fine farm buildings from tenant farming times – as well as other distinguished residences and abbeys – have been redeveloped for the rural tourism business, especially in the uplands of the four provinces. More information is available in Ancona, from: Agriturist (regional office, tel. 071 201763), Turismo Verde (Corso Stamira 29, tel. 071 202987); Terranostra (Via Pizzecolli 14, tel. 071 52319).

The seaside resorts: tradition and quality

That the region has a real vocation for tourism is confirmed by the 14,000,000 or more vacationers who, year after year, flock to its 180-km coastline, from Gabicce Mare to San Benedetto del Tronto. Tourism was born in the mid-19th century, with the new upper-class fashion of bathing in the sea, and the arrival of the first sports and amusement facilities and hotels along the beaches. After World War II, tourism really began to take off and the entire stretch of coastline was transformed: Gabicce Mare and the backdrop of the Colle San Bartolo nature park; the Conero promontory with its high cliffs and small beaches tucked away in corners of untamed natural beauty; the holiday resorts of Numana and Sirolo. The coast further south, with its lush vegetation, has been dubbed the Riviera of the Palms.

Marche has a well-established tradition of tourist facilities with over 1,000 hotels (offering a total of 58,000 beds), tourist villages, campsites, and nearly 25,000 self-catering apartments. For further information contact the Marche region's Tourism Service (tel. 071 8061, fax 071 8062154) or Faita Marche (tel. 0734 622333), which specializes in campsite accommodation. Communications have helped popularize the region in Italy and abroad (Germans form the largest group of foreign vacationers). Ancona has rediscovered its strategic role as a Mediterranean sea port, and is now a center for maritime tourism, and the unbroken sequence of resorts up and down the coast offers a whole range of attractions: high-quality beaches, marinas, cultural events, and countless artistic treasures in the hill towns a short drive inland.

The "Two Sisters" beach from the Conero promontory

A jewel-case of natural beauty

Monti Sibillini and Monti della Laga (and the not-to-be-missed excursion to the Volpara Falls) are a hiker's paradise.

The *Parco Nazionale dei Monti Sibillini* (for information: tel. 0737 95525, fax 0737 95532) is in the Ascoli Piceno and Macerata provinces. The *Monti della Laga e del Gran Sasso d'Italia* nature park comes under the authority of the town of Arquata del Tronto. The *Parco Regionale Monte Carpegna, del Sasso Simone-Simoncello*, with its 2,000 hectares of state-owned forest, is run from Carpegna (tel. 0722 770064). The *Parco Naturale Regionale Colle San Bartolo* (tel. 0721 952610), between Gabicce Mare and Pesaro, is an interesting wetland area that provides a winter home for herring gulls and cormorants. The *Parco Regionale del Monte Conero* (18 hikes through Mediterranean maquis, covering some 8,000 hectares) is run from Sirolo (tel. 071 9331161, fax 071 9330376). The *Riserva Naturale Gola della Rossa e Gola di Frasassi* (information from the mountain village of Esino Frasassi, Via Dante 268, tel. 0732 6951, Fabriano), includes an awe-inspiring series of underground caves. The *Riserva Naturale Integrale Montagna di Torricchio*, run by Camerino University (tel. 0737 2527, 637211) provides a natural habitat for hares, squirrels, foxes, and badgers. The *Riserva Naturale Abbadia di Fiastra* (tel. & fax 0733 202942, e-mail: pichin@mercurio.it) protects the flowering ash and several varieties of oak. There are 15 state-owned forests, and the WWF runs the *Oasi Naturalistica Bosco di Frasassi* (tel. 0732 22937, 21296).

Nature parks and protected areas

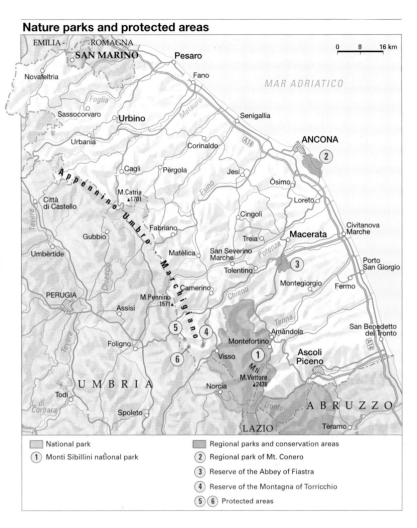

☐ National park	☐ Regional parks and conservation areas
① Monti Sibillini national park	② Regional park of Mt. Conero
	③ Reserve of the Abbey of Fiastra
	④ Reserve of the Montagna of Torricchio
	⑤ ⑥ Protected areas

Outdoor pursuits

Underwater fishing is popular in the rocky sea bed at Vallugola, around the Conero (Portonovo, Sirolo, Numana) and at Pedaso, while *angling* is possible along the whole coast, and in the region's rivers and lakes. There are many *yachting and recreational sailing schools* in the harbor towns (Porto San Giorgio has the biggest marina in the whole of the Adriatic). *Skiing* is one of the most popular mountain sports in the Apennines, at 2,000 m and above at Ussita and between 1,500 and 1,800 m at Pintura di Bolognola, Piobbico, Castelsantangelo sul Nera, Forca Canapine, and at Mt. Piselli near Ascoli Piceno. *Horse-riding* is offered by the expanding rural tourism industry.

Taking the waters

Mineral water cures, mud baths, aerosol therapy and other treatments are on offer at spas throughout the region: in Carignano Terme and Montegrimano; in San Vittore delle Chiuse di Genga; in Tolentino and Sarnano, in Torre di Palme and Acquasanta Terme.

Gastronomic delights

There are as many varieties of local cuisine in Marche as there are dialects, and – tongues being as much for speaking as for savoring flavors – it is hardly surprising that the local food and language have a common history. The region is a collection of gastronomic micro-climates each influenced by its neighbors, or from across the

Apennines and Mediterranean tastes on the coast. The area between the province of Ascoli Piceno and the Abruzzo region to the south features an inter-regional blend of hot, savory foods washed down with Montepulciano wines. The Montefeltro area has culinary links with Romagna to the north and Tuscany to the west, while the Macerata area has close ties with neighboring Umbria.

One of the Piceno area's most tempting specialties are fried olives *all'ascolana*, filled with a mouth-watering mixture of meats and the slender *maccheroncini* from Campofilone. Cured pork is widely used throughout the region's Apennine area: ham in Carpegna, salami in Visso, Macerata province and Fabriano, and *coppa* prepared using family recipes. Cheese production is closely linked to the ancient transhumance trails: *pecorino* varies from valley to valley, one of the tastiest being the type matured in tufa ditches. Many varieties of mushroom grow in the Apennine woods, and the prized white truffle, found in Montefeltro and the Pesaro uplands, is a delicacy used in Acqualagna, Sant'Angelo in Vado; black truffles meanwhile are eaten at Castelsantangelo sul Nera. Not surprisingly, fish reigns supreme along the coast. The local

Olives, Ascoli style

brodetto, or fish soup, appears in various forms. Ancona's main fish specialty in Ancona is without doubt *stoccafisso* (dried cod, or "stockfish"). *Vincisgrassi* is a rich first-course delicacy invented in the 18th century by Maceratese chef Antonio Nebbia (the Ancona variety is thought to have been invented by General Windish Candidus Grätz). The region also produces a Christmas cake made from dried fruit, chocolate, honey and fine bran flour, and variously referred to as *pistincu*, *crustingu*, *frustingu* or *figusu* in the Piceno and Macerata valleys, and known as *bostrengo* in the Pesaro area.

Marche produces no fewer than 11 wines of guaranteed origin: Verdicchio from Matelica and the Jesi Castles area, Bianchello from Metauro, Esino valley wines, wine from the Pesaro and Macerata hills, Falerio from the Ascoli hills, Piceno red (and high-quality red), Conero Red Vernaccia di Serrapetrona, and last but not least Lacrima di Morro d'Alba.

Michelangelo's delight

Michelangelo is known to have been involved with the people of Casteldurante all his life, although there is no record that he ever visited the town, or even nearby Urbino. His closest friends were Francesco Amatori – known as "l'Urbino" – and his wife Cornelia Colonelli, who, upon her husband's death, returned with her children (Michelangelo's godchildren) to Casteldurante. They began to correspond on a regular basis, and letters to the artist were nearly always accompanied by a gift of *casciotte di guaimo*, a typical cheese from the Urbino area. Nearly all the letters written between 1 January 1557 and 26 July 1561 mention that a consignment of this much-loved specialty was on its way. Cornelia refers to rounds of the cheese as *casci* or *casciotti* irrespective of their weight.

This was only one of the cheeses from this area. Others (still made to this day) included the pit cheese of Talamello, *pecorino* from San Leo and Casteldelci, and *bazzotto*, made in Fano, which was preserved in sheep's milk and eaten before it had fully ripened. So eager was Michelangelo to ensure himself a constant supply of *casciotta d'Urbino* at table that he came to a special arrangement with his contacts in Casteldurante, to the point of even buying up farms in the area. He was not alone in his love of the cheese: a document dated 29 October 1590 in the State Archive in Florence describes the dispatch of four *guaimo* cheeses by the senior priest of Mercatello to the Duke of Urbino, and in 1761 the future Pope Clement XIV sent his written thanks from Rome to the Abbot of Cagli for his most welcome gift of delectable *casciotta* cheeses.

1 Ancona and the Conero promontory

The area

Coastal navigators used to refer to Mt. Conero as *Monte di Ancona*, suggesting strong links between the mountain and the regional capital city that lies at its northernmost tip. The stretch of coastline from Ancona to the mouth of the Musone river is the most scenic and environmentally significant part of the region, and the area where its most picturesque seaside resorts are located. The Miocene massif of Mt. Conero, an isolated arm of the Apennines, sharply interrupts an otherwise straight stretch of coastline and the region's orderly pattern of rivers draining into the sea. The bora, mistral and sirocco winds, along with extremes of temperature and marine erosion, have created dramatic cliffs, natural caves and twisting shingly beaches. The area, which has been settled by man since Bronze and Iron Age times, is a sharply contrasting mixture of dark patches of centuries-old Mediterranean maquis and dazzlingly white limestone. Overhead, it is not uncommon to see the peregrine falcon gliding slowly and undisturbed, a sure sign that the protected parkland of Mt. Conero is still an unspoiled environment.

1.1 Ancona

Walking tour from Via Marconi to the War Memorial *(see plan pp. 34–35)*

Nestling in the hilly northern headland of the Conero promontory, the city slopes gently but rapidly down to the inlet of its port but comes to a much more abrupt end at the sheer drop of its cliffs overlooking the sea. In ancient times, the area in between was the marshy, reed-filled mouth of the Pennocchiara river, which lives on in certain place names, including the Calamo fountain (from the Latin word *calamus*, or reed). The course of the river is now occupied by Corso Mazzini.

Ancona (elev. 16 m, pop. 100,058), whose oriental origins are immediately apparent to visitors arriving from the sea, is theatrically situated. The sea approach almost suggests an acropolis, dominated by the cathedral of *San Ciriaco*,

which witnesses both the sunrise and the sunset in the waters of the Adriatic. The natural harbor, the only considerable seaport in the mid-Adriatic, is protected by the curve of the promontory (the name Ancona means "elbow"). For centuries the port was the basis of the city's commercial success, through ancient trading routes with the Dalmatian coast and Greece. From the 19th century Ancona also became a major rail intersection between the north–south coastal route and the Trans-Apennine railroad through the Tiber valley to Rome. Traces of early Villanovan and Picene settlements, which have been found over early Bronze Age remains on the southwest slopes of Mt. Cardeto (elev. 102 m), extend as far as the Guasco hill, from which the landing place

The cathedral of San Ciriaco dominates the Port of Ancona

below was controlled. It was to exploit the port and the trade in amber with the Baltic and Aegean seas that a colony of Syracusan exiles settled here in the 4th century BC. This is substantiated by the presence of Greek coinage, by architecture (most notably a temple to the goddess Cupra, protectress of sailors, ruins of which can still be seen beneath the cathedral) and by references in classical literature (*ante domum Veneris, quam Dorica sustinet Ancon*; Juvenal, IV 40). The Syracusans, living alongside the Picenes, established a thriving market with the East and a lively center for the production of Attic ceramics, purple, wool and cosmetics. Ancona was spared reprisals after the Battle of Sentinum (295 BC), but its strategic and commercial importance and extremely strong military power soon brought it under Roman control. It was involved as a *civitas foederata* in the wars of Hannibal and the Illyrian Wars, during which period the town and port grew. In 90 BC it was made a *municipium* and was already a naval base. As part of his plans to conquer Dacia, Trajan developed its maritime structures: the fine Trajan Arch is the greatest reminder of this period, but other vestiges of the Roman city also remain, notably the Forum (in what is now Piazza del Senato), the Temple of Venus beneath the cathedral, the amphitheater and the thermal baths (near the church of *SS. Sacramento*).

The shrine to St. Stephen, mentioned by St. Augustine, was well known in the East, an indication of the early arrival of Christianity in Ancona, Christian worship being practiced alongside the cult of the patron saint, St. Cyriacus. The city later fell under the sway of the Byzantine exarchs as part of the Pentapolis, was fought over in the Gothic War (6th cent.), sacked by invading Saracens in 839 and all but destroyed by a disastrous earthquake. It repopulated in the late 10th century, declaring itself a free municipality and re-establishing trading links with Dalmatia and the East. It heroically resisted two sieges: in 1167 by Frederick I Barbarossa, and in 1173 by his chancellor Christian of Mainz, who had the support of the Venetian fleet (Venice was opposed to Ancona becoming a maritime republic).

In the early 13th century Patrician villas were built within new, fortified walls whose gateways faced the sea. The city clashed with the territories held by Jesi, Osimo and Macerata over its expansion inland. In 1348 the city was betrayed and fell into the hands of the Malatesta; in 1355 it came under the sway of Cardinal Egidio Albornoz, and was

forced to obstruct attempts by the Malatesta, Alessandro Sforza and finally the Aragonese to expand along the coast. In 1447 Eugene IV reconfirmed its status as a republic under papal protection. The ship owners of Ancona subsequently contested the Venetian shipping routes, as it set its sights northeastward and the city was em-

Ancona. The cathedral porch

bellished with refined Gothic marble work. It was a prosperous but short-lived age: the wealthy port whetted the appetite of Pope Clement VII, who craftily sold it in 1532, when the fortress was being built by Antonio da Sangallo the Younger, offending rather than defending the population.

From that time on the city came under the control of the Church States, to which it wearily yielded until the Unification of Italy. In 1732 Pope Clement XII reversed its declining fortunes and upgraded the city by establishing the free port, for which Luigi Vanvitelli designed a series of new maritime structures. In 1799 Napoleon's troops entered the city through the new Porta Pia and Strada Pia, now Via Marconi and Via XXIX Settembre and proclaimed the Republic, but in 1799 the city succumbed to the siege by the Russian and Turkish fleets, and by the Austrians who with the French and the pope governed in turns until 1860. After making a patriotic contribution to the *Risorgimento*, Ancona was first occupied and then annexed by plebiscite to the Kingdom of Italy.

Much civil construction work followed, but

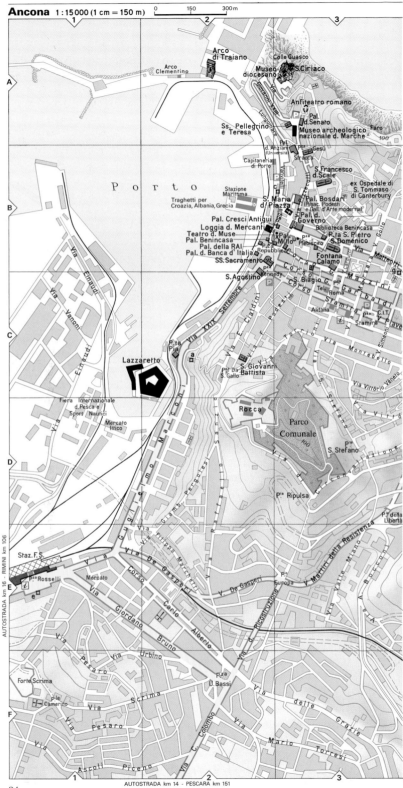

Ancona 1:15000 (1 cm = 150 m)

0   150   300 m

AUTOSTRADA km 14 - PESCARA km 151

AUTOSTRADA km 16 · RIMINI km 106

Arco di Traiano
Arco Clementino
Colle Guasco
Museo diocesano
S.Ciriaco
Anfiteatro romano
Pal. d.Senato
Ss. Pellegrino e Teresa
Museo archeologico nazionale d. Marche
Faro 100
Pal. d'Anziani (Università)
Pª Geso
S. Francesco d.Scale
Siracca
Capitaneria di Porto
ex Ospedale di S. Tommaso di Canterbury
Porto
Stazione Marittima
Traghetti per Croazia, Albania, Grecia
S. Maria d'Piazza
Pal. Bosdari (Pinac. Podesti e Gall. d'Arte moderna)
Pal. Cresci Antigui
Loggia d. Mercanti
Pal. d. Governo
Teatro d. Muse
Biblioteca Benincasa
Pal. Benincasa
Pal. Milo
Pª
P.ta S. Pietro
Pal. della RAI
Plebiscito
S.Domenico
Pal. d. Banca d'Italia
Republicca
Via
SS.Sacramento
Fontana Calamo
S. Agostino
Matteoti
Kennedy
S. Biagio C.
Via
S. Giovanni
Telc
Roma
Corso
Podesti
Stamira
Alitalia
C.I.T.
Stamira
Plave
P.ta Pia
Via L. Cialdini
Via XXIX Settembre
Lazzaretto
Pª Da S. Gallo
S. Giovanni Battista
Via Montebello
Via Vittorio Veneto
Fiera Internazionale d.Pesca e Sport Nautici
Rocca
Parco Comunale
100
Mercato Ittico
Pª Ripulsa
S. Stefano
Pª della Libertà
Staz. F.S.
Pª Rosselli
Via Guglielmo Marconi
Via Vittorio Marchetti
Via De Gasperi
Mercato
V. De Gasperi
Pª Europa
V. Martiri della Resistenza
Corso
Carlo
Albenio
Via Giordano Bruno
Via Urbino
Pª U. Bassi
Forte Scrima
Pªle Camerino
Via Pesaro
Via Scrima
Via C. Colombo
Via delle Grazie
Via Mario Torresi
Via Ascoli Piceno
Via Pesaro
Via Einaudi
Via Vanoni
Via Einaudi

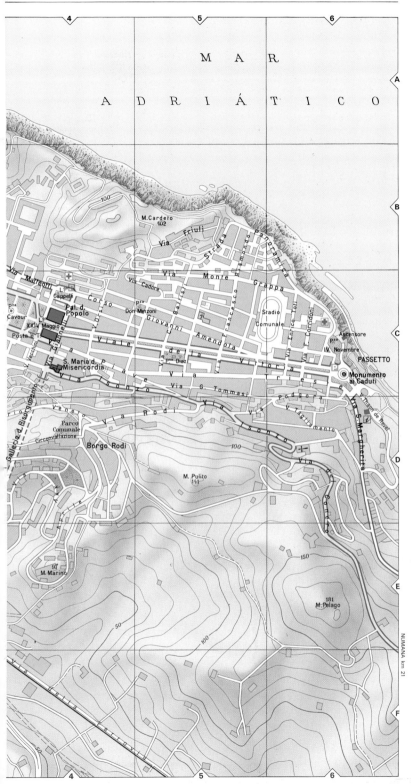

MAR

ADRIÁTICO

M. Cardeto
102

Via Friuli

Strada panoramica

Via Monte Grappa

Via Cadore

Corso

Pal. d.
Popolo

P.za
Don Minzoni

Stadio
Comunale

Cappelli

Lgo

P.za
Cavour

XXIV
Maggio

Posta e T.

Via Giovanni Amendola

Via Enrico Toti

Via F. Corridoni

Ascensore

P.za
IV. Novembre

PASSETTO

S. Maria d.
Misericordia

Viale

della

Vittoria

Monumento
ai Caduti

Via G. Tommasi

Via Isonzo

P.za Diaz

Via Piave

Galleria d. Risorgimento

Via Vecchini

Via Vanero

Via Rodi

Via Isonzo

Via Podgora

Via Tagliamento

Via S. Margherita

V. msgr. de Revel

Parco
Comunale

Circonvallazione

Borgo Rodi

M. Pulito
141

100

Via Conero

97
M. Marino

150

50

181
M. Pelago

100

NUMANA km 21

Via Flaminia

50

Stockfish, Ancona-style

Stockfish (or *stoccafisso* as it is known in Italian, perhaps from an old Dutch word "stoc," meaning rack) features prominently in Marche recipes and has particular associations with Ancona. The flourishing trade that grew up between the Adriatic seaport and the Baltic Sea led to the custom of sun-drying cod to provide food for the return journey south. The fish eventually found its way into Ancona's own cuisine, where it was enhanced with simple, but strong-flavored vegetables, herbs, oil and wine. Today's *stoccafisso all'anconetana* is still very much the original recipe prepared by Marche farming families on high days and holidays: vineyard owners would celebrate the end of the grape harvest, for example, with lavish meals centering around this main fish course.

The dried fish is left in cold water (for between three and eight days, with frequent changes of water) to restore the original wet-fish texture. It is then cut into chunks of about ten centimeters and cooked in a pan, together with thick-sliced potatoes, tomato and chopped mixed herbs. The mouth-watering result is seafood at its best.

the city was also reduced to a state of servitude and military occupation. It expanded beyond its walls in heavily-populated, rationally-planned districts which grew up around the major thoroughfares (Corso Garibaldi), large squares (Piazza Cavour, Piazza Roma) and the new railway station in the southwest. It suffered the first bombing of Italy by the Austrians (24 May 1915) and in the two decades that followed continued to expand outward: in the east it filled the plain with the elegant, airy residential Adriatico district. It suffered heavy Allied bombing in 1943–44 (160 air raids), and most of the medieval and Renaissance city was razed to the ground, destroying its historic image as an ancient maritime city, which hasty postwar reconstruction failed to save from disappearing altogether. Other natural disasters (including an earthquake in 1972) opened up new wounds, which have now largely been healed as major restoration and urban redevelopment work is slowly but surely carried out.

The walking tour starts at Via Marconi near the Lazzaretto and Porta Pia, from where Via XXIX Settembre leads to Piazza della Repubblica, defined architecturally by the Teatro delle Muse and the side of the church of *SS. Sacramento*. A detour up the Astagno hill leads along Via Cialdini to the fortress, while the main road continues along Via della Loggia, with its fine civil buildings (and the church of *Santa Maria della Piazza*), and Lungomare Vanvitelli: the Trajan and Clementine arches are clearly visible in the distance; to the right is the cathedral of *San Ciriaco*. From the church and adjoining bishop's palace, the road runs down the Guasco hill to the Roman Amphitheater, the church of *SS. Pel-*

legrino e Teresa and the Palazzo del Senato, the first of the monumental buildings on Via Ferretti and Via Pizzecolli: Palazzo Ferretti is now the home of the Museo Archeologico Nazionale delle Marche, Palazzo degli Anziani is used by the university (note the church of *Gesù* opposite). Beyond the church of *San Francesco delle Scale* is Palazzo Bosdari, containing the "Francesco Podesti" art gallery and the municipal modern art gallery. Another important building, Palazzo del Governo, leads to Piazza del Plebiscito, in which the Benincasa Municipal Library and the church of *San Domenico* stand. Via Gramsci leads back to Piazza della Repubblica, at the northwest extremity of Corso Mazzini, whose main monuments are the church of *San Biagio* and the Calamo fountain. This road continues beyond Piazza Cavour and Largo XXIV Maggio, as Viale della Vittoria, an avenue that terminates in the Passetto district at the War Memorial.

Via Marconi (C-E1-2). This continuation of the Adriatic highway runs from the railway station, past the Lazzaretto and becomes Via XXIX Settembre, ending at Piazza della Repubblica. The street, originally known as Strada Pia, was created by Pope Pius VI to facilitate access to the city after centuries in which the only way in and out of the city was across the Astagno hill.

Lazzaretto* (C1-2). This edifice, brilliantly executed by Luigi Vanvitelli (1733–43), was designed as a modern multi-purpose structure for military purposes and as the port's quarantine station. The pentagonal building encloses an inner courtyard around the ornamental Doric *Temple of*

San Rocco, which the huge warehouses and the merchant's homes overlooked. Once totally cut off from city life, it is now the venue for major cultural events.

Porta Pia (C2). This grand gateway, built in Istria stone between 1787–89 by Filippo Marchionni, was built as a new entrance to the city at the end of Strada Pia and formed part of the wall leading up to the citadel (see p. 38). Its inner section, made of blocks of tufa, was designed in a more sober style by Scipione Daretti.

Piazza della Repubblica (B2-3). This square occupies a pivotal point between the Astagno hills (where the citadel stands) and the Guasco hills (dominated by *San Ciriaco*). the side overlooking the port and the sea offers glimpses of *Vittorio Emanuele Wharf*, formerly *Portella della Beccheria*, which recalls the arrival of the king in 1860, a few days after the city surrendered.
Palazzo della Banca d'Italia (B2) was rebuilt after World War II, partly by Marcello Piacentini (1951–53). *Palazzo della RAI*, opposite, is the work of Gaetano Minnucci (1948–56), who built it over the remains of the eighteenth-century Palazzo Trionfi.

Teatro delle Muse (B2-3). This theater dominates the square with its imposing neoclassical facade. It was built between 1822 and 1825 to a design by Pietro Ghinelli (and was the region's largest theater) and inaugurated with Gioacchino Rossini's *Aureliano in Palmira* in 1827. Badly damaged during the war, it has remained unused for over half a century, but plans are soon to get under way to restore it in a manner that does justice to its exterior: its austere Palladian design contrasts with the six huge Ionic columns in Istrian stone and the pediment, decorated with a bas-relief depicting *Apollo and the Nine Muses* by Giacomo De Maria.

Church of SS. Sacramento (B2). Built in 1539 (portal), it was restored in 1771–76 by Francesco Maria Ciaraffoni, when the twisted *campanile* of Borrominian inspiration was added, and the interior was redesigned in the shape of a Latin cross with a deep choir. Note the *Statues of the Apostles* in the niches along the nave by Gioacchino Varlè; the *Four Evangelists* in the pendentives under the dome were painted by Francesco Podesti (1880); the *Preaching of John the Baptist* (first altar on the left) is by Filippo Bellini.

Via Cialdini (B-C2) is the main artery of the three roads that climb the *Astagno* hill (from *ad stagnum*, "toward the marsh," but also known as Capodimonte) and until the late 18th century provided the only, and difficult access to the city from the coast and Rome. It is lined with a whole series of 16th- and 17th-century palaces, whose interiors were completely restored after the 1972 earthquake; its lower part crosses the area of the Roman Baths and the Jewish Ghetto.
At the bottom of the street is the former church of *Sant'Agostino*, built by the Augustinians (1338–41) and originally called *Santa Maria del Popolo*. This church, which stands at the point

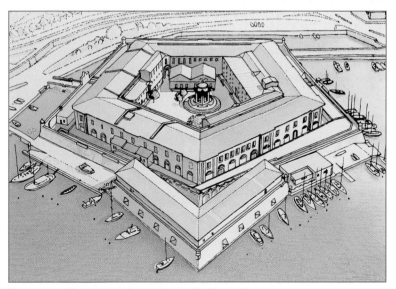

The pentagonal Lazzaretto in Ancona, designed by Vanvitelli

where travelers and pilgrims from Rome and the coast converged, was enlarged by Luigi Vanvitelli between 1751 and 1764. The splendid **portal*** survives. Begun by Giorgio da Sebenico (1460–75), it was completed in part by Michele di Giovanni (1494). The statues under the baldachins of the pillars represent *Santa Monica and San Nicola da Tolentino* (bottom, left to right) and *San Simpliciano and Beatified Agostino Trionfi* (top, left to right). The large festooned lunette in the center – a masterpiece of the ornate Adriatic Gothic style by the Dalmatian sculptor – depicts in dramatic relief *St. Augustine Showing the Holy Scriptures to the Heretics*. The interior is empty (in 1861 it became state property and was turned into a barracks). Still adjoining the church is a square convent *cloister* with Tuscan columns.

Further on, the road widens out into a small square, overlooked by the Romanesque portal of the 13th-century church of *San Giovanni Battista* (C2). The apsed interior, remodeled by Lorenzo Daretti (1782), has two fine canvases: *Christ with St. Charles Borromeo and St. Ubaldo* by Andrea Lilli and an *Ecce Homo* by Federico Zuccari.

At the top of the hill, the **Rocca** (C-D2-3) was built at the order of Pope Clement VII in 1532–38, by Antonio da Sangallo the Younger, who also supervised the project: a brilliantly-executed irregular polygon from which seven ramparts of different shapes and sizes and at different heights radiate out. Throughout the 16th century it was extended with the addition of a vast system of *trenches*, which encircled its perimeter four times, creating the complex that came to be known as the *Cittadella*. No longer used for military purposes, it will now house the offices of the Marche Regional Authorities.

Via della Loggia (B2-3). This is a stretch of the old *Via Publica*, one of Ancona's most ancient thoroughfares and the main artery of the medieval and Renaissance city, running parallel to the coast inside the walls. The first part was extended with the construction of the Teatro delle Muse, continuing (as Lungomare Vanvitelli) into the port district to the Trajan and Clementine arches, and beyond to the end of the quay (see p. 39).

Palazzo Benincasa (B2). Commissioned by wealthy ship owner and trader Dionisio Benincasa to unify his property facing the sea, this building is the largest private civil edifice in the old town. It was designed by Giorgio da Sebenico, who Benincasa probably met on his travels to Venice where the Dalmatian architect was working on the Doges' Palace; note the Benincasa crest on the facade. The palace, which originally had three stories above ground level, with lancet ground floor openings (still visible) and biforate windows on the two floors

above (the present windows are period remakes from 1926), was raised at the end of the 18th century, when the new ceilings were frescoed by Giuseppe Pallavicini with rare *Views of Ancona*.

Loggia dei Mercanti* (B2). This is the city's greatest civil monument and the very symbol of its lively mercantile past. The decision to construct a covered loggia in which to display merchandise and bargain over sales prices was decided as early as 1392 by the Council of the Elders, and work was completed with the addition of the roof in 1443; the facade, which had remained unfinished, was redesigned in stone by Giorgio da Sebenico (1451–59) at great cost. The secular themes agreed upon with the artist for the facade's sculptures represented the Christian virtues of *Hope, Fortitude, Justice* and *Charity*, with the city symbol of the rampant knight in the center of the middle span. After a fire, Pellegrino Tibaldi redesigned the lowest order with typical mannerist faces (1556), also reorganizing the new front of the opening facing the sea and the interior in the Doric order, (1944 air raids destroyed much of the ceiling and their paintings) adding the daring hanging sculpture (1561), later incorporated by Gioacchino Varlè. The *Portella della Loggia* for the unloading of goods can be seen on the side facing the port.

Palazzo Cresci Antiqui (B3). This building, with 15th-century lancet arches in decorated brick, faces the loggia. The entrance hall, courtyard and elegant monumental staircase are clear indications of the changes made to the 15th-century building in the late 1700s; traces of Venetian-Dalmatian sculpture remain on the *portals* on Via della Catena and on Via Bonda (dated 1454), onto which the inner courtyard formerly opened through three ogival arches.

Santa Maria della Piazza* (B3). Originally built over an early Christian basilica from the 4th or 5th century, which in turn is thought to have been built over Trajan walls and towers, this Romanesque church (formerly *Santa Maria del Canneto* or *del Mercato*) probably dates back to the 12th century. By 1223 the naves and central apse had been extended with the creation of the inscribed transept; later the central nave was raised up on octagonal pillars. The Romanesque *facade** is one of the most interesting in the region: it is in three sections around an Apulian-style splayed portal, and has four elegant orders of blind arcades with spoil material inserts (Byzantine-style *Figure at Prayer*); it is signed Filippo and dated 1210. The truncated gable roof is, like the upper part of the campanile, evidently the result of reconstruction after the 1691 earthquake. Inside, glass slabs in the floor allow visitors to see the remains of the early Christian place of worship.

Lungomare Vanvitelli (A-B2-3). Along Via Saffi, Via del Porto and Via Sottomare – numerous gateways and tower houses were opened from the 13th century onward in the walls facing the sea with ogival arcades, often with their own private jetties for the unloading of goods directly into private warehouses. The only public *quay* was that owned by *the Municipality* or the Customs, opposite Santa Maria della Piazza, and of which remains are still visible along the surviving part of Via Sottomare. Continuing toward the North Quay, a number of monuments are visible to the left: the remains of *Portella Palunci*, enclosed within the harbormaster's office area, the so-called *Casa del Capitano del Porto* (the harbormaster's office) with double lancet opening, like the *Portella di Pier Greco* further north, and finally *Arco Capoleoni*.
Opposite the old walls halfway down the quayside are the remains of two important buildings bombed in 1944: the 16th-17th-century *Palazzo Mancinforte*, incorporated with its decorative remains into the Hotel Palace, and *Palazzo Leonardi,* probably designed by Carlo Marchionni, and now used as a garage by the tax authorities.

Arco di Traiano＊＊ (A2). The most important Roman monument in the Marche region, this 14-m-high triumphal marble arch was built between 100 and 115 in honor of Trajan, who had rebuilt the port at his own expense. The construction, whose slender Corinthian proportions were necessitated by the narrowness of the quay below, is perhaps the work of Apollodorus of Damascus. It was originally topped by three bronze statues of the prince, his wife and his sister, but these were stolen by the Saracens, who also took the rostra and the bronze letters in the 9th century. The present flight of steps dates back to 1852.

Arco Clementino (A2), This Istrian-stone arch with delicate chiaroscuro Doric moldings was built by Luigi Vanvitelli in 1738 as a symbolic gateway to the city from the *North Quay* (A1-2) for Pope Clement XII. A statue of the pope, which was originally to have graced its attic story, was more wisely placed in what is now Piazza del Plebiscito.

Cathedral of San Ciriaco＊＊ (A3). The cathedral, one of the finest examples of the Italian Romanesque and a symbol of the fusion of Adriatic and eastern artistry, proudly stands on the acropolis of the Doric city overlooking the sea. It was built over the foundations of the temple of Venus Euplea (4th cent. BC), which was also the site of a subsequent (6th cent.) early Christian place of worship dedicated to St. Lawrence. Toward the beginning of the 11th century the church became the third episcopal see of Ancona. When the relics of the city's patron saint Judas Cyriacus and those of St. Mar-

The Romanesque facade of Santa Maria della Piazza in Ancona

cellinus were brought to the church to join those of St. Liberius, the presbytery was raised to create the new martyr's crypt below. For reasons of space a new transverse extension was added between the late 12th and early 13th centuries, forming a cross with the original basilica; both parts were covered with wooden Venetian ogival vaulting and a southwest door was opened. This brilliant new design created a church in the form of a Greek cross having raised apsidal transepts and facing the port and the new road into the city.

The large splayed Verona marble *porch* with columns resting on lion figures was added in the 13th century to embellish the *portal**, which has clustered columns supporting ogival arch decorated with animals and heads of saints. The ogival ribbed dome, on a twelve-sided drum and pendentives supported by Byzantine-style figures of praying angels, rests on cruciform polystyle pillars and was completed in the 16th century. The detached campanile was built on the foundations of a late 13th-century military tower. Inside the cathedral note in the south transept the *Chapel of the Crucifix*, whose transennae are made from late 12th-century parapet tiles; on the left wall of the presbytery the *Sepulcher of the Blessed Ginelli* by Giovanni Dalmata (1506); and in the north transept the *Chapel of the Madonna*, with a sumptuous altar by Luigi Vanvitelli (1739).

Museo Diocesano (A3). Many of the cathedral's treasures are now kept in the former *Episcopio,* a 15th-century building (guided tours Sat and Sun afternoons), which became a bishop's palace in 1834. It contains the 15th-century *Reliquary of St. Stephen*, the *Shroud of St. Cyriacus* (10th cent.), the **Sarcophagus of Flavius Gorgonius** (4th cent.), and 17th-century Rubens-style tapestries. There is also an Art Gallery (works from the 14th–19th centuries), a large *Lapidarium*, and many rare parchments, medals and religious vestments.

Roman Amphitheater (A3). This elliptical theater, which nestles in the depression between the Guasco and Cappuccini hills, was built in the time of Augustus and enlarged under Trajan; it could seat some 8,000 spectators. The site was abandoned in the 4th century and later used as a burial ground and sub-structure for building work. In 1810 it was rediscovered and excavation work began after World War II. It will now form part of an archaeological park extending to the cliffs in the northeast of the city.

An exhibit in Ancona's Museo Diocesano

SS. Pellegrino e Teresa (A3). This church, which adjoins Palazzo Ferretti (see below; nobles residing in the palace could attend services in private), was begun for the Discalced Carmelites in 1706 and completed in 1738 in Baroque style; its circular plan beneath a solid drum and dome contains a *St. Teresa in Ecstasy* by Francesco Solimena in the choir stalls above the entrance and, on the high apsidal altar, a late 12th-century wooden *Crucifix*.

Palazzo del Senato (A3). Formerly known as Palazzo dei Pilestri, this palace was built in the area of the Roman forum before 1225 and used as the Senate House. It originally had four stories above ground level (an extra story was later added and restored during postwar restoration) and now, though part of its south wing is missing, it is one of the best examples of civil Romanesque architecture in the region for the sober elegance of its front (the only surviving example). It houses the Marche Region's Architectural and Environmental Heritage Department.

Palazzo Ferretti (A3). One of the best examples of civil mannerist architecture, this palace was built for Count Angelo Ferretti by Pellegrino Tibaldi (around 1560–66), who also frescoed the frieze on the *piano nobile* with *Scenes from Mythology and the History of Rome*; the Fireplace Room has frescoes by the Zuccari brothers. Renovated in 1759 with addition of an extra floor and the creation of the hanging garden, it was bought by the State after the war and since 1958 has housed **the Museo Archeologico Nazionale delle Marche*** (visits 8.30am–1.30pm).

The museum, which reopened in 1988 after lengthy restoration following the earthquake, has a large collection of finds from excavations and other sites in the Marche that have helped to reconstruct the history of the region from prehistoric times to the Late Middle Ages. Among the most important exhibits are funerary offerings from the early and late Bronze Age, items from Picene and Senonian-Gallic civilization, including decorated *Attic vases*, Etruscan *bronze* masterpieces, oriental *silverware* and *ivory*, and Celtic *jewelry*. A special controlled-climate display case on the ground floor was designed for the Cartoceto bronzes (see p. 78), currently being restored in Florence.

Palazzo degli Anziani (B3). The origins of this historic home of the civic judiciary are steeped in legend (the palace has been associated with the Roman princess Galla Placidia). Giorgio Vasari recounts how after its demolition at the hands of the Saracens in 839, it was rebuilt by Margaritone d'Arezzo (1270) in Romanesque-Gothic style. Important traces of this work can be seen both on the side facing the sea (high lancet arches and crossed-arch windows) and on the side facing Piazza Stracca (two orders of stone lancet loggias and sculpted panels with *Biblical Stories*). It suffered damage by fire in 1348, part of its east front was buried in 1563 to level the square, and the part remaining above ground level was restored in 1564–71 to a design by Tibaldi with windows having broken pediments. The Pamphilj fleurs-de-lis are a reminder of 1647 renovation

Vanvitelli's Gesù church in Ancona

work, during which the staircase was added and the central part of the roof raised to create the Hall of Honor, now the *aula magna* of the university faculties of Economics and Commerce.

Chiesa del Gesù (B3). This church, a building with a tall Tuscan pronaos that makes contrastive use of Istria stone and brick, looks proudly out to sea. It was designed by Luigi Vanvitelli for the Jesuits together with the adjoining convent over the foundations of an earlier (1605) place of worship, and was completed in 1743. With its light-filled Vignola-style interior in the shape of a Latin cross, shallow transepts and four communicating chapels, it is a minor masterpiece from the architect's early career. Although deconsecrated, it still contains a *St. Francis Saverius* by Sebastiano Conca.

Via Pizzecolli (B3). This road (once called Via del Comune) and its continuation (Via Gramsci), form the city's main monumental thoroughfare, and runs from the Roman forum to Piazza della Repubblica.

San Francesco delle Scale (B3). Franciscan friars, who first settled here in the late 13th century, built the church and convent of Santa Maria Maggiore in 1323. By the 15th century it had already grown to such importance that the area became known as the "Island of St. Francis." In 1455–59, when the church had already changed its name to *San Francesco*, Giorgio da Sebenico was commissioned to build the magnificent portal with baldachin, in ornate Gothic style modeled on the Porta della Carta gateway to the Doges' Palace in Venice, but its grandeur was dimmed by the major renovation of the complex carried out by Francesco Maria Ciaraffoni between 1777 and 1790. It was later used as a barracks and hospital by Napoleonic troops and the Piedmontese, badly damaged during 1943–44 air raids, but restored, reinstated and reconsecrated in 1953. Inside is a plaster *Glory* by Gioacchino Varlè (high altar), an *Assumption* by Lorenzo Lotto (apse), a *Baptism of Christ* by Pellegrino Tibaldi (1st altar on the right), and a *Madonna of Loreto* by Andrea Lilli (1st altar on the left).

Palazzo Bosdari (B3). This conspicuously-situated palace overlooking the sea, was the residence of a family of Dalmatian origin which bought it in the mid-17th century and renovated it with windows and an entrance portal echoing the style of Pellegrino Tibaldi. More Pamphilj fleurs-de-lis can be seen in the inner courtyard, which is reached by an elaborate entrance way. Bought by the city authorities in 1963, since 1973 it has been the home of the "Francesco Podesti" municipal art gallery, which adjoins the Modern Art Gallery.

Pinacoteca Comunale "Francesco Podesti." This collection, created in 1888 from the painter's artistic bequest, was originally housed in the former convent of *San Domenico*, then in the convent of *San Francesco delle Scale* (1919–58) and in Palazzo degli Anziani (1958–73), before moving to its present home. The gallery (open Tue to Sat 10am–7pm; Sun and Mon 9am–1pm) contains some fine paintings, although it does not provide a complete account of Ancona's artistic history. Among the most noteworthy works are those by Carlo da Camerino (*Dormition of the Blessed Virgin* and *Circumcision*), Arcangelo di Cola (*Madonna of Humility*), Neri di Bicci (shrine with *Madonna and Child*), Carlo Crivelli (*Madonna and Child*), Sebastiano del Piombo (*Portrait of Francesco Arsilli*), Lorenzo Lotto (*Sacred Conversation*), Titian (*Apparition of the Virgin*), Pomarancio (*Adoration of the Magi*), Antonio Tempesta, Andrea Lilio (*Ecstasy of St. John the Baptist, St. Francis, St. Bernardine of Siena and St. Paul, Angel Musicians, Scenes from the Life of St. Nicholas, Crucifixion with St. John the Baptist and St. Nicholas of Tolentino*), Angelo Caroselli (*Necromancer*), Giovanni Francesco Guerrieri (*Madonna and Sleeping Child with St. Anne*), Guercino (*Immaculate Conception and St. Palazia*), Ciro Ferri (*Mystic Marriage of St. Catherine*), Orazio Gentileschi (*Circumcision*), Carlo Maratta (*Madonna with St. Ambrose, St. Francis of Sales, and St. Nicholas*), Francesco Podesti (*Deposition*, preliminary sketch for *The Dogma of the Immaculate Conception, Eteocles and Polynices*); sculptural frag-

ments attributed to Margaritone d'Arezzo. The adjoining **Galleria Comunale d'Arte Moderna** (open Tue to Sat 10am–7pm; Sun and Mon 9am–1pm) was created in 1967 from a small collection of acquisitions made with Premio Marche funds, and now contains around 300 works by local and Italian artists, chosen for being representative of the century, most notably Adolfo De Carolis, Anselmo Bucci, Luigi Bartolini, Massimo Campigli, Virgilio Guidi, Ivo Pannaggi, Carlo Levi, Aligi Sassu, Ennio Morlotti, Orfeo Tamburi, Corrado Cagli, Pietro Annigoni, Bruno Cassinari, Emilio Tadini, Piero Dorazio, Gio Pomodoro, Getulio Alviani, Arnaldo Pomodoro, and Valeriano Trubbiani.

Palazzo del Governo (B3). This building was the hub of urban life in the Renaissance and the symbol of the balance of political and administrative power between the two hills of the city when, after the fire at Palazzo degli Anziani (1348) the seat of local government was transferred here. The original 1381 edifice was enlarged between 1418 and 1450, incorporating a medieval tower. In 1484 it was redesigned by Francesco di Giorgio Martini in Renaissance style (note the windows and string courses) and the twin classical portal was opened in the north facade; inside, Michele di Giovanni and his son Alvise di Michele created the arcaded courtyard (1493–94), and the rooms were renovated by Melozzo da Forlì (work that has since been lost). Bought from the papacy after 1532, it was the seat of the apostolic governors up to 1860; today it houses the Prefecture.

The *Civic Tower* (14th cent.) next to the palace kept its original medieval appearance until 1581, when it was rebuilt; the clock was built in 1611 and restored in 1808, and in 1612 the balcony with mannerist portal was added.

Piazza del Plebiscito (B3). Popularly known as Piazza del Papa because of

Painting by Titian in the "Francesco Podesti" Art Gallery, Ancona

the statue of Pope Clement XII, the square's form and geographical position make it the most important space in the city. It was created in the 15th century as a result of an enlargement scheme that incorporated the built-up area outside the walls of the Astagno hill and led to the construction of the Palazzo del Governo; it took on in its final form in the early 19th century.

The semi-circular *Pius VII Fountain* is by

palace in Via della Loggia. After being donated to the city authorities, it was transferred to Palazzo degli Anziani in 1750 (with a collection of 2,634 printed books and manuscripts mainly on civil and canon law, history, geography, and commerce) and moved to its present home in 1950. Although the library has suffered wartime losses of over 8,000 books, the collection currently numbers 135,000.

Ancona: Piazza del Plebiscito, with the church of San Domenico in the background

Pietro Zara (1818); the *Fountain of the Beheaded* is from the same period, but uses a 16th-century frieze which is traditionally believed to depict the heads of the young noblemen slain in 1534 during the taking of Ancona. The *Statue of Pope Clement XII* was sculpted in Istrian stone by Agostino Cornacchini (1737), originally for the basilica of St. John Lateran in Rome, then as an adornment for the Clementine Arch; the steps were not added until 1818.

Former Ospedale di San Tommaso di Canterbury (B3). Built in 1394 (using late Roman and 12th-century columns and capitals), this hospital contained a chapel with oratory dedicated to the *Virgin Enthroned*, as a reminder of miracle which took place in 1470. A large *Fish Market*, designed by Pietro Zara, partly below ground, was added on the south side in 1817. Both structures are to be used for the city museum.

Biblioteca Comunale Benincasa (B3). The mannerist *Palazzo Mengoni Ferretti* (1592) is the home of the municipal library, which was created from a 1669 bequest and opened to the public in 1671 in the family

Adjoining the library is *Porta San Pietro*, popularly known also as *Arco di Garola* and dating back to 1221, one of the few surviving traces of the 13th-century city walls; it is decorated by two leonine protomai.

San Domenico (B3). This church, whose facade is unfinished, was built between 1761 and 1783 on the site of the 13th-century church of the same name, to a design by Carlo Marchionni. The interior is a single vessel having eight deep side chapels and is decorated by nine statues and ten stucco medallions with *Dominican Saints* by Gioacchino Varlè, but more significantly by two important paintings: Titian's **Crucifixion** (1588; high aitar) and Guercino's *Annunciation** (1656; 1st altar on the left). The large adjoining convent – now a tax office – was used by the dreaded Inquisition in the 16th century.

Palazzo Millo (B3). This palace, at the end of *Via Gramsci*, also part of the ancient Via del Comune, was built between 1759 and 1770. The Vanvitelli-style design is attributed to Carlo Marchionni, the then director of the work on the port, who built it with his son Filippo, together with Francesco Maria Ciaraffoni. It has a large staircase with entrance way and inner courtyard; its upper rooms were frescoed (*mythological scenes*) by Giuseppe Pallavicini.

Corso Mazzini (B-C3). The winding "Corso Vecchio," the only road running east until the creation of the parallel *Corso Garibaldi* (1867) and *Corso Stamira* (1931), follows the old Via del Calamo, so called after the marshy cane thicket (or *calamus*) that once covered the site at the end of the Pennocchiara valley.

On the left is the late baroque church of *San Biagio* (B3), built 1745–48 by Ancona's Dalmatian community; the *Madonna and Child with Saints* inside is a rare painting by Francesco Maria Ciaraffoni.

A little further on is the *Calamo Fountain*, or *Fontana delle Tredici Cannelle*, so named after the thirteen bronze water spouts in the form of the heads of fauns; the vigorous but skillfully executed Mannerist rusticated ashlar work was taken from an illustration by Pellegrino Tibaldi of around 1559.

Piazza Cavour and Largo XXIV Maggio (C3-4). The square centers around the 1867 statue of Piedmontese statesman Aristodemo Costoli; the road runs between the Sacconi-style *Palazzo delle Poste and Telecomunicazioni* (Guido Cirilli, 1926) and the *Palazzo del Popolo* (1931).

The church of *Santa Maria della Misericordia* (C4) is worth a short detour: the fine Gothic-Renaissance *portal* by Marino di Marco Cedrino (1475) belonged to the previous church, destroyed in 1944.

Viale della Vittoria (C4-6). This major thoroughfare, laid out as part of major urban expansion work between the wars, is lined with Art Nouveau *villas* and features an elegant tree-lined avenue. The quiet *Piazza Diaz* (C5), a traditional meeting place for the city's youth, leads to the city's third coastal area, set against the blue backdrop of the sea and sky: the Passetto (C6).

Monumento ai Caduti (C6). The city's war memorial is a light-filled peripteral temple in Istrian stone of elegant Doric proportions, designed (1927–33) by Guido Cirilli. Its eight fluted columns support the frieze with the epigraph in the Leopardi song "All'Italia."

1.2 The Conero Promontory
From Ancona to Numana, 24.5 km

The Conero Riviera, which is quickly reached from the city by road, is an area of outstanding natural beauty with a wealth of prehistoric sites that is quite unique on the Adriatic coast.

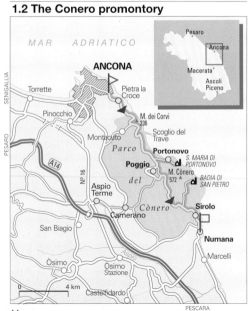

1.2 The Conero promontory

The drive begins at Passetto, from where Via S. Margherita follows the coast to the hamlet of Pietralacroce (3.5 km) and after another 7.5 km meets the road leading down (2 km) to Portonovo. At Poggio (2 km) drive straight on past the road leading off to the right to Camerano and Aspio Terme (10 km), and after another 6 km to the turn-off (to the left) for the Abbey of *San Pietro* (3 km). 3 km further on the road reaches Sirolo and, after another 5 km, Numana.

La strada del Monte
This extremely picturesque seaside road offers splendid views of the coast

The Conero regional park

When ruling no. 21 of 23 April 1987 came into effect, the Marche Region finally won the long, hard battle for its first public nature park. A year later, the Conero Landscape Development Plan made a real contribution to safeguarding and protecting one of the Adriatic's most beautiful natural environments. Though relatively small in size (approx. 5,800 hectares), the park contains – in the area between the Gallina cliffs in Ancona to the mouth of the Musone river – rare geological formations, wildlife, Picene and Roman archaeological remains and monuments to medieval and military architecture that make it an oasis of truly outstanding natural beauty and cultural interest. Dominated by the characteristic dark outline of Mt. Conero (572 m; the name comes from the Greek word *komaros*, the arbutus), whose raw white limestone heart is revealed before it sinks into the Adriatic's emerald waters, this nature park offers something for all tastes: hill walking (there are more than 18 walks along breathtakingly scenic paths), cave exploration (in underground caverns and passages often shrouded in myth and legend) and other outdoor pursuits (such as bird watching). For the more culturally minded there are artistic treasures galore, while the seaside resorts offer vacationers splendid secluded beaches and coves as well as sailing facilities (the marina at Numana has room for 800 boats). Portonovo Bay is also renowned for its gastronomic delights.

The Torre Clementina "towers" over Portonovo beach

beginning at Pietralacroce (m 170). The razor-sharp *Scoglio del Trave* juts out into the foamy sea, just before *Mezzavalle Beach*.

Portonovo*

The beach, surrounded by modest bathing establishments and excellent restaurants overlooking the sea, is one of the gems of the regional park of Mt. Conero. Above is the *Napoleonic Fortress*, a coastal battery and military bulwark for 600 soldiers built in 1808 to defend the supplies of drinking water during Napoleon Bonaparte's naval blockade of the British fleet. Further along is the *Torre Clementina*, built by Pope Clement XI in 1716 to defend the coast against marauding pirates. This tower was restored at the end of the 19th century by Adolfo De Bosis, who converted it into a quiet, secluded home.

On a spur of the harbor, against the imposing backdrop of Mt. Conero, sits the church of Santa Maria di Portonovo*, with dazzlingly white limestone walls. This combination of a basilica and Greek cross plan with dome and trumpet arches was built before 1050 using Lombard building methods (suspended arches and pilaster strips) by Benedictines possibly of Franco-Norman provenance and is a minor masterpiece of Romanesque architecture. Enlarged in 1225 to accommodate a convent (now destroyed), it was abandoned in 1320 following a landslide; after looting by the Turks, it was restored in 1897 and reconsecrated in 1934.

Poggio

This is one of the small inland historic towns (186 m) that grew up between the 11th and 12th centuries to protect the coast and was the scene of countless raids by marauding Turkish pirates, who plundered the town.

A 10-km detour to the southwest leads to the Aspio river and two interesting towns outside Ancona.
The first (6 km) is Camerano (elev. 231 m, pop. 6,659), an industrial and wine-producing center first inhabited in Neolithic

times, then by the Picenes, and later grew into a flourishing fortified town which owed allegiance to Ancona. It was the birthplace of painter Carlo Maratta, who is remembered by a bust in Piazza Roma. The 13th-century church of *San Francesco* betrays its 12th-century foundation in the Gothic portal and adjoining cloister; the interior was redesigned by Francesco Maria Ciaraffoni. *Palazzo Mancinforte*

Beached boats in Numana

(18th–19th cent.) has a fine Italian garden. Camerano is also noted for the caves that extend under the town of Castelvecchio, in which the population probably sought shelter from pirate attacks. The impressive sequence of underground rooms were carved out of the tufa in the 17th and 18th centuries.

Four km further along the road is Aspio Terme (33 m), a verdant spa resort with four cold mineral water springs (Regina Coeli, Santa Maria, Nuova and Forte).

Badia di San Pietro

This Romanesque abbey church, built by Benedictine monks in the first half of the 11th century, was a Camaldolese hermitage from 1558 to 1860. The present facade dates back to 1651, the fine decorated capitals on the pillars and the columns of the three naves inside (visits by prior arrangement, apply to APT, Ancona) document their earlier history. The adjoining convent is now a hotel.

The stretch of coast below tells a fascinating story of geological happenings (picturesquely described in such names as *Devil's Hollow, Slave Caverns, Papal Seat, Sail, Black Rocks,* and *Two Sisters*). The formations have always fired the popular and poetic imagination, with no end of historical and scientific conjecture as to their origin and use; each has contributed to the charm of the Conero's "enchanted castle."

Sirolo*

One of the most picturesque corners of the Adriatic coast, this village was fortified in the 11th century by the Franco-Teutonic Cortesi family and ceded to Ancona in 1225.

This resort (elev. 125 m, pop. 3,137) retains the old castrensian layout. The characteristic campanile belongs to the church of the *Madonna del Rosario* (containing 16th - cent. frescoes). Note also the churches of *SS. Sacramento* (with 15th-century portal) and the parish church of *San Nicolò* (1765). Sections of the medieval wall can be seen in Piazza Teatro including the *Torrino rampart*; the *Cortesi Theater* dates back to 1908.

Villa Vetta Marina, on the road to Numana, was built at the beginning of the 19th century on the site where St. Francis founded a convent in 1215.

Numana*

An ancient Picene port (8th century BC), the town (elev. 56 m, pop. 3,038) was refounded by the Syracusans (4th cent. BC), then became a Roman colony (269 BC) and later a *municipium* (91 BC). In 558 and 1292 it was ravaged by an earthquake and plundered by the Saracens, and gradually declined until it came under the control of Ancona in 1404.

The *Shrine of the Crucifix* was reconstructed in a somewhat pretentious modern style (1969) over the previous 1561–66 shrine (Pellegrino Tibaldi?). Visitors come to see the miraculous late 12th- early 13th-century Romanesque wooden *Crucifix*. In the same square is the former Bishop's Palace (1773). The Antiquarium (open 9am–7pm) has a rich collection of funerary offerings from recently-excavated Picene tombs. Via Roma, from which the characteristic flight of steps of Via IV Novembre known as the *Costarella* rises, leads to a small square with the Pincio Tower (decapitated in 1930 and with remains of an ogival arch), part of the medieval fortifications.

2 Around Ancona

The Province

Created with the territorial reorganization following the Unification of Italy, the Ancona province (1,940 km²) is the smallest of the four that make up the Marche region. The provincial capital is still the most populous city – although Jesi and Senigallia are quickly catching up – but only the third largest municipal area after Fabriano and Arcevia. This is emblematic of an historical, economic and cultural situation that has turned the regional capital's attentions toward the sea rather than toward land ownership and farming, which is the economic base of most of the towns and cities in the surrounding area. Ancona has had a contradictory and often conflicting relationship with its neighbors, who have suffered rather than acknowledged its supremacy. Nonetheless, the city has determined the commercial development of the other towns and cities in the province by virtue of its position at the inevitable point of convergence of all trade in the area, especially following the creation of the free port by Pope Clement XII in 1732.

Today the administrative borders that mark out the province of Ancona (composed of 49 municipal areas) often have little bearing on local history and geography. The border does, it is true, follow the clear-cut, natural border of the Cesano river valley in the northwest and, in the southwest, gains the deep wedge created by the quiet Esino river valley and the arable land in the Apennine foothills up to the *Gola della Rossa* (although Fabriano and Sassoferrato, to the west of this gorge would seem to fall more logically into Umbrian territory). But the southeast border, which jumps from one side of the Musone river to the other and, just before reaching the coast, twists artificially to include Loreto, is the result of a contrived and historically largely unjustified redefinition of boundaries. Indeed Loreto was once an enclave that enjoyed certain extra-territorial privileges: as the site of the holy shrine of the Santa Casa, elevated by Sixtus V to the status of *felix civitas lauretana*, it no longer came under the natural and episcopal jurisdiction of Recanati, although it retained cultural links with the province of Macerata.

The municipal area of Osimo, which comprises Castelfidardo and Offagna and is largely given over to farming, has a certain degree of independence and cultural identity, the town of Osimo in particular having a rich historical tradition of its own. But the area's real center of gravity – since ancient times, when it separated the 5th and 6th Augustus *regio*, and later the food-producing Piceno from suburbicarian Piceno – is the Esino valley. Fertile and with a rich medieval history (Benedictine abbeys), the area enjoyed the benefits of closer links with Rome after the Via Clementina was opened (1732). Communications were further improved in the mid-19th century when the Esino valley was cho-

The Santuario della Santa Casa, Loreto, in an 18th-cent. print and today

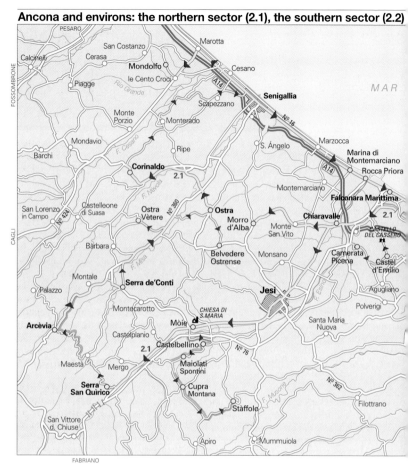

Ancona and environs: the northern sector (2.1), the southern sector (2.2)

sen in preference to the Potenza valley further south for the new railway line. The Esino valley is dominated by Jesi and its castles, a rapidly expanding town abounding in well-preserved monuments from Roman times to the Renaissance. It also documents the culture of the wealthy nobility in the 18th century (the Pergolesi Theater is one of the finest and most active in the region); and since the early 19th century it has been a competitive industrial center. Senigallia, in the northern part of the province, has been the site of a famous market from the 13th century (the *Fiera della Maddalena*). In Renaissance times it was a small workshop of military architecture and in the second half of the 18th century a model of neoclassical townplanning. Inland, between the Misa, Nevola and Cesano valleys, lie the historical towns of Ostra, Ostra Vetere, Castelleone di Suasa, and Corinaldo, whose marginal position led to their frequent use as military bases.

2.1 The north of the province
Circular tour from Ancona, 153 km

The driving tour passes through the vine-covered hills of the Verdicchio wine-making area and ends on the east coast with its splendid beaches after passing though gentle rolling hills topped by perfectly walled towns (the walls of Corinaldo are undoubtedly the best known and most striking, but those of Jesi are also worthy of note) and with holy shrines that have drawn pilgrims for centuries (the Cistercians founded the abbey at Chiaravalle and the church of Santa Maria in Moie). The tour is no less rich in artistic treasures: Jesi art gallery has works by Lorenzo Lotto, Luca Signorelli's polyptych can be seen in the church of *San Medardo* at

and from here the road makes its way back to the coast and Senigallia (17.5 km), from where it is worth continuing up the coast and a little way inland (13 km) to Mondolfo. In the opposite direction the SS16 leads (15.5 km) to Falconara Marittima, and after another 10.5 km back to Ancona.

Chiaravalle

This town (elev. 22 m, pop. 13,729), which grew up on the 16th century (it was the site of largest tobacco factory in the papal state), has the remains of one of the three abbeys founded by the Cistercian monks in Italy from Clairvaux (which translates into Italian as *Chiaravalle*). In 1126 Benedictine monks from France laid the foundation stone for **Santa Maria in Castagnola** (open winter 6.30–11am and 5–6.30pm; summer 6.30–11am and 5–7pm), reutilizing a Benedictine monastery dating back to the 7th century. The Gothic style has the simple lines typical of the order's architecture, seen in the facade, with its narthex and rose window, in the buttressed sides, and in its interior, whose three naves are punctuated by 12 cruciform pillars. The *altars* in the arms of the transept are Baroque.

Twelve km to the west is **Morro d'Alba** (elev. 199 m, pop. 1,689), a small historic town surrounded by 15th-century walls and a steep escarpment; the *Museo della Cultura Mezzadrile Utensilia* (open Sat 4pm–6pm, Sun 10am–noon; 15 Jun–15 Sep 4pm–7pm, Sun 10am–noon and 4pm–7pm) has a collection of old agricultural implements.

A 15-km excursion southwest of Chiaravalle takes in a number of castles. The castle at *Camerata Picena* (elev. 125 m, pop. 1,472), is a 14th-century manor-house with the typical circular layout of the hill towns. **Castel d'Emilio** (elev. 157 m) takes its name from one of the area's Roman colonizers: the medieval *fortress* is reached by a crenelated brick tower, with an lancet arch opening. Finally, *Castello del Cassero*, with its clearly recognizable entrance tower, dates back to 1375.

Arcevia, while Senigallia boasts a Renaissance fortress, the Foro Annonario market complex and the arcaded Portici Ercolani. The SS16 (Adriatica) highway runs northwest out of Ancona and after 11.5 km meets the SS76 (Val d'Esino), which follows the course of the Esino river. The first stop (6.5 km) is Chiaravalle – from where excursions can be made to Morro d'Alba (12 km) and to the east of the river to explore the ancient castles (15 km). Further up the Esino valley is Jesi (11.5 km) and the church of Santa Maria in Moie (10 km), from where a 22.5 km detour leads into the Verdicchio hills. 12 km further on, at Serra San Quirico, a winding scenic road leaves the Esino and after 16 km reaches Arcevia, before turning northeast onto the SS360 (Arceviese) towards Serra de' Conti (13.5 km). 10 km further on is the turn-off for Ostra Vetere (3 km), and then, after another 6 km, Ostra, from where a 4-km detour to the south leads to Belvedere Ostrense. 13.5 km northwest of Ostra is Corinaldo

Jesi *

Some years ago this town (elev. 97 m, pop. 39,502; see plan p. 51) was dubbed the "Milan of the Marche" because of its hard-working reputation. This is partly due to its position on a low hill in the Esino valley first settled by the Umbrians, who founded *Aesis*. But it was the Romans who understood the strategic importance of the town and the valley below. In 247 BC they took over a colony, and established a branch of the Via Flaminia along the river and then the border of the V and VI *re-*

giones of Augustus. Jesi was also a border town at the time of the food-producing Pentapolis, separating the Longobards from the Byzantines.

The town took on a more recognizable form in the 11th century; in the 12th century it acquired municipal status and was the unexpected birthplace of Frederick II; the cathedral and the walls were built in the centuries that followed. In the 1300s and 1400s the town was caught up in the bitter war between the Guelphs and the Ghibellines, which came to an end with the return to church rule in 1447. This was followed by the so-called second communal age, in which the walls and other buildings were restored and the town expanded with the addition of the area around Via Sabella (now Corso Matteotti). The State of Jesi, which had been taken away from the Marca governor in 1586 and put under the control of a pontifical prelate, survived until the Napoleonic occupation. Its subsequent return to papal control was accompanied by an intense development in farming, and later the creation of spinning mills and factories in the valley. This gave rise to Jesi's industrial vocation, which firmly established itself after World War II.

The walls* (A2–3). These still encircle the original town center and are a significant example of a defense system. They are the result of renovation work (ramparts and blockhouses) on a 14th-century fortification built over the remains of a similar Roman structure.

A view of the walls in Jesi

This work was carried out in 1488 by Baccio Pontelli, who also built a stronghold that was demolished a few decades later. There are fine views of the walls from the public park (A3), where the late 15th-century round *keep* stands, and from *Via Garibaldi* (A2-3), where houses have been built over the former defense systems.

Before visiting the historic center, note the church of *San Marco* (A2; visits by prior arrangement, tel. 4334), originally built by the Benedictines in the 13th century and given a new facade in the mid 19th century; the original Gothic style is still clearly visible inside. The 14th-century *fresco* at the end of the south aisle is from the Rimini school.

Piazza Federico II (A2-3). This square in the center of the town, on the site of the old Roman forum has a 19th-century *obelisk-fountain*. Tradition has it that Costanza d'Altavilla gave birth to Swabian Emperor Frederick II in a tent in the square. The town's architecture is predominantly 18th and 19th century. In the early 1700s, Andrea Vici built the former church of *San Floriano* as part of a convent over an earlier place of worship. Note the Baroque *Palazzo Balleani** (A3), with *balcony* held up by large caryatids, and *Palazzo Ripanti* (the windows have mixtilinear Borromini-style pediments). The *Duomo*, founded in the 13th century, has a neoclassical facade; the single-nave interior with large dome was remodeled in the 18th century; the two Verona brocatello marble *stoups* to the sides of the entrance are by Giorgio da Como.

Palazzo del Vecchio Seminario houses the *Museo Diocesano* (A3; open Mon, Tue, Thu and Fri 10am–noon), whose collection includes a 14th-century wooden *Crucifix*, a 16th–17th century gold *Processional Cross* and five canvases by Ercole Ramazzani.

Via Pergolesi (A2). This street, which became the town's main thoroughfare after a mid-15th century reorganization, follows the Roman *cardo* and contains a sequence of interesting Renaissance architecture, notably *Palazzo Amici* (A2-3), which dates back to 1526. An inscription in a small square to the right marks the birthplace of 18th-century composer *Giovanni Battista Pergolesi*.

Palazzo della Signoria* (A2-3). This building, in Piazza Colocci, is also known as *Palazzo dei Priori*, and was built by Francesco di Giorgio Martini in 1486–98. The Tuscan architect's style can be seen in

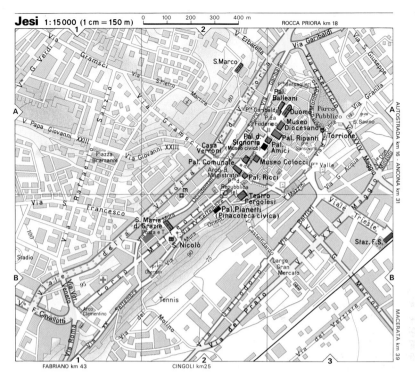

the solemn, elegant lines of the **facade**, which has, inside a frame also by Martini, a crowned *lion rampant* (the symbol of the city), the work of Michele di Giovanni and Alvise di Michele; the windows have the typical Guelph cross pattern. The tower on the left-hand side of the facade – which was rebuilt in 1661 – was originally designed by another Tuscan architect, Andrea Sansovino, to whom the first row of loggias in the inner courtyard have also been attributed. The palace, which was originally the city hall and from the late 16th century the seat of the pontifical governors, today houses the *Municipal Library* (with over 100,000 books, manuscripts and incunabula, as well as a large collection of essays by Gaspare Spontini) and the **Museo Civico** (open 9am–noon and 3pm–6pm; Sat 9am–noon): the archaeological exhibits come from the ancient settlement of *Aesis* (note the group of headless *imperial Statues* and the *portraits of Augustus, Tiberius* and *Caligula* discovered in the area of the former convent of San Floriano), but there is also an in-

The lion rampant, symbol of Jesi

teresting collection of 80 *Apulian vases* made between the 1st century BC and the 2nd century AD. Other exhibits include two 15th-century *bas-reliefs*, a polychrome terracotta (*Nativity* and the *Annunciation to the Shepherds*) attributed to Pietro Paolo Agabiti, and a collection of *apothecary vases** made in Urbania in 1747.

Opposite Palazzo della Signoria is the *Museo "Antonio Colocci"* (visits by request, apply at the Pinacoteca Civica), housed in Palazzo Colocci, and with an interesting 18th-century apartment; on loan a collection of archaeological finds and an exhibition of weaponry.

Piazza dell'Indipendenza and Piazza Spontini (A2). These two squares lie at the end of Via Pergolesi (note *Casa Verroni*, an interesting example of Renaissance architecture with a triumphal Roman arch doorway) and are graced with two 16th-century buildings: *Palazzo Comunale* and *Palazzo Ricci*, which has a rusticated facade. The two are separated by the *Arco del Magistrato*, the ancient gateway to the Roman and medieval towns.

51

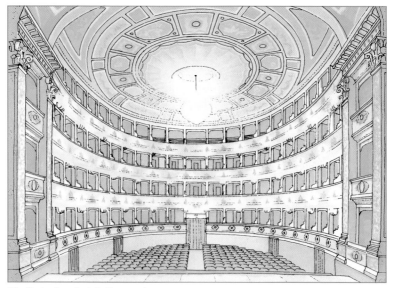

The Teatro Pergolesi, Jesi's opera house

Teatro Pergolesi (A-B2). This important Italian opera house built between 1791 and 1796 to a design by Francesco Maria Ciaraffoni on the southeast side of Piazza della Repubblica, is named after the great composer Giovanni Battista Pergolesi, who was born in Jesi. It is the venue for a major opera season in October.

Leading off from the square are *Corso Matteotti* (A-B1-2), the road along which the town expanded and today one of Jesi's busiest streets, and, running parallel to it, *Via XV Settembre*, where the Art Gallery is located (see below).

Palazzo Pianetti* (B2). This is the most important palace belonging to the rich local nobility which settled here between the 17th and 18th centuries and was designed in the early 18th century by a member of the Pianetti family, who was the architect of Charles VI Hapsburg. The profound influence his experience at the Austrian court had can be seen in the side facing the street, which has no fewer than 100 windows, and in the **gallery*** on the *piano nobile*, a celebration of Baroque stuccowork of central European inspiration.

Pinacoteca Civica*. Jesi's most prestigious institution (open 9.30am–12.30pm and 5pm–8pm; Jul–Aug 9.30am–12.30pm and 5pm–midnight; closed Mon), this art gallery

Giovanni Battista Pergolesi

has an extensive collection of paintings, most notably those painted by Lorenzo Lotto between 1512 and 1532. Here is the **polyptych*** (*St. Lucy before Judge Pascasio*; in the predella, *St. Lucy at the Tomb of St. Agatha*, *St. Lucy Condemned*, *St. Lucy Being Dragged by Oxen*), a work considered to be one of the artist's masterpieces for the freshness of its color and detail (1531–32); also here are *Gabriel* and the vividly colored *Lady of the Annunciation* (ca. 1526), an extraordinarily realistic *Visitation* (ca. 1531), a *Madonna and Child with St. Joseph and St. Jerome* and *St. Francis Receiving the Stigmata with St. Clare* (1527), with superb chiaroscuro effects. There are four small paintings on wood (*Nativity, Epiphany, St. Jerome, Sts. Sebastian and Roch*) by Pietro Paolo Agabiti; *Mary Magdalene Visited by Angels* from the Guercino school, and works by Pomarancio and Carlo Cignani. A large part of the gallery is devoted to contemporary art, with works by Renato Guttuso, Ennio Morlotti, Bruno Cassinari, Virgilio Guidi, Enrico Paolucci, and Michelangelo Pistoletto.

Santuario di Santa Maria delle Grazie (B2). Preceded on Piazza Pergolesi by the *Monument to the Composer* (1910), it was built as a votive chapel following the 1454–56 plague but was rebuilt in the mid-

18th century; the fresco in the chapel to the right of the high altar (*Madonna of Mercy*) is probably from the 15th-century Umbria-Marche school.

The church of *San Nicolò*, was founded in the 12th–13th centuries, while the *Arco Clementino* (B1), which marks the end of the 15th-century expansion, was opened in 1734 in honor of Pope Clement XII.

Down in the modern town, the abbey of *Santa Maria del Piano* (B3, off map) is reached by taking Via Marconi and turning left into Via Santa Maria. Although Romanesque in origin, it is clearly Gothic in style; inside is an 8th-century *sarcophagus* *, one of the finest examples of Marche medieval art.

Santa Maria

This church, near the village of Moie (elev. 9 m), formed part of a 12th-century abbey complex and was the second Cistercian settlement along the Esino river. The fine interior has a nave and two aisles divided by cruciform pillars, with a combination of barrel- and cross-vaulting.

From the church, a 22.5 km detour winds its way up the southern side of the valley through the celebrated Verdicchio hills, and after 6 km reaches **Castelbellino** (elev. 261 m, pop. 3,304), whose medieval origins are seen in the layout of the town and in the traces of the old walls; the *Museo Civico* (visits by appointment, 8am–2pm) has a *Madonna of the Rosary* by Benedetto Nucci, a *Crucifix and Saints* and an *Archangel Michael, St. Charles Borromeo and St. Bernardine of Siena* by Ernst Van Schayck. 3.5 km further up is **Maiolati Spontini** (elev. 405 m, pop. 5,449), the birthplace of the celebrated composer Gaspare Spontini. The *Museo Spontiniano* (visits by request, apply at the Town Hall), has a collection of manuscripts and memorabilia as well as Spontini's own personal library; his *tomb* in the church of *San Giovanni*, has a medallion decoration by Antonio Canova.

At 14 km is **Cupra Montana** (elev. 505 m, pop. 4,794), a holiday resort of Picene origin, whose name derives from a temple to the goddess Cupra, a symbol of plenty. Indeed the fertility of the surrounding area is seen each year in the abundant wine crop, which is celebrated in a well-known festival and documented by the fascinating *Museo Internazionale delle Etichette dei Vini* (open 10am–noon and 5pm–7pm; summer 10am–noon, 5pm–7pm and 9pm–11pm; closed Mon), whose collection of wine labels from around the world includes some from the early 19th century. The *Collegiata*, or collegiate church, rebuilt in the 18th century, has a 15th-century silver *Cross* and Baroque works by Antonio Sarti. Finally, at 22.5 km lies **Staffolo** (elev. 441 m, pop. 2,115), an interesting town

mostly still surrounded by its old walls (the keep was built by Egidio Albornoz); the *Museo del Vino* built into the walls (open on request) offers wine-tasting, and has a superb oak and stone *wine-press* from 1695.

Serra San Quirico

This town (elev. 300 m, pop. 2,997) has made remarkable use of its fortifications: the houses are built over the walls, thereby creating covered streets known locally as *copertelle*. The attractively situated church of *Santa Lucia* was rebuilt in the second half of the 17th century; the *Cartoteca Storica Regionale* (open 9am–noon and 4pm–7pm) has maps dating from around 1200 to the present day.

Arcevia

Situated on a rocky spur overlooking the upper Misa valley and once famed for its impregnability, Arcevia (elev. 535 m, pop. 5,704) is now better known as a pleasant holiday resort. Gone are the days of opulence as a bastion of the Papal State, when after being granted municipal status at the end of the 12th century, it played an active

Il Verdicchio

Verdicchio wine-growing was introduced to the Marche region by the Etruscans, whose techniques were later perfected by the Senonian Gauls (hence the vine's Latin name *arbustum gallicum*). The original clone acclimatized well to the slopes of the Esino valley. The combination of good loamy soil, plentiful sunshine and regular weather patterns led to the creation of a clear white wine with a pale yellow-green color, rich, fragrant bouquet – not unlike apricot – and an agreeably full-bodied, fruity flavor that lingers on the palate.

Today's Verdicchio (photo) comes in three denominations of guaranteed origin (DOC): Castelli di Jesi Classico, Castelli di Jesi and Matelica. They account for 80% of the region's DOC wine output and make a substantial contribution to the local farming economy.

The houses in Sera San Quirico were built straight onto the walls

part in the political life of the Marca. Despite urban redevelopment, the town retains its medieval layout, based around a central thoroughfare that runs along the spur (today's Corso Mazzini), and the appearance of a walled town (to which its old name Rocca Contrada testifies) and the 15th-century *walls*, with four well-preserved gateways (note in particular the Santa Lucia gate). The town's most significant monument is the **Collegiata di San Medardo**, rebuilt in 1634, and having two works by Luca Signorelli: polyptych of *God the Father, the Virgin and Child with Saints* in the apse, and *Baptism of Christ* in the baptistery; there is also a late 15th-century carved wooden *choir*, a Michelangelo-inspired *Last Judgment* by Ercole Ramazzani on the left-hand wall of the presbytery; a glazed terracotta *dossal* by Giovanni della Robbia (1513) on the altar of the left transept; and a *Meeting of King Lothair and St. Medard* by Claudio Ridolfi.

Running along the left flank of the church is *Via Ramazzani*; follow this street to the left and then turn right into Vicolo Santa Maria where the early 15th-century church of *Santa Maria* has a Della Robbia *Annunciation* (1528).

Corso Mazzini runs along the right of the church of *San Medardo*. A doorway on the left marks the entrance

to the *Museo Archeologico Statale* (open 9am–1.30pm), which has a collection of prehistoric and protohistoric remains; the medieval *Palazzo Comunale* stands on the right.

Serra de' Conti

As its name suggests, this town (elev. 216 m, pop. 3,367) has medieval origins: it was a feudal town until 1238 when it became a free commune. It too has **well-preserved defensive walls**, over which the 15th-century monastery of *Santa Maria Maddalena* was built near Piazza Leopardi.

On the way to Ostra, it is worth making a detour to **Ostra Vetere** (elev. 250 m, pop. 3,530), which contends with its neighbor the distinction of having been founded by the inhabitants of Ostra Antica. The dome and campanile that rise above its rooftops belong to the church of *Santa Maria della Piazza*, a modern imitation of Gothic style. The Municipio has two detached *frescoes* by Dionisio Nardini and Fabrizio Fabrizi (1470).

Ostra

This well-preserved walled town (elev. 188 m, pop. 5,901), which until 1881 was called Montalboddo, looks down over the Misa valley. It is believed to have been founded by the inhabitants of Ostra Antica, and was sacked and destroyed many times in its history.

Arcevia: porta di S. Lucia

The central *Piazza dei Martiri* is dominated by the *Torre Civica* (15th–16th cent., but later altered) and a portal belongs to the church of *San Francesco*, little of whose 14th-century origins remain. It is decorated with frescoes by Filippo Bellini (3rd chapel on the right) and various canvases by Ercole Ramazzani. *Corso Mazzini*, which runs from the square between the church and Palazzo Comunale, is lined with 18th-century buildings; note in particular *Palazzo Luzzi* (nos. 66–68) and *Palazzo Pericoli* (no. 73).

Four km to the south lies **Belvedere Ostrense** (elev. 251 m, pop. 2,178), also partly enclosed by 15th-century walls; its *Museo Internazionale dell'Immagine Postale* is worth a visit (open Mon, Wed, and Fri 4pm–7pm; other days by prior arrangement).

Corinaldo*

The town's main attraction are its **walls****, arguably the best preserved in the whole region. The walk around these old fortifications (part of which was the ancient sentry patrol route) is the best way of getting to know the long, eventful history of the town (elev. 203 m, pop. 5,234), which was already quite eventful as early as the mid 14th-century, when it was destroyed by Egidio Albornoz and rebuilt in a way more suited to the morphology of the area. The dense fabric of the town is indeed the result of Corinaldo's role as a stronghold both for the Malatesta family, who ruled the town from 1366 to 1440, and for Pope Sixtus IV, under whom the walls were completed in 1490.

The solid, 912-meter-long defense structure is punctuated by towers (the *Sperone* is traditionally attributed to Francesco di Giorgio Martini) and gateways (*Porta di Sotto* dates back to 1366; *Porta Nuova* was built in 1490). Construction work proceeded within the walls in the centuries that followed, and a rectilinear road network was laid out (the **Piaggia**, or "One Hundred Steps") leading up to the *Terreno*, the modern town center.

The main religious building is the 17th-century *Santuario di Santa Maria Goretti* (reached from the Terreno by Via Santa Maria Goretti), dedicated to the young martyr whose house and monument are at the entrance to the town. In *Piazza del Cassero*, next to il Terreno, is the former Benedictine convent, which houses the *Civica Raccolta d'Arte "Claudio Ridolfi"* (open Sat and Sun 10am–12.30pm and 4pm–7.30pm; mid Jun–mid-Jul and mid Aug–mid-Sep 10am–12.30pm and 4pm–7.30pm; mid Jul–mid-Aug 10am–12.30pm, 4pm–7.30pm and 9pm–11pm), which contains a collection of wooden *statues of saints*, *reliquaries*, embossed *silver*, and altarpieces from between the 16th and 18th centuries.

Another good reason to visit the town is to witness the *Festa del Pozzo della Polenta*, held in memory of an episode in which a thief who had made off with a sack of maize flour, fearing he was going to be caught, tipped his booty into the fountain.

Senigallia

A memorable advertising slogan describing Senigallia's "velvet beach" highlights one of the main economic resources of this town (elev. 5 m, pop. 41,511; see plan

Corinaldo, the "Piaggia"

p. 56), which straddles the Misa river. In the 20th century Senigallia has put behind it its commercial past (based on the port and the famous market that once attracted all comers) and has taken off as a tourist resort, helped to no small degree by the extremely fine sand of its beaches. The fortunes of *Sena Gallica* have been linked to its wharves since at least the 14th century, although its history can be traced back to the 4th century BC, and the Senonian Gauls. It was an important center under the Romans and as part of the maritime Pentapolis. The port flourished under the aegis of Sigismondo Malatesta and Giovanni Della Rovere, and from the mid 17th century to the end of the following century – thanks also to the presence of the *Fiera della Maddalena*, the famous market that originated in the 13th century, and to exemption from duties – saw the arrival of no fewer than 500 sailing vessels, generating trade worth some 10 million

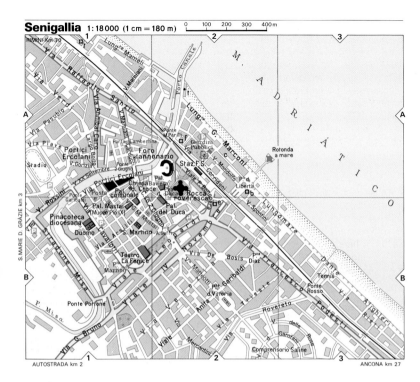

scudos. The Renaissance walls (parts of which still exist with their gateways) were fortified in the late 15th century with the building of the castle (the Rocca Roveresca), but by the 18th century could no longer contain the rapidly-growing population, and urban expansion was accompanied by the building of the Portici Ercolani, the Foro Annonario and the La Fenice theater. Senigallia was also the birthplace of Giovanni Maria Mastai Ferretti, who became Pope Pius IX.

Rocca Roveresca** (A2). The castle is named after Giovanni Della Rovere, who commissioned Baccio Pontelli to design the stronghold, construction of which began in 1480. The Florentine architect, perhaps influenced by Luciano Laurana, devised a square structure, with four cylindrical towers at the sides. Inside (open 9am–7pm; Jul and Aug 9am–1pm and 5pm–10pm, Sun 9am–7pm), it is possible to visit the underground passages and patrol trenches, and study the history of the Della Rovere family and restoration work in a *permanent exhibition.*

Piazza del Duca (A-B2). This square, in front of the castle, is decorated with the fountain of the same name, also called *Fountain of the Lions* (1596). It has two im-

portant buildings: *Palazzo del Duca,* built in the 16th century as a residence of the dukes of Urbino (the coffered ceiling decoration on the *piano nobile,* is attributed to Taddeo Zuccari); and **Palazzetto Baviera** (open winter 8.30–12.30pm and 3.30pm–6pm, closed Thu afternoons, Sat and Sun; summer 8.30am–12.30pm and 3.30pm–7pm, closed Sat morning and Sun), of 14th-century origin but modified at the end of the following century, six rooms decorated in stuccowork (mythology and biblical scenes) by Federico Brandani.

Foro Annonario* (A2). This neoclassical building, which is still used as a market, was built by Pietro Ghinelli in 1831. Its exedral structure consists of 30 Doric columns in brick.

Portici Ercolani* (A1). This long row of buildings, punctuated by openings in white Istrian stone, was built in the second half of the 18th century to serve the intense traffic attracted by the fair and is dedicated to the cardinal in charge of the extension of the city at the time. The *Biblioteca Comunale Antonelliana,* which opened in 1767 and contains over 50,000 volumes, is housed in part of the first block.

Behind the Portici is the 16th–17th century *Chiesa della Croce,* whose high altar is

56

decorated by a *Bearing the Body of Christ* by Federico Barocci (1579–82).

Palazzo Comunale (B1). Senigallia's city hall building is by another member of the Della Rovere family: Francesco Maria II commissioned Muzio Oddi to design the palace, which was built in the 17th century. The *Fountain of Neptune*, to the right of the entrance, was probably made using a Roman statue.

Palazzo Mastai (B1). This building belonged to another important family in the city, the Mastai Ferretti, who lived in the building from the 17th century. One member of the family, Giovanni Maria, who was born here, became Pope Pius IX in 1846. Memorabilia of this pontiff can be seen at the *Museo Pio IX* (open 9am–noon and 4pm–7pm; closed Mon in winter).

Follow Via Mastai to the left of the palace as far as Via Marchetti, in which the 18th-century church of *San Martino* (B1) is interesting for two works: a *Madonna and Child with St. Anne* by Guercino (1642–43; 2nd altar on the right) and a *Madonna and Child with Saints* by Palma Giovane (1580; 3rd on the left).

The street that runs off in line with the church leads to Via Battisti. To the right is the *Teatro La Fenice**, which after remaining unused for 60 years reopened on 5 December 1996, thereby rekindling a musical tradition that began back in 1838, when the original theater opened. In its first one hundred years it saw performances by many famous singers, often under the direction of such *maestri* as Giuseppe Verdi, Pietro Mascagni, and Ruggero Leoncavallo.

Behind this modern building is the *Museo Comunale d'Arte Moderna e dell'Informazione* (open Tue–Fri 8.30am–12.30pm), which documents the relationship between word and image, from 16th-century engravings (16th cent.) to graphic art and more recent media (photography, copy art, visual poetry, computer art).

Duomo (B1). This is the most recent of Senigallia's cathedrals, although it was originally built in the 18th century for the Jesuit congregation and only later was transformed into a cathedral. The facade was ordered by Pio IX, who was baptized in the pool that can still be seen in the chapel of the baptistery (3rd on the left). Two other important works are the *Madon-

na and Child** by Ercole Ramazzani in a chapel in the right-hand transept and the 6th-century *Sarcophagus of St. Gaudentius* in the sacristy.

Pinacoteca Diocesana (B1). The collection (open 10am–noon and 4pm–6pm; Jul–Aug 10am–noon and 5pm–7pm; closed Sun), which has been displayed in the old bishop's palace since 1992 has 16th-century paintings, including the *Madonna of the Rosary* (1588–92) by Federico Barocci, a *Baptism of Christ* attributed to Andrea Lilio, a *Madonna and Child with Saints* from the Parmigianino school, a *Lady of the Assumption* from the school of Guido Reni, a *Nativity* by Ercole Ramazzani, and *Lot and His Daughters* by Palma Giovane.

On the hill where the cemetery is situated is the church of **Santa Maria delle Grazie** (B1, off map), designed by Baccio Pontelli (Giorgio Vasari attributed it to Girolamo Genga, however). The *Madonna di Senigallia* by Piero della Francesca has been moved to the Galleria Nazionale della Marche in Urbino, but a splendid *Madonna Enthroned with Saints*** by Perugino behind the high altar remains in the church.

The old market in Senigallia

The adjoining convent, whose two *cloisters* are attributed to Pontelli, houses the *Museo di Storia della Mezzadria* (open 8.45am–12.15pm, closed Mon; 16 Jun–15 Sep 8.45am–12.15pm and 4pm–7.15pm), which traces regional farming history through its agricultural implements.

Thirteen km to the northwest, beyond the Cesano river in the province of Pesaro and Urbino, Mondolfo (elev. 144 m, pop. 10,698) looks down over the sandy coastline. Its history can be traced back to the 12th century; from 1631 it was controlled by the church; the old town is enclosed by a double medieval *wall*, rebuilt in the 16th century at the same time as the 13th-century church of *Sant'Agostino*.

Farming in the Marche region was characterized for 600 years by an agricultural system known as "mezzadria," whereby tenant farmers worked the land without owning it. The system, which is similar to sharecropping, dominated peasant life from the 14th century until its abolition in 1964.

Since the tenant farming family were required to furnish all the everyday items needed to run the

farm and the household, they were involved not only in producing crops and rearing livestock, but also in a range of other manual, mechanical and creative skills, including building, plumbing, weaving and carpentry.

Senigallia's museum of the history of "mezzadria," a busy study and research center, traces the development of the culture that grew up around this system of farming.

Falconara Marittima

Approached on the northern side of the Esino river by two fortifications (at Marina di Montemarciano, elev. 4 m), this is the *Mandracchio,* or mooring basin, ordered by Sigismondo Malatesta. At the mouth of the Esino, *Rocca Priora* (built in 1198 and converted for agricultural use), divides into two distinct parts: the more modern part by the sea is organized both for industry (oil re-

fining) and tourism. Falconara (elev. 5 m, pop. 29,820), has a historical upper town, with a medieval *Castle* and the medieval church of *Santa Maria delle Grazie,* interesting for its Gothic *portal* and a baptismal *font* made from a Byzantine-style capital.

A little further inland is the *Paese dei Bimbi* (open Apr-Sep 9am–8pm, closed Tue), a highly popular children's play land.

2.2 The south of the province

From Ancona to Loreto, 36.5 km *(see map pp. 48–49)*

This driving tour takes in two places of regional and national pilgrimage. Osimo is the site of the holy shrine of St. Joseph of Copertino, a foretaste almost of the splendors to come at Loreto, whose cult of the Virgin Mary has acquired such significance as to have taken over the entire town. Nearby are Offagna, with its splendid castle, and Castelfidardo, famous for the manufacture of piano accordions.

Take the SS16 which heads southeast out of Ancona, and after 17.5 km turn right (at the railway station) to Osimo (4 km), from where the excursion (10 km) to Offagna begins. Osimo is just 5.5 km from Castelfidardo, on the road (9.5 km) to Loreto.

Osimo

The people of this town are jokingly referred to as the "headless," after the decapitated statues now in the Palazzo Comunale. These Roman sculptures mark one of the most important episodes in the history of the town (elev. 265 m, pop. 28,631; see plan p. 59), which lies high in

the hills between the Aspio and Musone rivers inland from Ancona. It was founded in the 7th–6th centuries BC by Greek and Sicilian colonizers who had already settled along the coast, and although virtually nothing remains of *Auximum* (from which the modern name Osimo derives), the Roman town already had a sizable population. In 539 AD it was at the center of a fierce war against the Goths and later belonged to the maritime Pentapolis. The granting of municipal status soon after 1100 ushered in a period of economic prosperity, and saw the promulgation of the statutes, which were revised over the years. The *contrade* were ruled over by the Malatesta and the Church State, which at the end of the 15th century commissioned Baccio Pontelli to build a castle (later demolished) and in the late 18th and 19th century employed the townspeople in the construction of major public works. The 19th century also brought new industries (spinning in particular) to what had always been an important farming area. With the rapid industrial growth after World War II the town expanded rapidly; in 1975 it became famous as the place where the treaty ratifying the postwar border between Italy and Yugoslavia was signed.

Duomo* (A-B1). A church dedicated to the town's first bishop St. Leopardus was built in the 8th century (or perhaps as early as the 4th) on the hill once occupied by a Roman temple. Nothing remains of this early place of worship, but the 12th-century Romanesque style is still clearly visible both in the south transept (arched corbel table, and rose window surrounded by feline protomai) and in the windows of the apse, framed partly by human figures. The interior is in the shape of an Egyptian cross with three naves. The crypt contains the 4th-5th century *Sarcophagus of St. Leopardus*, a *Pastor's Tombstone* dating back to the same period surmounted by a 13th-century *arch,* and a 4th-century **sarcophagus** with the relics of local saints (on the sides are *Scenes in the Hellenistic tradition;* the lid has *biblical scenes*).

The adjoining bishop's palace is to become the home of the **Museo Diocesano d'Arte Sacra** (A-B1-2), whose collection includes a polyptych (*Enthroned Madonna and Child with Saints*, 1418) by Pietro da Montepulciano, a *ciborium* (1547) by Franco Battista Semolei, a *Madonna and Child* by Sermoneta (1551), a *Virgin and Child with St. Philip and St. James* by Simone De Magistris (1585) and, in the Treasury, a silver *lamina of St. Leopardus* (9th cent.), a 15th-century *Station Cross* in gilt copper and a Byzantine-style *triptych with hinged panels* (15th–16th centuries).

Baptistery (B1-2). This building, with a characteristic stone and terracotta facade, was founded in the 12th century but repeatedly remodeled. The coffered *ceiling* is 15th century (the paintings are from two centuries later); the *baptismal font** was cast in bronze by Pier Paolo and Tarquinio Jacometti in 1627.

Via Goremo leads down to Piazza Gramsci. Here, a panoramic view takes in Castelfidardo, Loreto, Recanati and Cingoli.

Palazzo Comunale (B2). The seat of municipal power is the result of a long building process which began in the 16th century (the facade, designed by Pompeo Floriani, took almost a century to complete) and ended in the second half of the 18th century. The entrance hall is decorated with 12 Roman headless *statues* found in the forum; the rooms have a 12th-century stone *Madonna* and a *polyptych* (ca. 1464) by Antonio and Bartolomeo Vivarini.

Via Pontelli (B2), part of the Roman *decumanus,* leads from the left-hand side of the palace to *Via di Fonte Magna* (A2-3), which follows the late 13th-century walls; the square tufa blocks are Roman (3rd–2nd cent. BC), as is the **Magna Fountain** (A2), after which the street is named. It is the only remaining vestige of *Auximum* and was probably part of a 1st-century BC nymphaeum, which

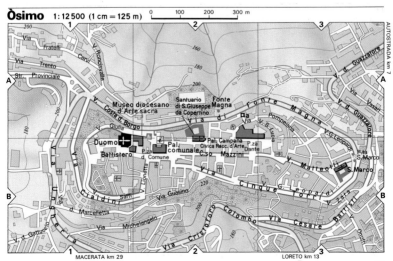

*Osimo Cathedral:
rose window*

legend has linked both to Pompey the Great (or *Pompeius Magnus*, hence the name) and to Belisarius, who in 539 AD is said to have poured poison into the fountain to wear down the resistance of the besieged.

Santuario di San Giuseppe da Copertino

(A-B2). The Counter-Reformation appearance of this religious complex belies its 13th-century origins and connections with the followers of St. Francis of Assisi. The building that survives is the result of unrestrained remodeling begun in the 16th century and finished in the second half of the 18th century by Andrea Vici, which left the east side of the cloister intact, but little else. The work was in part linked to the arrival of Giuseppe da Copertino, who spent his last years and also died in the adjoining convent.

The interior is mostly decorated with white stuccowork; the most important painting is a 16th-century canvas: *Madonna and Child with Saints* (2nd altar on the left), attributed to Antonio Solario with the help of Giuliano Presutti; the coves of the vault in the sacristy are frescoed with *Evangelists* from the early 15th-century Giotto school; the canvas (*The Ecstasy of St. Joseph of Copertino*) is by Ludovico Mazzanti.

The saint's body lies in the *crypt*, opened in 1963, while the *Museo San Giuseppe da Copertino* (open 7.30am–noon and 3.30pm–7pm) contains the rooms in which the saint supposedly rose into the air in ecstasy, as a result of which he became the patron saint of airmen; the collection of heraldic university hats and other votive items meanwhile recalls how the friar assisted scholars in their studies.

Palazzo Campana

(A2-3). This building was originally a boarding school (built in 1714 and designed in part by Andrea Vici; its pupils included Aurelio Saffi and future popes Leo XII and Pius VIII), but in recent years has been turned to other cultural uses. The *Biblioteca Comunale*, a library founded in 1667, is now housed there, together with the *Archivio Storico Comunale* (whose so-called Red Book has documents concerning city life dating back to the 11th and 12th centuries) and the **Civica Raccolta d'Arte*** (visits by request, apply at the Municipal Library). Paintings include three fragmentary frescoes (*Coronation of the Virgin, Christ the Judge, Angel Musicians*) attributed to Andrea da Bologna, a *Beheading of St. Denis* attributed to Giacinto Brandi, an *Our Lady of Sorrows with Angels and Symbols of the Passion* attributed to Odoardo Vicinelli, and a *St. Nicholas and Saint* possibly by Claudio Ridolfi. The contemporary graphic art, paintings and sculpture are mainly by Marche artists, although there are also eight prints by G. B. Piranesi. The local archaeological finds range from the 8th to the 1st centuries BC.

A fresco (*Madonna and Child with Saints*; 1st altar on the left) attributed to Arcangelo di Cola and a *Madonna of the Rosary* by Guercino (high altar) can be seen in the Baroque interior of the church of *San Marco* (B3).

Ten km to the northwest lies Offagna (elev. 306 m, pop. 1,615), a town centered around its castle, or *Rocca*** (open 25 Apr–30 Jun, Sat and Sun 9.30am–12.30pm and 4pm–7.30pm; 1 Jul–30 Sep 9.30am–12.30pm and 4pm–8pm), which the city of Ancona built between 1454 and 1456 to

The Monument to Enrico Cialdini, Castelfidardo

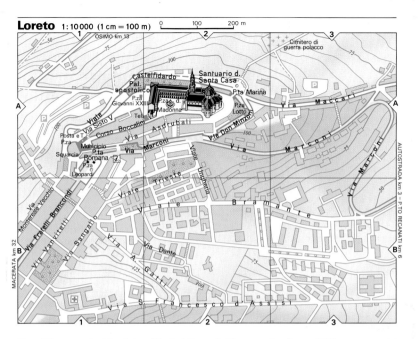

thwart the expansionist policies of its rival Osimo. Although the architectural lines of this mighty quadrilateral are medieval in style, the defense structures were designed to withstand attack not from stones or boulders but from the new firearms (hence the 50 cannon emplacements). Near the castle is the *Museo di Scienze Naturali "Luigi Paolucci"* (open Oct–May 9am–noon, Sun 10am–noon and 4pm–7pm, closed Mon; Jun & Sep 4.30pm–7.30pm, holidays 10am–noon and 4.30pm–7.30pm, closed Mon; Jul–Aug 10am–noon and 4.30pm–7.30pm, closed Mon), which displays examples of local flora and fauna.

Castelfidardo

Although this town (elev. 199 m, pop. 15,640) is best known in and outside Italy as a piano accordion manufacturing center, it also has its place in Italian history as the scene in 1860 of a decisive battle during the struggle for the political unification of Italy (or *Risorgimento*), in which forces loyal to the Savoy family clashed with those supporting the pope.

The event is remembered by the *Monument to Enrico Cialdini* (Vito Pardo's dramatic sculpture depicts the general on horseback leading his troops into battle) and, in the 16th-century *Palazzo Mordini*, at the *Museo Risorgimentale della Battaglia* (open summer 10am–noon and 4pm–7pm, Fri 10am–noon and 5pm–midnight; winter 10am–noon and 4pm–7pm, closed Tue). The town's musical instrument manufacturing history is documented in the Museo Internazionale della Fisarmonica (open 9.30am–noon and 3pm–6pm) in Palazzo Comunale, with a collection of more than 150 instruments, the oldest dating back to the opening of the first workshop in 1863. The building's Coat of Arms Room has the crest of the Marche cities that "sponsored" the monument to Cialdini.

The square in front of the Municipio is the heart of the town; its mainly 18th-century appearance is the result of the major urban redevelopment of the town's palaces and churches carried out in that century. All that remains of the castle (other than the reference to it in the name of the town) are the four gates and fragments of the walls, which have been built over.

Loreto**

Second perhaps only to Lourdes in Europe in the numbers of pilgrims it attracts, Loreto (elev. 127 m, pop. 11,053; see plan above) is a much older place of pilgrimage than the French town, and grew up around a quite different event. Records of a holy site in Loreto can be traced back as far as 1294: tradition has it that the house in Nazareth where Jesus lived after his return from Egypt was transported by angels first to Istria and then here.

A town grew up on the site, especially when Pope Paul II took it upon himself to build the new fortified basilica, and granted the first plenary indulgence to those

61

The Sanctuary of the Holy House of Loreto: plan of marble bas-reliefs

North face   West face

a Birth of Mary

b Marriage of Mary

c Annunciation

d Visitation

e Mary and Joseph present themselves for Augustus' census

f Birth of Jesus, with Adoration of the Shepherds

g Adoration of the Magi

h Ecstasy of Mary

i Translation of the Holy House

l Agony in the Garden, and Flagellation

m Way to Calvary, and Crucifixion

n Annunciation and Adoration of the Shepherds

o Adoration of the Magi, and Jesus in the Temple

Statues of Sibyls

1 Hellespont

2 Frigian

3 Tiburtine

4 Libyan

5 Delphic

6 Persian

7 Pontic

8 Erythraean

9 Cumaean

10 Samian

Statues of Prophets

I Isaiah

II Daniel

III Amos

IV Jeremiah

V Ezekiel

VI Zacharia

VII David with head of Goliath

VIII Malachi

IX Moses

X Balaam

who came here on pilgrimage. The construction of the new place of worship brought together the leading architects of the day: Baccio Pontelli, Bramante, Andrea Sansovino, Giuliano da Sangallo and Antonio da Sangallo the Younger, to name but a few, hence the lack of architectural unity. The pope also ordered other buildings needed for the reception of pilgrims (a hospital, shops and hotels) and lodgings for those officiating at religious services. By the time of Pope Gregory XIII these structures were already insufficient, but it was not until the time of Pope Sixtus V that extensive expansion work began on the castle, which had been enclosed by walls in 1520. The town, described as the *felix civitas lauretana* in honor of the pope (Felice Peretti), spread northwest toward

The Church of Loreto

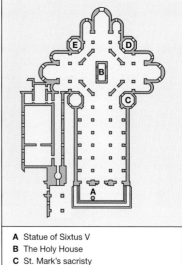

A Statue of Sixtus V

B The Holy House

C St. Mark's sacristy

D St. John's sacristy

E St. Luke's sacristy

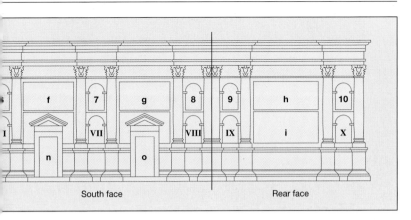

| | f | 7 | g | 8 | 9 | h | 10 |

| I | VII | | VIII | IX | i | X |

| n | o |

South face | Rear face

the Montereale hill, along what is now Via Fratelli Brancondi. Since that time town and shrine have coexisted in harmony, with subsequent expansion work taking account of plans made under Sixtus. Now, at the turn of the third millennium, the holy shrine dominates the town's economy to such an extent that, as Montaigne commented back in 1581: "There is hardly a person in the town who is not involved in the various services of this place of pilgrimage."

Piazza della Madonna* (A2). At the end of *Corso Boccalini* (A1-2), the

Loreto: the Santa Casa

town's main thoroughfare, is the monumental yet harmonious space around which Loreto's architectural masterpieces are situated.

The *Fontana della Madonna**, designed by Carlo Maderno and Giovanni Fontana, has graced the square since 1614; the eagles and cherubs under the upper basin, the winged dragons and crests under the lower basin, and the tritons riding dolphins around were added in 1622 by Tarquinio and Pier Paolo Jacometti.

Santuario della Santa Casa** (A2; see plan p.6). Preceded, on the steps, by the bronze *statue of Sixtus V* giving blessings from the gestatorial chair (A; Antonio Calcagni, 1589), the late-Renaissance fa-

cade in Istrian stone was begun by Giovanni Boccalini in 1571 up to the lower cornice and completed in 1587. The lower order is divided up by four pairs of pilasters, echoing the three-part inside. The four bronze *doors** are from the school of sculpture that flourished in Recanati between the late 16th- and early 17th-centuries: the door on the right (1600) is by Calcagni, Sebastiano Sebastiani and Tarquinio Jacometti; the center door (1611) is by the Lombardo family; and the door on the left (1596) is by Tiburzio Vergelli and G. B. Vitali; the *Statue of the Madonna and Child* above the main door dates from 1583. The 18th-century *campanile* to the left was added (1750–54) by Luigi Vanvitelli; the heaviest bell weighs 7.3 tons and is affectionately nicknamed *Loreta*.

Around the outside of the church note Baccio Pontelli's terracotta *sides*, and the **transepts*** and **apses*** of the presbytery, where the fortified structure, designed to protect the holy site from marauding pirates, is clearly visible (the high Gothic windows are the only concession to decoration); and Giuliano da Sangallo's Brunelleschi-inspired **dome*** (1500).

The spacious **interior*** (93 x 60 m) with 12 pillars supporting Gothic arches, was designed to accommodate large numbers of pilgrims; the chapels in the transept and apse are named after the countries which contributed to their decoration (the central chapel is by Ludovico Seitz); the dome was refrescoed (*History of the Dogma of the Virgin and the Loretan Litanies*) by Cesare Maccari.

Beneath the dome is the **Santa Casa**** (B), of Holy House. The beautiful marble screen (see plan pp. 62–63) was designed by Bramante in 1509 as a monumental shrine and built under the supervision of Giovanni Cristoforo Romano, Andrea Sansovino, Raniero Nerucci, and Antonio da Sangallo the Younger – it celebrates the **Earthly Life of the Virgin Mary***, revealed by *sibyls* (upper niches) and by *prophets* (lower niches) and depicted in the bas-relief *stories*; Sansovino's *Annunciation** (c) is considered to be a masterpiece of the decorative composition. The House of the Virgin inside, with its strikingly bare walls, contrasts sharply with the exterior; the altar has a *Statue of the Madonna and Child*, remade after the 1921 fire by Enrico Quattrini; on the left wall is a 14th–15th century *Madonna and Child with Two Angels* and an *Enthroned Madonna and Child with St. John the Evangelist and St. Catherine of Alexandria*, a 14th-century fresco from the Umbria-Marche school; on the wall in front of the altar is a 13th-century painted *Cross*.

The **Sagrestia di San Marco** (C) was frescoed by Melozzo da Forlì between 1477 and 1480: the vault has *Angels Bearing the Instruments of Christ's Passion* and *Prophets*; on the walls below is *Christ's Entry into Jerusalem* (note the way the countryside is depicted, and the figure in the bottom right-hand corner, believed by some to be the artist himself). From 1479 Luca Signorelli decorated the **Sagrestia di San Giovanni*** (D) with, among other works, *Doubting Thomas* and the *Conversion of Saul*, and in the vault *Angel Musicians*; the *lavabo* is by Benedetto da Maiano, the intarsia *benches* and *wardrobes* are attributed to Domenico di Antonio Indivini, the majolica-tiled *floor* is 16th century. The **Sagrestia di San Luca**

(E) has a terracotta *St. Luke the Evangelist*, attributed to Benedetto da Maiano.

The **Treasury**, reached from the north transept by the first door on the right in the corridor, is better known as the *Sala del Pomarancio* because it was frescoed by the artist with lively *Scenes from the Life of Mary** (1605–10; note the daringly foreshortened figure of the Virgin), alternating with six *Prophets* and six *Sibyls*; Pomarancio also painted the *Crucifixion* on the altar; Andrea Costa's *wooden furniture* was designed to contain votive offerings (the most exquisite of which were removed by Napoleon Bonaparte following the Treaty of Tolentino).

Palazzo Apostolico (A2). Four architects worked on this unfinished building, whose sides facing Piazza della Madonna are characterized by a rhythmical sequence of arches and pilaster strips. It was begun by Bramante (1509) and continued by Antonio da Sangallo the Younger, Giovanni Boccalini completed the upper floor and Luigi Vanvitelli designed the elegant avant-corps on the west side.

Inside is the *Archivio Storico della Santa Casa*, whose earliest document is the 1507 *Bull of Pope Julius II*, and the **Museum-Art Gallery** (open spring–summer 9am–1pm and 4pm–7pm, closed Mon; Nov–Mar, visits by request tel. 977759). Its collection includes paintings and other artifacts no longer used at the Santa Casa (ceramics, furniture, liturgical ornaments). The prize exhibits are the eight **canvases*** by Lorenzo Lotto, some of them painted here, and nearly all dated between 1549 and 1556: *Baptism of Christ*, *Christ and the Adulteress*, *Sts. Roch, Christopher and Sebastian* (1531), *St. Michael Driving out Lucifer*, *Adoration of the Magi*, *Adoration of the Child, Sacrifice of Melchizedek* and *Presentation in the Temple*. There is also a large collection of **apothecary ceramic ware*** (over 500 items from the Urbino workshop of Orazio Fontana), and a priceless collection of *tapestries*** woven in Brussels and based on cartoons by Raphael.

3 Pesaro and its surroundings

The province

Pesaro was aptly described in the mid-1970s – a period of cultural and economic expansion and extensive urban redevelopment – as the "city that mediates between the province and the rest of the world." Some of the initiatives begun at that time have continued and become well established; others, inevitably, have been scaled down or fallen victim to industrial and general economic recession. Pesaro is a border city that relates both to the Marche region of which it is a part and its northern neighbor, Romagna. Although it does differ in many ways from "the Marches," it also has historical ties with the region and the one hundred cities of the Marche under papal rule, which Stendhal described in 1821 as "shrewd government by priests." Its duality also comes across in its cuisine, which combines seafood specialties such as *brodetto* with the traditional fare of its farming traditions (white meat, salami and other cured meats). Its economy is split between a well-established furniture-making industry, high-quality farming and an expanding services sector. Likewise, tourism combines seaside vacationing – begun in the early 20th century when bathing in the sea became popular and seaside residences such as the enchanting Villa Ruggeri were built – with the tourism that attracts visitors to the city's historic center and its high-profile cultural events (the Cinema Festival and the Rossini Opera Festival). The city's heritage begins with pre-Roman and Roman remains (the Museo Archeologico Oliveriano, the cathedral), and continues with the Malatesta gateways, the splendors of the city under the Sforza family, the lavish legacy of the Della Rovere

Piazza del Popolo in the center of Pesaro

seignory, through to the composed neoclassical architecture produced during papal rule in the 18th and 19th centuries. Pesaro boasts a harmonious urban layout, which derives from the organization of the ancient town that grew up in successive layers over the basic Roman grid plan. But the city has, of course, also produced "harmony" of a musical kind, through the works of Gioacchino Rossini. The medieval castles (Gradara) and churches in the immediate environs are yet more reminders of the seigniorial age up to 1631.

Fano has a somewhat different history. After the splendors of ancient Rome and the aristocratic rule of the Malatesta came the period of *Libertas Ecclesiastica*, leading to a less formal spirit and sense of humor that survives in its Carnival traditions.

The Adriatic Sea, from Gabicce Mare to Fano, has been influential in many ways: it has favored the development of customs and traditions, awakened a desire to escape, or had a calming influence. In the 20th century alone, its presence can be felt from Ercole Luigi Morselli and Fabio Tombari through to the contemporaries.

The sea is, of course, also the end of the road that leads here from Rome, the old *Via Flaminia*, which has recently been rediscovered in an admirable project that has drawn attention to the many layers of civilization in the area, from the earliest settlers of the Metauro river valley to the present day. From Pesaro and Fano, the Flaminian Way leads past countless ancient stopping-places to Fossombrone, the Furlo gorge (traversed through the Roman tunnel) at Cagli. The area is dotted with small towns full of artistic treasures waiting to be discovered. And a rich legacy from the years of papal rule can also still be seen in a number of unexpectedly beautiful palaces and churches.

3.1 Pesaro

Circular walking tour from Piazza del Popolo *(see plan pp. 68–69)*

The Rossini Opera Festival (ROF), held every year under the auspices of the Italian President, has become an internationally acclaimed event, with music lovers flocking to the Teatro Rossini, the Pedrotti Auditorium and the more modern Palafestival to enjoy the music of Pesaro's most illustrious son. The city (elev. 11 m, pop. 87,703) does indeed owe much of its fame and prestige to Gioacchino Rossini, but it also thrives on its industrial activities – especially modular kitchen production – the modern descendants of a long craft tradition dating back to the 16th century when majolica manufacture was at its height.

The area was quite a different place in 184 BC, when the Romans founded *Pisaurum*: the plain, already inhabited by Picene tribes, was such an insalubrious, marshy area – partly because of the presence of clay (later used for ceramics manufacture) – that in the time of Augustus a second group of settlers had to be sent. The Roman grid layout forms the basis of the present-day town, as it did also for the medieval settlement, which was long contested by the Goths and the Byzantines, the Longobards and the Franks (Pepin the Short donated it to the Church in 774). The town enjoyed municipal status from the 12th to the end of the 13th century, when the Malatesta family from Rimini took control. They were followed by the Sforza, who built the mighty castle and Palazzo Ducale, and then by the Della Rovere, who ruled until 1631. In this period majolica production (well documented in the Musei Civici) developed, the last part of the Foglia river was turned into a canal harbor and new walls were built, although these were almost totally destroyed at the beginning of the 20th century when the city discovered its potential as a seaside resort and began to expand seaward. This aspect of the city is testified to by the charming villas between Viale della Vittoria and the beach and is one that contributes in no small measure to Pesaro's prosperous economy.

The walking tour begins in the square at the heart of the city, Piazza del Popolo, from which Via Branca, Via Zongo and Via Sabbatini lead to the Conservatorio Rossini. The street on the left-hand side of the conservatory leads to the Museo Archeologico Oliveriano in Via Mazza, which runs southwest toward the church of *San Giovanni Battista* and the Orti Giuli. In the opposite direction Via Mazza meets Corso XI Settembre, in which the church of *Sant'Agostino*

The Rossini Opera Festival

"In its eighteen editions, the ROF has not only unearthed the forgotten Rossini repertoire but also brought together a wealth of professional skills and revived a real sense of craftsmanship. This is particularly significant at a time when the disappearance of traditional arts and crafts has become a worrying social problem in Italy. The Festival has done much to develop the artistic and technical workmanship that goes into stagecraft, creating whole new professions that will become more numerous as technology progresses ... [and brings with it] new skills that can be marketed at home and abroad, but which can only be learned through workplace experience." This was how superintendent Gianfranco Mariotti introduced the 1997 edition of the event, highlighting how the "Festival Corporation" does much more than its original aim of reviving Gioacchino Rossini's vast and largely unknown musical legacy. The scientific, historical and publishing work is done by the Fondazione Rossini, which since 1974 has been engaged in the publication of a critical edition of the composer's complete works. The ROF (see logo below) was set up in 1980 by the city authorities to work alongside the foundation and bring its activities to life in the theater. The result is a modern interactive musicology workshop that has put Pesaro on the world's musical map and aroused a great deal of cultural interest.

stands, with the *Nome di Dio* church nearby. Halfway down Via Castelfidardo, a turning to the right (Via Mazzolari) leads to the Musei Civici, and on to the junction with Via Rossini, at the point where the composer's house stands. Beyond the Cathedral – and the turn-off for Marina di Pesaro – is Viale Don Minzoni, which runs past the Rocca Costanza and leads to Piazza Matteotti, from where Via San Francesco leads to the church of *Santa Maria delle Grazie*, and back to Piazza del Popolo.

Piazza del Popolo (D2-3). The historical and political hub of the city is graced with a *fountain* with tritons and sea horses (Lorenzo Ottoni, 1685). Behind the *Municipio* (D3; 20th cent.) is the little church of *Sant'Ubaldo* (1605); the 16th-century *Palazzo della Paggeria* is unfinished, and the neoclassical *Palazzo della Direzione Provinciale Poste e Telecomunicazioni* (D2) incorporates on its right-hand side the terracotta facade with Gothic stone *portal** (1395) of the former church of *San Domenico*. But the square's and indeed the city's most impressive building is **Palazzo Ducale***, now the seat of the *Prefettura*. It was ordered by Alessandro Sforza in the second half of the 15th century and renovated in the following century for the Della Rovere by Bartolomeo and Girolamo Genga. The Renaissance lines of the facade echo in one respect at least the ducal palace in Urbino: the five windows, framed and crowned by festoons (Domenico Rosselli) of the *piano nobile*. The portico below has six arched openings between imposing pillars; the top of the facade is crenelated.

Conservatorio Gioacchino Rossini (D2). This "conservatory of music and *bel canto*," as Rossini himself described it, was built using part of the bequest left by the composer to the city in 1868. However, it did not open until 1882 and only moved to its present home (*Palazzo Olivieri*, designed by Giovanni Andrea Lazzarini) in 1892. The interior is given over entirely to the composer's memory: in the courtyard is the *Monument to the Composer* (Carlo Marocchetti, 1864), the *Fondazione Gioacchino Rossini* and adjoining *Tempietto Rossiniano* (admission on request, apply at the Foundation), with scores, manuscripts and memorabilia; the *Auditorium Pedrotti* retains a 19th-century appearance.

The composer is also remembered in the nearby *Teatro Rossini*, which opened in 1815.

Museo Archeologico Oliveriano (D2). Hidden away in the 17th-century rooms of *Palazzo Almerici* is a collection of ancient works that deserve to be discovered. They include Italic, Roman, and Greek *bronzes* (note in particular two ornaments for a 5th-century BC hydria), a bilingual *inscription** in Etruscan and Latin; Etruscan, Greek and Roman *coins*; the 2nd-3rd century AD *Boscovich anemoscope**, an instrument used extensively to establish conditions before putting out to sea; early-Christian cemetery *glassware*. But the prize exhibits at the museum (admission on request, weekdays 9.30am–noon) are unquestionably the stelae from the necropolis of Novilara, an expression of Picene culture between the 8th and 5th century BC: richly decorated with geometric patterns and human figures, they document the close contacts with Danubian-Balkan culture across the Adriatic, and have little in common with the Greek and Etruscan idioms of the time. They also display the repetition of ornamental motifs of the Bronze Age; the *stele with navigation scene** deserves particular attention. The *Biblioteca Oliveriana*, which opened in the late 18th century in the same building, has a collection of over 150,000 books. There are 5,000 16th-century volumes, many incunabula and illuminated manuscripts, as well as documents bearing the signatures of Torquato Tasso, Giacomo Leopardi, and Giosuè Carducci.

The southwest end of Via Mazza ends at Via Passeri. To the right lies the church of *San Giovanni Battista* (D2), which was probably intended as the Della Rovere family mausoleum. Begun by Girolamo Genga in 1543, it was completed by his son Bartolomeo, with the exception of the facade; inside, on the second altar on the right, is a wooden *Crucifix* by Innocenzo da Petralia Soprana.

Continue down Via Passeri and turn right into Via Belvedere to *Orti Giuli* gardens (C-D1) created over the ramparts of the wall. The *Museo Scientifico "Luigi Guidi"* (closed to visitors) occupies the rooms of the *Osservatorio Valerio*, founded in 1861, which has a collection of old instruments used for measuring seismic, geomagnetic, astronomical, and meteorological phenomena (records of rainfall and wind intensity have been kept since the institute was founded), and of 19th-century maps and pressed flowers.

Sant'Agostino (C2). Despite the alterations made in the 18th century, the church still displays its early 15th-century origins in the Venetian Gothic *portal**, in Istria stone and decorated with lions and statues in niches and tabernacles. Exquisitely carved, inlaid **choir stalls** (beautiful views

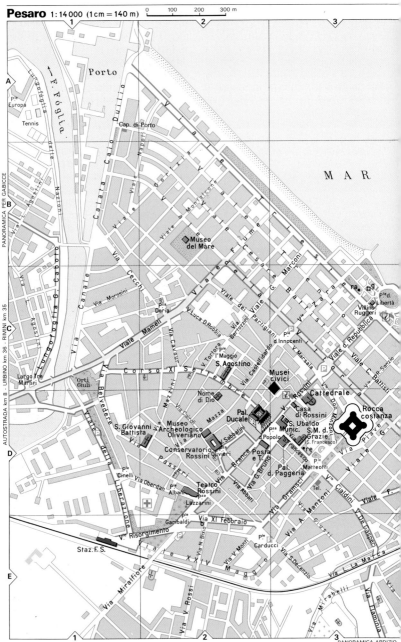

Pesaro 1:14 000 (1 cm = 140 m)

of the city) from the late 15th– early 16th-centuries enclose the presbytery.

Musei Civici* (C-D2-3). (open Oct–Apr 8.30am–1.30pm, Sun 9am–1pm, closed Mon; May–Sep 9am–7pm, Sun 9am–1pm, closed Mon).
The art gallery has works from the Venetian, Tuscan and Bolognese schools, including Vitale da Bologna, Giovanni Bellini (**Coronation of the Virgin**, known also as the *Pala di Pesaro* and dated 1474, generally recognized as his masterpiece), Marco Zoppo, Jacobello del Fiore, Domenico Beccafumi and Guido Reni.
The exhibits in the Museo delle Ceramiche come from Urbino, Castel Durante, Faenza, Deruta, Gubbio, Castelli, and Pesaro it-

in 1792 – in the street that was named after him – has been transformed, in his honor, into a small museum (open Oct–Apr 8.30am–1.30pm, Sun 9am–1pm, closed Mon; May–Sep 9am–7pm, Sun 9am–1pm, closed Mon). Displayed along with various memorabilia are the home's original furnishings. The nearby *cathedral* displays its Romanesque origins in the column-bearing lions to the sides of the portal, while the facade is clearly influenced by the Gothic style. Inside, a temporary floor conceals the remains of the Roman building over which the church was erected, and which the floor *mosaics** are a part of; the *Crucifix of St. Bernard* (chapel to the right of the main chapel) is an example of 15th-century Venetian art.

The road continues towards the sea beyond Largo Moro as *Viale della Repubblica* (C3), and, after crossing Marina di Pesaro's main thoroughfare *Viale Trieste* (A-E1-5), ends at *Piazza della Libertà* (C3): to the left note the art nouveau Villa Ruggeri, from 1904–08; Arnaldo Pomodoro's *Large Sphere* was replaced at the center of the space in 1998.

The northwest section of Viale Trieste and, to the left, Via Pola lead to the *Museo del Mare* (B2; open: October–April 8.30am–1.30pm, Sun 9am–1pm, closed Mon; May–September 9am–7pm, Sun 9am–1pm, closed Mon), installed in 1986 in the early 20th-century *Villa Molaroni*. It traces the history of Pesaro's canal-harbor.

Rocca Costanza* (D3). This stronghold has all the typical elements of 15th-century military architecture: a deep moat, four imposing round towers and a square plan; these are also the distinguishing features of the style of Luciano Laurana, who built the edifice between 1474 and 1487 for Costanzo Sforza.

Santuario della Madonna delle Grazie (D3). Although the revered image to which the complex is dedicated did not arrive here until 1922, the church itself dates back to the 13th century (it was commissioned by the Malatesta, who dedicated it to St. Francis), as the Gothic *portal* decorated with reliefs and sculptures testifies. The interior is Baroque, but traces of 14th- and 15th-century frescoes can be seen on the wall behind the facade and the first arches of the right-hand aisle. The 16th-century *Image of the Madonna delle Grazie*, protectress of the city and believed to have miraculous powers, is in a marble temple in the apse. A room to the left of the high altar has frescoes taken from the walls of the church and a painting of *St. Ursula* by Palma Giovane.

self; they bear the signatures, among others, of Francesco Xanto Avelli, of Alfonso Patanazzi, Carlo Antonio Grue, and Nicola da Urbino. There is also a glazed terracotta tondo by Andrea della Robbia and a *bas-relief* by Francesco Laurana.

Casa di Rossini (D3). The simple home in which the composer came into the world

3.2 The northern coast

From Pesaro to Gradara 33.5 km *(see map p. 73)*

This short itinerary affords splendid views as it winds its way along the beautifully scenic stretch of green, rocky coastline north of Pesaro. The two main towns here are popular tourist destinations: Gabicce Mare, a seaside resort with an excellent beach; and the walled town of Gradara a little way inland, made famous by Dante's story of the doomed lovers Paolo and Francesca.

The road leads northwest out of Pesaro, first passing Villa Imperiale (3.5 km), and then through Fiorenzuola di Focara and Casteldimezzo before reaching Gabicce Mare (22.5 km), right on the border with the region of Emilia-Romagna. Gradara lies 5.5 km inland.

The panoramic road*
to Gabicce Mare

Although rather tortuous, this road is a much better choice than the SS16 further inland. The views and the interesting works of architecture along the way make the sharp

bends and gradients well worth the effort. **Villa Imperiale*** (open in summer, apply at the APT), is a living reminder of how Renaissance high society spent its leisure time. Set in a lush pinewood, it consists of two main blocks, one built in the 15th century by Alessandro Sforza and the other by Girolamo Genga in the 16th century. Its name derives from the fact that Hapsburg Emperor Frederick III stayed here on his way to Rome for his coronation, and laid the foundation stone. The rooms have 16th-century paintings by Genga, Bronzino, Raffaellino del Colle, Perin del Vaga, and Francesco Menzocchi.

Fiorenzuola di Focara (elev. 177 m) is a medieval town surrounded by walls and towers. Its name is a reminder of the *fuochi*, or beacons, once lit to guide seafaring vessels. *Casteldimezzo* (elev. 197 m) is interesting for its houses perched high above the sea, and the *Parish Church*, with a *Crucifix* carved by Antonio Bonvicino and painted by Jacobello del Fiore.

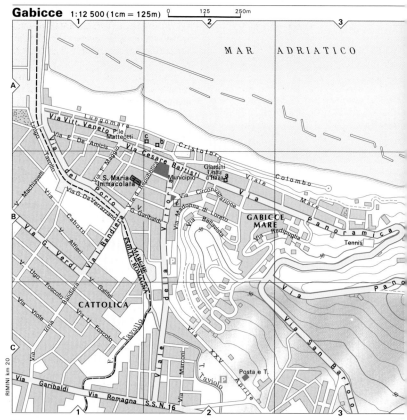

The walled town of Gradara, dominated by its castle

Gabicce Mare

This thriving seaside town (elev. 11m, pop. 5,466; see plan pp. 70–71) with its beautiful sandy beach, hotels and holi-

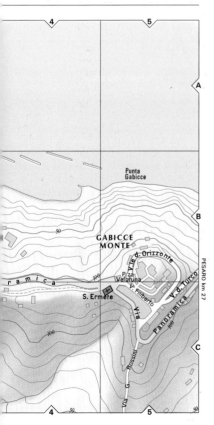

day atmosphere, is the Marche region's main resort north of Pesaro, and is divided from the adjoining town of Cattolica (in the Romagna region) by the Tavollo river. Its days as a seafaring town are over, but the past lives on in *Gabicce Monte* (elev. 144 m), the *Castellum Ligabitii* mentioned in historical records (the earliest references to a settlement here date back to 998). The promontory on which it stands is the last piece of high ground on the coast before it flattens out into the endless expanse of the Po plain.

Gradara**

The approach from the coast offers perhaps the best view of the walls, which are one of the main attractions of this small town (elev. 142 m, pop. 2,850). The walls and the castle they enclose create a small, intact medieval world which restoration work in 1923 has helped to preserve. Records speak of a settlement on this hill near the Tavollo river as early as 1032; construction of the stronghold began in the 13th century. The defense walls were raised in the 14th century by the Malatesta, who ruled the town until 1463, whereupon it passed into the hands of the Sforza, the Della Rovere and, from 1631, the Church.

The **walls**** are punctuated by square crenelated towers (the panoramic walk affords good views of these). Entry to the historic center is through the *Porta dell'Orologio*, which has always been the only access to the town.

71

An inner set of walls separates the town from the Castle** (open winter 9am–1.30pm, summer 9am–7pm), which is square in plan and has an imposing polygonal keep on the northeastern side. The historical importance of this complex, built by the Griffo family and altered first by the Malatesta and then the Sforza, is somewhat overshadowed nowadays by the story of the tragic kiss between Paolo and Francesca told by Dante in the 5th *canto* of "Hell" in his Divine Comedy. Although it has been established that the ill-fated gesture did not in fact take place here (Dante himself never came to Gradara), the legend lives on in the *inner court*, with its portico and loggia, and in the rooms, many of them still with 15th- and 16th-century furniture. The *chapel* has an altar made from a sarcophagus with bas-reliefs, behind which is a glazed majolica *Madon-na and Child with Saints* by Andrea della Robbia; the *Sala della Passione* has frescoes depicting the *Passion of Christ*, attributed to Amico Aspertini; the *Camerino di Lucrezia Borgia* was possibly also frescoed by Aspertini; the *Sala dei Putti* has *frescoes* and a *St. Paul*, attributed to Francesco Zaganelli and Girolamo Marchesi; the *Battle Scene* in the *Sala del Consiglio* is again by Aspertini; the walls in the *Camera di Francesca** are decorated with Malatesta emblems; the *Madonna and Child* is a painting on wood from the 15th-century Marche school; the *Sala di Giustizia* has a 1484 *Madonna and Child with Saints* by Giovanni Santi; the *Archangels* are German works from the 15th and 16th centuries. Francesca's Room also contains the trap door through which the lovers are said to have tried in vain to escape her brother's vengeful wrath.

3.3 From Fano to Urbino through the Metauro valley

137-km itinerary *(see map p. 73)*

Although somewhat off the beaten track, this excursion takes in a series of small, out-of-the-way towns whose appeal lies precisely in the authentic atmosphere they have preserved as little-known places without the crowd-pulling masterpieces of art and architecture. Even sprawling Fano has succeeded in preserving a historical center that offers the rare pleasure of a quiet stroll, discovering such minor gems as the Arch of Augustus, the nearby complex of *San Michele* and Palazzo Malatesta. Venturing inland reveals Mondavio castle, the charming solitude of the Fonte Avellana hermitage or the beautiful works of Gaetano Lapis in Cagli. The itinerary also goes on the trail of Francesco di Giorgio Martini and Girolamo Genga: nearly every town and village has a building either built or renovated by one of them. Nature lovers will enjoy walks through the Mt. Catria woods.

From Pesaro, the SS16 arrives after 11.5 km in Fano; nearby is the Mt. Giove hermitage (5.5 km) and Carignano Terme (10 km). The SS3 *Flaminia* leads (13 km) to Calcinelli, then across to the right bank of the Metauro river and, after 11.5 km, to Orciano di Pesaro, just 2 km from Mondavio. After another 3 km, the SS424 runs southwest (8.5 km) to San Lorenzo in Campo, from where it is worth making the 7-km detour northeast to ancient *Suasa*. 11 km southwest of San Lorenzo is Pergola, from where the road leads up to the monastery of Fonte Avellana (18 km). A rather tortuous 25-km stretch of road leads down to Cagli on the *Via Flaminia*, which, after the Furlo Gorge tunnel, becomes the express highway just outside Fossombrone (20 km). From here the SS73bis (*Bocca Trabaria*) leads after 18.5 km to Urbino (see itinerary 4.1).

Fano*

Little could Julius Caesar have imagined as he crossed the Rubicon in 49 BC that the small settlement of *Fanum* he occupied would have eventually become the city with the third largest number of residents in the Marche region, and one of the most dynamic centers of the regional economy. In the 1st century BC, Fano (elev. 12 m, pop. 54,962; see plan p. 76) was little more than a village that had developed around a temple to Fortuna (*Fanum Fortunae*, hence the city's name) erected as a reminder of the victory against Hasdrubal in 207 BC, across the Flaminian Way, which reached the Adriatic here before turning northwest toward *Ariminum* (Rimini). The only certain date is that of the foundation of the *Julia Fanestris* colony by Augustus. The town was organized in the Roman grid pattern, and this is still visible despite major changes to the historic fabric, and surrounded by its first wall, only part of which survives since parts of it were used for later defense structures. No other public Roman buildings remain (gone is the famous basilica built by

Vitruvius on the Forum): after destruction by fire and wholesale ravaging by the Goths, it did not rise up again from its ruins until two centuries later, when it became one of the maritime pentapolises.

After gaining the status of a free municipality (in the late 15th cent.) the town sided with Frederick I Barbarossa and was inevitably caught up in the wars between the Guelphs and the Ghibellines. It also rapidly established contact with the Dalmatian coast across the Adriatic and built the cathedral. The city center shifted to Piazza Maggiore (now Piazza XX Settembre), where the Palazzo della Ragione was built, and, more significantly, the residence of the Malatesta, who were lords of Fano from 1357 to 1463. During this time they extended the walls and built the Castle, close to the Metauro river. Of the grandiose plans to strengthen the defense systems devised by the papal gov-

Pesaro and environs: the northern coast (3.2), from Fano to Urbino along the Metauro valley (3.3)

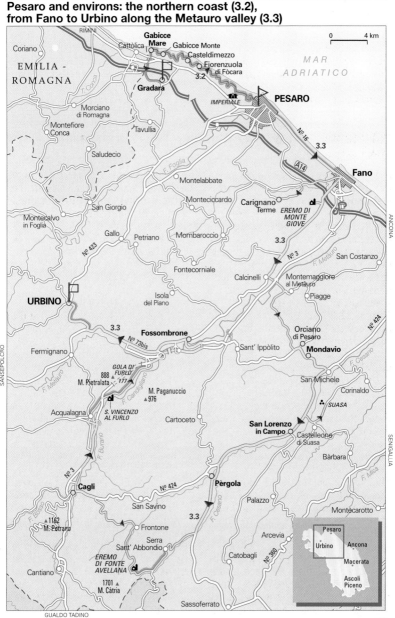

ernment in the 16th century, only the bastion by Sangallo was realized. Throughout the 18th century the historical fabric of the town underwent considerable change as buildings were pulled down and others built in their place. The creation of the Marina, preceded in the early 17th century by the opening of the canal-harbor, dates back to the 19th century, when the first bathing establishments led to the beginning of high-class tourism. Tourism has since grown and today Fano is not only a major fishing port and busy trading center but also a popular holiday resort.

Largo di Porta Maggiore (C1). This road junction is the point where the *Via Flaminia*, now Via Roma, entered the city. The gateway after which it is named is gone, but it is still possible to see the bastion of which it was a part, built by Matteo Nuti in 1464 as part of the reinforcement of the defense structure ordered by the Malatesta and now used as gardens.

Arco di Augusto* (B-C1). A memorial inscription recalls that this monumental sandstone arch clad in white travertine was dedicated to the first Caesar in 9 AD, although it was originally built to give thanks for the foundation of the city in 2 AD. It is classical in structure: the two smaller fornices at the sides spanned footpaths; the large central arch, decorated with a cornice, was a driveway.
The attic story was demolished in 1463 by Federico da Montefeltro during a siege, although traces of it remain in the adjoining facade of the former church of *San Michele** (C1), where a bas-relief to the right of Bernardino di Pietro's fine **portal** (1512) reproduces the Roman arch in its original form.
The **Logge di San Michele*** (B1), beyond the arch, is a building with an airy *arcade** (1495) and graceful *courtyard**, whose 15th-century arcade is surmounted by a 1920 loggetta in the style of the period.

Via Arco d'Augusto (B1-2). This is the continuation of the old Roman road inside the city walls, but is also the *decumanus maximus* of the first settlement, and now a pleasant shopping street.

Cathedral (B2). This heavily remodeled church, which dates back to the 10th century, was rebuilt for the first time in 1140. The Romanesque interventions made at that time can be seen in the facade, added during restoration, and, inside, in the *high reliefs** on the pulpit. The 17th-century *Cappella Nolfi** (1612, 3rd chapel on the right), has wall and ceiling frescoes by Domenichino, the *Madonna in Glory* on the altar of the chapel to the right of the high altar is by Ludovico Carracci and the *Lady of the Assumption* in the main chapel by Sebastiano Ceccarini.

Palazzo Montevecchio (B2). The street crosses *Corso Matteotti* (B-C1-2) – originally one of the *cardines* of the Roman settlement leading to the colony's forum – and leads to Piazza degli Avveduti, which the rear of this building overlooks. One of the most imposing and sumptuous of Fano's patrician palaces, it was erected in the mid - 18th century, possibly with the assistance of Alfonso Torreggiani. The front of the building is on Via Montevecchio: the portal is connected to the large first-floor window and the second-floor balcony, and encloses an impressive *Monumental Staircase** lined with statues.

Piazza XX Settembre (B-C2). Once known as Piazza Maggiore, this square has been the hub of city life since the Middle Ages. The picturesquely named *Fontana della Fortuna*,

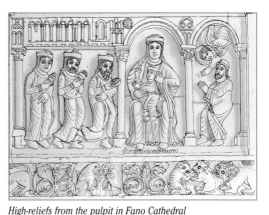

High-reliefs from the pulpit in Fano Cathedral

Fountain of Good Fortune, dates back to the 16th century; the *Palazzo della Ragione* (B2), which is two centuries older, was begun in 1299, and houses the *Teatro della Fortuna*, a theater with a splendid neoclassical auditorium constructed between 1845 and 1863 by Luigi Poletti; the lofty *Civic Tower* is a postwar addition to the square.

Fano: the canal-harbor

Palazzo Malatesta* (B2). The late 15th-century *Borgia-Cybo Arch* to the right of Palazzo della Ragione leads to the *Corte Malatestiana*, a beautiful open-air space used for theatrical performances and other events. It is lined by the two wings of the palace that was the Malatesta residence until 1463, then the City Hall and from the early 20th century the city museum and art gallery (see below). The different periods of its construction can be seen in the facades: the lower part, with a Gothic portico topped by merlons is 15th century; the airy Sansovino loggia on slender columns is from the following century.

Museo Civico and Pinacoteca. The museum and art gallery are housed in the 15th-century part of Palazzo Malatesta and form a single institution (open 8.30am–12.30pm, Sun 8.30am–13; closed Mon). Exhibits range from Neolithic times to the present day.

The archaeological section documents pre- and protohistorical settlements through local Neolithic and Iron Age finds; the remains of Roman civilization include *statues* (most notably the incomplete statue of *Emperor Claudius* and one of a young boy thought to be the grandson of Augustus), mosaics (note the excellent panther) and a collection of stone inscriptions. The coin collection boasts a fine set of Malatestian **medals*** coined by Matteo de' Pasti (those portraying Isotta degli Atti and Sigismondo Malatesta are dated 1446) and many others minted in Fano between the 15th and 18th centuries.

One of the most important paintings is a triptych (*Madonna Suckling the Infant Christ with Sts. Michael and Paul*) attributed to Guglielmo Veneziano, a polyptych by Michele Giambono (ca. 1420) showing the *Madonna of the Rose and Child with Saints*, and an *Enthroned Madonna and Child with Saints* painted around 1487 by Giovanni Santi, a *Guardian Angel* by Guercino, and an *Annunciation* by Guido Reni, *David with the Head of Goliath* by Domenichino and a *Nativity* attributed to Pietro Paolo Agabiti. Alongside these masterpieces are works by Giovanni Francesco Guerrieri, Simone Cantarini, Mattia Preti, Andrea Lilio, Corrado Giaquinto and by 18th century artists Antonio Amorosi, Sebastiano Ceccarini, Francesco Mancini and Pietro Tedeschi. 19th- and 20th-century works include those by Gerolamo Induno, Antonio Mancini, Giovanni Pierpaoli and Ettore Tito.

Rounding off the museum collection is the typical set of 18th-century ceramics, including works from the old hospital apothecary and Venetian *tableware*.

San Pietro ad Vallum (B2). Known also as *San Pietro in Valle*, this 16th-century church by G. B. Cavagna is in *Via Nolfi*, another Roman *cardo* (visits: apply at the Culture Office). Its sumptuous Baroque *interior*, is richly decorated with stuccowork, gilding, frescoes and paintings.

The street along the right-hand side of the church leads to the **Biblioteca Federiciana** (B2), a library founded by Domenico Federici, with over 200,000 volumes (including 3,000 from the 16th cent.); two 1688 *globes* (of the earth and the heavens) in the room of the same name, with carved *shelves* of a slightly earlier date.

Arche Malatestiane* (B-C2). In the 17th century, two monumental Malatesta tombs, originally inside the church of *San Francesco*, were relocated beneath the portico of the now deconsecrated 14th-century church. One of the tombs, in Gothic style, is of the first wife, Paola Bianca, and is by Filippo di Domenico (1416–21); the other, in Renaissance style, is the tomb of Pandolfo III, and is attributed to Leon Battista Alberti (1460).

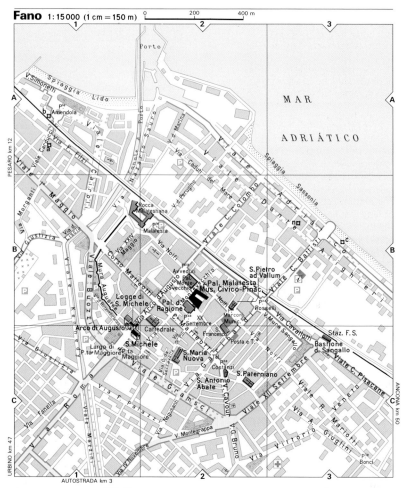

Fano 1:15 000 (1 cm = 150 m)

Santa Maria Nuova (C2). Nothing remains of the medieval origins of this church, more correctly known as *San Salvatore*, since it was rebuilt first in the 16th century (with the addition of the porch and the Renaissance *portal*, by Bernardino di Pietro) and again in the 18th century, when stuccowork was added to the interior. The 3rd altar on the right has works by Perugino (**Madonna with Saints**; a *Pietà** in the lunette; and, on the predella, **Scenes from the Life of the Virgin**, apparently executed with the help of a very young Raphael in 1497). The 2nd altar on the left has a 1489 **Annunciation**, and the *Visitation* in the 1st altar is by Giovanni Santi.

San Paterniano (C2). This church, beyond the 18th-century temple of *Sant'Antonio Abate*, is dedicated to the patron saint of Fano and attributed to Sansovino; the adjoining cloister is also Renaissance in style.

Bastione del Sangallo (C3). An angular bastion, decorated on the outside by the stone crest of Julius III, marks the eastern corner of the Malatestian walls, and was built in 1552 as part of an unfinished scheme to strengthen the city's defenses.

Rocca Malatestiana (B1-2). The most imposing element in the city's defense system lies at the northern corner. This trapezoid stronghold, commissioned by Sigismondo in the mid-15th century and surrounded by a moat was for many years used as a prison.

A road leads down from the castle to the *canal harbor* (A1-2), opened between 1612 and 1616 by Girolamo Rainaldi. Overlooking the harbor is the Institute of Marine Biology, the home of the *Museo del Mare* (A2; open: Sat 3pm–6pm, Sun 9am–noon), which illustrates the Adriatic Sea through its marine life.

To the south of the castle is a fine section of the **Augustan Walls** (B1), built in sandstone and punctuated by towers and gateways, leading back to Largo di Porta Maggiore.

There are two interesting excursions just outside Fano. The first, 5.5 km away, is to the **Eremo di Monte Giove** (C1, off map), a 1650 Camaldolese monastery; the church of *San Salvatore* is 18th century. The second (10 km), leads to **Carignano Terme**, which has special plants to recover waters rich in alkaline bicarbonate, chlorinated magnesium, sodium bromide and sulfur.

Toward Mondavio

This route, which passes through a variety of landscapes, begins on the old *Via Flaminia* (now the SS3). The parallel express highway to Fossombrone in the valley bottom serves the plain southwest of Fano, which has become a center of small and medium-sized industry. Further inland, the old Roman road runs closer to the river and the small hill towns perched on the lower slopes begin to come more clearly into view. The hills rise up to *Orciano di Pesaro* (elev. 264 m, pop. 2,313), a village interesting for the Renaissance church of *Santa Maria Nuova**, attributed to Baccio Pontelli.

Mondavio (elev. 280 m, pop. 3,834) is surrounded ancient walls. The mighty *Rocca** (1482–92; open: 9am–noon and 3pm–7pm) shows the hand of Francesco di Giorgio Martini. It houses the *Museo di Rievocazione Storica* and the *Armeria*, with mannequins displaying costumes and weaponry from the 15th to 18th centuries. In Piazza Matteotti stand the Palazzo Municipale (which has a *Madonna and Child* by Carlo da Camerino) and the cloister of the Convent of *San Francesco*, home of the *Museo Civico* (open 9am–noon and 3pm–7pm), whose collection includes canvases by Giuliano Presutti and Federico Barocci, together with Marche ceramics and an exquisite wooden *tabernacle* from 1610.

San Lorenzo in Campo

Although the castle stands in ruins, the walls of this ancient little town (elev. 209 m, pop. 3,360) survive. Official documents mention the town around the year 1000, but it was first settled much earlier around the 7th–8th century church of **San Lorenzo** (admission by prior arrangement, tel. 776825), originally part of a Benedictine monastery. This church, after which the town is named, is an outstanding example of the Romanesque-Gothic, despite changes made in the 13th and 14th centuries. This style is best exemplified in the side portal, the minor apses and the lower, three-apsed part of the crypt. Four of the columns dividing the interior into three naves are hewn from a single piece of Egyptian granite and are dated as early as 1550 BC (they were taken from the Temple of Adonis in nearby *Suasa*).

In the medieval center, the 1565 *Palazzo Della Rovere*, previously called Palazzo Pretorio and Palazzo delle Milizie, houses the *Musei Comunali Laurentini* (admission on request, tel. 776814), which comprise the *Museo Archeologico di Suasa* (with a Roman tomb and funerary offerings), the *Museo Etnografico Africano* (exhibits illustrate customs and traditions in Sierra Leone) and a *collection of fossils and minerals*.

The countryside between Fano and Pesaro

The ancient city of *Suasa* – or *Suasa Senonum*, to give it its full name – lies 7 km northeast of San Lorenzo in Campo, on the right-hand bank of the Cesano river, across the boundary in the province of Ancona. This settlement, founded by the Senonian Gauls, later became a Roman town and was destroyed in 409 by the Goths under Alaric; excavations (closed to visitors) have revealed remains of the *amphitheater* and of a patrician *domus* with mosaic floor.

Pergola

Pergola (elev. 265 m, pop. 7,115) probably owes its foundation in the early 13th century not to the people of the Marche but to the Umbrians. At the behest of the town of

The library in the Fonte Avellana hermitage

Gubbio, the inhabitants of the surrounding mountains moved down into the small plain formed by the confluence of the Cinisco and Cesano rivers, settling at a strategically favorable point for commerce between Umbria and the upper Adriatic. The trading activities which ensued encouraged the development of crafts and architecture, with the foundation in the Middle Ages of many churches (although these were nearly all remodeled between the 1500s and 1800s) and, in the 16th–18th centuries, of middle-class and patrician residences.

At the beginning of the town, the former church of *San Giacomo* displays its 13th-century origins in the portals on the facade and on the right-hand side of the exterior; the Baroque interior has a fresco in a niche on the left (*Crucifixion*) attributed to Lorenzo d'Alessandro. The *Duomo*, on Via Don Minzoni, has a neoclassical facade and a 17th-century interior. The only reminder of its Romanesque origins is the campanile; the 14th-century painted wood *Crucifix* is influenced by the Rimini school. The most interesting example of secular architecture is the 18th-century arcaded *Municipio* on Corso Matteotti.

The museum center in Largo San Giacomo is soon to become the home of the **Cartoceto bronzes*** from the Julio-Claudian age: this equestrian group, discovered in 1946, consists of two female figures and two figures on horseback, and is extraordinary not only for the fact that the bronze was gold-plated, but also because it is one of the few works to have survived the widespread medieval practice of melting down ancient statues as a source of raw material.

Eremo di Fonte Avellana*

This secluded place of meditation (elev. 680 m), set in an isolated wooded valley at the feet of the rugged *Mt. Catria* (elev. 1,701 m), dates back to the arrival here of St. Romuald in 980. Dante, who stayed at the monastery, mentions it in the 21st *canto* of his "Paradise." The abbey, which has seen periods of glory and of crisis, has belonged to the Camaldolese order since the 17th century.

The Romanesque-Gothic **church** is in the shape of a Latin cross, and has a raised presbytery over an 11th-century crypt; the *Crucifix* on the high altar is 16th century. To the right of the church is the chapel of *San Pier Damiani*, opened to celebrated the 900th anniversary of the death of the saint who retired here in 1035, and the entrance to the **monastery** proper (open weekdays 9am–11am and 3pm–5pm, Sun and holidays 3pm–5pm). Also to the right is the *Sala San Pier Damiani*, whose barrel vaulting is similar to that of the church, followed by the *scriptorium* (where the amanuenses worked) and the *Biblioteca Dante Alighieri* (many of the over 10,000 volumes date back to the 16th and 17th centuries). The small *cloister*, with Romanesque and Gothic arches, leads to the chapter-house and Baroque *Refectory*, and to the cells, which date back to the monastery's foundation: a bust of Dante and a stone tablet indicate the cell where the poet stayed.

Mt. Catria is ideal for hiking enthusiasts, who can enjoy walks of varying difficulty through the mountain's dense woodland.

Cagli

There was a time when the drive for independence of this town (elev. 276 m, pop. 9,356) reached such an intensity that it successfully opposed the threats of nearby Gubbio and the lordship of Montefeltro. This was the high point in the history of Cagli, a town inhabited by the Umbrians that had already gained importance in Roman times (just outside the town is the *Mallio Bridge*, built over the Flaminian Way and restored in Augustan times). In the mid-14th century Francesco di Giorgio Martini was ordered by the Montefeltro to design a stronghold, of which only the ellipsoidal *Tower** survives (admission on request, tel. 791232), because the dukes preferred to destroy it themselves rather than let it fall into the hands of the rival Borgia. Cagli, which is famous for the *Gioco dell'Oca*, a game held there in August, also attracts lovers of 18th-century art with an unusual urban itinerary, which follows the trail of the works by Gaetano Lapis.

Palazzo Comunale*. From 1476 Francesco di Giorgio Martini worked on the reconstruction of this 13th-century building, which overlooks the central *Piazza Matteotti*. Some of its rooms house the *Museo Archeologico e della Via Flaminia* (open Oct–May, Sat and Sun 10am–noon and 3pm–6pm; Jun–Sep 10am–noon and 4pm–7pm), which illustrates the important role played by the Via Flaminia in the history and communications of the town; the rest of the collection of the former Museo Civico, awaiting relocation, includes a fresco fragment (*Head of St. Sebastian*) by Giovanni Santi, a canvas (*Evening*) from the school of Gherardo delle Notti, and *drawings* by Antonio Canova.
On the corner of the same square is the *Duomo*, or cathedral, originally a Romanesque-Gothic building but remodeled in the 17th and 18th centuries. The canvas in the second altar on the right and those in the chapel on the left of the high altar are by Gaetano Lapis.

From the square take Vicolo Luzi and turn right into Via Purgotti, to *Palazzo Tiranni-Castracane*,

a 16th-century palace decorated with stuccowork by Federico Brandani. This is to house the *Diocesan Collection*, with works by Claudio Ridolfi and Girolamo Cialdieri di Bartolomeo, and rare 13th-century **religious objects**.
Take the road running along the left-hand side of Palazzo Comunale, turn left into Via Gucci and then right, to the Romanesque-Gothic church of *San Francesco*, whose bare facade has a lunette frescoed in the 14th century. Inside, note the 15th-century *frescoes* to the left of the first altar on the right (attributed to Antonio Alberti); the third altar has a *Madonna della Neve* by Gaetano Lapis; the first on the left has a *Madonna and Child with Saints* by Raffaellino del Colle.

San Giovanni Battista*. From Piazza Matteotti, *Corso XX Settembre*, which begins to the left of the cathedral, leads down to Via dell'Ospedale on the right, onto which this Romanesque church faces. Known also as the church of *San Domenico*, it contains works by Gaetano Lapis (1st altar on the right), Girolamo Genga (to whom the *Annunciation and God the Father** are attributed) and Giovanni Santi (**Madonna and Child, Saints and Resurrection** in the 2nd altar on the left and *Christ at the Tomb between two Saints* above the nearby sepulcher).

At the end of Via dell'Ospedale stands the church of *Santa Chiara*, with female saints in the wall medallions and the *Triumph of St. Clare* in the ceiling by Gaetano Lapis.

Gola del Furlo*
Mt. Pietralata (elev. 888 m) and *Mt. Paganuccio* (elev. 976 m) seem almost to swallow up the Candigliano river, which, before the construction of a dam, could hardly find a course between the two eminences. Opening a road through this narrow ravine was never going to be easy, but the Romans, undaunted by the task, continued the *Via Flaminia* by simply digging their way through; Emperor Vespasian completed the **Galleria del Furlo***, in 76–77 AD. This tunnel was known in ancient

Art within Art
The Torrione di Cagli (right) is the home of the Centro di Scultura Contemporanea. And what better use could have been found for this splendid tower than as a permanent study and documentation center of modern sculpture in the unique context of a masterpiece of Renaissance architecture by painter, sculptor and architect Francesco di Giorgio Martini? The center publishes its own *Quaderni di scultura contemporanea*, which present the latest research into the plastic arts, with critical reflections on events now enshrined in history.

times as *petra pertusa* or *forulus*, from which the Furlo gorge gets its name.

To drive through the tunnel, leave the expressway at Acqualagna and continue along the old Flaminian Way. This leads first to the Romanesque church of *San Vincenzo al Furlo* (part of an 8th-century abbey), then alongside the lake formed by the dam and into the Roman tunnel; a road to the right just before the entrance leads to a smaller gallery, cut by Gaius Flaminius in 217 BC.

Fossombrone

The architecture and indeed the whole mood of this Metauro valley town (elev. 118 m, pop. 9,507) is very reminiscent of nearby Urbino, whose lords used it as their country residence. The Montefeltro arrived in 1444, when it was sold to them by a member of the Malatesta family (the owners in the previous century), who fortified it by building the castle in the citadel. Historically, Fossombrone had been part of the Pentapolis and was an important town in Roman times, at least from 133 BC, when Gaius Sempronius Gracchus arrived here to enforce his land reform laws. The town's name derives from the tribune known at the time as *Forum Sempronii* (remains of *Roman baths* and a *Roman road* have been discovered along the road to Pesaro).

Corso Garibaldi. This partly arcaded main street is lined with 15th- to 18th-century palaces and churches. The church of *Sant'Agostino* is 14th century in origin but was remodeled in the 18th century; behind the high altar is a *Nativity* by Federico Zuccari. Immediately beyond is the *Corte Rossa*, a 16th-century residence of the dukes of Urbino. The short street along its left-hand side leads to the *Corte Bassa** (admission by prior arrangement, tel. 740377), one century older, designed by Francesco di Giorgio Martini and Girolamo Genga.

The continuation of Corso Garibaldi has an interesting series of rusticated facades: the 16th-century **Palazzo Cattabeni** or *Palazzo del Monte di Pietà* (rusticated sandstone); the late 15th-century *Palazzo Staurenghi* (smooth rustic work); the 16th-century *Palazzo Comunale* (rusticated sandstone); and the late 15th-century *Palazzo Vescovile* (Florentine rustic work).

Cathedral. Originally part of a Benedictine abbey, the church was redesigned by Cosimo Morelli. It has a neoclassical facade. The interior decorations are mainly 16th- and 17th-century, but note the 14th-century fresco *Madonna della Provvidenza* in the 1st chapel of the left-hand nave; the sacristy has a sandstone reredos by Domenico Rosselli (1480).

Corte Alta*. This building, also known as the *Palazzo Ducale*, is reached by a flight of steps in the cathedral square. It was begun in the 13th century by the Malatesta and enlarged between 1466 and 1470 by Francesco di Giorgio Martini and Girolamo Genga for Federico da Montefeltro. It houses both the *Pinacoteca Civica* (closed in 1997 for reorganization) and the *Museo Civico "Augusto Vernarecci"* (open Sat and Sun 3.30pm–6.30pm), which has archaeological material from prehistoric times, sub-Apennine culture (fragments of bowls) and Picene culture (fibulae in the form of arches and leeches, 6th–4th century BC bronzes, 5th-century BC bronze pans); a large section on the Roman *Forum Sempronii* illustrates the town and the area through epigraphs on public buildings, judicial and sacred inscriptions, memorials to emperors, and 1st- to 4th-century sculptures, everyday objects (weighing-scale and loom weights, Republican and Imperial coins, vases, oil-lamps and personal adornments) and funerary practices (stelae, late Roman sarcophagi, cineraria, inscriptions, embalming articles).

The **Cittadella**, which overlooks the rooftops of the town, is reached either by a difficult path or by steep steps. Here are the remains of the 13th–15th century *Rocca Malatestiana*: a pentagonal stronghold enclosed by imposing towers and a keep. Inside is the courtyard of the Baroque church of *Sant'Aldebrando* (admission by prior arrangement, tel. 740377), which contains early 15th-century frescoes by Antonio Alberti.

Fossombrone's other main collection is in the 16th-century *Palazzo Pergamino-Simili*, on Via Pergamino leading in the direction of Urbino. This is the **Quadreria Cesarini** (open Sat 9am–12.30pm; and 3pm–6.30pm on the 1st and 3rd Sunday of the month), an art gallery with over 60 paintings and the complete graphic art works of Anselmo Bucci; the gallery also has modern and contemporary artworks by Giorgio Morandi, Achille Funi, Arturo Tosi, Marino Marini, Francesco Messina, Gino Severini, and Aldo Carpi.

4 Urbino and environs

"On the slopes of the Apennines, almost in the center of Italy toward the Adriatic, is situated, as everyone knows, the little city of Urbino. Although it is surrounded by hills which are perhaps not as agreeable as those found in many other places, none the less it has been favored by Nature with a very rich and fertile countryside, so that as well as a salubrious atmosphere it enjoys an abundance of all the necessities of life."
Baldassare Castiglione's *Book of the Courtier* (trans. George Bull, Penguin) offers interesting insights into Urbino – the *urbs bina*, or city on two hills – and the duchy of the Montefeltro family, a branch of the Carpegna counts, in the valley of the Metauro and Foglia rivers. Before he even mentions the palace, "the most beautiful in all Italy," Castiglione widens the view, in space and time, toward Fermignano, Urbania, Sant'Angelo in Vado, Mercatello sul Metauro; and toward Montecalvo in Foglia, Tavoleto, Sassocorvaro, Lunano, Piandimeleto, Belforte all'Isauro. These fortified towns were owned by Duke Federico da Montefeltro, and some still have the castles he ordered Francesco di Giorgio Martini to design for them. This historical and artistic galaxy revolved around Duke Federico, the politician, patron of the arts and the inspiration behind the cradle of culture and humanistic civilization that was Urbino in the 15th century. And he surrounded himself at court with geniuses from all fields: scientists, architects, painters, sculptors, theoreticians, novelists and treatise writers.
Here, a form of humanism developed that was the most rational and abstract, the most harmonious and balanced in its links with nature of the entire Renaissance. It found its outward expression in the Ducal Palace, whose facades faced onto the city, and whose hanging gardens with their false windows overlooked the surrounding countryside. Its architecture exemplified human triumph over the divine forces of mathematical and geometrical proportion. Henceforth the city would be associated with the grandeur of its golden age in the 15th century, in the later times of crisis of the Della Rovere seignory, emerging even through the melancholy of Federico Barocci, who depicts the palace's twin turrets as the backdrop to

scenes of Crucifixions and Annunciations. In the 18th and 19th century Urbino became an isolated provincial town and fell into decline, only to be brought back to life in the 20th century by the free university, whose students now outnumber the local population by almost two to one. Urbino is the "windy city" of Giovanni Pascoli's youthful memories, and the town Paolo Volponi loved, left and inevitably returned to with bitterness and regret ("As I stand motionless on the round hill behind Urbino, far from that sharp diamond-shaped town, from the clear-cut shafts of light that close every street, I hear the infinite voices of the two valleys of the Metauro and Foglia rivers"; from "Le Porte dell'Appennino," 1955–59).

The church of San Bernardino degli Zoccolanti, outside Urbino

81

4.1 Urbino**

Itinerary from Piazza del Mercatale *(see plan p. 83)*

Federico da Montefeltro succeeded in doing what few people in history have ever done: he identified himself so closely with a city as to become virtually synonymous with it. In redesigning Urbino (elev. 485 m, pop. 15,171), he totally erased its previous history and made it all but impossible for anyone to change its layout thereafter. The ideal city and art capital he created was no less rich in artistic monuments and masterpieces than the much larger cities of Venice, Florence and Rome. His strong personality, and his moral and intellectual energy, so well depicted in the Piero della Francesca portrait of him that hangs in the Uffizi Gallery in Florence, are clearly visible still today within the walls of his city, perpetuating the associations between the man and the town and highlighting the genius of this 15th-century patron of the arts. It was during the years of his rule as a duke (1442–82) that the city took on its final form. Some doubt remains as to the true origin of the name: some have suggested that it derives from *urvum* (the curved handle of a plow – a reference to the shape of the hill on which it stood), others explain the name as a contraction of *urbs bina* (twin city). Whichever is true, the area is known to have been densely settled by Umbro-Picene populations, and it was certainly an important town in Roman times (as its raising to the status of *municipium* in 46 BC suggests). Little remains of this early historical period, other than the Roman Theater and the finds now exhibited in the archaeological museum, although the *Poggio*, the hill on which Palazzo Ducale was later built, retains the typical roman *cardo* and *de-*

cumanus layout (the Forum is now occupied by Piazza Duca Federico). That destruction came about during the Gothic-Byzantine wars, from which Urbino did not recover until the 12th–13th centuries when it passed into the hands of the Montefeltro, a branch of the noble Carpegna family. The 14th century is better documented architecturally, through the churches of *San Domenico* and *San Francesco* and the gradually urbanization of the *Monte*, the hill to the northwest of the *Poggio*, which offered a foretaste of the cultural and artistic splendors to come during Urbino's golden age a century later. That earlier age begins with the cycle of frescoes, still in the Gothic style, of the Oratory of *San Giovanni Battista* and, after Pope Eugene IV bestowed on Oddantonio da Montefeltro the title of Duke of Urbino (1443), concludes with the building of the Renaissance Palazzo Ducale, by Luciano Laurana and Francesco di Giorgio Martini. The magnificence did not come to an end when Federico died, though: his son Guidobaldo raised the walls around the historic center, founded the University (originally established in 1506 as a College of Doctors for the administration of judicial matters), and two great Italian artists, Raphael and Bramante, worked here. When Guidobaldo died without direct heirs, the duchy passed to his nephew Francesco Maria I, a member of the Della Rovere family, who moved his court to Pesaro, and left Urbino in decline.

It was not until the 1700s that the city showed the first feeble signs of reawakening (Urbino is one of the few places in Italy to have been only marginally influenced by

The rooftops of Urbino

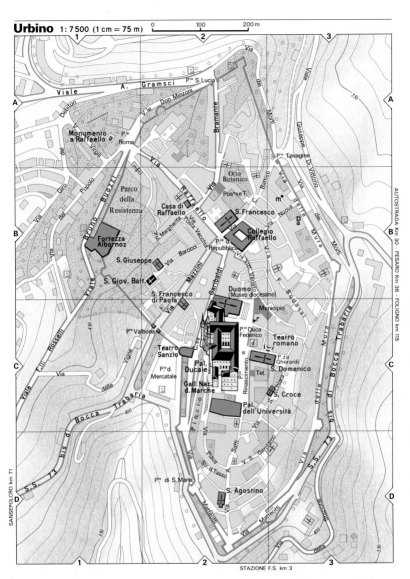

Urbino 1:7500 (1 cm = 75 m)

(map of Urbino with labeled streets and landmarks including Monumento a Raffaello, Parco della Resistenza, Fortezza Albornoz, Casa di Raffaello, S. Francesco, Collegio Raffaello, S. Giuseppe, S. Giov. Batt., S. Francesco di Paola, Duomo (Museo diocesano), Municipio, Teatro romano, Teatro Sanzio, Pal. Ducale, Gall. Naz. d. Marche, S. Domenico, S. Croce, Pal. dell'Università, S. Agostino, Orto Botanico, and others)

AUTOSTRADA Km 30 - PESARO Km 36 - FOLIGNO km 115

SANSEPOLCRO km 71

STAZIONE F.S. km 3

the Baroque) through the patronage of the Albani. One member of this family had already been pope, another transformed Urbino and renovated its churches and palaces, always showing deference to the Renaissance image Federico had created. Respect also guided construction work in the 19th century, when historical buildings were converted and new ones built (the university colleges) that have become milestones in contemporary architecture. The walking tour begins at Piazza del Mercatale, from where both the theater steps and a spiral staircase lead up to Corso Garibaldi, past the west front of Palazzo Ducale through the Pincio gardens and into Piazza Rinascimento, which is bordered on its south side by Palazzo dell'Università. The square is dominated by Palazzo Ducale and the Galleria Nazionale delle Marche; streets also lead off to the southeastern quarters of the city. After the visit to this major artistic complex and the nearby cathedral, the tour continues down the slopes of the *Poggio* hill (Via Vittorio Veneto) to Piazza della Repubblica, then up the *Monte* hill to Raphael's birthplace and the monument to the artist. After the Fortezza Albornoz, Via dei Maceri leads to the churches of *San Giuseppe* and *San Giovanni Battista*, and finally to Via Mazzini, which leads back down to Piazza del Mercatale. Automobile users may also like to visit the University halls of residence and the church of *San Bernardino degli Zoccolanti*, just outside Urbino.

The walls* (A-D1-3). Enclosing Urbino in a kind of spindle-shaped pattern, the walls correspond to what was until World War II the city's outermost boundary. The architectural methods which the Montefeltro used to build them in the early 16th century were way ahead of their time: with their heart-shaped ramparts and rounded trunnions this was one of the first modern defense systems to encircle an entire town.

Decoration in the Ducal Palace library, Urbino

Piazza del Mercatale (C1-2). This square, once the site of a market outside the walls, is now the main point of access to the historic town, especially now that it serves as a parking lot. Entrance is through the 17th-century *Porta Valbona* (C1) and the *theater steps*, which just inside the walls climb to the right along the steeply sloping path between the square and Corso Garibaldi, past the houses perched beneath the palace. Alternatively, visitors may use the ingenious **spiral stairway**, which Francesco di Giorgio Martini designed inside the 15th-century semi-cylindrical bastion to the right of the gateway.

Corso Garibaldi (B-C2). Both ascents lead into this street, which offers a good close-up view of Palazzo Ducale's west front, with its slender flanking turrets and three-tiered loggia. Note also the *Teatro Sanzio* (C2; 1853), built close by the semi-cylindrical stairway bastion.
Away to the south are the *Pincio Gardens* (C-D2), laid out in 1840 over Federico da Montefeltro's stables, which opened onto Piazza Mercatale below; it affords an excellent *view** of the Apennine mountains.

Palazzo dell'Università (C2). This building is the headquarters of Urbino University, one of the driving forces of the local economy and a focus for the city's cultural life, and is joined to Palazzo Ducale by a barrel-vaulted arch; the two buildings dominate Piazza Rinascimento (see below). A stone coat of arms in Via Saffi serves as a reminder that this was the first residence of the Montefeltro.

Before embarking on the tour of the duke's palace, it is worth paying a brief visit to the southeastern quarters. The church of *Sant'Agostino* was converted into a university building by Giancarlo De Carlo (1973). Its medieval origins can still be seen in the terracotta wall, topped by a series of small arches.
The *Oratorio di Santa Croce** (open on request, tel. 327731) is thought to have been designed by Francesco di Giorgio Martini; it was frescoed in the cross vault near the entrance by Giorgio Picchi (*Stories of the Holy Cross*); note the fresco (*St. Sebastian*) by Giovanni Santi on the right-hand wall, and a fresco of the *Madonna and Child with Angels* by Ottaviano Nelli on the left-hand wall. From Piazza Gherardi, Via San Domenico leads off back to Piazza Rinascimento, past the sunken remains of the *Teatro Romano* (on the right).

Piazza Rinascimento (C2). This is the name of the southern section of the square at the monumental heart of the city. The Egyptian *obelisk* was brought here in 1737 to celebrate the pontificate of Pope Clement XI and the urban redevelopment work carried out by the Albani. The former Gothic church of *San Domenico* (C2-3), stands "defiantly" opposite Palazzo Ducale and the Duomo (see below). It has a 1451 portal, decorated in the lunette by a copy of the *Madonna and Saints* by Luca della Robbia (the original is in Palazzo Ducale).

Palazzo Ducale** (C2). "It seemed more like a city than a mere palace," said Baldassare Castiglione, marveling at Federico da Montefeltro's residence (now the home of the Marche's Artistic and Historical Monuments Department, National Gallery and Archaeology Museum). French essayist Montaigne, who visited the city when the last of the Della Rovere family was still alive, commented that it "contained as many rooms as there are days in the year"; Giorgio Vasari described it as "wondrous." The palace (visits by prior arrangement 9am–7pm, Sun and Mon 9am–2pm), is no less awe-inspiring today, both as a feat of architectural engineering and as the first example of a princely residence in the form – not of an austere, impenetrable fortress along medieval lines – but of a palace that welcomed in the outside world, a place of intellectual ferment and the perfect setting for the humanistic culture and ideals of its patron Federico. When he was summoned to start work on the palace in Urbino in 1465, architect Luciano Laurana was not starting from scratch: the original core of the residence (corresponding to the elegant paired windows overlooking Piazza Rinascimento) had already been begun around 1444. It was Laurana, however, who decided on the central courtyard and solved the problem of building on such an awkward, uneven site, creating the celebrated **west front**, which looked out toward that other Renaissance capital, Florence, as if in an attempt to forge some kind of link between the two courts. He also designed the **twin turrets*** that have since become the very symbol of the city. The winged **facade*** enclosing Piazza Duca Federico was by another great 15th-century architect, Francesco di Giorgio Martini, who took over from Laurana in 1472, when the latter left for the Aragonese court in Naples.

In this part of the building the portal of the south wing, which was decorated (as were the windows) by Ambrogio Barocci, leads to the heart of the residence, the **Cortile d'Onore**** (or Courtyard of Honor, see plan p. 86 a), which symbolizes and perfectly embodies not only Urbino culture but Italian 15th-century art and civilization as a whole, in the geometric discipline of its proportions, its balanced use of light stone and red brick, and the sheer formal order it offers. The Latin inscriptions on the string courses above the portico and the *piano nobile* celebrate Duke Federico.

The former public areas surrounding and opening onto the courtyard included the duke's Library, where the illuminated codices of the Lord of Urbino (now in the Vatican Library) were kept. Exhibited in adjoining rooms are 71 *panels** depicting the machinery of war and peace executed by Ambrogio Barocci (second half 15th cent.) from a design by Francesco di Giorgio Martini and originally on the backrests of the seat running round the winged facade.

Near the courtyard's well is the entrance to the **Museo Archeologico Urbinate**, which grew out of the Epigraphic Museum founded in 1756. The exhibits, some of which were found by Raffaele Fabbretti, include tombstones and memorial inscriptions, inscribed pillars, and

The Courtyard of Honor in the Ducal Palace, Urbino

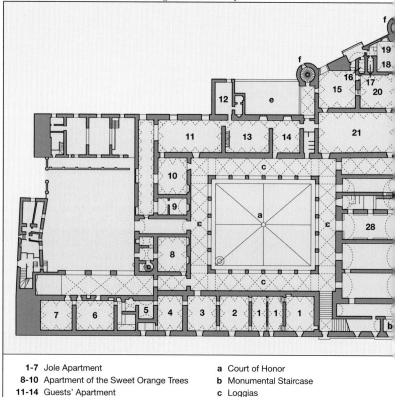

1-7   Jole Apartment
8-10   Apartment of the Sweet Orange Trees
11-14   Guests' Apartment
15-21   Duke Federico's Apartment
22-27   Duchess' Apartment
28   Throne Room

a   Court of Honor
b   Monumental Staircase
c   Loggias
d   Hanging garden
e   Cockerel Court
f   Twin towers

decorated pagan and Christian urns; there is also a remarkable relief work (*Ulysses and the Sirens*; 1st century AD) and the early 4th-century *Marmorarius Eutropus Slab*.

The courtyard also provides access to the **basement areas**, ancillary rooms serving a variety of functions: stable, cattle shed and *neviera* (a cold store where snow from the gardens above was collected), and the duke's kitchens and bathrooms, both equipped with heating, drainage and waste disposal systems.

Galleria Nazionale delle Marche**. The monumental **staircase*** (b), created by Luciano Laurana and decorated by Ambrogio Barocci to celebrate the patron (note the stone crest and the *statue* of the duke in a niche on the first landing by Girolamo Campagna), leads to the so-called *soprallogge** (c), upper corridors overlooking the courtyard, and embellished with finely inlaid doors.

This is the palace's *piano nobile*, and home of the region's most prestigious museum since 1912 (the year it was founded). Its im-

portance lies not only in the wealth of artworks by the most prominent artists of the day – the combined collections of the Montefeltro and the Della Rovere – but also in the setting in which they are exhibited, its architecture and decoration, which together give one of the most comprehensive pictures of Italy's artistic output from the Middle Ages to the Renaissance.

The east wing of the palace – the oldest – is taken up by the *Appartamento della Jole* (1-7), so named after the mythological figures of Hercules and Iole carved on a fireplace by Michele di Giovanni in the room of the same name; here too is the original glazed terracotta *lunette** (*Madonna and Saints*) by Luca della Robbia from the facade of the former church of *San Domenico*, a *Head of the Madonna* by Agostino di Duccio, a bas-relief of *Federico da Montefeltro and his secretary Ottaviano Ubaldini* attributed to Francesco di Giorgio Martini. The other rooms in the apartment have a number of interesting, albeit damaged

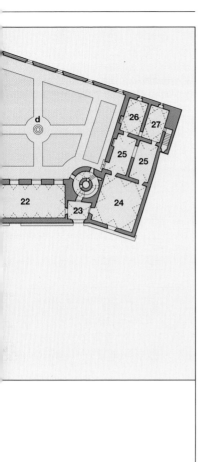

ries from the Life of Christ; 1345) by Giovanni Baronzio, a painted *Crucifix* by the "Maestro di Verucchio," a triptych (*Coronation of the Virgin*) by the "Maestro dell'Incoronazione di Urbino," and a *Madonna and Child* by Allegretto Nuzi. The *Appartamento degli Ospiti*, (or Guest Apartment; 11-14), includes the so-called King of England's Room decorated by Federico Brandani with stuccoes depicting the symbols of the houses of Montefeltro and Della Rovere, and contains a variety of artworks. They range from 15th-century wood sculptures (with a remarkable Annunciation from the Abruzzo school), a chest containing 103 15th-century gold coins found at Mondavio, paintings attributed to Carlo and Vittore Crivelli (*St. James of the Marca*), Giovanni Bellini (*Sacra Conversazione*) and by Alvise Vivarini (polyptych with *Madonna and Saints*, 1476).

Duke Federico's **Apartment*** (15-21) is the most sumptuously-decorated part of the entire palace. Finely inscribed stone cornices decorate the *Audience Room**, with Piero della Francesca's two masterpieces: the **Flagellation**** (an extraordinary work that combines the scientific precision of perspective science with the allegorical significance of the subject) and the **Madonna of Senigallia**** (a Renaissance icon in which the theme of Mary's motherhood is tinged with forebodings of death). Brandani created the stuccowork on the ceiling of the *Guidobaldo Chapel*. The wall decorations in Duke Federico's **Study*** were inlaid by Baccio Pontelli (probably designed by Sandro Botticelli, Francesco di Giorgio Martini and Bramante); Joos van Gent painted the **Portraits of Illustrious Men*** in the upper section (14 of the original 28 are now in the Louvre), a compendium of the greatest geniuses of ancient and modern times. The tiny *Chapel of Forgiveness** is next to the *Temple of the Muses*, once decorated with paintings of the same name by Giovanni Santi (these are now at the Corsini gallery in Florence), which leads out onto the loggias of the west front. The Duke's bedchamber is decorated with a carved stone fireplace

frescoes (*Men at Arms*), attributed to Giovanni Boccati, *Duke Federico's Alcove** – a splendid example of a 15th-century piece of furniture, with rare tempera decorations (*viridarium*) attributed to Giovanni da Camerino – a painting on wood (*Scenes from the Life of Saint Savinus*) by Boccati, part of the predella for Orvieto Cathedral, a *Crucifixion* and *Madonna and Child* by Girolamo di Giovanni. The so-called Appartamento dei Melaranci (or "Orange-Tree Apartment"; 8-10) has 14th-century works, including a Polyptych* (*Madonna and Child with Saints*, and Sto-

Annunciation (Carlo da Camerino)

(attributed to Domenico Rosselli and Francesco di Simone Ferrucci), a *Portrait of Federico da Montefeltro and his Son Guidobaldo*** by Pedro Berruguete and a painting on wood (*Madonna and Child*) from the Verrocchio school. The beautiful *Angel Room* has a *fireplace* with a frieze of cherubs by Rosselli; *inlaid doors** attributed to Botticelli; the *Communion of the Apostles** painted by Joos van Gent around 1473; the *Profanation of the Host** by Paolo Uccello, the predella of the work mentioned above by Joos van Gent; the **Ideal City*** attributed to Luciano Laurana or Piero della Francesca (one of the highest achievements of the formal culture, perspective science and aesthetic aspirations of the day); the bas-relief (*Madonna and Child*) by Tommaso Fiamberti; and a 15th-century carved, inlaid chest (perspective of the city). The works in the *Room of Musical Gatherings*, chosen by Baldassare Castiglione as the setting for his *Book of his Courtier*, are late 15th century. They include a *Crucifixion* and a *Pentecost* by Luca Signorelli and the Buffi altarpiece (*Madonna and Child with Saints*; 1489) by Giovanni Santi. The *Duchess' Apartment* (22-27) was decorated later. It now contains works from the 16th century. In the vestibule is a stained-glass *Annunciation* by Timoteo Viti, while the adjoining duchess' drawing-room (note Francesco di Simone Ferrucci's *stucco ceiling**) marks the beginning of a series of world-famous masterpieces, most notably Raphael's **The**

Mute**, (this portrait of a gentlewoman, probably painted around 1507, at the end of his stay in Florence is seen by scholars as one of the highest expressions of the Urbino master's art – see p. 89) and *St. Catherine of Alexandria*** (an early work of his), while the **Christ Blessing**, a highly evocative work of fine pictorial expression, is attributed to Bramantino, and *Sts. Thomas à Becket and Martin between Archbishop Arrivabene and Duke Guidobaldo* was painted by Timoteo Viti. The works in the duchess' bedchamber date back to the mid-16th century, and include a **Last Supper** and *Resurrection* by Titian (both part of a processional standard made around 1544), the *Madonna of Succor with Saints* by Raffaellino del Colle, an *Annunciation* by Vincenzo Pagani and Flemish tapestries. Works by Pellegrino Tibaldi, Taddeo Zuccari and Federico Brandani are in the wardrobe in the adjoining room, while the seven Tapestries of the **Acts of the Apostles**, woven in the 17th from cartoons by Raphael, decorate the walls of **Throne Room*** (28), the solemn hall (35 x 15 m) which the duke used for festivities: note the initials F.C. (Federicus Comes) in the ceiling roses and the inscriptions FE DUX (Federicus Dux) on the fireplaces and over the doors.

The second floor of the Palazzo Ducale, designed by Bartolomeo Genga, was built at the behest of Guidobaldo II Della Rovere, hence the name *Appartamento Roveresco*. It divides into two parts. The first, dedicated to painting,

Inlay work by Baccio Pontelli in the Studialo, or Duke's Study, in the Ducal Palace, Urbino

has some noteworthy paintings by Federico Barocci (the unfinished *Assumption* is one of his last works; there is also an interesting *Immaculate Conception**, *St. Francis Receiving the Stigmata*, and a *Crucifixion*). Other works by his pupils include a *Madonna and Child with St. Francesca Romana* by Orazio Gentileschi, a *St. Roch*, by Andrea Lilio, a *St. Jerome* by Simone Cantarini, monochromes with *Stories from the Life of St. Paul* by Claudio Ridolfi, and others by Giovanni Francesco Guerrieri and Mastelletta. The second section illustrates the wide-ranging ceramic output of the day through examples, displayed in rotation, from local kilns, and from Faenza, Deruta, Siena, and Castelli; it also has a collection of drawings and prints.

The long Pasquino gallery, with 15th-century crenelations filled in during the reign of

A fireplace in the Ducal Palace

Guidobaldo da Montefeltro, was decorated by Ridolfi and Girolamo Cialdieri di Bartolomeo with paintings to celebrate the wedding of Federico Ubaldo Della Rovere to Claudia de' Medici (1621).

Duomo (B-C2). The cathedral, another of Federico da Montefeltro's major projects for Urbino, was designed by Francesco di Giorgio Martini alongside the family residence, on the site of the present cathedral, which was rebuilt in neoclassical style by Giuseppe Valadier after the 1789 earthquake; the facade was added in 1802.

The aisled interior has a large dome over the crossing. The most interesting works are in the chapels to the side of the main chapel and in the apse. In the *Cappella della Concezione*, to the right of the high altar, the canvases on the right- and left-hand walls are by Carlo Maratta (*Assumption*) and Carlo Cignani (*Birth of the Virgin*) respectively. An *Assumption* by Cristoforo Unterbergher decorates the altar in the main chapel. The *Cappella del Sacramento* to the left of the high altar survived the earthquake: on the left-hand wall is a *Last Supper* by Federico Barocci.

The north transept leads to the Museo Diocesano "Gianfrancesco Albani" (open 9am–noon and

Raphael's Mute

This portrait (right) is one of Raphael's most complex and enigmatic paintings. It marks the culmination of his portrait painting work and of a category of painting which in those very years was becoming established as a genre in its own right. This masterpiece, from the artist's Florentine period (it is dated around 1507), has been the subject of countless studies that have attempted to shed light on some of its hidden secrets. Historical investigations have attempted to determine the identity of the woman portrayed. Studies of its style have extolled the sublime perfection of the portrait's construction, the modest, unassuming elegance of the figure and her intensely introspective countenance, which shows clear Leonardesque influences. Diagnostic analyses have revealed an earlier version showing a much younger woman, painted in a quite different style: the features are less angular, and the lower-necked dress is adorned with numerous tapes tied across the shoulder, a fashion of the day. Her jewelry has also come under close scrutiny, in particular the chain and pendant, which seem to be a later addition to the portrait. She wears three rings: the first has a ruby (a stone believed to bring prosperity to the wearer), of a shape and size frequently found in the 15th century; the second has a sapphire, traditionally associated with the idea of chastity; and the third, on her right hand, shows Nordic influences, especially in the use of the typically north European "en rende bosse" enameling technique.

2pm–6pm). It contains 14th-century frescoes removed from the walls of the former church of *San Domenico*, the Treasury (with an exquisite 13th-century English bronze *lectern** and an 18th-century Saxon porcelain altar service), 14th–17th century paintings (including works by Andrea da Bologna and Barocci), a paschal candelabrum, also in bronze, possibly designed by Francesco di Giorgio Martini, illuminated hymnals and Casteldurante majolica work (16th–17th cent.).

The custodian also takes visitors to the crypt, where a 16th-century marble *Pietà** by Giovanni dell'Opera can be seen.

Piazza della Repubblica (B2). This square acts as a central point from which tourists may visit Palazzo Ducale or the Albornoz Fortress.

The austere building on its northeastern side is the early 18th-century Collegio Raffaello, in which the *Museo del Gabinetto di Fisica* (open 8am–2pm; Tue–Fri also 3pm–6pm; closed Sat and Sun) displays a collection of scientific instruments from the 17th century to the present day. To the left is the wide-arched portico of the church of *San Francesco*, founded in the 14th century but rebuilt in the 18th century;

Palazzo Albani, Urbino

the *Cappella del Sacramento*, to the right of the presbytery, has an elaborate marble arch (1516–27) from an earlier ducal chapel; the *Forgiveness of St. Francis* in the apse is by Federico Barocci (1576–81).

Via Raffaello (A-B1-2). The portico of *San Francesco* marks the beginning of this characteristic street lined with a sober row of brick-built houses leading up the hill.

The **Casa di Raffaello** (open weekdays 9am–1pm and 3pm–7pm, Sun and holidays 10am–1pm), is the birthplace of the artist (in the room in which he was born hangs an early *Madonna and Child* fresco by the young painter). The little museum contains engravings and reproductions of his masterpieces, and a number of paintings by Raphael's father Giovanni Santi, Giulio Romano, and Timoteo Viti, and is the home of the Accademia di Raffaello. The plan of the house is interesting since it documents the typical layout of a 15th-century house, designed around a small courtyard.

Nearby, in the picturesque *Via Bramante* (A-B2), is the *Botanical Garden* (open 8am–12.30pm and 3pm–5.30pm; closed Thu and Sat afternoons), which was inaugurated in 1806.

Monument to Raphael (A1). This 1897 work stands in the public gardens at the end of Via Raffaello just outside the walls on a 16th-century bastion; the view extends over the modern quarters to the Montefeltro hills.

The other park, which affords a truly breathtaking view of the cathedral and the Palazzo Ducale, contains the *Fortezza Albornoz* (B1; 14th–16th cent.), with semicircular towers and imposing bastions.

Via dei Maceri (A-B1-2). This road, to the right of the fortress park descends steeply down to the quarter of *San Giovanni*, where it becomes Via Santa Margherita. The elegantly paved flight of steps, or *piola*, of the same name leads to Via Barocci (Barocci was born at no. 18).

Oratorio di San Giuseppe (B2). This oratory (open weekdays 10am–12.30pm and 3pm-5.30pm; Sun and holidays 10am–12.30pm) was built by the Confraternity of St. Joseph in the 16th century. It consists of two chapels: the main one, which constitutes the church proper, was rebuilt in Baroque style at the end of the 17th century; the smaller chapel, which remains intact, contains a *Presepio** by Federico Brandani, an elaborate stucco nativity scene.

Oratorio di San Giovanni Battista* (B2). The cycle of **frescoes*** in this late-14th-century church (open weekdays 10am–12.30pm and 3pm–5.30pm; Sun and holidays 10am–12.30pm) have been described as the most outstanding example of the International Gothic style in Italy. This 1416 representation of the *Life of St. John the Baptist*, which decorates the entire inner nave, topped by a wooden vaulted *ceiling**, is by Jacopo and Lorenzo Salimbeni; on the back wall is the impressive *Crucifixion*, which shows a certain Nordic influence.

San Francesco di Paola (B-C2). The steps of *San Giovanni*, which offer another attractive view of the twin turrets of Palazzo Ducale, lead down to Via Mazzini; almost in line with the steps rises this 16th-18th century church; the ceiling frescoes (*Stories from the Life of the Saint*) are the most important work of Antonio Viviani (1614).

The visit to Urbino ends with the University Colleges and an important church, just outside the town.
From Piazza del Mercatale, take the SS73bis in the direction of Arezzo and turn right at the first crossroads to the *Collegi Universitari** (D1, off map), designed by Giancarlo De Carlo and begun in 1966.
Leave Urbino from Porta Lavagine in the direction of Ancona as far as a junction of three roads; here, take the road that leads up to the church of *San Bernardino degli Zoccolanti* (B3, off map; 1482-91), the mausoleum of the dukes of Montefeltro ordered by Federico himself and variously attributed to Francesco di Giorgio Martini and Bramante; this poised Renaissance building contains the Baroque monuments to Federico and Guidobaldo da Montefeltro. There is a good view of Urbino from the esplanade.

4.2 The upper Metauro valley
From Urbino to the Abbey of Lamoli, 34.5 km

This itinerary follows the course of the first stretch of the Metauro river almost to the border with Umbria and Tuscany, through the lands of the medieval Massa Trabaria. The region, which extended from Mt. Carpegna in the northwest to Mt. Catria to the south, comprised the upper Metauro and Marecchia valleys, almost bordering on Sansepolcro. The first part of the name is a reminder that the land was originally owned by monasteries and abbeys (the word *Massa*, which features in many Italian place names, is a medieval term for a rural community), while Trabaria is a reference to the *travi*, or beams used in building and made by cutting down the fir trees that grew abundantly in the area. While Urbania was influenced by the splendors of the nearby palace of Urbino – indeed the same architects who built for Federico da Montefeltro worked here – the higher the road climbs into the Apennines, the more mountainous the landscape becomes and the more the traces of the medieval past are felt.
The SS73bis (Bocca Trabaria) leads out of Urbino, from which a more tortuous but more scenic road leads after 17.5 km to Urbania. Back on the SS73bis, the town of Sant'Angelo in Vado is reached after another 9.5 km. 7.5 km further on the road reaches the town of Mercatello sul Metauro, and after another 13 km, the Abbey of Lamoli.

Urbania

This town was known in the Middle Ages as Castel delle Ripe, whose craftsmen were already turning out ceramics as early as the 13th century. It was rebuilt by Guglielmo Durante, who renamed it Castel Durante, and continued the majolica activity. The arrival of the Montefeltro in 1424 gave the industry a tremendous boost, and by the following century no fewer than 32 enterprises were at work, selling their refined products the

4.2 The upper Metauro valley

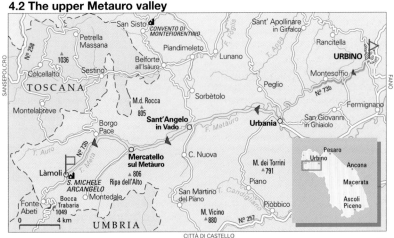

CITTÀ DI CASTELLO

Casteldurante majolica

In the 16th century the Montefeltro hills boasted a flourishing majolica tradition that was one of the best-known and most distinguished in the whole of Italy. Thanks to the clays of the Metauro river used in their manufacture, Casteldurante ceramics were of particularly high quality. They were also imaginatively decorated, and became a particularly sophisticated form of the so-called historiated genre, whose stylistic features and iconographical symbols were profoundly influenced by the Raphaelesque style that developed under the Renaissance dukes of Urbino. Urbania, as Casteldurante is now called, is the only town in the region – and one of just 26 in Italy – that has been officially designated as an ancient ceramics making center, not only because of its glorious past but also thanks to the ceramists who today ensure that the tradition lives on.

length and breadth of the peninsula. Production continued even when the town changed its name yet again (to Urbania; elev. 273 m, pop. 6,459), at the order of Pope Urban VIII, who in 1636 declared the town an independent municipal authority.

Piazza San Cristoforo. The main streets of the historical town converge on this central square; the statue of the patron saint and the Teatro Bramante are 19th century.

Along Via Roma is the church of the *Crocifisso*, where Francesco Maria II Della Rovere, last Duke of Urbino is buried; the *Madonna in the Clouds* (right-hand chapel) is by Federico Barocci.
In Via Garibaldi, which leads off from Piazza San Cristoforo, stand the oratory of *Corpus Domini* (open on request, apply at the Pro Loco), a 14th-century church modified in the following century (the prophets and sibyls in the lunettes are by Raffaellino del Colle), and the church of **Santa Chiara**, founded in the 13th century as part of a convent, but remodeled in 1626; the altarpiece (*Madonna and Child in Glory with Saints*) on the high altar is the masterpiece of Girolamo Cialdieri di Bartolomeo (1629).

Palazzo Ducale*. One side of Urbania's most important civil building is on Corso Vittorio Emanuele, which also leads off from Piazza San Cristoforo, but the main facade is on the street at right angles to it, Via Piccini. This all-brick palace, originally the 13th-century residence of the Brancaleoni, was transformed by Francesco di Giorgio Martini and Girolamo Genga. Its most elaborate facade overlooks the Metauro river, and features an overhanging loggia and two cylindrical towers; the inner courtyard is surrounded by columns with graceful capitals.
The palace now houses a number of cultural institutions (open 10am–noon and 3pm–6pm; closed Mon). The *Library* was founded by Federico da Montefeltro himself, but many of its volumes were taken away to form the Biblioteca Alessandrina in Rome. The **Museo Civico** has detached 14th-century frescoes and a rich collection of paintings by Marche and non-Marche artists from the 16th and 17th centuries, including Giovanni Francesco Guerrieri, Federico Zuccari, Amico Aspertini, Palma Giovane, Domenico Peruzzini, and Federico Barocci (sketches); note also *Mercator's Globes** (*terrestrial globe*, 1541; *celestial globe*, 1551), a collection of 16th–17th century maps and the traditional collection of local period ceramics*. The downstairs rooms house the *Museo dell'Arte Contadina*, devoted to the ethnography of the upper Metauro valley.

Via Crescentini, which runs off from Corso Vittorio Emanuele just before Palazzo Ducale, leads to the **Cathedral**, in Piazza Bartolomei, and dedicated to the town's protector. The Romanesque campanile of this 18th-century church testifies to its older origins. The most interesting painting inside is the *Crucifix**, on wood, by Pietro da Rimini (1320) above the high altar. The church also has an *Urn with the Humerus of St. Christopher*, attributed to Antonio Pollaiuolo.

Palazzo Comunale. This elegant 16th-century building stands in Piazza della Libertà, at the end of Corso Vittorio Emanuele.

From the square, follow Via Bramante and, after Largo Scirri, turn right into Via Urbano VIII, to the former *Palazzo Vescovile*, the old bishop's palace built by Francesco di Giorgio Martini and Girolamo Genga. It houses the **Museo Diocesano** (open on request, tel. 319643, 319463), which has an epigraphic museum and an art gallery, and sections on silverware, sacred ornaments and ceramics. Not to be missed here are: two 1282 *capitals* from the church of *San Francesco*; an early Christian stone *Crucifix**; fragments of 14th-century *frescoes* from the Fabriano school; a plaster *bas-relief* by Benedetto da Maiano; a *Madonna and Child* by Antonio Alberti; and canvases by Claudio Ridolfi and Giorgio Picchi. The *ceramics** illustrate local manufacture from earliest times to the present day.

San Francesco. From Piazza della Libertà, Via Ugolini leads to this church, which originated in the 13th century but was transformed in 1762 (open on request, apply at the Pro Loco). It is one of the most interesting examples of Marchigian Baroque style.

Nearby is the remodeled *Church of the Dead* (open 10am–noon and 3pm–6pm), whose medieval origins can still be seen in the Gothic portal on the facade; the painted decorations inside date back to the late 16th–early 17th centuries. Behind the altar is the *Cemetery of the Mummified Bodies**: thanks to a rare chemical process, the corpses found in the burial site under the church were in an excellent state of preservation.

One km outside Urbania along the road to Sant'Angelo in Vado is the Parco Ducale or *Barco*, used by the dukes of Urbino. The hunting lodge was begun by Francesco di Giorgio Martini and finished by Girolamo Genga (1535); the adjoining church of *San Giovanni Battista*, a Vanvitelli-inspired building dating back to 1765, uses as its sacristy the mausoleum built for Federico da Montefeltro by Martini.

Sant'Angelo in Vado

The Truffles Festival, held every year between October and November (see p 94), celebrates the prestigious produce of this town (elev. 359 m, pop. 3,787), known in ancient times as *Tifernum Mataurense* and, after a period as capital of Massa Trabaria, became an integral part of the Duchy of Urbino from 1437. The choice white truffle that grows here is the *tuber magnatum pico*, for which an experimental truffle-growing center has been established. Connoisseurs of the delicacy describe the taste as more sophisticated and less pungent than that of the black truffle.

Visitors first come to the church of *Santa Maria dei Servi* (open on request, apply at the Municipio), a 14th-century edifice remodeled during the Renaissance, as the two portals on the side testify. The interior is a treasure house of paintings and sculptures: the bronze bas-relief (*Madonna in Glory**) on the altar to the left of the main entrance is attributed to Lorenzo Ghiberti; the painting on wood (*Madonna and Child with Saints*) immediately after the side entrance door is signed by Raffaellino del Colle and dated 1543; Francesco Mancini (who was born in Sant'Angelo) painted the *Vision of St. Philip Benizi* in the 4th altar on the left.

Standing opposite each other in the small main square (*Piazza Pio XII*) are the *Palazzo della Ragione*, whose foundation stone was laid in the 14th century and which has a distinctive tower, and the *Duomo*, whose original 12th-century plan was extended in the 17th century; the *Triumph of St. Michael* in the apse is another painting by Mancini.

The Ducal Palace near Urbania, residence of the Montefeltro

On the truffle trail

Of all the Marche region's typical produce, the black and white truffles (below) are without question the most celebrated. Their growth here is favored by a combination of soil, climate, exposure and the woody or grassy plant forms the tuber grows on. White truffles are found mainly in marlacious, chalky and clayey soils; black truffles occur in soils with a particularly high chalk content. The whole Pesaro Apennine area – especially Acqualagna, Sant'Angelo in Va- do and Sant'Agata Feltria – is rich in the prized white, and in the black truffle. The autumn months, during which they are collected, have long been a very special time of the year in the Marche region, and the occasion for many national festivals, most notably the ones held in Acqualagna, Sant'Agata Feltria, and Sant'Angelo in Vado. The latter is the home of an experimental truffle-growing center that leads the way in the study of mycorrhizae and fungal growth.

On Corso Garibaldi is the entrance to the *Museo dei Vecchi Mestieri* (open on request, apply at the Municipio), which explores the history of arts and crafts in this part of the region.

Via XX Settembre leads to Piazza Umberto I, where stands the 17th-century octagonal church of *San Filippo*, and the Palazzo Comunale from the same period, which has a 1603 canvas by Federico Zuccari.

Mercatello sul Metauro

Mercatello (elev. 429 m, pop. 1,496), which was one of the main walled towns of Massa Trabaria, still exudes a medieval air: some of its houses still maintain the "Door

The hills around Pesaro

of Death" tradition, whereby one door of the house is opened exclusively for the passage of the deceased.

The *Collegiate Church* in Piazza Garibaldi is an imposing, originally Romanesque edifice, with Gothic windows on the sides; the canvas of the *Madonna delle Grazie* in the presbytery dates back to the 11th century, while sacred artistic objects from the 13th to 17th centuries can be seen in the *Museo della Collegiata* (open on request, tel. 89640). Note the elegant loggia of the 17th-century *Palazzo Gasparini* in the same square.

The town's most impressive work of architecture is the church of **San Francesco***, a Romanesque-Gothic gem that could almost be described as a museum of central Italian art from the 14th to the 17th centuries: two medallions with Federico da Montefeltro and Ottaviano Ubaldini on the wall behind the facade are attributed to Benedetto da Maiano; the triumphal arch with two robust statues of saints is late Gothic; on the crossbeam is a *Crucifix** painted on wood by Giovanni da Rimini; above the altar is an exquisite early 14th-century *polyptych** (*Madonna and Child with Saints*) attributed to Giovanni Baronzio; to the right of the altar a 13th-century painting on wood (*Madonna and Child**) by Bonaventura di Michele; to the left, a 14th-century *Madonna and Child with St. Anthony* on wood by Luca di Tommè; the vault of the apse may have been frescoed by Girolamo Genga (evangelists); the *St. Clare* on the left-hand wall of the nave is attributed to Lorenzo Salimbeni. In the sacristy is a *Virgin and Child with St. Sebastian* attributed to Giovanni Francesco Guerrieri (1630), a *Baptism of Christ* by Claudio Ridolfi (1612), and a *Circumcision* by Giorgio Picchi (1586).

Some 13 km further up the valley, at Lamoli (elev. 600 m), lies the church of *San Michele Arcangelo*, part of a Benedictine abbey founded between the 16th and 18th centuries; considerable rebuilding work was carried out in the mid-20th century on the interior, which has 14th–16th century frescoes.

5 Montefeltro country

The area

Montefeltro is a beautiful, rugged highland area between the upper valleys of the Foglia and Marecchia rivers in the northwest corner of the Marche region, on the border with Tuscany and Emilia-Romagna. It is an area rich in culture and history with many historic walled towns atop its rocky limestone spurs that provide a living legacy of its past. In its golden age – the late Middle Ages – Montefeltro offered an abundance of woods and farmland, and its fortified towns were safe havens for the population during the dark years of the Barbarian invasions. It was also crossed by Christian pilgrims making their way from eastern Europe to the Eternal City: from Rimini they would head up the Marecchia valley, then cross Montefeltro country to the Viamaggio Pass through the Apennines before descending the Tiber valley to Rome.

The towns are organized into two mountain communities. San Leo, Talamello, Pennabilli, Casteldelci, Maiolo, Novafeltria, Sant'Agata Feltria form the Community of Alta Valmarecchia; while Montegrimano, Mercatino Conca, Sassofeltrio, Villagrande di Montecopiolo, Monte Cerignone, Tavoleto, Auditore, Pietrarubbia, Carpegna, Macerata Feltria, Sassocorvaro, Frontino, Belforte all'Isauro, Piandimeleto and Lunano form the Community of Montefeltro. Although the former officially belongs to the Marche region, its people have much in common with their immediate neighbors, relations with whom have always been quite natural, given the road network linking them and occasions like markets and local festivals. The Montefeltro community, too, often seems to have more in common with Romagna, as indeed do Pesaro and Urbino, which also lie close to the Romagna border.

The towns themselves are a living reminder of the trials and tribulations the area suffered as the Montefeltro of Urbino, the Malatesta of Rimini, and the grand dukes of Tuscany vied for power. Towns were built and razed to the ground in the many disputes that decided the fates of the fortified towns and their lands. And with each transfer of power, the laws, the taxes and the very way of life changed: a checkered history that seemed almost to mirror the area's chaotic geological origins.

The fortress of San Leo stands on a rocky spur

The landscape is the result of the "gravitative flow" of the Valmarecchia, which, as a result of a succession of substantial landslides under the surface of the prehistoric sea created the Marche countryside; the enormous spurs of rock were subsequently covered by scaly clay formations, which eventually enveloped them completely and once the sea bed emerged were eroded by rain to a greater or lesser degree, depending on their resistance, which led to the creation of crags that seem to slash through the earth's surface. Curiously, nearly all the sheer faces are oriented toward the Adriatic, the side least subject to erosion. This explains why the marl limestone massif of Mt. Carpegna is found alongside the limestone Simone and Simoncello rocks, the peaks of San Leo and San Marino, and the brown pudding-stones of Pietrarubbia, which at sundown take on the appearance of mysterious ruined towers.

But there is much more to the Montefeltro area than rugged scenery and troubled history. Take, for example, the typical farm produce of the area, which reflects the variety of its mountain agriculture. Mushrooms grow in abundance, and salami and other sausage-meats are produced as well as local bread and cheeses (including the fresh *raveggiolo*, *ricotta* and *pecorino* cheeses, and the special Talamello "pit cheese," which derives from the ritual of hiding the rounds of cheeses from thieves in safe holes dug out of the rock). And although the old mountain master craftsmen have long since disappeared (a museum of peasant life in the castle of Piandimeleto gives a moving account of the old farming methods), craft traditions are kept alive at the artistic metalworking school (TAM) set up in 1990 in Pietrarubbia, under the direction of Arnaldo Pomodoro.

Montefeltro country
Itinerary from Urbino to San Leo, 87 km

This excursion begins on the minor, winding road that heads northwest out of Urbino. After 23.5 km it arrives in Sassocorvaro, from where roads lead off to Piandimeleto (11 km) and Casinina (11.5 km). 5.5 km after Sassocorvaro lies Macerata Feltria, from which a 25.5 km detour runs mostly along the left bank of the Conca river as far as the border with Emilia-Romagna; in the other direction a 12.5 km dri-

5. Montefeltro country

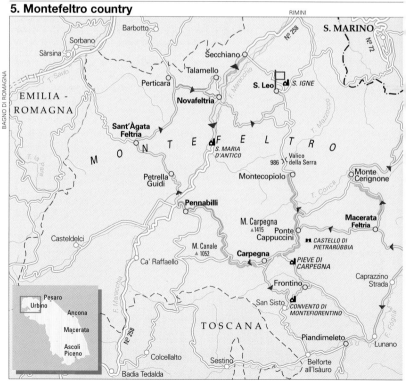

ve leads to Carpegna, a base for mountain walks and a 6.5 km excursion to the convent of Montefiorentino.

A scenic 11-km drive with splendid views of Mt. Carpegna leads to Pennabilli, to Sant'Agata Feltria (9.5 km) and, after a brief detour to Perticara, to Novafeltria (12.5 km). Talamello (2 km), the parish church of Secchiano (4 km) and the church of Santa Maria d'Antico (4 km) are also worth a visit. Finally, high up on the other side of the river, a 12.5-km drive away, is San Leo, with its impregnable fortress.

Sassocorvaro*

The Montefeltro and Malatesta fought a long, hard battle to win control of this rocky spur overlooking the Foglia river valley, which has been dammed to form a reservoir. At that time Sassocorvaro (elev. 326 m, pop. 3,493) was little more than a village, before Francesco di Giorgio Martini arrived to build what was an exemplary piece of military architecture, the **Rocca Ubaldinesca*** (open: Apr–Oct 9.30am–12.30pm and 3pm–7pm; Nov–Mar Sat 2.30pm–6.30pm, Sun 9.30am–12.30pm and 2.30pm–6.30pm). Curiously boat-shaped in plan, it is surrounded by imposing cylindrical towers, the only openings being diagonal slits in the upper part, which made it impossible to see the besieging forces. The interior is based around the Courtyard of Honor, from which the various rooms lead off (some now taken up by the art gallery, with a noteworthy *Christ* attributed to Guido Reni) and a loggia; the upper floor, reached by a spiral staircase, has an 18th-century *Teatro* and the *Museo "L'Arca dell'Arte,"* which recalls the "safety operation" carried out during World War II by the then Fine Arts Commissioner of Urbino to keep safe over 10,000 works of art in this fortress (see p. 98); the museum also has a *Crucifix* on wood from the Rimini school of the 1300s and a canvas by Evangelista di Piandimeleto.

Nearby is Palazzo Battelli, home of the *Museo della Civiltà Contadina* which documents local farming history (open: Apr–Oct 9.30am–12.30pm and 3pm–7pm; Nov–Mar Sat 2.30pm-6.30pm, Sun 9.30am–12.30pm and 2.30pm–6.30pm), while the nearby collegiate church of *San Giovanni Battista* has 14th- and 15th-century bas-reliefs and frescoes. From the belvedere it becomes clear how Sassocorvaro got its nickname "The Montefeltro Sentinel": the view takes in the lake and the Foglia river, which abounds in fish, and beyond the hills, with Mt. Carpegna. rising above them in the distance.

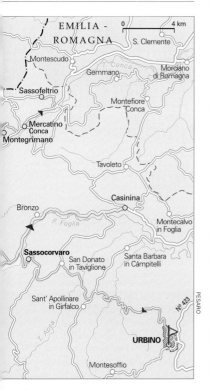

The road leading up the valley on the left bank of the Foglia river leads after 11 km to **Piandimeleto** (elev. 319 m, pop. 1,849), known in ancient times as *Planus Mileti*, a medieval town whose houses are huddled around the *Castle* (open: 9am–noon and 3pm–7pm). The fortress, which is thought to date back to the time of Charlemagne, was rebuilt in the late 15th century and is now the residence of the Oliva family, whose ancestors arrived in Italy before the year 1000; note the Renaissance *fireplaces* and *portals* that decorate its rooms, some of which are taken up by the *Museo del Lavoro Contadino* and the *Museo di Scienza della Terra* (farming history and methods), and a *herbarium* where the Marche's main botanical species are displayed. The two Gothic *tombstones* and 15th–16th century *frescoes* are worth visiting in the nearby church of *Sant'Agostino*. The *Art Collection* (open: Mon 3pm–7pm, Wed 8.30am–7pm, Fri 8.30am–1pm), in the house of the *Settima Opera di Misericordia* in the new part of the town, has mainly 19th- and 20th-century works, but also an interesting 18th-century Slavic *icon*.

A road follows the Foglia river down valley from Sassocorvaro and after 11.5 km arrives in Casinina (elev. 167 m), home of the *Museo Storico della Linea Gotica* (open: 9am–noon and 3pm–7pm), which commemorates a short but bloody World War II battle between Germans and allied troops along the river, then part of the Germans' "Gothic Line" defense system; edu-

"Ark" for Art's Sake

The new museum dedicated to art-works in danger, housed in Sasso-corvaro's *Rocca Ubaldinesca*, was originally created as a way of re-membering the World War II effort to save 10,000 masterpieces of Italian art, masterminded by the then Fine Arts Commissioner for Urbino. To-day's "Art Ark" museum, sponsored by the Montefeltro mountain com-munity is divided into sections: the museum proper, with life-size repro-ductions of the works saved; a per-manent "Art in the War" exhibition on the techniques used during World War II to protect the works; a tempo-rary "Art in Danger" exhibition on masterpieces at risk; the rooms of "Art's Saviors," dedicated each year to the different winners of the Pasquale Rotondi Award (a sculpture designed by Arnaldo Pomodoro awarded for outstanding achieve-ment in "the art of saving art"); and Save Montefeltro, exhibitions of works and local crafts in need of help.

cational in intent, the museum relives the dra-ma of the episode through original documents (newspapers, magazines, schoolbooks, and let-ters from soldiers taken prisoner), photographs and other items (weapons, means of commu-nication, and uniforms).

Macerata Feltria

For visitors arriving from Sassocorvaro the approach to this town (elev. 321 m, pop. 2,002), built in the late Middle Ages on the steep banks of the Apsa river, near the Roman settlement of *Pitinum Pisaurense* and contested in the 14th century by the Malatesta and the Montefeltro, is through its old **Borgo**. On the main street (*Via Antimi*) stands the 19th-century parish church of *San Michele Arcangelo* (inside note the *Crucifix** on wood, painted by Carlo da Camerino in 1396) and the *Terme Pitinum*, thermal baths with sulfur-rich waters.

The road widens to become Via Gaboardi, which after a bridge, leads to the **Castle**, the medieval heart of the town built on higher ground and partly surrounded by walls. Beyond the former church of *San Francesco* (14th century; the portal is Gothic), is the *Arco dei Pelasgi*, which recalls the legendary founders of the town, from where a steep cobbled street leads through the *Porta Castellana* gateway into a small square. A Gothic sandstone portal on the left marks

the former *Palazzo del Podestà* (11th–12th cent.), for centuries the center of civic pow-er and now the *Museo Civico-Archeologico-Paleontologico* (open: May–Sep 10am–noon and 3.30pm–7.30pm): the collections com-prise the prehistoric age (flints), Roman times (finds from *Pitinum Pisaurense* and the surrounding area), the Middle Ages (tombs) and the Renaissance (ceramics). On the right, the church of *San Giuseppe* al-so has a late Gothic portal decorated with ornate terracotta rustic figures. The *keep*, all that remains of the castle at the highest point of the town, now contains the muse-um's palaeontological collections.

A scenic road heads north out of town toward the Conca river valley, in which a number of small towns lie. The first (7.5 km) is **Monte Cerignone** (elev. 528 m, pop. 675), whose me-dieval layout remains virtually unchanged, with much of the old wall defense system also intact. A road spirals up to the 12th-century *Rocca**, now the Municipio, partly rebuilt in 1478, at the order of Federico da Montefeltro, by Francesco di Giorgio Martini or, according to some sources, Leon Battista Alberti; it affords fine views of Mt. Carpegna. Opposite is the Renaissance *Palazzo Begni*. The 17th-century church of *San Biagio* and the church of *Santa Maria del Soccorso* contain works by Bartolomeo Vivarini. Nine km downstream on a spur overlooking the valley stands Montegrimano (elev. 536 m, pop. 1,121), an old town with steep narrow streets. Its 15th-century *bell tower* was the castle keep; a canvas by Barocci (*Madonna delle Grazie*, 1607) is kept in the church of *San Silvestro*. The area was known already in medieval times for its al-kaline waters rich in sulfur, bromine and iodine that gush from springs on the slopes of Mt. San Paolo; their curative properties are exploited at the *Terme di Montegrimano*, a thermal estab-lishment 2 km outside the town.

A further 2.5 km along the road lies *Mercatino Conca* (elev. 275 m, pop. 1,092), the busiest town in the upper Conca valley, 6.5 km from which is *Sassofeltrio* (elev. 466 m, pop. 1,273), whose fortified stronghold, first mentioned in 962 and rebuilt at the order of the Montefeltro by Francesco di Giorgio Martini, has all but disappeared; the *panorama** extends from the Adriatic to the peaks of Mt. Titano and over the entire Conca valley to Mt. Carpegna.

Toward Carpegna

The road to Carpegna just outside Mac-erata Feltria passes close by the church of *San Cassiano al Pitino* (open on request: apply at the Museo Civico-Archeologico-Paleontologico), thought to have been built in around 1000: the portal is Gothic, the aisled interior Romanesque. Archae-ological excavations have revealed the re-mains of what was probably a Roman ther-mal bath, confirming the theory that this was the site of *Pitinum Pisaurense* (open on request: apply at the Museo Civico-Archeologico-Paleontologico).

Ahead are fine views of *Mt. Carpegna* (elev. 1,415 m); to the left are the picturesque remains (a 14th-century square *tower*) of the *Castle of Pietrarubbia**, just before which is an abandoned town, particularly atmospheric in the late afternoon when the setting sun brings out the deep red color of the stone, a reminder of the origin of the name (originally *Petra Rubea*); the streets are "furnished" by a number of Arnaldo Pomodoro stone sculptures.

A little further on, on an isolated crag, stands the Romanesque church of *Sant'Arduino*.

At the Ponte Cappuccini junction, the road heading north leads to San Leo (see p. 102), but first (6.5 km) passes through the scattered town of *Montecopiolo* (elev. 296/1,406 m, pop. 1,226), once a fortified stronghold but now a winter and summer holiday resort.

The *Serra Pass* (elev. 986 m) to the north affords splendid views over a sequence of mountains dotted with villages.

Carpegna

The chief town of the Montefeltro area (elev. 748 m, pop. 1,580), on the southern slopes of Mt. Carpegna, is another typical hill town at the center of a territory that remained independent of the Church State from the Middle Ages right up to 1819, thanks to an imperial privilege.

The Montefeltro themselves are believed to be descended from the Carpegna family, which gave its name to the town and is remembered in the majestic *Palazzo Carpegna* (open on request: tel. 77114), built in 1675; its facade is decorated with gray stone architectural elements and a fine double staircase. The parish church of *San Giovanni Battista* dates back to 1323; the church of *San Leo* has a canvas by Evangelista di Piandimeleto.

The many paths and tracks in the surrounding mountain area are a paradise for hill-walkers, horse-

riders, and mountain bike enthusiasts. The climb to *Sasso Simone* (elev. 1,204 m) is a particularly interesting walk leading up to the remains of a Benedictine *abbey* and a *fortress* built by the Medici (1566–72).

A 6.5-km detour to the southeast leads to the **Convent of Montefiorentino**, founded by Franciscan monks in the 13th century and much remodeled since. It stands in a leafy woodland setting at the end of an avenue of cypress trees. In the church, the *Chapel of the Oliva Counts** (to the right of the entrance) is a harmonious space, square in plan, with a hemispherical dome inspired by Brunelleschi, thought to have been designed by Francesco di Simone Ferrucci; he also designed the *Oliva Tombs* (1484), while the painting on wood (*Enthroned Madonna and Child with Angels, Saints and Patron**; 1489) on the altar is considered to be Giovanni Santi's masterpiece. Three and a half km to the northeast lies *Frontino* (elev. 519 m, pop. 373), a medieval village with intact walls (note the interesting pentagonal *tower*; the artworks in the *museum* (open: 4pm–6pm; closed Sun), who was particularly fond of the place.

The road back to Carpegna from here (6.5 km) goes past the **Pieve di Carpegna*, a 1323 church subsequently remodeled; the rectory has a fresco (*St. John the Baptist*) dated 1539.

Pennabilli*

This town (elev. 629 m, pop. 3,098) lies between two rocky outcrops, one called *Roccione* (formerly known as *Penna*) the other *Rupe* (previously *Billi*). Although both were fortified in the 14th century, castle ruins survive only on the latter, now topped by a cross. The original settlement at the foot of the *Roccione* hill did not expand into the area between the two hills until the 15th century. According to a local tradition (which is, however, vehemently contested by the Verucchio family from Romagna) the Malatesta, who later became the lords of Rimini, originated here in the 12th century; Pennabilli re-

The "Roccione" hill in Pennabilli

Minimal Museums

These installations – in and outside Pennabilli – would perhaps better be described as "Sites of the Soul." For in their simplicity they offer the chance to rediscover aspects and angles on life and the past on which few of us ever take the trouble to stop and ponder.

The *Garden of the Forgotten Fruits* in Pennabilli, for instance, is a "museum that recreates yesterday's flavors" (Tonino Guerra), with a collection of fruit trees that once grew spontaneously in Montefeltro's orchards. *Sundial Street* is an idea in the main street of the old town, on whose palaces are reproductions of famous works of art that now measure time (the arrows mark the hours in the copy of Antonello da Messina's *Martyrdom of St. Sebastian*). The tiny Church of the Fallen is the home of the world's "most empty and poetic museum": the *Angel with Whiskers*, named after the painting of the same name in-

spired by a poem by Guerra. The *Thought Sanctuary* consists of seven enigmatic sculptures that make up a place of meditation with a vaguely oriental feel. The inspiration behind the *Refuge of the Forsaken Madonnas* is no less poetic: Guerra imagines that all the sacred representations of the Virgin Mary that have been abandoned in the many shrines around the countryside have gathered here to escape man's indifference.

In the town of Petrella Guidi, the *Field of Names* consists of two white memorial tablets to film director Federico Fellini and his actress wife Giulietta Masina.

At the foot of a millenary tower in Bascio, almost on the border with Tuscany, the *Giardino pietrificato*, or *Petrified Garden (photo)* consists of seven carpets of artistic ceramic work dedicated to seven historical figures who passed through this area.

mained in Malatesta hands until 1468, when Federico da Montefeltro took control; thereafter they were subject to the laws of the duchy of Urbino. It was a member of this duchy who "compelled" Pope Gregory XIII to move the seat of the Montefeltro diocese here from San Leo in 1572. The town is famous for its National Antiques Fair, held each year in July, and the out-of-the-ordinary "Minimal Museums" in the center of town and in the surrounding area, which derive from Tonino Guerra's love of the area (see above).

From Piazza Vittorio Emanuele, with its 16th-century (but much remodeled) *Cathedral*, Via Carboni leads up to the **Roccione**, around which the oldest part of the town grew up. The road passes through two gateways: the 15th-century *Porta Carboni*, which has a crumbling Montefeltro escutcheon (1474), and the *Porta Malatesta*, decorated with a similar crest. A little further on, to the right, is the church of *Sant'Agostino*, or *Santuario della Madonna delle Grazie*, begun in the 15th century; the intaglio works inside are early 17th century, the altar on the left has a *Madonna and Child* attributed to the school of Antonio Alberti but reworked in the 16th century. In the nearby Vicolo Som-

ina, the Seminario Feretrano houses the *Museo Diocesano "A. Bergamaschi"* (closed for repairs), which contains works of art and other items from different periods taken from various churches and chapels in the Montefeltro area.

Further down the Marecchia river is an 11th–12th century Romanesque *church* (open on request, apply at the Pro Loco), whose facade, decorated in the lower part with geometric motifs, has a portal with porch; the altar is supported on a Roman *ara*; note also the 11th-century fragment with two intertwined peacocks and the base of the 1st pillar on the right, which testify to an even older place of worship on the site. At Ponte Messa (elev. 373 m), is Europe's only information technology museum, the *Museo di Informatica e Storia del Calcolo* (visits by arrangement: tel. 922172).

A pleasant walk through oak woods, fields of corn, junipers and other conifers leads gently up to *Mt. Canale* (elev. 1,052 m).

Sant'Agata Feltria

Shortly after the semi-abandoned town of *Petrella Guidi* (elev. 578 m), now the haunt of intellectuals and writers and the setting for one of Tonino Guerra's "Minimal Museums" (see p. 100), the picturesque fortified town of Sant'Agata Feltria (elev. 607 m, pop. 2,364) begins to appear on the horizon. The earliest settlers were Umbro-Sabellians, but it was already a Roman colony in 206 BC; the history of the fortress is that of the families who owned it: the last being the Fregoso, who received as a dowry with the wedding of the daughter of Federico da Montefeltro. The highly popular National White Truffle Fair, held here between mid-October and mid-November is a reminder that the town is the local capital of this prized tuber.

The first building of interest on entering the town is the *Convent of San Girolamo* (open on request: apply at the Municipio), whose church, built in 1568, has on its high altar a *Madonna with St. Jerome and St. Christine** which the Fregoso family commissioned Pietro da Cortona to paint between 1630 and 1640 (their coat of arms can be seen on the base of the altarpiece).

The **Rocca Fregoso*** (open: summer 9am–12.30pm and 3pm–6.30pm; winter, Sat and Sun 9.30am–noon and 3pm–6.30pm), perched high on a crag known as Sasso del Lupo, was originally a 14th–15th century manor house probably belonging to the Malatesta, to which some changes were made by Federico da Montefeltro (1472), and others by the Fregoso in the 16th century; the interior, used also for temporary exhibitions, has a collection of art nouveau *posters*, a *Tailoring and Dressmaking Exhibition*, illustrating sartorial history from pre-industrial times to the present day; and an *Alchemy Exhibition*, on the precursor of modern chemistry.

At the foot of the castle, in Piazza Garibaldi, is the collegiate church of *Sant'Agata*, rebuilt in 1776, whose 3rd altar on the right has a 15th-century wooden *Crucifix* by a German sculptor; the *Palazzo del Municipio*, built in 1603 by the Fregoso, contains a small theater (1727) with three tiers of boxes, and having a curtain and stage scenery painted by Romolo Liverani. The same family commissioned the church of the *Cappuccini* (built 1575–77, but radically restored in the 19th and 20th centuries), a short walk up from the square.

Seven km along the road to Novafeltria, a turn-off to the left leads (1.5 km) to **Perticara** (elev. 655 m), surrounded by mountains from which sulfur was extracted until the 1960s. The history of this thriving economy is traced in the *Museo Storico Minerario* (open: 10am–noon and 3pm–6.30pm; closed Mon and Fri), with sections on archaeology, geology and mining life; there is an interesting reconstruction of part of an entrance gallery into the bowels of the earth.

Novafeltria

Along with San Leo and Pennabilli, this town (elev. 275 m, pop. 6,577), is one of the main towns of the Montefeltro area. Until 1941 it was called Mercatino Marecchia. The chief monuments are in the main square: the 17th-century *Palazzo Municipale*, a small arcaded building which belonged to the Segni counts, and to the right, at the top of a flight of steps, the 14th-century *Chapel of Santa Martina* (the dome-vaulted campanile was added in the 16th century).

Interesting excursions lead off from Novafeltria in all directions. Two km to the north is **Talamello** (elev. 386 m, pop. 950), a 15th-century Malatesta stronghold known for its pit cheese. On the high altar of the parish church of *San Lorenzo* is a shaped wooden *Crucifix**, long attributed to Giotto but in fact painted by Giovanni da Rimini around 1320. Near the cemetery, the so-called *Cella* (open on request; apply at the Municipio, tel. 920736) was completely frescoed in 1437 by A. Alberti.

Four km to the northeast, at *Secchiano* (elev. 216 m), is a *church*, under whose apse an ancient crypt has been found; the church contains the Roman *Sinifia Severina ara*, now used as a holy water stoup.

Four km to the southwest lies the church di **Santa Maria d'Antico**, built thanks to the generosity of the Oliva counts: the facade is adorned by a 15th-

A view of Sant'Agata Feltria, with the Rocca Fregoso

century *portal* in stone, surmounted by a sculptured lunette, inside is a glazed terracotta tondo (*Madonna and Child*, 1450) by Luca della Robbia.

San Leo**

From every approach, San Leo lives up to its reputation ("There is but one pope, there is but one God, there is but one fortress of San Leo," "the finest, biggest military machine in the whole region," to quote two tributes). The town (elev. 589 m, pop. 2,594), which sits atop an enormous limestone outcrop, remains inaccessible to this day, which is precisely what makes it such a tourist attraction, both for its natural beauty and for its monuments.

The name of the mountain occupied by the town – and the entire Montefeltro area – is thought to come from the Latin *Mons Feretri* or *Feretrius* (according to one tradition, a temple to Jupiter – *Iuppiter Feretrius* – once stood on the site of the cathedral); alternatively it may derive from the Sabellian term *Fell-eter* ("shepherd mountain"). The origin of the name of the town is clearer: it derives from a Dalmatian saint and companion of St. Marinus, who in the 4th century, is traditionally believed to have converted the area to Christianity and become the first bishop. A long, hard war was waged between Longobards and Byzantines for control of the land (one of the earliest records is of the siege of Berengar II by Otto I, in 962–963), and later between the Guelphs and the Ghibellines. The Ghibelline Carpegna family took control of the San Leo estate from the early 13th century to the early 16th century, by which time they had become dukes of Montefeltro and then of Urbino. It later passed into the hands of the Della Rovere and, after 1631, of the Church. The town was now no longer a defensive fortress but a prison, a function it retained until the early 20th century.

Piazza Dante. The town is made picturesque both by its imposing fortress, but also by the buildings that form the architectural backdrop. The *Porta Sud*, or South Gate, is the only access to the historic center. On the left is *Palazzo Municipale*, the residence of the counts of Montefeltro and dukes of Urbino. A little further on, on the right-hand side of the square, is *Palazzo Nardini*, where St. Francis stayed on 8 May 1213 (marked by a plaque) and where he received Mt. Verna as a gift. *Palazzo Mediceo*, also in the square, was commissioned by the Della Rovere but rebuilt by the Medici (1517–21). This palace houses the *Museo d'Arte Sacra** (open weekdays 9.30am–6.30pm, Sun and holidays 10am–7pm), organized chronologically from the 8th to 19th century. The oldest exhibits are the fragments of the *ciborium* from the early-medieval cathedral of Montefeltro, but there is also

A disconcerting character

Giuseppe Balsamo (right) is better known as Alessandro, the Count of Cagliostro. This flamboyant character fled his native Palermo, where he had been accused of theft, and took refuge in Rome before setting off around Europe to give vent to his natural inclinations for magic and exotericism. He would introduce himself as an alchemist, a medium, a clairvoyant, or thaumaturge and was much revered – and indeed feared – as a powerful figure in the century of adventurers who roamed the courts of Europe.

But the Count of Cagliostro was also a leading freemason who in Rome started a lodge based around the Egyptian rite that ran counter to Catholic thinking. Betrayed by his wife, he was arrested and sentenced to death by the Inquisition. Pope Pius VI had him locked up in the fortress of San Leo, where he served four years, four months

and five days of his sentence. He spent the first six months in a cell of the Treasury, then three years and ten months in the so-called *Pozzetto* (bottom left) where he was basically buried alive and obliged to gaze through double iron bars at nothing but consecrated sites. It is said he went on inveighing against the clergy and that when he died no one dared to bury his body, which was in fact never found. And his soul, so the story goes, still haunts the fortress, in search of justice.

a memorable altar-piece (*Sts. Leo and Marinus beside the Virgin and Child*) by Luca Frosino and a *Deposition* by Guercino.

An open area behind the apse of the church, beyond the solitary Romanesque bell tower (12th cent.), affords a magnificent view of the Marecchia valley and San Marino.

La Pieve*. This church completes the architecture of the square with its apses decorated by small arches and pilasters, which date back to an extension of the original 10th-century place of worship (although its foundation has been put as early as the 8th century, confirming this as San Leo's oldest church) almost entirely in ashlar stone, with some use of spoil.

The entrance is on the left-hand side (the unadorned main facade is without portal). The basilica-plan interior has an aisled nave divided by pillars and columns (some from imperial Rome, like the time-worn capitals),

The ciborium in a church in San Leo

and a truss roof. Over the presbytery, raised on the three-apsed crypt, stands the 11th-century **ciborium**, supported on columns with early-medieval capitals; at the beginning of the right-hand aisle, steps lead down to a sacellum, thought to have been built by St. Leo in the 4th century.

Duomo*. The cathedral, which occupies a higher position on the edge of the crag, was begun in 1173 over a 9th-century building and finished in the 13th century. Built in sandstone, with the addition of various salvaged materials, it shows Lombard influences in its Romanesque style, in particular the arched corbel table and slender, splayed one- and two-light windows.

In contrast with the decorated apse, the interior is solemn and austere: the nave and aisles are divided by clustered piers (the date 1173, the year of construction is inscribed on the 4th on the right) and by two Roman columns, with 3rd-century capitals). A 16th-century staircase leads up to the high presbytery with its three apses: the central apse has in its semidome a much reworked *Crucifix*, possibly originally from the 13th century. Two flights of steps (the lid of San Leo's sarcophagus is beneath those on the left) lead into the atmospheric triple crypt, supported on pillars and columns with Byzantine and Barbarian capitals.

The fortress* (open: winter 9am–noon and 2pm–5pm; summer 9am–noon, 2pm–6pm). Entered just beyond the South Gate from Via Leopardi, this stronghold stands majestically at the highest point of the crag, and is the valley's main landmark. It was given its present form by Francesco di Giorgio Martini; the mighty cylindrical towers and the long curtain wall connecting them are also attributed to the Siena-born architect (though Giuseppe Valadier made considerable changes to both), as well as the triangular wall section, similar to the prow of a ship, facing the valley. The building enjoyed a reputation as an absolutely impregnable fortress, and was thus also used as a prison for Count Alessandro di Cagliostro (who also died here in 1795; see p. 102) and many other anti-papal patriots.

While the Treasury and Dungeon in which Cagliostro was held recall the fortress's past as a prison, other rooms contain the *Museo, Pinacoteca* and *Galleria d'Arte Contemporanea*. The latter has frequent temporary exhibitions, the others have 16th- and 17th-century paintings, 17th–19th century prints, 16th–19th century furniture, 15th–19th century weapons, wrought-iron and brass, pottery and ceramics from the 3rd century BC to the 19th century; and an extensive collection of documents on the *Risorgimento* (the taking of the town by the Cacciatore di San Leo battalion in 1866), and on Berengar II, Otto I, St. Francis, and the Montefeltro.

In the immediate vicinity, the *Convento of Sant' Igne* (1.5 km to the north; open on request, tel. 916277) is worth a visit. Founded by St. Francis in 1213, it has an elegant cloister with hexagonal columns.

At Belvedere, the *Roman Column* used as a war memorial was embellished in 1997 with a sculptured scepter by the contemporary artist, Arnaldo Pomodoro.

6 From Fabriano to Camerino

The area

The area from Fabriano to Camerino lies between two almost parallel Apennine chains: to the west is the chain that culminates in the summit of Mt. Maggio (1,361 m) straddling the Umbria-Marche border; to the east is the chain that runs from Mt. San Vicino (1,479 m) to Mt. Canfaito (1,111 m). The depression separating the two, technically known as the "Camerino syncline," is traversed by a series of other smaller ridges that gives the area a hilly, submontane appearance. Fabriano spreads out down in the plain; Camerino sits on a hill in an isolated position inside a large basin bounded to the south by the Sibillini mountains that stretch out behind the town of Visso.

Fabriano, which lies in the Giano valley to the east of the Umbria-Marche section of the Apennines, has a population of nearly 30,000, and is Italy's third largest municipal area (269 km²). As early as the Middle Ages this ancient town was famous for its iron foundries (the town's crest still features a *fabbro*, or blacksmith), and for its paper manufacturing industry, which is still the mainstay of the local economy, along with wool and leather processing. The Giano river flows into the Esino river at Albacina, close to the site of the Roman colony *Tuficum*. A little further down the Esino valley (near the famous Frasassi Caves) is the confluence with the Sentino, the river on which the towns of Genga and Sassoferrato lie. The latter was built on the ruins of the Roman *Sentinum*, the theater of a battle in 295 BC in which the Romans and

The hall of candles in the Frasassi Caves

their Picene allies vanquished the Samnite alliance; this battle played a crucial part in the history of the area, since it marked the beginning of Roman penetration into the Marche area.

The ever-isolated, solitary town of Camerino sits proudly atop its hill overlooking the surrounding fortified villages. Repeatedly mentioned in antiquity, particularly during Roman times, (when it formed an equal-status alliance with the Romans, the so-called *aequus foedus*), the town became one of central Italy's major political and cultural centers in later centuries. Camerino's long-time enemy, the Ghibelline town of San Severino Marche, lies to the northeast at the end of the upper Potenza valley, and is surrounded by the natural beauties of the Grilli valley and the centuries-old Canfaito beech woods on Mt. San Vicino.

An important town in Picene and Roman times (as the remains of *Septempeda* just outside the town demonstrate), it was influential in the 14th and 15th centuries in the development of the International Gothic style in European painting, through the brothers Lorenzo and Jacopo Salimbeni. Still today, the aristocratic appearance of San Severino Marche, with its palaces and frescoed churches, blends beautifully with the medieval atmosphere created by the many lookout towers and ruined castles in the surrounding area.

South of Camerino is the town of Visso, the Roman *Vicus Elancensis* and today the gateway to the Sibillini mountain national park away to the east. Visso, which lies in a depression between the Ussita and Nera rivers, once belonged to the duchy of Spoleto, and on gaining independence found itself constantly at odds with the neighboring towns of Montefortino, Norcia, and Camerino itself. It was granted gubernatorial powers under the pontifical legate of Umbria, and the town was not annexed to the Marche region until 1860. Today its natural and cultural attractions make it one of the area's more secluded but popular vacation centers.

6.1 Fabriano and environs
Circular tour from Fabriano (47.5 km)

This tour, which begins and ends in Fabriano, includes the old hill town of Sassoferrato, the Frasassi caves and surrounding woodland, and Fabriano itself, a town renowned for its long paper-making traditions. A road heading west out of town follows the Riobono river for 8 km. A right turn at the road junction leads to Sassoferrato, 10 km to the north. Continuing east along the Sentino river, the road arrives after 8 km at Genga, a center for excursions to the nearby Frasassi Caves – one of the most complex karst formations in the whole of Italy and a major tourist attraction. The road then joins the SS76 (Val d'Esino), and heads south back toward Fabriano. A 10 km detour along a tortuous but scenic road lead up to the ruins of the important Benedictine abbey of Val di Castro. Rejoin the SS76 for the last 9.5 km to Fabriano.

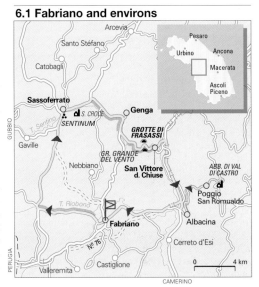

6.1 Fabriano and environs

Fabriano*

Ever since its earliest days, Fabriano has been an industrial town whose wealth has derived not from control over the surrounding area, but from manufacturing and trading activities. Iron, wool, tanning and above all paper-making soon led to the creation of a merchant and artisan class, which by the 13th century enjoyed considerable municipal power. Further testimony of the city's prosperity is provided by its school of painting, which found expression in the refined, cultured style of the International Gothic, examples of which can still be seen in the city's churches and, more importantly, its art gallery. Fabriano reached the peak of its economic development under the Chiavelli seignory, which came to an end in 1435. After a brief period of rule by Francesco Sforza, the town was annexed to the Papal State, a change that ushered in a long period of decline from which the town did not emerge until the late 18th century, when it rediscovered a spirit of enterprise in its traditional paper-making activities. Local industry received a major boost in the second half of the 19th century with the arrival of the railroad. Today Fabriano (elev. 325 m, pop. 29,058; see plan p. 106) shows signs of the considerable expansion of the last forty years, during which time major industrial estates have grown up not only in and around the town itself but along the entire Giano valley. One of the main events in the town's calendar is the Feast of St. John the Baptist (24 June), in which costume parades are held in the flower-decked streets. The celebrations culminate in the *Sfida del Maglio*, a traditional contest between the wards of the town.

The Fabriano crest

Piazza del Comune* (B2). More a triangle than a "square," this hub of town life is closed on the northwest side by the **Palazzo del Podestà** (1255), one of the oldest examples of medieval civic architecture in the entire Marche region, with a characteristic archway passing over the street. In front of the palace, is the so-called *Sturinalto Fountain* (the name means "upward-spouting"). Originally constructed in 1285 and remodeled in the mid-14th century, its concentric basins recall those of the Fontana Maggiore in Perugia. Next to the long *Loggiato di San Francesco*, a 17th-century construction with 19 arches, is the **Palazzo Comunale**, which dates back to the 14th century but was extensively restored in 1690; in the courtyard is the entrance to the **Teatro Gentile**, one of the region's most interesting 19th-century theaters, with a large curtain painted by Luigi Serra. On the opposite side of the square, next to the *Clock Tower*, is the facade of the **Palazzo Vescovile**, the bishop's palace which was built in 1545 and made higher in the 18th century.

Behind the Loggiato di San Francesco, in the old Convent of the Lesser Friars, is the so-called *Grande Museo* (open Sat and Sun, 5pm–7.30pm), an eclectic collection of photographs and old views of Fabriano, farming tools and equipment, old musical instruments, stuffed animals, masks and nativity scene statuettes from around the world. The most unusual section is the extensive collection of characters and costumes from fantasy and horror movies, the only one of its kind in Europe. Almost opposite is the former **Oratorio della Carità** (1587–97), an interesting example of Marchigian Mannerism.

Piazza Umberto I (B2). Adjoining Piazza del Comune is the area known today as Poio, once occupied by the Castelnuovo, and one of the strongholds around which the town grew up. Here are the Duomo and the former **Hospital of Santa Maria del Buon Gesù**, a late-Gothic work of civil architecture built in 1456 to combine three earlier hospitals (since 1994 it has been the home of the art gallery, see below). The **Duomo**, dedicated to St. Venanzius and rebuilt in the first half of the 17th century. All that remains of the 14th-century structure is the polygonal apse. The single-nave interior has chapels decorated with stuccowork and gilded friezes: the paintings include, in the 4th chapel on the left, a *Crucifixion* by Orazio Gentileschi, who also painted the *frescoes* on the walls (1620). The choir leads into two

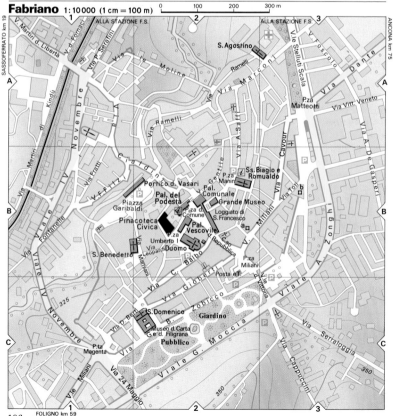

Fabriano 1 : 10 000 (1 cm = 100 m)

FOLIGNO km 59

narrow rooms, the remains of 14th-century chapels radiating out from the apse: the one on the right contains frescoes by Allegretto Nuzi depicting *Scenes from the Life and Martyrdom of St. Lawrence**, painted around 1365.

late 16th-century collection has large altarpieces produced under commission by non-local artists (toward the end of the 16th century the artistic activity in Fabriano died out almost completely). Note in particular the *Nativity with St. Francis of As-*

Palazzo del Podestà (behind the fountain) in Piazza del Comune, Fabriano

Pinacoteca Civica "Bruno Molajoli"* (B2). Founded in 1862 and enlarged in 1912 with the collection of tapestries and paintings from the Cathedral Chapter, this art gallery (open 10am–noon and 3pm–6pm; Jun–Sep 10am–noon and 3.30pm–6.30pm; closed Sun afternoon and all Mon) has an important collection of works from the Fabriano school of the 14th and 15th centuries in the International Gothic style. The first rooms have fragments of frescoes from churches in the town and exquisite 14th-century polychrome wood sculptures, most notably a *Pietà Group** from the Oratorio dei Beati Becchetti in the convent of *Sant'Agostino*. There are many works by Allegretto Nuzi, who was extremely active in Fabriano: they include a *Madonna and Saints** and a painting on wood of *St. John the Baptist and St. Venanzius*. All the works by Gentile da Fabriano, one of the main exponents of the International Gothic, disappeared when Napoleon's troops plundered the town, but the gallery does have two impressive works by Antonio da Fabriano, the best-known local artist from the 15th century: a fresco with *Madonna and Saints* and a *Dormition of the Blessed Virgin** on wood. Note also the *Virgin in Adoration with St. John the Baptist and St. Catherine of Alessandria* by the Maestro di Staffolo, a late Fabrianese imitator of Gentile. The

sisi by Andrea Boscoli, a *Virgin of the Rosary with Sts. Dominic and Catherine** by Orazio Gentileschi and a *Presepe* by Simone De Magistris (1570). The 16th- and 17th-century Flemish **tapestries*** in one of the rooms are from the Cathedral Chapter.

San Benedetto (B1-2). Via Leopardi leads from Piazza Umberto I to this church, once part of a monastery complex rebuilt in the 16th century over a 13th-century predecessor; the interior (open on request, apply at the monastery of *San Silvestro*, tel. 21631) is Baroque, but the semi-circular apse has frescoes by Simone De Magistris with *Stories from the Life of St. Sylvester*. Nearby, on a lower level than the square, is the 1636 *Oratorio del Gonfalone* (open on request, tel. 709259).

An important testimony of the power achieved by the guilds can be seen in **Piazza Garibaldi** (B1-2), once the center of the town's manufacturing and trading activities: the Potters' Portico, built in 1364 as a Shoemakers' Hospital and sold to the potters in the mid-15th century. Beneath the portico is a fresco from the school of Allegretto Nuzi.

San Domenico (C2). This disused church displays its 14th-century origins in its left-hand side, polygonal apse and campanile. The interior, now used for exhibitions, was redesigned in the 18th century, but the

Fabriano and paper-making

In Italy, the town of Fabriano is synonymous with the art of making paper, which was introduced to the western world by the Arabs between the 7th and 8th centuries. It was in Fabriano that master paper makers in the 13th century devised the basic manufacturing techniques. The invention of the watermark, a distinguishing image imprinted into the paper itself and visible when held up to the light, was something

of a revolution. These marks designated ownership (or patronage) of the paper produced, and went on to become an art form in their own right. In more modern times the Europe-wide launch of Fabriano paper came about thanks to the enterprising spirit of Pietro Miliani, who in 1782 decided to put his energies into establishing the Cartiere Miliani. In 1796 this became the first paper mill to produce the so-called *Carta di Francia* tissue paper, known also as "flimsy" because of its delicate manufacture. It was followed later by the mass production of the celebrated Fabriano sketchbooks, which are still made to this day.

Paper-making in Fabriano

chapel of *Sant'Orsola* – reached through a small door in the apse – has remains of *frescoes* from the school of Allegretto Nuzi. The beautiful spaces of the former convent of *San Domenico* provide the setting for the **Museo della Carta e della Filigrana** (open 9am–1.15pm and 3pm–7pm; Sun, 9am–12.30pm and 3.30pm–7pm; closed Mon; in winter open until 6pm) which illustrates traditional paper-making processes, the creation of watermarks and the evolution of the art, for which Fabriano is world famous.

Via Verdi leads from Piazza del Comune to the church of *SS. Biagio e Romualdo* (B2), an elegant example of late-Baroque architecture, built by the Camaldolese in the 15th century, enlarged in 1511 and 1660, and rebuilt in the 18th century. Note inside, on the wall above the entrance, the sumptuous *organ*, built by Gaetano Antonio Callido (1790).

Sant'Agostino (A2-3). This huge convent (open on request, tel. 23021), used as a hospital until 1874, stands by the walls in the northeastern quarter of the town. The 13th–14th century church, rebuilt in the second half of the 18th century, has on one side a 14th-century *portal* and, inside, two Gothic chapels with important 13th-century *frescoes* * in Giottesque-Riminese style. The cloister contains the former *Oratorio dei Beati Becchetti*, a small late Gothic room with a large monochrome fresco (*The Tree of Life*).

Sassoferrato
The town still has reminders of the old Umbro-Roman settlement *Sentinum* with remains of buildings, paved streets and walls, and of a famous battle that took place on the banks of the Sentino river in 295 BC, in which the Romans overcame the Gauls and the Samnites. The town also became the byname of G. B. Salvi (Sassoferrato), a 17th-century painter known for his delicate classical style, who was born here in 1605. Today's town (elev. 386 m, pop. 7,020) divides into two parts, the new town and the old medieval town on the hill, dominated by the austere *Rocca* built in 1368 by papal ambassador Cardinal Egidio Albornoz.

Castello. The highest and oldest part of the town retains its medieval character. At the entrance to the ancient fortified area is the church of *San Francesco*, a 13th–14th century Romanesque-Gothic building (open on request, tel. 9354) containing a 14th-century *Crucifix* * on wood attributed to Giuliano da Rimini, and remains of *frescoes* of the 14th- and 15th-century Fabriano school. *Via Don Minzoni*, the main road through the old town leads to *Palazzo Montanari*, built in the 13th century as a convent and later rebuilt. It is now the home of the **Museo delle Arti and delle Tradizioni Popolari** (open on request: apply at the Tourist Office, tel. 956231), and is soon also to house the *Galleria Civica d'Arte Contemporanea*, created to display the paintings, sculptures and graphic art work entered for the G. B. Salvi Award, an event that has been held in Sassoferrato since 1950. The 15th-century *Palazzo Oliva*, in the main square, contains the *Biblioteca Comunale*, a library with over 10,000 books, ancient incunabula, 16th-century books, and manuscripts. Also in the square is the 14th-century **Palazzo dei Priori**, altered in the 16th century and remodeled in the 20th. Inside, the Museo Civico (open at Easter, from 25 April to 25 May, in August, at Christmas, 9am–1pm and 2pm–7pm, and at other times of the year 9am–1pm, except Sun). It is in two parts, the first with archaeological material from the Roman colony of *Sentinum*, the second with Byzantine and Flemish relics, sacred objects and paintings, including two works by Pietro Paolo Agabiti and a *Crucifixion*, an early work by G. B. Salvi. Two other paintings by Sassoferrato (*Virgin at Prayer* and *Mater Dolorosa*) are kept in the nearby monastery of *Santa Chiara* (open on request: apply at the Tourist Office, tel. 956231), founded in the 13th century.

A turn-off from the main road near the medieval church of *Santa Maria del Ponte del Piano* (rebuilt several times up to the 17th century) crosses the Sentino river and runs along the right bank. A brief detour to the right leads up to the church of **Santa Croce***, built in the 12th century for the Camaldolese monks, partly from spoil recovered from Roman *Sentinum*. This Lombard-Romanesque construction has a fine *portal* with carved stone cornices and decorated capitals hidden away in a kind of atrium. The interior (open on request: tel. 629450, 959030), in the shape of a Greek cross, has sculptured capitals, fragments of 14th-century frescoes, and Roman and medieval marble.

Genga

Set in the dense woodland on top of a hill in the upper Esino valley, this town (elev. 322 m, pop. 2,006) is still surrounded by its ancient fortifications. It was the birthplace of Annibale Della Genga, who became Pope Leo XII (1823–29). But the town is best known as a base for excursions to the highly popular Frasassi Caves, which lie within its territory. At the end of the town is the deconsecrated medieval church of *San Clemente*, now used as a *Museum* (open Jul–Aug, 1pm–7pm; closed the rest of the year except Sun: 10am–1pm and 3pm–6pm), it has sacred ornaments and objects belonging to Leo XII, a 1474 *triptych* by Antonio da Fabriano, who also created a wooden *processional standard* painted on both sides, and a marble statue from the workshop of Antonio Canova (*Madonna and Child*), from the small octagonal church built in a grotto in the Frasassi gorge.

Just outside the town is the 2-km-long **Gola di Frasassi**, the high-walled limestone gorge cut by the Sentino river whose rather inaccessible caves open off to the sides. Evidence of prehistoric settlements have been found inside. The large *Grotta del Santuario* (open in summer on request: apply at the Consorzio Grotte di Frasassi, tel. 167013828) contains the *Chapel of Santa Maria intra Saxa*, part of a Benedictine monastery in the Middle Ages, and a small octagonal *church*, designed by Giuseppe Valadier in 1828 at the order of Leo XII.

San Vittore delle Chiuse*

This church, near the thermal spa of *San*

The apse of the church of San Vittore delle Chiuse

Vittore delle Chiuse (elev. 204 m), is one of the most important Romanesque monuments in the entire region. The church, which was probably founded in the 11th century, is similar in plan to *San Claudio al Chienti* (see p. 126). The facade has an ogival vestibule enclosed by an imposing truncated campanile and a graduated cylindrical tower. The *interior* (open 9am–1pm and 3pm–7pm) is in the shape of a Greek cross inscribed within a square in the-

The grotte di Frasassi: Large Wind Cave

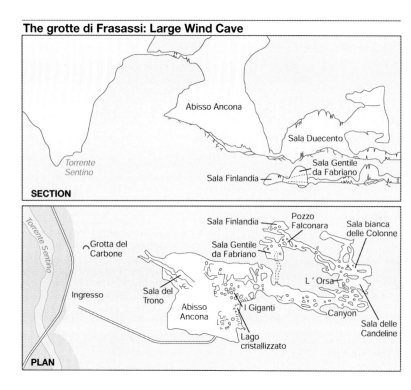

Byzantine style; the three naves are divided by sturdy cylindrical pillars. To the right of the facade are the remains of the ancient convent, in which a speleo-palaeontological museum is to be created; nearby is the entrance to the Frasassi Caves.

The Grotte di Frasassi**

The celebrated Frasassi caves (guided tours: Nov–Feb, 11am, 3pm and 4pm; Sun, holidays and Christmas, Mar–Jul and Sep–Oct, 9.30am, 11am, 12.30pm, 3pm, 4.30pm and 6pm; August, non-stop 8am-6.30pm; 19 July-24 August, 8am-6.30pm and 8pm-10.30pm; see plan and cross section above), are one of the most complex, best-known karst systems in Italy: an intriguing underground world of lakes enclosed by crystal arabesques, stalactites suspended like daggers, pillars towering up toward majestic vaulted caverns and beautiful transparent alabaster formations. The long underground route winds through a network of caves. The main cavern, the *Grotta Grande del Vento* (or "Large Wind Cave"), was discovered in 1971 by the Marche Speleology Group, part of the Ancona division of the Italian Alpine Club (CAI); the caves were subsequently organized for visits with walkways and the 1,500-m sequence opened to the public

in 1974. It begins at the *Abisso Ancona*, a vast space measuring (180 x 120 m) and probably the largest of its kind in Europe; from here other underground caves are reached, whose imaginative names (*Hall of the Two Hundred*, *Hall of the Candles*, *Hall of the Bear* and *Hall of Infinity*) were suggested by the spectacular formations they contain, and whose effect is heightened by the atmospheric lighting.

Before returning to Fabriano, a 10-km detour to the left of the SS76 leads to the abbey of Val di Castro, an ancient Benedictine settlement. To the south the side road leads to **Albacina** (elev. 286 m), founded in the Middle Ages by refugees fleeing the nearby town of *Tuficum*, which was razed to the ground by the Goths. This little town at the foot of *Mt. Maltempo* (elev. 1,088 m) still has the appearance of an ancient walled town clustered around its austere castle. A tortuous scenic road leads up to *Poggio San Romualdo* (elev. 936 m) and on to the **Abbey of Val di Castro**, founded in 936 by St. Romuald, who died here in 1027. Of the monastic complex which enjoyed a position of prestige and authority until the mid-15th century, the square tower that was part of the fortified walls survives, as does the 13th-century *church*, with 15th-century *frescoes* on the walls and an even older *crypt* (11th cent.). Note also the little 13th-century *cloister*, the monks' *refectory* and the *Chapter House*, whose cross vault is supported on polygonal pillars.

110

6.2 Camerino and environs
From Camerino to the Sibillini mountain national park, 103.5 km

This itinerary, which begins with the noble charm of the ancient ducal town of Camerino, traverses the relaxing green countryside as it heads to the hill towns to the north, in particular Matelica, set among the Verdicchio-producing vineyards and San Severino Marche, perched high on an isolated hill; and to the western section of the Sibillini mountain national park in the south.

The suggested tour visits the towns in a clockwise fashion starting with Pioraco, 15.5 km to the northwest of Camerino, and from there along the SS256 (Muccese), which links the Potenza and Esino valleys, to Matelica. Nineteen km from here lies San Severino Marche, from where the road runs south, past Serrapetrona, then along the SS77 (Val di Chienti), past the Da Varano castle and the Polverina lake, to the junction (7.5 km) with the SS209 (Valnerina). As the road once again turns south, the landscape gradually becomes more mountainous; after 20.5 km the road arrives at Visso, from where excursions can be made to Ussita (5 km) and the villages in the Sibillini mountain national park.

Camerino*

With its houses huddled against the old walls, its narrow, winding lanes, and long irregularly shaped street blocks interrupted by short, steep alleys, the old town of Camerino (elev. 661 m, pop. 7,361; see plan p. 112), has retained an almost perfect medieval layout. The skyline of the town, which stretches out along the ridge between the Chienti and Potenza valleys, is still dominated by the noble architecture of what was the capital of the Da Varano duchy, whose troubled history spans three centuries. Camerino was the birthplace of Arcangelo di Cola, Giovanni Boccati, and Girolamo di Giovanni, the main exponents of the school of Camerino which in the 15th century were a landmark in the figu-

rative arts of central Italy. The city's cultural traditions live on in the famous university, which was recognized by Pope Benedict XIII as a direct descendant of the flourishing 14th-century *studium*. On the Sunday following the town's local feast day (17 May), a magnificent procession of over 600 townsfolk dressed in splendid Renaissance costumes marks the beginning of the *Corsa alla Spada*, the traditional "Sword Race" contest between the town's wards.

Piazza della Vittoria (C1). This square stands in the southwest corner of the historic center, on the site of the moat that once surrounded the castle but was filled in the late 17th century. This part of the town, once outside the walls, was also the site of the convent of *San Pietro in Muralto*, built in 1480 over a previous

6.2 Camerino and environs

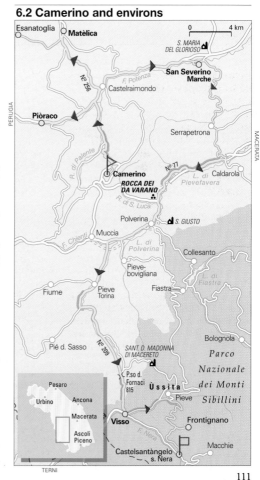

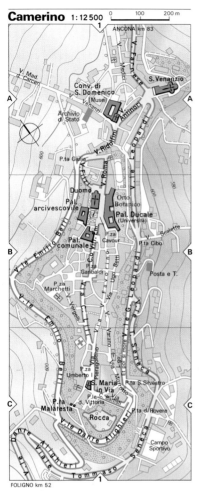

Camerino 1:12 500

FOLIGNO km 52

monastery. One wing of the convent is preserved inside the imposing **Rocca**, or fortress, built by Cesare Borgia in 1503 to defend the western slopes of the hill (extensive views over the Sibillini mountains). Nearby is the *Porta Malatesta*, Renaissance in style but medieval in origin.

The old part of the town begins to the north of Piazza della Vittoria, *Piazza Umberto I* (C1), is a medieval square that was heavily remodeled between the 17th and 19th centuries. The Baroque church of *Santa Maria in Via*, begun in 1639, has a 13th-century painting on wood (*Madonna and Child*) by the Maestro di Camerino, which, according to tradition, was brought here by crusaders returning from Smyrna in the mid-14th century.

Corso Vittorio Emanuele (B1). This is the ancient *Arengo*, the medieval center of town life, and is lined by a number of ancient patrician residences. *Palazzo Co-*
112

munale, which also stands in the street, was once the bishop's palace; its present appearance is the result of major remodeling carried out in the 19th century. The courtyard leads to the *Teatro "Filippo Marchetti,"* built in the mid-19th century to a design by Vincenzo Ghinelli.

Piazza Cavour (B1). This fine 16th-century square, the hub of town life, has a bronze *Statue of Sixtus V*, by Tiburzio Vergelli (1587). The square is bounded by the Archbishop's Palace, the Ducal Palace and the Duomo, rebuilt by Andrea Vici in 1802–32 to replace the ancient **cathedral** destroyed in the 1799 earthquake. Inside is a 15th-century *Statue of the Madonna of Mercy*, a wooden sculpture from the local artistic tradition; in the crypt is the *Tomb of St. Ansovinus** (14th cent.), the 9th-century bishop of Camerino, in Tuscan Gothic style. The porticoed **Palazzo Arcivescovile** (Archbishop's Palace), built 1572–80 and possibly designed by Vignola, houses on its first floor the *Museo Diocesano* (open on request) with frescoes, paintings, sculptures, silverware, and sacred items from churches in the diocese. The two main works are the large *Madonna in Glory with St. Philip**, painted by G. B. Tiepolo in 1739–40, and a *triptych* by Girolamo di Giovanni.

The Tomb of St. Ansovinus in Camerino Cathedral (14th cent.)

20th-century poets

20th-century poets

In February 1892 playwright and poet Ugo Betti (below) was born in Camerino, not many miles from the birthplace of Giacomo Leopardi, Recanati. Betti was the chief exponent of the so-called "theater of words," theatrical performances based on poetry and spiritual introspection in which the stage is interpreted as the home of human reflection. In "An Italian Town" Ugo Betti offers a lyrical description of Camerino, which strikes the visitor as a "castle with very high, irregularly-shaped walls ... surmounted by stony buildings with few windows ...; to anyone beholding the town at twilight from the west, it stands golden almost, high over the other hills over which night has already fallen (reminiscent of that golden Camerino that the town's patron saint – Venanzius – holds in the palm of his hand in an ancient statue)." The playwright's name lives on in the National Ugo Betti Stagecraft Award, held every two years.

The Marche Region and Matelica in particular are the setting for some of the works of Libero Bigiaretti, one of Italy's main postwar poets and narrators, who always carried with him the memory of his native town, a true "place of the soul" and the atmosphere of provincial life. Matelica and the Marche Regional Authorities jointly dedicate to Bigiaretti the National Narrative Fiction Award, held every year between May and June.

Palazzo Ducale (B1). This vast complex to the east of the square and now the seat of the university, has an original core remodeled in the late 14th century. Inside is the *Biblioteca Valentiniana*, founded in 1802, which has an important collection of books and some beautiful rooms. The porticoed courtyard, perhaps designed in part by Baccio Pontelli (15th cent.), leads to various rooms, including the so-called *Hall of the Bride and Groom*, with 15th-century frescoes, and to the panoramic terraces overlooking the hills. The university's *Botanical Gardens*, beneath the palace's high walls (open 9am–1pm and 3pm–5pm; Sat 9am–1pm; Sun closed), were opened in 1828.

Convento di San Domenico (A1). This quadrilateral complex with a large courtyard, is owned by the University of Camerino, which in 1994 began a restoration program to create a new home for all the city's museums. Built at the end of the 13th century around an existing church, it was run by Dominican friars until 1811, and, after the Napoleonic occupation, was taken over by the Augustinians, who held it until 1860. Thereafter the convent fell into a state of disrepair together with the churches of *San Domenico* and *San Sebastiano* (now multi-purpose halls), and was used as barracks, a warehouse, a school and even as a railway station. The north wing of the convent houses the **Museo e Pinacoteca "Girolamo di Giovanni"** (opening spring 1998, prior to which it was housed in the former church of *San Francesco*). Exhibits include archaeological finds, ceramics, bronzes, coins, frescoes and paintings from different periods, including works from the 15th-century Marche schools. There is a 1st–2nd century Roman *mosaic* found in the town itself, and a 12th-century bas-relief depicting *The Archangel Michael Slaying the Dragon*. Note also the interesting works by Girolamo di Giovanni: an *Annunciation* and a *Deposition* in the lunette, a 1449 *Enthroned Madonna with Saints*, the *Gonfalon of Tedico*, signed and dated 1463, and a fresco from the shrine of Bolognola (*Madonna and Child with St. Catherine of Alexandria**).

Special spaces have also been set aside for Bruno Bartoccini's *collection of sculptures*, donated by the artist to the town. The two other museums to be rehoused in one wing of the convent when restoration work is completed, are the *Museo di Scienze Naturali dell'Università* (currently in the basement of the Ducal Palace) with geo-paleontological and zoological collections; and the Museo Diocesano (see p. 112).

San Venanzio (A1). A high classical-style pronaos has much altered the appearance of this ancient church, rebuilt after the 1799 earthquake. Once surrounded by porticoes – of which only a short section remains – the building still has its 14th-century *portal** in ornate Gothic style, which survived remodeling work and the devastation caused by the earthquake.

In a wooded valley near Renacavata 3.5 km to the east of the town is the **Capuchin Convent**, built in 1531 over an existing abandoned hermitage. Inside, a small *museum* (open on request, tel. 644480) with liturgical ornaments and everyday objects from the life of the friars between the 15th and 18th century. The high altar of the adjacent *church* has a 16th-century glazed majolica previously attributed to Mattia della Robbia and now considered to have been executed by Santi Buglioni.

Pioraco

Paper mills powered by the waterfalls of the Potenza river still operate in this village at the beginning of the Pioraco Gorge. The first were opened as early as 1360, but the village itself (elev. 441 m, pop. 1,320) is even older and was a Roman settlement on the *Via Prolaquense*

The organ in the church of San Filippo, Matelica

which connected Umbria with the Adriatic. The 1327 church of **San Francesco**, in the leafy Piazza Leopardi, has a Baroque interior with a detached fresco (*Crucifixion*) attributed to Girolamo di Giovanni. Traces of frescoes can also be seen in the *cloister* of the adjoining convent, in which the **Museo della Carta e della Filigrana** (papermaking and watermarks; open 10am–12.30pm; closed Sun) and the *Museo dei Funghi and dei Fossili* (mushrooms and fossils; open Jul–Sep, 11am–12.30pm; Sun, 11am–12.30pm and 5pm–7pm). The *Ponte Marmone* on the main road is a Roman bridge restored in the 15th century.

Matelica*

The main square is dedicated to Enrico Mattei, to recall how the founder of Italy's national petroleum group, ENI, spent his youth in this town on a spur over a bend in the Esino river, at the confluence with the Braccano. But wine connoisseurs associate the name of the town more readily with the prized Verdicchio white wine produced in the valley. Today, Matelica (elev. 354 m, pop. 10,042) is a center of industry, although its many monuments are a reminder of its ancient past. A Roman

municipium and episcopal see from the 5th century, it was sacked by the Longobards and annexed to the duchy of Spoleto; it gained free municipal status in 1160 and was ruled between the 15th and 16th centuries by the Ottoni, a powerful Guelph family. Its manufacturing traditions are also steeped in history: in the Middle Ages the town was already a thriving center for the production of woolen cloth.

Piazza Enrico Mattei. This square, in the center of town, is surrounded by noble buildings and decorated by an octagonal *fountain* (1619). On one side stands **Palazzo Pretorio** (1270), with the *Torre Civica*, and the elegant *Loggia degli Ottoni* (1511); on the other the 19th-century *Palazzo Comunale* and the 15th-century *Palazzo Ottoni*, in the courtyard of which the remains of two rooms from a Roman dwelling have emerged (2nd century AD). The Baroque church of the *Suffrage* contains in the chapel on the right a painting with *Crucifix and Souls in Purgatory* attributed to Salvatore Rosa. A short way along the main street, *Corso Vittorio Emanuele*, is the **cathedral**, rebuilt in the 19th and 20th centuries, with an unusual facade that incorporates the 1474 campanile.

Museo Piersanti*. This museum, in Via Umberto I 11, in the 15th-century *Palazzo Piersanti* (open 10am–noon and 5pm–7pm; closed Mon; winter, Sat and Sun, 10am–noon and 4pm-6pm) contains paintings and other objects from the Marchigian school from the 15th–17th centuries, many of which belonged to Monsignor Filippo Piersanti in the 17th century. Particularly noteworthy is a *Crucifix** on wood (signed and dated 1452), considered to be one of the masterpieces of Antonio da Fabriano, who probably also painted the finely executed *Madonna and Child*. Note also a *Madonna and Child* and *St. Anne with other Saints* by Lorenzo d'Alessandro, a small painting on wood of *St. Sebastian* by Vittore Crivelli, and a triptych on a gold background by Arcangelo di Cola. Some rooms in the palace still have their original 18th-century furnishings together with miniatures, ivory objects, French and Flemish tapestries, sacred gold ornaments, and 18th-century curios.

Opposite Palazzo Piersanti stands the 19th-century *Teatro Condominiale*, built to a design by Giuseppe Piermarini. The 14th-century church of **Sant'Agostino** (note the richly decorated Romanesque portal) is in the nearby Piazza Lorenzo Valerio.

San Filippo. Built by the Oratorians between 1655 and 1660, this church in Via Oberdan has a Borromini-style terracotta facade that does little to prepare visitors for the decorative exuberance inside. Angels, saints, cherubs, festoons, and floral motifs in plaster and wood decorate the six side chapels, frame a number of canvases in Baroque cornices in a sumptuous display that culminates in the ornamentation surrounding the organ above the door. Continuing along Via Oberdan, past a 15th-century *arch* with *loggetta*, turn right into Via San Francesco, in which the church of the same name stands.

San Francesco. The Romanesque portal is the only indication of the 13th-century origin of this church, whose 18th-century interior contains some notable works of art. In the 1st chapel on the right, beside the entrance, is a *Purgatory* by Ercole Ramazzani (1586), who also painted two canvases in the 5th chapel (*Immaculate Conception* and *Ascension*); in the 2nd, an **Enthroned Madonna and Child with Sts. Francis and Catherine of Alexandria***, an exquisite composition by Marco Palmezzano (signed and dated 1501); in the 4th, a triptych with *Madonna and Franciscan Saints* by Francesco di Gentile. In the 3rd altar on the left is an *Epiphany* by Simone De Magistris (1566); in the 1st chapel on the left, an altarpiece by Simone Cantarini (*Madonna and Saints*, 1st half 17th cent.).

Six and a half km to the west lies the little town of **Esanatoglia** (elev. 446 m, pop. 1,911), on the slopes of a hill at the beginning of the valley of *San Pietro*, where the Esino river has its source. The town still has numerous medieval houses and ancient churches. *Palazzo del Pretorio* is 13th century, and the Romanesque *parish church* in the upper part of the town has a 13th-century portal and a Roman inscription in the base of the campanile.

San Severino Marche*

This town falls into two distinct parts: the medieval *Castello* area, high on the Montenero hill, built around the old Romanesque Cathedral; and the *Borgo*, founded in the 13th century for reasons of trade and general convenience, and dominated by the large, elliptical Piazza del Popolo, the medieval *platea mercati*. The numerous architectural episodes in the late 16th century, the Baroque transformations, and the 19th-century palaces give the town (elev. 235 m, pop. 13,018) a monumental appearance that is highlighted by the many works of art to be seen here. San Severino was home to an important school of painting, and the frescoes of Lorenzo and Jacopo Salimbeni can still be seen in some of the town's churches and in the large art gallery, while the Roman remains in the archaeological museum tell the story of the birth of the town, which was founded by refugees fleeing the nearby settlement of *Septempeda*, which was razed to the ground in 545 by Totila, King of the Ostrogoths.

The Palio delle Torri, San Severino Marche

Piazza del Popolo. This elongated elliptical square is the center of the town. On the south side stands *Palazzo Comunale* (1764), designed by Clemente Orlandi; opposite is the Rococo facade of the 1768 church of *San Giuseppe*. Other noteworthy buildings are the 16th-century rusticated terracotta *Palazzo Servanzi Collio*, and the **Palazzo dei Governatori** (also 16th cent.), with a 19th-century clock tower by Ireneo Aleandri, which marks the entrance to the 14th-century church of *Santa Maria della Misericordia*, rebuilt in the 17th century (one intrados has *frescoes* by Lorenzo Salimbeni, signed and dated 1404).

At the end of the arcaded section on the south side of the piazza is the **Teatro Feronia** (1827), also designed by Ireneo Aleandri.

the year 1000. The ground floor houses the **Museo Archeologico "Giuseppe Moretti"** (open on request, 9am–1pm; Jul–Sep, 9am–1pm and 4.30pm–6.30pm; closed Mon), with pre- and proto-historic materials (weapons and pottery), items of everyday use, inscriptions and memorial stones from the Roman town of *Septempeda*, and Picene burial goods from the Mt. Penna and Pitino necropolises (6th cent. BC). The palace is also the home of the **Pinacoteca Civica "Tacchi Venturi"*** (open on request, 9am–1pm; Jul–Sep,

The Da Varano Castle in the upper Chienti valley

Along Via Rosa, and across from Viale Bigioli stands the church of *San Domenico*, built together with its adjoining convent in the first half of the 13th century, but rebuilt in the early 14th century and restored in 1664. Nearby, not far from Via Bigioli, is the *Museo del Territorio* (open on request, tel. 638377), with a collection of farming implements and equipment.

Duomo Nuovo. Dedicated to St. Augustine, the new cathedral has 15th-century elements on its facade and a late-Gothic terracotta portal (1473), which survived the various reworkings of the 13th-century church, enlarged in the 15th century. The interior, which was remodeled in 1776 and in 1827, contains 16th- and 17th-century paintings, including a 1548 *Madonna del Carmine with Saints* on wood, (2nd altar on the right) and a *Noli me tangere* canvas, attributed to Pomarancio (3rd altar on the right).

Palazzo Tacchi-Venturi. This palace was built in the 15th century, using a lookout tower that possibly dated back to before

9am–1pm and 4.30pm–6.30pm; closed Mon), which has an interesting collection of the works the brothers Lorenzo and Jacopo Salimbeni. There are also paintings by Paolo Veneziano, and by Alunno, a *polyptych* by Vittore Crivelli, and a painting on wood by Pinturicchio (**Madonna della Pace***), considered to be one of the masterpieces of the Perugian artist, together with works by Lorenzo d'Alessandro (*Nativity*). Continue along Via Salimbeni and turn left to visit the church of San Lorenzo in Doliolo.

San Lorenzo in Doliolo. Tradition has it that this church was founded by Basilian monks in the 6th century over the ruins of a pagan temple; the present church is, however, 12th century and has been much remodeled. The 14th-century campanile forms the facade of the church and is similar to that of the Duomo Vecchio (see below). It has an atmospheric interior, with raised presbytery and a 1572 baptismal *font*. The *crypt*, supported on sturdy pillars and columns, has remains of frescoes by Lorenzo and Jacopo Salimbeni.

Castello. Perched high on the hill (elev. 343 m), this was the original town, but is now reduced to a collection of monuments. Beyond the *Porta delle Sette Cannelle*, named after the nearby seven-spouted Gothic *fountain*, the road leads up in between the old houses to an open area which affords fine views* over the new town and the surrounding hills. On the right, at the base of the early 14th-century *Torre Comunale,* is the wall of the *Monastery of the Poor Clares*, of 14th-century origin but rebuilt in the 18th century, which terminates against the remains of the *Palazzo Consolare* (13th cent.). On the left stands the **Duomo Vecchio**, possibly founded in the 10th century, but rebuilt in 1061, and enlarged and remodeled several times. Its 14th-century facade has a remarkable *portal* topped by a small shrine; the campanile, from the same period, whose upper section has two large bifora windows, was the prototype for the other bell towers in San Severino. The interior was transformed in 1741; note the *choir**, begun in 1483 and completed in 1513, and, in a chapel at the base of the campanile, remains of frescoes* by Jacopo and Lorenzo Salimbeni.

The SS361 toward Macerata arrives after 1 km at the church *of Santa Maria della Pieve*, which retains the apse and right-hand side of the original Romanesque structure; the interior (open on request, apply at the Municipio, tel. 641184), has 14th–15th century votive *frescoes*. Near the river lie the remains of the Roman town of **Septempeda** (open on request: apply at the Museo Archeologico).

On the road to Cingoli is the church of *Santa Maria del Glorioso*, built 1519–22 on the site of an ancient chapel in which a miracle is said to have taken place.

The Upper Chienti valley

Beyond the San Luca river, where the Chienti valley widens out, rises the **Rocca dei Da Varano** (apply at the Town Hall in Camerino, tel. 636245, 632534). This fortress was originally built in the 13th century and restored in the 14th. A little further along the road, a turn-off to the left

leads up 2 km to the 12th-century domed church of **San Giusto***, designed on a circular plan, with four radiating chapels. Inside are remains of 14th-century *frescoes*. The main road leads on to the village of *Polverina* (elev. 377 m), and **Polverina Lake**, a hydroelectric reservoir with a capacity of almost 6 million cubic meters of water.

Visso

This town, lying in a wooded depression in the upper Nera river valley, became important because of its position on the main communications route between Camerino and Foligno. Its ancient history is testified to by its noble 15th- and 16th-century architecture and the numerous medieval stone houses that still line its old narrow streets. The center of this little town (elev. 607 m, pop. 1,290), known as the gateway to the Sibillini Mountain National Park, is **Piazza dei Martiri Vissani***, on which elegant 15th- and 16th-century palaces stand. A 14th-century *portal**, with an *Annunciation* attributed to Paolo da Visso in the lunette (1444), belongs to the **Collegiata di Santa Maria**, built in the 12th century but later remodeled. The interior, transformed in the 17th century, has 14th- and 15th-century *frescoes*, traces of the original decoration (note in particular those in the apse, with their remarkable chromatic effects); the Romanesque *Chapel of the Baptistery* has capitals, reliefs, a holy water stoup and a font from the 12th century, taken from the original church.

The **Museo-Pinacoteca** (open on request, tel. 95200) is housed in the 14th-century church of **Sant'Agostino**. This museum and art gallery has mainly religious works (frescoes, paintings on wood, wood sculptures, astylar crosses in silver and bronze) gathered from churches in Visso and the surrounding area; they include the 12th-century *Madonna di Mevale* on wood, and 12th–13th century *Madonna and Child* sculpted in wood. The nearby *Piazza Capuzi* is remarkable for its architecture: note the porticoed *Palazzo dei Governatori*, a medieval building remodeled in 1579, and the *Palazzo dei Priori* (1482), now the town hall, with Gothic portal and Renaissance windows.

Santuario della Madonna di Macereto*

This Bramantesque church (1528–38) stands on a solitary plateau on the western foothills of the

The Santuario della Madonna di Macereto

117

Sibillini Mountains (elev. 998 m). The Greek-cross interior contains a 14th-century oratory re-clad in 1585–90. Near the church stands the *Palazzo delle Guaite*, built in 1583, which affords a splendid view over the rocky crags of Mt. Bove (elev. 2,112 m).

Ussita

Now a favorite vacation destination and winter sports resort, Ussita (pop. 468) is scattered over the northwestern slopes of Mt. Bove, and based in the hamlet of *Pieve* (elev. 744 m). Of interest here is the church of *Santa Maria Assunta*, which has remains of the original 14th-century building and, inside, *frescoes* attributed to Paolo da Visso, Camillo di Gaspare, and Fabio di Gaspare Angelucci. The *frescoes* in the 13th-century Romanesque church of *St. Stephen*, in the hamlet of Sorbo (elev. 832

Marche section of the Apennines, between the Visso pass (elev. 816 m.) to the north and the Forca Canapine (or San Pellegrino) pass (elev. 1,541 m) to the south. These mountains, which form the watershed between the Adriatic and the Tyrrhenian Seas, rise to an average altitude of 2,200-2,300 (Pizzo Regina 2,334 m, Mt. Vettore 2,476 m) are mostly limestone, with rocky walls, narrow gullies, ravines, rivers, and karst formations.

An 8.5 km road leads from Ussita to **Frontignano** (elev. 1,342 m.), one of central Italy's best-known ski resorts, on the slopes of Mt. Bove, whose summit is reached by cable car. Seven km further on is Castelsantangelo sul Nera (elev. 780 m, pop. 386), a tiny medieval village which still has sections of 15th-century walls and Romanesque churches (open on request, tel. 970063): the parish church of *Santo Stefano*

The unspoiled natural environment of the Sibillini mountains. Bottom: an eagle and an Apennine gentian

m), are possibly also by Paolo da Visso. Ussita is the base for excursions in the **Parco Nazionale dei Monti Sibillini**, a nature reserve covering area of 60,000 hectares spread over the Sibillini mountain range, a 40-km-long chain of the Umbria-

has a 14th–15th century *baptismal font*; the nearby church of **San Martino** has *frescoes* from the school of Paolo da Visso.
The nearby convent of **San Liberatore** (open on request, tel. 970063), has a church with *frescoes* from the Umbria-Marche school (15th–16th cent.).

7 The Macerata district

Profile of the district

For those reaching the area from over the Apennines, the district of Macerata offers a gradual shift from hewn stone to manmade brickwork. The most memorable feature of this land lies in the domestication of its characteristically sweet, natural environment – the fruit of the steady, patient work of the inhabitants in their attempt to maximize the farming. These changes, which apply also to the band of the Marche highlands, can be seen in the stratification of the many historical elements corresponding to each of the different eras that have succeeded each other.

Rather than the aftermath of the violent events in history, the dominating role of the district capital is the upshot of widespread schemes of administrative reorganization of the territories along the Adriatic lying within the compass of papal political influence. Macerata today has lingering intimations of the town's layout as a free commune, but in its overall appearance today, its form is clearly determined by the conjugation of the two preceding physical focuses: on the one hand the "podium" built on a geographical high point; and on the other the cathedral, with its bishop's residence alongside, lying on lower ground. The piazza's importance to the citizenry is the outcome of progressive alterations made from the 1500s to 1600s. These include the construction of the Loggia dei Mercanti – a response to the growing Florentine trade ethic; the Palazzo Apostolico (now the Prefettura); the Torre Civica; and the redesign of the town's central thoroughfare (now Corso della Repubblica). The district capital shares a certain chromatic *persona* with its neighboring towns that stems from a common use of brick. But many variations of hue can be appreciated, due to the different types of clay used and the time of baking; this is invariably a soft rose color, varying gently from a rough ocher to a burnt sienna, and is a characteristic of a kind of brick that endows the architecture with a warm, craftsman's feel – witness to a centuries-old tradition and deep, reciprocal familiarity with the very earth of the district.

7.1 Macerata and environs

A walking tour through Macerata
A circular tour from Macerata, 83.5 km *(see map on pp. 120–21)*
A tour from Macerata to Civitanova Marche, 49 km *(see map pp. 120–121)*

The intact city walls that still enclose the historic center of Macerata, the noble palazzi, the hushed ancient streets, the Neoclassical "stadium" known as the Sferisterio – built for the games but now a venue for opera music – our chapter on Macerata proposes two itineraries for discovering the town and its surroundings.

The first starts in Macerata itself and proceeds in a westerly direction, leading to Pollenza (9 km) via the inland roads. The route leads up to the gentle hills of the valley of the Palazzolo, reaching the town of Treia (4 km); continuing along the inland roads, the route leads to Cingoli (19 km), famous for its sweeping views of hills sloping down toward the Adriatic Sea. At a distance of 21.5 km lies Filottrano, where the route turns once again toward Macerata amid the billowing hills that border the coast.

The second itinerary unravels toward the Adriatic along the SS485. Leaving from Macerata, the route crosses over the state road to Carridonia (11 km); another detour leads to the important church of San Claudio al Chienti. A further 7 km's drive brings us to Monte San Giusto, from where we proceed along the state road to the church of Santa Maria a Pie' di Chienti. Further on, another turnoff to the left provides an alternative circuit down to the sea: in 5 km it proceeds to Montecosaro, whence, on the left, it continues to Morrovalle (6 km) on the right, and Civitanova Alta (4.5 km), the medieval section of the town of Civitanova Marche, at a distance of a little more than 4 km.

Macerata *

Perhaps the best-known of the city's monuments is the spectacular Sferisterio, originally a sports arena erected in the early 1800s to hold the characteristic local game of ball (*pallone al bracciale*) and now an important summer venue for concerts and

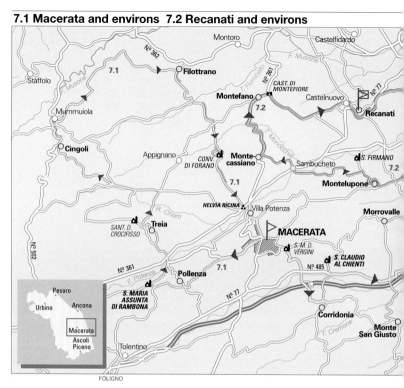

FOLIGNO

opera. The opera season runs July through August. The city walls, dating from the 15th and 16th centuries, are virtually intact and neatly enclose the historic center. Within the walls, the town itself (elev. 314 m, pop. 42,824; see plan on p. 122) is laid out around Piazza della Libertà, with elegant churches and palazzi in the Mannerist and Baroque styles. The first settlement was established here by refugees from the Roman *Helvia Ricina*, a township destroyed in the year 408; Macerata became a free commune in the year 1138, and was officially recognized as a bishopric in 1320 by John XXII, the second Avignon pope. After a period of seigniorial rule, in 1445 the city returned to the Church, which made it the seat of the Marchigian legation, thereby bringing a long period of isolation that did not end until the Napoleonic period, when the town was absorbed into the Kingdom of Italy.

Piazza Garibaldi (A1). The busy Piazza Garibaldi provides a point of convergence for the main circulation routes and the modern neighborhoods that have grown up on the west side of town. The straight thoroughfare Corso Cavour terminates in a *Monument to the Fallen* (1928–32) by C. Bazzani. An iron gate marks the entrance

120

to the ancient core of the town, to which leads Corso Garibaldi: at no. 77 stands a fine 18th-century building, *Palazzo Torri*, fronted by a semicircular facade; at no. 20 stands the *Palazzo dei Tribunali*, formerly the convent of Santa Chiara, built in 1661 and completed in the first decade of the ensuing century.

Corso Matteotti (A2). A key thoroughfare serving the old city center, Corso Matteotti boasts several prime examples of 16th-century architecture, such as the *Palazzo Consalvi* (no. 62) attributed to Pellegrino Tibaldi, who may well also have designed the *Palazzo Rotelli* (1570) at no. 41. A little further on at no. 33 rises the *Palazzo Mozzi*, also known as the *Palazzo dei Diamanti* for its diamond rustication. The avenue ends in Piazza della Libertà, close to the **Loggia dei Mercanti***, an elegant construction in the Tuscan Renaissance style, constructed in 1504–05.

Piazza della Libertà (A2). This square is the very heart of Macerata, from which radiate the various routes in and out of town. On the west side stands the arcaded **Palazzo dei Priori**, now the seat of the municipality, built in the first half of the 17th century, its facade remodeled in 1820; installed in the

entrance hall and courtyard of the building is an *archaeological collection* with fragments of sculptures, statuary, and inscribed slabs from Roman times originating from the colony of *Helvia Ricina*. The northern end of the square is closed by a 16th-century building, now the Prefettura, and formerly the residence of the papal legates; the building contains a fine marble portal of 1509, and traces of the lancet arches be-

longing to an earlier construction (13th cent.). On the opposite side of the square rises the *Torre Civica*, also known as the *Torre dell'Orologio*, begun in 1485 but not completed until 1653. Alongside stands the *Teatro "Lauro Rossi"* (A2), built in 1767 to designs by Antonio Bibiena. Abutting the east side of the square is *San Paolo* (A2-3), built in 1623–55; on the right an archway marks the entrance to the *University*, instituted in 1540 by Pope Paul III on the *Studium Legum* that had existed since 1290.

From the stepped incline to the right of the Torre Civica one descends to the church of *Santa Maria della Porta* (B2), a remarkable construction with a Romanesque lower story (11th cent.) and a Gothic upper story, characterized by a splendid *portal* dating from the end of the 13th century.

Corso della Repubblica (A-B2) also converges on the square. Here stands the church of *San Filippo* (B2), built to designs by G. B. Contini over the period 1697–1730. The boulevard leads to Piazza Vittorio Veneto, which is overlooked by the collegiate church of *San Giovanni*, begun in 1539 but not completed until later under the architect Rosato Rosati, in 1660. Alongside stands the former *Jesuit College*, a vast 17th-century complex with a facade from 1854, now housing the various civic museums and the municipal library. Among the sectors of the museums that deserve a visit is the **Pinacoteca Comunale**, or council art gallery (open 9am–1pm, 4pm–7pm; closed Sun afternoon and Mon morning); the gallery is divided into two sections: the first, dedicated to the art of antiquity, accommo-

Aerial view of Macerata, showing the Sferisterio

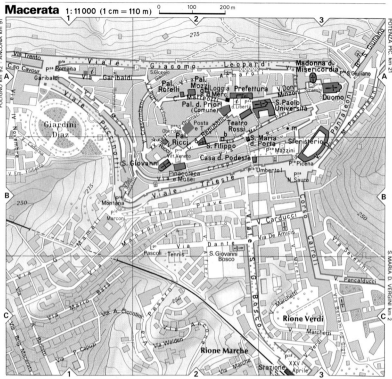

Macerata 1:11000 (1 cm = 110 m)

dates paintings of Umbro-Marchigian origin from the 14th to 19th centuries, with works by Giacomo da Recanati, F. Barocci, Sassoferrato, S. Cantarini, C. Maratta, and an exquisite *Madonna and Child** (1470) by Carlo Crivelli. The second section vaunts a collection of modern and contemporary art, with paintings by E. Prampolini, L. Spazzapan, B. Cassinari, D. Cantatore, E. Vedova, and the local Futurist painter Ivo Pannaggi. The **Museo Civico** (open 9am–1pm, 4pm–7pm; closed Sun afternoon and Mon morning) boasts not only archaeological finds from the ancient colony of *Helvia Ricina*, but also sundry objects, photographs, and documents on the history, customs, and traditions of the town. Flanking the museum is the *Museo delle Carrozze*, with vehicles and sedans of various types and eras. In the 18th-century halls of the first story is the public library, with manuscripts, precious incunabula, and *cinquecentine*, and books published in the 1500s. Also accommodated in the building is the *Museo Regionale del Risorgimento e della Resistenza* (closed for alterations), which boasts an armory collection, military uniforms, autograph letters and manuscripts by some of the leading figures of the country's history.

A short way up Via Ricci stands the *Palazzo Ricci*, built in the 1500s but remodeled in 1772; the building now houses the **Galleria d'Arte Contemporanea** (visits on application to the local Cassa di Risparmio bank, Tue and Thu 4pm–6pm, Sat 10am–noon), with a commendable collection of artists' work from the Italian

The Spheristerium of Macerata

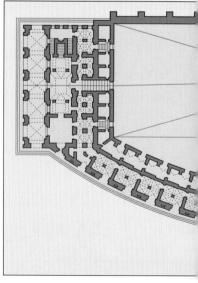

Novecento. When, between 1763 and 1772, the Ricci marquises had the building constructed, their wealth and political status would normally have allowed them something far more grand. But the family favored a more feudal style and, rather than emulate the grandeur of the upper classes, preferred a building that conformed with a more bourgeois outlook. Consequently, the nameless architect they commissioned adopted the classicizing style that prevailed in the town, following a basic geometrical pattern of sobriety. The Ricci family was far from being imitative. One of the most noted exponents of the family was Matteo Ricci (1552–1610), a Jesuit who served as the first Italian ambassador to the East. At the start of the 19th century the brothers Amico and Domenico Ricci made a name for themselves – the former was an art historian, the latter a patriot and creator of the first children's preschool institution for the Papal States (1841). Now the property of the Fondazione Carima, Palazzo Ricci has not betrayed its original modernist outlook, and houses a noteworthy collection of paintings from the Italian Novecento, including an important group of works by the Macerata-born painter Scipione.

Via Don Minzoni (A2-3). Lined with various faculties of the university, this avenue which runs from Piazza della Libertà toward the cathedral has become a sort of "university stronghold." Beyond the arcades of the *Foro Annonario* (1874) rise various 18th-century buildings, including the *Palazzo Compagnoni Marefoschi*, built to designs by Luigi Vanvitelli; and the *Palazzo Buonaccorsi* (early 18th cent.), now the seat of the Fine Arts Academy

and the Accademia dei Catenati, which was founded in distant 1574.

The Cathedral (A3) Founded in the 15th century, but extensively reworked in 1771–90 to designs by Cosimo Morelli, the cathedral's facade remained unfinished; the campanile alongside dates to 1478. In the church's vast interior hang canvases from the 17th to 18th centuries. Overlooking the square outside is the sanctuary of the **Madonna della Misericordia**, erected in 1736–41 on the site of a votive chapel dating to 1447. The harmonious interiors are the work of Luigi Vanvitelli. In the presbytery are two huge 18th-century canvases by Sebastiano Conca; a large inconostasis, or screen, protects the venerated image of the *Madonna of Mercy*, which dates to the 15th century.

The Sferisterio (A-B3; see plan), from the Latin *spheristerium*, was built as a venue for the popular "bracciale" ball game. The remarkable arena (90 x 36 m) was built in 1820–29 to designs by Ireneo Aleandri, who styled it on Palladio's work. With a capacity of 7,000 spectators, in the past the stadium has hosted tournaments and equestrian circuses; since the 1920s the sferisterio hosts important opera performances each year. Alongside the arena stands the *Porta Picena* (1823), whence stretches from **Piazza Mazzini** (B2-3), with the so-called *Casa del Podestà*, an unprepossessing building erected in 1373.

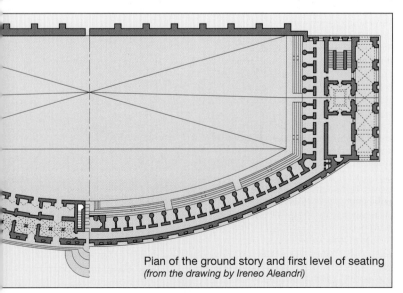

Plan of the ground story and first level of seating
(from the drawing by Ireneo Aleandri)

Leaving the town from Porta Picena and continuing for 2 km, passing the cemetery, we come to the church of **Santa Maria delle Vergini** (C3, off map), a fine piece of Bramantesque architecture with an engaging brickwork facade and slender octagonal dome (1550–65). Inside one may admire stuccoes and frescoes from the 16th to 18th centuries, plus a fine *Epiphany* (1581) by Tintoretto and assistants.

The hills between Macerata and Cingoli

Pollenza

The town of Pollenza (elev. 341 m, pop. 5,630) commands a panoramic ridge that separates the lower valleys of the Potenza and Chienti rivers. When in the Middle Ages the township was founded, it bore the name Montemilione; its present name (adopted in 1862) comes from the earlier Roman appellation *Pollentia*. In the historic center, which is still largely enclosed in the old city walls, worth visiting are the church of *San Giuseppe*, having a handsome 16th-century portal, and the church of *SS. Francesco e Antonio*, whose facade by Cesare Bazzani boasts a superb *Gothic portal*, all that remains of the original construction. In the Piazza della Libertà, where stands the *Palazzo Comunale*, rises a bust in memory of Giuseppe Verdi carved in 1913 by Vittorio Morelli.

Santa Maria Assunta di Rambona*

This sandstone church was founded in the 8th century by the Longobard queen Ageltrude on the ruins of a temple attributed to the goddess Bona (whence the name "Rambona," a contraction of *Ara Bonae*); the outward aspect of the building, however, is the result of various alterations made in the 11th and 12th centuries, when the three radial apses were added. The interior (visits on application, tel. 5493346) has tracts of 16th-century votive *frescoes* and a fascinating *crypt** with twin aisles divided by columns salvaged from Roman monuments.

Treia

The defensive walls, towers, gates, and ancient houses of Treia (elev. 342 m, pop.

9,321) have retained the spirit of medieval life in this town. The town's name derives from *Trea*, a Roman *municipium* that actually stood lower down the hillside, but was abandoned for a more secure site. The medieval settlement bore the name of Montecchio, and remained so until 1790, when Pius VI awarded the locality full status as a town. A token of the town's ancient heritage is the "Disfida del Bracciale," a game played with a small, heavy ball on the first Sunday of August, in which each of the town's four wards take part.

At the center of Treia lies **Piazza della Repubblica**, enclosed in a tall balustrade designed by Andrea Vici. Among the buildings of special interest abutting the square is the arcaded *Palazzo Municipale* (16th–17th cent.) housing the *Museo Civico Archeologico* (visits on application, 10.30am–1pm; tel. 215117), in which various material from the Roman settlement of *Trea* and surroundings are on exhibition. Opposite the 18th-century church of *San Filippo* stands the compact *Accademia Georgica* (1823), the work of Giuseppe Valadier. Along Via Lanzi, passing by the *Monument to the Fallen* by Cesare Bazzani, the road proceeds straight to the **Cathedral**. Of the original structure (12th cent.), only the bell tower has survived, while the rest is the upshot of reconstruction work

Pollenza: crypt of Santa Maria Assunta di Rombona

done in the 18th century by Andrea Vici; inside stands a bust of *Sixtus V* attributed to Giambologna.

A short distance from the town in the direction of Chiesanuova rises the sanctuary of the **SS. Crocifisso** built by Cesare Bazzani in the early 1900s on the site of an older parish church. Inside can be admired a fresco of the Umbrian school (16th cent.) featuring a *St. Sebastian* (2nd altar on right) and on the high altar a 16th-century *Crucifix*. Numerous architectural and sculptural fragments of the Roman period provide reminders that this was once the site of the Roman colony *Trea*.

Cingoli*

Perched on the eastern flank of Mt. Cingoli, this town (elev. 631, pop. 10,051) commands a fabulous view of woodlands, fields and distant farmlands that lead right to the sea: among the panoramic centers of the Marchigian interior, this is perhaps one of the most noted for its view from Mt. Conero to the Sibillini, a vista so expansive Cingoli has been likened to a balcony over the Marche. Still enclosed in its city walls, the town conserved a quiet, out-of-the-way atmosphere with Renaissance palazzi and medieval churches, many of which were later remodeled in the Baroque style. Founded in the 3rd century BC, the Roman settlement of *Cingulum* was razed by the Goths and Longobards, and the district became a feudal territory of the bishop of Osimo; subsequently it became a free commune, but the rivalry between the town's leading families kept Cingoli under the power of the papacy. From the 16th to 18th centuries, as part of the Papal States, a long period of peace ensued during which the arts and sciences were encouraged, and many noble palaces were constructed.

Cingoli, the so-called Fontana del Maltempo

Piazza Vittorio Emanuele II. The square occupies what was formerly the site of the Roman acropolis. Facing each other across the square are the cathedral and the **Palazzo Municipale**, built in the 12th century on the foundations of a Roman edifice and rebuilt in the Renaissance in 1531; the *Torre dell'Orologio*, a Romanesque tower was raised in 1482 and furnished with a fine clock-face in stone. The aforementioned palace now houses the *Museo Archeologico Statale* (open 9am–1.30pm). On the opposite side of the square stands the mighty 17th-century **Cathedral**, its facade unfinished (1830), and transformed inside in 1938.

Left of the cathedral lies Via Foltrani with a line of splendid Renaissance palazzi that belonged to the town's noble families (note

nos. 5, 6, and 9 in particular). Just past *San Domenico*, erected in the 13th century but with an 18th-century interior, on the right stands *San Benedetto*, of Romanesque origin but, like many other churches, reworked in the 17th century; note the canvas on the high altar by Annibale Carracci (*Deposition from the Cross*).

In the Biblioteca Comunale (public library), which is reached from Piazza Vittorio Emanuele II along Via del Cassaro, stands the **Pinacoteca Comunale** (open 10.30am–12.30pm; closed Sun). The gallery boasts a good collection of works by the local artist Donatello Stefanucci, and other paintings from the churches across the Cingoli district, including a splendid *Madonna of the Rosary with Saints** (1539) by Lorenzo Lotto.

Via del Podestà With its ancient houses and handsome buildings, the street is one of Cingoli's most memorable. Overlooking the street is the *Seminario Vescovile*, originally belonging to the Order of St. Philip Neri and adjacent to a church dedicated to the saint, built in the 13th century but completely reworked in the 1500s, and then reconstructed once more in 1695. The *portal* is of 14th-century Romanesque design, the interiors are an example of late Marchigian Baroque, with alcove chapels adorned with stuccoes and frescoes.

Corso Garibaldi. The street is lined with some very smart palazzi built in the 16th and 17th centuries, original residences of Cingoli's patrician families. At no. 85 rises the *Palazzo Castiglioni* (visits on request, tel. 602531), the birthplace of Pope Pius VIII, with fine 19th-century furniture and a picture gallery. Opposite the *Palazzo Mucciolanti* (18th cent.) Via Cavour leads to *San Francesco*: from the original 14th-century structure the church has kept a fine *Romanesque portal* in one side wall and a tall polygonal apse. The street ends at the **Balcone delle Marche***, so-called because of the striking view it affords of the surrounding hilltop towns and farms extending as far as the sea, with Mt. Conero rising in the distance.

At the end of Corso Garibaldi, turning left, one comes to the little church of *San Nicolò*, built in the 13th century, having a Romanesque *portal* transferred from the church of San Esuperanzio (see below). A little further on stands the *Porta Pia*, raised by Ireneo Aleandri in 1845 in honor of Pope Pius VIII.

Sant'Esuperanzio*. On the road to the cemetery, stands this collegiate church of Romanesque-Gothic style built in the second half of the 12th century to house the tomb of the bishop and saint, Esuperanzio, protector of the town. The presbytery is raised over a *crypt* (1777) with votive *frescoes* (15th–16th cent.), some of which are badly worn; on the right wall, between the 4th and 5th arches, lies the *Altare del Sacramento*, an altar enshrined in a marble arch (1537).

Filottrano

Tradition has it that this town (elev. 270, pop. 9,066) was founded by the sons of the Longobard Ottran; one thing is sure: the town was besieged on several occasions in an effort to contain certain powerful lords contesting the area. The town's more recent history has also seen heavy battles: one during the Italian campaign of the French cavalry leader Joachim Murat between the Austrian troops and the Italian brigades; the other in 1944, when Filottrano was snatched from the Germans during a series of bloody assaults. The most important monument here is the **San Francesco**, with its (unfinished) brickwork facade and stone *portal* of

Triple apse of the church of San Claudio al Chienti

1531. The interiors are 18th century, and offer an interesting example of Marchigian Baroque (morning visits on application, tel. 7127560).

In Vicolo Beltrami stands the Palazzo Beltrami Lucchetti, which houses the *Museo del Biroccio* (open Tue 3pm–6pm; Wed 9.30am–noon,

3pm–6pm; Fri 9.30am–noon); the collection is devoted to the history of the regional farm cart and the farming community; there is also an *archaeological section* that displays tribal objects from the Indians of the Mississippi.

The road that leads out from Filottrano toward Macerata passes close to the **Convent of Forano**, originally 13th century, and famous for a visit made by St. Francis of Assisi.

The remains of the Roman colony of *Helvia Ricina*

On the site once occupied by the Roman town *Helvia Ricina*, razed by the Visigoths in the 5th or 6th century, now stands *Villa Potenza* (elev. 95 m), a small town lying on the junction of numerous roads. Within the present ward the vast ruins of the Roman *Theater* (2nd cent. AD) can be admired; opposite stand marble reliefs, epigraphs, and architectural fragments of Roman buildings found in the Potenza river.

From Macerata to the Adriatic

San Claudio al Chienti*

A charming cypress-lined avenue leads up to this venerable temple, which is one of the most captivating examples of local Romanesque. Its singular structure comprises two vessels of the same dimensions built one above the other. Raised in the 5th or 7th century on the ruins of Roman *Pausulae*, but reworked from the late 9th to the early 12th centuries, the church has a narrow facade pierced by single- and two-light windows. The *lower church*, which is preceded by a foresection with a large portal, is on a square plan; in the central apse are two *frescoes* dating from 1468. Two spiral stairways in the corner towers ascend to the terrace, which introduces the *upper church* through a remarkable Romanesque doorway.

Corridonia

Until 1931 the site was known by its old Latin name, *Pausulae*. The present name pays homage to the local-born statesman Filippo Corridoni (d. 1915). Corridonia (elev. 255, pop. 12,703) conserves stretches of the old walls and a handful of buildings of historical interest, including the Neoclassical *SS. Pietro e Paolo*, built to designs by G. Valadier; the church contains two wood *Crucifixes* (respectively 1400s and 1500s). The rectory alongside houses an interesting **Pinacoteca** (visits on request, tel. 431832) having a collection of altarpieces and paintings of the 14th to 17th centuries, including a *Virgo Lactans** by Carlo Crivelli; a *Madonna del Carmelo* by Pomarancio; and a *Madonna of Humility* by Andrea da Bologna, signed and dated 1372.

Monte San Giusto

This town (elev. 236, pop. 7,155), whose economy is based on shoe production, has a very well-conserved historic center. The **Palazzo Municipale**, perhaps begun in the year 1494 and terminated in 1513, bears on its main facade a tall frieze* and five large windows in the Guelph style. In the narrow Via Tolomei rises the church of *Santa Maria Telusiano*, founded in the 14th century and remodeled in the 16th; the interior contains a large **Crucifixion*** (1531), an important work by Lorenzo Lotto.

Santa Maria a Pie' di Chienti*

According to a long-standing tradition, it was the great Carolingian king Charlemagne who had the temple built to celebrate a victory against the Saracens. Actually, Santa Maria was erected in the 9th century, and later remodeled. The unostentatious facade (17th–18th cent.) has a an apse section* of Nordic inspiration with radial chapels surmounted by the main apse of the upper church. The fine **interior*** (see plan) has an aisled nave. In the *lower church* the front section of the nave continues up to the church's exposed-truss ceiling, and proceeds to the broad, low presbytery, deambulatory and three radial chapels; the *upper church* comprised the presbytery and ambulacra reserved for the monks. On the right wall and main apse a series of fine 14th-century *frescoes* have been brought to light; among the works kept in the church are a wooden *Crucifix** from the 15th century, and two small terracotta statues (*Virgin Annunciate* and an *Angel*), also dating to the 15th century.

Montecosaro

In the Middle Ages, the ancient *Mons Causarius* was enclosed in the fortified castle and was involved in endless territorial conflicts with nearby Civitanova. Today the town (elev. 252, pop. 4,884) has managed to conserve part of its original 14th-century walls and the basic layout established in the 17th century. On the edge of town rises the octagonal church of *San Rocco* having an admirable *fresco* by Po-

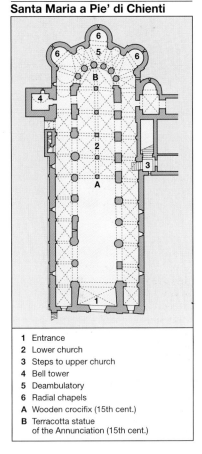

Santa Maria a Pie' di Chienti

1 Entrance
2 Lower church
3 Steps to upper church
4 Bell tower
5 Deambulatory
6 Radial chapels
A Wooden crocifix (15th cent.)
B Terracotta statue of the Annunciation (15th cent.)

marancio on the high altar. As with Santa Maria a Pie' di Chienti, the foundation of **Morrovalle** (elev. 245 m, pop. 8,674) has been tied to the great Charlemagne. Town life revolves around the main square, *Piazza della Libertà*, with its 14th-century *Torre del Comune*, and arcaded *Palazzo Municipale*; and the *Palazzo Lazzarini*, erected in the 14th century and later altered. In the vicinity of Piazza San Bartolomeo stands the *Museo Internazionale del Presepe* (visits on request, tel. 221420), a museum with examples of the art of crib design from all over the world.

Civitanova Alta

Straddling the crown of a hill (elev. 160 m), and still partly enclosed in its castle walls (15th cent.), the town was founded in the Middle Ages by refugees from the troubled coastal towns. Since 1938, however, it lies within the administrative aegis of Civitanova Marche, its ancient port. The heart of the town is **Piazza della Libertà**, onto which abuts

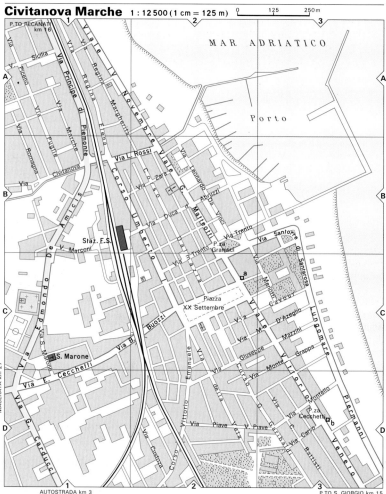

Civitanova Marche 1 : 12 500 (1 cm = 125 m)

MAR ADRIATICO

P.TO RECANATI km 16

MACERATA km 27

AUTOSTRADA km 3

P.TO S. GIORGIO km 15

the former *Palazzo Comunale*, a 16th-century building which now houses the **Civica Galleria d'Arte Moderna "Marco Moretti"** (open 8am–1pm; closed Sun) in which a substantial collection of contemporary Italian paintings are on exhibition, including works by Carlo Carrà, Mario Sironi, Giorgio Morandi, Antonio Ligabue, Giacomo

Manzù, and Orfeo Tamburi. Alongside the art gallery stands *San Paolo*, rebuilt midway through the 18th century; opposite rises the church of *San Francesco*, which has retained its original 14th-century Gothic portal together with remains of a Romanesque-Gothic decoration along its flanks and a handsome bell tower. At the corner of Corso A. Caro stands the *Palazzo Cesarini*, dating from the 13th century but completely rebuilt twice, once in the 1500s and again in the 19th century. A little way on rises the church of *Sant'Agostino*, erected in the 15th century, its interiors reworked during the 1600s.

Civitanova Marche

Fishing, general commerce, and a flourishing shoemaking industry have secured the town's growth (elev. 3 m, pop. 37,906; see street plan above), particularly after

Boats in construction at Civitanova Marche

128

World War II. The town has become a thriving seaside resort owing to its beaches and extensive catering facilities. At the heart of town life lies *Piazza XX Settembre* (C2), dominated by the *Palazzo Comunale* built in 1862. Also on the square is the once Romanesque *San Marone* (C1). Traces of the ancient burgh of the Roman settlement *Cluana* have been brought to light between the church and the railway.

7.2 Recanati and environs
Circular itinerary of 60 km *(see map on pp. 120–121)*

From the birthplace of the poet Leopardi to the sea, and then back to the interior along minor roads through gentle hills graced with vineyards and olive groves whose peaks are capped with small towns and villages of considerable scenic charm.

After Recanati the itinerary follows the SS77 seaward to Val di Chienti, reaching Porto Recanati after 11 km. From here it continues as far as Porto Potenza Picena, before turning back inland. The route then climbs the Potenza valley reaching Potenza Picena after 8 km. After 5.5 km it climbs further to Montelupone, and from here Montecassiano. After a drive of 19.5 km in all, the route returns to Recanati, passing through Montefano and by the castle of Montefiore.

Recanati *

The ancient tower of the convent of Sant'Agostino, the noble and severe palazzo which still contains the papers of the Leopardi family library – streets, squares, monuments of the birthplace of the poet Giacomo Leopardi evoke ideas of such impact that one forgets that Recanati (elev. 293, pop. 19,489; see map below) was an antique township on the crest of a hill. The expansion in the 15th and 16th centuries bears witness to the thriving business of the town's tradesmen, but did not detract from the elegant atmosphere of the town center, the measured prospects of 18th- and 19th-century palazzi along the main thoroughfares, and the substantial collection of art works in the churches and mu-

---

From Recanati on the trail of Lorenzo Lotto

Though born in Venice, like his illustrious predecessor Carlo Crivelli, in 1508 Lorenzo Lotto created his first painting in the Marche: the grand polyptych of the *Madonna and Saints*, now kept in the Pinacoteca Civica alongside other superb masterpieces, such as the *Transfiguration* (1512), and the *Annunciation* (1528 ca.). From Recanati, Lotto's work took him to various other towns in the region, where he remained until his death. These include Jesi, whose picture gallery hosts the *St. Lucy Polyptych* (1531–2; see illustration), a work of signal importance in the Italian Renaissance; Loreto, where he spent half of his life, and where the later works are kept, including the *Presentation*

in the Temple; Ancona, where the picture gallery has a *Sacra Conversazione*; and Cingoli, with its *Madonna of the Rosary* (1538) in the Pinacoteca Comunale. Some of the churches dotted around the region also contain works by Lotto: the high altar in Santa Maria in Telusiano at Monte San Giusto is home to a *Crucifixion* which Berenson has described as one of the greatest portrayals of the tragedy of Golgotha in the story of painting, and one of the absolute masterpieces of the Renaissance; in Mogliano, in the apse of the church of Santa Maria Assunta, hangs an *Our Lady of the Assumption* (1548); and another painting of this subject on the high altar of San Francesco delle Scale in Ancona.

seums; finest of these are the works by Lorenzo Lotto in the public art gallery. But while the town resounds with reminders of the lofty and rather pessimistic lyrics of Leopardi, this was also the birthplace or the great Beniamino Gigli, to whom the town has dedicated a museum.

Piazza Leopardi (B2-3). Reworked in the last decades of the 1800s, the square is dominated by the classicizing *Palazzo Comunale*, which, together with *Monument to Giacomo Leopardi* in front was inaugurated in 1898 on the occasion of the celebrations for the first centenary since the poet's birth. The building houses the public picture gallery and museums (see below). Slightly isolated on the left rises the 13th-century *Torre del Borgno* (B2), the only surviving part of the original Palazzo Comunale (the clock-face dates from 1562). On the right of the square is the flank of the church of **San Domenico** (B3), a temple of Romanesque construction reworked in the 14th century, with a distinguished *portal** created in 1481 by Lombard master sculptors to designs that have been attributed to Giuliano da Maiano; the roomy

interiors, reworked in the 18th and 19th centuries, contain a detached fresco by Lorenzo Lotto featuring *St. Vincent Ferrer in Glory* (1515; 2nd altar on left).

Pinacoteca Civica* Set up in 1898 within the Palazzo Comunale (open Oct–Mar 10am–1pm, 3pm–6pm; Apr–Sep 10am–1pm, 4pm–7pm; closed Mon) boasts a rich collection of important works, including a fine *polyptych* (1422) by Pietro da Montepulciano, and a *wood bas-relief* of 1395; the most important work in the gallery is undoubtedly the magnificent *Madonna with Child and Saints**, a huge polyptych by Lotto; plus the *Transfiguration** panel of 1512 inspired on Raphael's model; a *St. James Pilgrim*, and a superb **Annunciation***, a signed canvas painted around 1528 in which the lively narrative is epitomized by the cat, alarmed by the sudden appearance of the angel. The palazzo also houses other collections of the *Musei Civici*, with documents relating to local history, a modern art section, and the *Museo Beniamino Gigli* (open Oct–Mar 10am–1pm, 3pm–6pm; Apr–Sep 10am–1pm, 4pm–7pm; closed Mon), with photographs, personal memo-

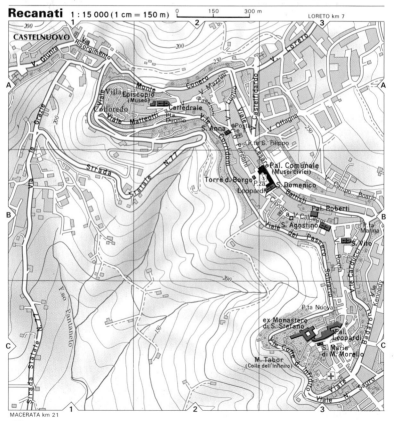

Recanati 1 : 15 000 (1 cm = 150 m) 0 150 300 m LORETO km 7

MACERATA km 21

Recanati: Piazza del Sabato del Villaggio

Presentation at the Temple (1582) by Pomarancio.

Piazza del Sabato del Villaggio (C3) is reached at the end of Via Roma. In this compact square stand the town's main monuments to Leopardi. The piazza is dominated by the poet's birthplace, **Palazzo Leopardi**, which is still inhabited by his descendants. The building houses a fine *library* set up by Monaldo Leopardi (open spring and autumn 9am–noon, 3pm–6pm; summer 9am–noon, 3pm–7pm; winter 9am–noon, 3pm–5pm), and boasts antique books, incunabulas, and rare texts; naturally, the library also contains memorabilia that belonged to the poet himself and an assortment of youthful manuscripts. Also bordering the square are the house of the famous Silvia, daughter of Leopardi's coachman, and the church of *Santa Maria di Monte Morello*, built in

rabilia, and costumes worn by Gigli in his performances.

Near the Torre del Borgo starts a broad, straight thoroughfare called **Corso Persiani** (A-B2), the town's main boulevard whose frontage incorporates the facade of *Sant'Anna* (A2), built in the 15th century but remodeled in the 1700s. At the end of the *corso* lies *Via Falleroni**; at nos. 25–37 one can glimpse traces of the arcades that graced the original housing. The street leads to the *cathedral*, rebuilt in the 18th century; the facade was incorporated into the adjacent bishop's palace (17th cent.), where now visitors can explore the **Museo Diocesiano** (open Jun–Sep 9.30am–noon, 3.30pm–7pm; Oct–Mar 9am–noon, 4.30pm–7.30pm; the entrance is to the left of the vestibule); the museum conserves paintings, sculpture, religious objects, including the remarkable *teche**, or vitrines, in gilded glass worked by craftsmen of the Umbrian school of the 14th century; other works include a Guercino featuring *St. Lucy* (1665) ; a *Sacra Famiglia* attributed to Mantegna; and a *Crucifixion* of the Caravaggio school.

Sant'Agostino (B3). From Piazza Leopardi the street leads up along Via Cavour and Via Calcagni. Beyond the Baroque frontage of the *Palazzo Roberti* (no. 19) with its eye-catching facade by Ferdinando Bibiena, to the right of Sant'Agostino, which was built with the attached convent at the end of the 1400s and reworked in the ensuing century: the ancient *portal* in Istrian stone set into the facade is by Giuliano da Maiano; the church's belfry, visible from the cloister of the convent, is the same ancient tower that occurs in one of Leopardi's verses ("Passero Solitario"). Continuing up the flank of the church and turning right into Via Roma, we reach the church of *San Vito*, dating from the 11th century but remodeled several times and having a facade redesigned by Luigi Vanvitelli after the earthquake of 1741; in the *oratory* annexed to the church hangs a

Beniamino Gigli, world-famous tenor

With over 40 years of success all over the world, 61 operas performed, 300 recordings, 16 films made between 1935 and 1951, Beniamino Gigli holds his place alongside Caruso as the greatest tenor of the century. In the space of a few years Gigli passed from singing as choirboy in the cathedral of Recanati to being a star of opera, and obtained great acclaim in 1918 in Bologna and Milan with his interpretation of *Mefistofele* by Arrigo Boito. An almost mythical interpreter of *bel canto*, Gigli achieved recognition all around the globe, and for 12 consecutive seasons was engaged by the Metropolitan, New York. Spiritually tied to Recanati, the great Gigli had a villa built (60 rooms) at Porto Recanati, close to the sea, Loreto, and in "Leopardi" country. In honor of the tenor, Recanati has built a full-fledged museum, the only one of its kind in the history of opera music.

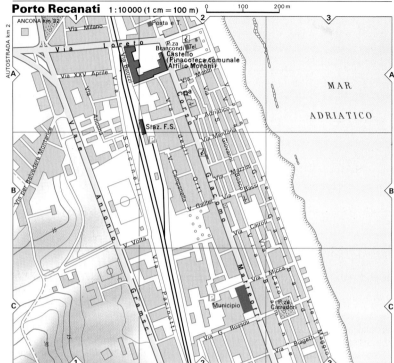

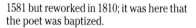

1581 but reworked in 1810; it was here that the poet was baptized.

From the square a signposted tour route flanks the right side of the building housing the *Centro Nazionale di Studi Leopardiani*, leading up to **Mt. Tabor** (C3). The hilltop, crowned by the former monastery of *Santo Stefano* of 15th-century origin, affords a magnificent view of the Potenza river valley and surrounding hills.

A pleasant walk of 2 km in the northwest direction leads to **Castelnuovo** (elev. 235 m; A1), a suburb of Recanati. On the edge of town stands *Santa Maria di Castelnuovo*, originally built in the Romanesque style, with a gabled facade and portal surmounted by a lunette adorned with reliefs (1253); the interiors, transformed in the 1800s, contain fragments of 15th-century frescoes.

Porto Recanati

Distributed along the coast a short distance from the mouth of the Potenza river, Porto Recanati owes its recent development to its long beach, which has made it one of the region's most frequent venues for tourism (see street plan above). Porto Recanati (elev. 6 km, pop. 8,514) continues as a major fishing town. It was established by Frederick II as the port of Recanati proper, a short distance from the site of the Roman colony *Potentia*, founded in 184 BC and de-

stroyed in the 5th century. The old **Castle** (A1-2), erected in the 15th century to ward off the continuous incursions of Turkish pirates, houses the *Pinacoteca Comunale "Attilio Moroni"* (visits on request, tel. 9799018, 7591283), which contains works by Rosso Fiorentino, Spagnoletto, Salvatore Rosa, Antonio Canova, and an important collection of Italian paintings from the 1800s, particularly those of the Macchiaioli group.

Continuing up the coast with its long white beaches the itinerary reaches Porto Potenza Picena (elev. 3 m), a tourist resort with some light industry.
In the 19th-century parish church, freely inspired upon Romanesque-Gothic form, hangs a large canvas by Pomarancio (*Madonna with Sts. Anne and James*); alongside the church rises a fine 17th-century *tower*, the only remains of a former fortress.

Potenza Picena

A mere 8 km from the sea, Potenza Picena was founded on a hilltop by refugees from the Roman colony of *Potentia* after the town's destruction in the 5th century, which was accompanied by the population's flight inland from the coast. Razed to the ground by order of Henry V in the year 1116, the burgh was rebuilt twelve years later at the behest of the bishop of Fermo, who called it Montesanto, a name it maintained through until 1862. Still enclosed in its defensive walls, the town (elev. 237 m, pop. 13,851) is known for its fine silk damask and brocades.

In the center of town, the reconstructed *Palazzo del Podestà* has conserved part of its original structure, though only the decoration around the central doorway; dating from the 19th century is the *Palazzo Municipale*. In Via Trento is the **Pinacoteca Comunale**, the public art gallery (open Wed 4pm–7.30pm; Sat 5pm–7.30pm), with paintings by Pomarancio, Simone De Magistris, Pietro Tedeschi, and Adolfo De Carolis.

Near the cemetery stands the church of the **Zoccolanti**, whose high altar is hung with a *Deposition* by Simone De Magistris, author also of the panel featuring a *Madonna and Saints* (1576) in the first chapel on the left; note on the left wall a small panel with a *Sacra Famiglia and the Young St. John Baptist*, by Santi di Tito.

Montelupone

Ancient defensive walls with look-out towers and gates enclose this small medieval burgh (elev. 272 m, pop. 3,107).

In the central square the 14th-century *Palazzo del Podestà* boasts a fine tower with Ghibelline crenelations; a short way off stands the rather unprepossessing church of *San Francesco*, dating from the mid-13th century.

Near the banks of the Potenza river, some 3.5 km out of town, rises *San Firmano*, part of an abbey erected in the 10th century by the Benedictine Order, which systematically reclaimed the land around this site. Rebuilt in the 13th century, the church has a superb lunette over the portal with a primitive-style *Crucifixion* stemming from the original building.

Montecassiano

Concentric streets converge on the central square of the burgh (elev. 215 m, pop. 6,153). According to local tradition, the place was founded by people who had fled the destruction of the ancient *Helvia Ricina*. At the entrance to the town is the oratory of *San Nicolò*, dating from the 13th century and having *frescoes* of the Umbro-Marchigian school (15th cent.). In the central square rises the 15th-century *Palazzo Municipale*. By means of steps one can ascend to the parish church of *Santa Maria Assunta* (apply to the Municipio, tel. 598135), built in the second half of the 1400s. In the aisled interior hangs a large *altarpiece* (1527) in glazed terracotta by Mattia della Robbia, and a panel by Giacomo da Recanati, the *Coronation of the Virgin* (15th cent.).

Montefano

The crenelated tower featured in the town's heraldic device is actually the one at the nearby castle of Montefiore, while the oak tree is a reminder of the welcome given to a member of the powerful Della Rovere family, who was refused hospitality at Osimo. Straddling the hilltop, Montefano (elev. 242, pop. 3,042) affords a view as far as the Sibillini mountains. The *Palazzo Municipale* (19th cent.) incorporates a fine 19th-century theater – one of the hidden treasures of the region – whose design is based on that of the Fenice in Venice.

At the town gates, on the road to Recanati, rises the imposing **Castle of Montefiore**, raised at the end of the 13th century by the people of Recanati as an outpost to defend their territories bordering with Osimo. Reworked in the 1400s and seriously damaged during World War II, the castle has long perimeter walls and a tall castle keep.

7.3 Tolentino and environs

Circular itinerary of 81 km *(see map on p. 134)*

Tolentino is the starting point for this circular itinerary, which meanders amid gentle hill slopes and broad valleys characterized by intensive agriculture. It is hard to imagine that these same territories were once malaria-ridden and uncultivated, but this was the scene that met the Cistercian monks who in the 12th century founded a large and important abbey. The monks were responsible for the general reclamation of the land, and the creation of the first fields of crops. To this day the area is a dense checker work of carefully tended fields amid the rolling hills.

Having visited the historic part of Tolentino and its imposing basilica, the itinerary continues in a northeast direction to the Val di Chienti, reaching the Rancia castle. At the station of Urbisaglia the route continues right and joins the SS78 Picena, which leads to Fiastra and then follows a turnoff toward the abbey of Fiastra (4.5 km) before leading off to Mogliano. After another 4 km it reaches Urbisaglia, where the remains of important Roman remains can be seen; from here the itinerary proceeds along the bed of the Fiastrella as far as Passo Sant'Angelo (13 km). By means of smaller in-

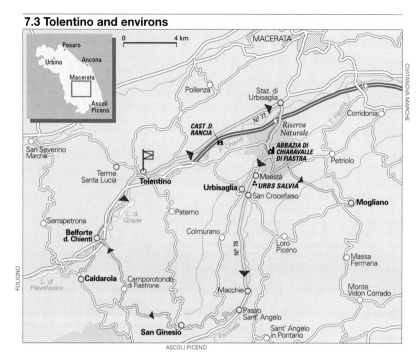

terior roads it reaches San Ginesio (7.5 km) and Caldarola (11.5 km), and after passing through Belforte and Chienti (4 km), the route returns to Tolentino (7 km).

Tolentino*

The precious frescoes in the basilica of San Nicola, the sarcophagus of St. Catervo in the cathedral, the Romanesque churches, the medieval houses, the stretches of ancient defensive walls: there are various attractions in the historic center of Tolentino (elev. 228, pop. 18,386), whose name is tied to that of a hermit, preacher, and thaumaturge who lived here for some thirty years and was already considered a saint before he died. To St. Nicholas is dedicated the vast basilica, one of the most important sanctuaries in central Italy. But Tolentino (see plan on p. 136) is also famous for an event in 1797 when Napoleon Bonaparte forced the pope to hand over both land and money for a battle in 1815 in which the Austrians crushed the troops of Joachim Murat. Also of local interest is the Biennale Internazionale dell'Umorismo nell'Arte, an international festival of humor held on alternate years. Situated in a strategic position in the Chienti river valley, the site has been inhabited from remote times; in the mid-14th century the Chienti was exploited for its

fast-flowing water to drive mills for tanning factories, the production of cloths, and other industrial activities. Even recent years have seen consistent growth in local activities such as the production of leather goods. As a result, in the 1950s the town's population increased substantially with the creation of numerous peripheral wards and the replacement of old buildings with modern constructions.

Piazza della Libertà (C2). Partly arcaded, the square is the hub of town and has marked the center of civic life ever since Roman times. Abutting the square are *Palazzo Sangallo*, attributed to Antonio da Sangallo the Younger (additional story added in 1932); and the *Palazzo Municipale*, rebuilt in the 1800s over the 4th-century public hall. On the northern flank of the square rises the characteristic *Torre dei Tre Orologi*, a tower built in the 1500s but heavily reworked in the 19th century.

The second story of the Palazzo Municipale houses the **Museo della Caricatura e dell'Umorismo nell'Arte** (open Mar & Fri 4pm–7pm; Sat & Sun 9.30am–12.30pm, 4pm–7pm) which, inaugurated in 1970, offers an overview of Italian and foreign humor, with many works donated by artists who have participated in this biennial event.

San Nicola** (C2-3). For thirty years, the Augustinian friar Nicholas was stationed here, where he died in 1305. The church itself dates from the 13th century, but was remodeled in the 14th and completed with the construction of the **portal*** in late Gothic style (1432, Nanni di Bartolo), set into the Baroque facade. The aisleless **interior** has a set of side chapels, a polygonal apse, and a coffered ceiling from 1628. In the first chapel on the right hangs a *St. Anne with an Angel** (1640) by Guercino; in the fourth hangs a *Madonna of Peace* by Giuseppe Lucatelli. At the end of the right wall one accesses the Gothic **chapel of St. Nicholas**, entirely decorated with a vast **cycle of frescoes**** by the Riminese school of the early 14th century, one of the highest expressions of Marchigian painting: in a double series of sections in the style of Giotto, the walls are painted with *Scenes from the Life and Miracles of the Saint* (lower register) and *Scenes from the Life of Jesus* (upper register) as a reminder that the friar lived in perfect imitation of Christ. At the center of the chapel stands the Renaissance *Arc of St. Nicholas* (1474) fashioned by a follower of Agostino di Duccio, above which stands a coeval *Statue of St. Nicholas* carved from Venetian stone. Adjacent is the **chapel of the SS. Braccia**, designed to accommodate the relics of the saint. The three intercommunicating chambers boast a sumptuous marble decorative program of statues and stuccoes that was not completed until the 19th century. From a doorway in the chapel a broad staircase descends to the *crypt*, built in 1932, where, below the original sepulcher, stands an urn in sculpted silver containing the relics of St. Nicholas.

From the steps to the crypt one accesses the **Museo dell'- Opera del Santuario** (open 9.30am–noon, 4pm–7pm) which exhibits paintings, detached frescoes, goldwork, and religious furnishings, early pieces of furniture, and liturgical items. Displayed on the right is a *collection of ceramics*, with early

Tolentino: portal of the basilica of San Nicola

pieces from Faenza, Savona, Deruta, Casteldelmonte, and Gubbio; together with examples of Japanese and Chinese pottery, 18th-century majolica from Pesaro, and some very rare examples of Moorish plates from Iberia. Among the works displayed in the museum, particularly worthy of note are the lunette with a *Pietà* by Vittore Crivelli; a *Madonna and Child with Sts. Simon and Liberato* by Simone De Magistris; and a wonderfully delicate *Reclining Madonna with Child**, a wooden statue of the Sienese school, early 14th century (though the figure of St. Joseph is perhaps from a little later). Also of interest is the ample collection of votive items left by devotees from the 15th to the 19th centuries.

From the chapel one reaches the **cloister**, created in the 13th–14th centuries (side adjacent to the church reworked in 1640–47). The walls and part of the vaults bear fresco decorations from 1689–90, painted over previous fresco work (of which traces remain here and there). A small doorway in the wall adjacent to the church provides access to the **saint's oratorio**, which is frescoed throughout. On the south side of the cloister stands a Romanesque portal with a handsome terracotta surround, formerly the entrance to the refectory.

Cathedral (B3). Founded in the early Middle Ages (8th–9th cent.) but extensively altered in the 1200s, and subsequently completely reworked round 1830, the cathedral is dedicated to St. Catervo, the patron saint of the city. Of the original Romanesque church, only the bell tower and the portal of the abbey church (side entrance) have survived. To the left of the presbytery lies the *chapel of St. Catervo* with two chambers: the second, in later Gothic style, is decorated with frescoes (early 14th cent.) by Francesco da Tolentino, and behind the altar, resting on four Romanesque lions, stands the huge **sarcophagus of Sts. Catervo, Settimia, and Basso*** (4th cent.), richly adorned with relief carvings.

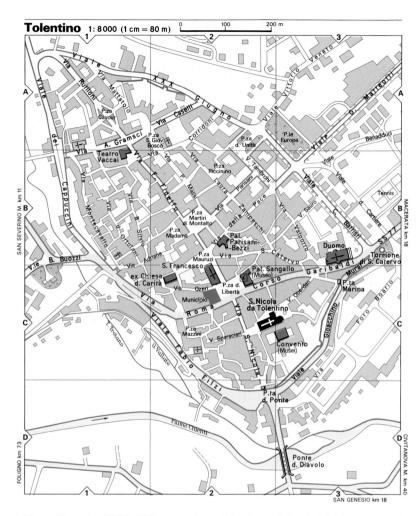

Tolentino 1 : 8 000 (1 cm = 80 m)

Piazza Mauruzi (B-C2). This square is reached by proceeding along Via Catervo past fine old buildings. On the left rises the church of **San Francesco**, built in the 13th century and remodeled in the 1700s. Of the original building, the present church has conserved the polygonal apse and, in the interior, a tall chapel with cross-vaults decorated with 14th-century *frescoes* (right of the presbytery); opposite the church stands the 16th-century *Palazzo Antici Mattei*, flanked by the older *Palazzo Mauruzi* (13th cent.). At the eastern end of the square stands the Romanesque church of the Carità (C2), which boasts an elegant coffered ceiling dating from the 15th century.

Palazzo Parisani Bezzi (B2). In the nearby Via della Pace 20 rises a building known also as the Palazzo della Pace, because it was here that Napoleon forced the hapless Pope Pius VI to sign a treaty, the so-called Peace of 136

Tolentino, which included the restitution of Avignon to France, together with the Venosino *contado* and the legations of Bologna, Ferrara, Ravenna, and Forlì. The building is now the seat of the *Museo Napoleonico* (visits on request, tel. 969797), and contains memorabilia and documents of the era.

Proceeding from Piazza Martiri di Montalto along Via Fidelio, the itinerary reaches the *Teatro "Nicola Vaccai"* (B1) designed in 1780–95 by Giuseppe Lucatelli.

On the road to San Severino Marche, 3.5 km northwest of Tolentino, lies the thermal spa of Santa Lucia, with a hotel and treatment center set in a magnificent oak grove. The center makes use of the local water, which is sulfur-rich with traces of alkaline bicarbonate; the water is taken from three different sources.

The Rancia Castle*

The four-sided castle stands alone, not far from the motorway. The original building was a fortified farmstead belonging to the Fiastra abbey (end 12th cent.), and was transformed into a castle in 1353–57 for the Da Varano, lords of Camerino (visits on request, tel. 973349). Of the many armed clashes that took place in the vicinity of the castle, the most important was the so-called Battle of Tolentino (2–3 May 1815), in which Joachim Murat's troops were crushed by the Austrian army.

The Abbey of Chiaravalle di Fiastra*

It was the Cistercian monks of Clairvaux who founded this abbey in 1142, dedicating their time to reclaiming the surrounding terrain, which was marshy and untilled. For three centuries the abbey was a crucial religious center with over 200 monks. Devastated in 1422 by mercenaries in the employ of the indomitable *condottiere* Braccio da Montone, the abbey fell into swift decline; in 1581 it passed to the Jesuits, who kept it until the eventual suppression of the order in 1773. It was then bought by the marquises Bandini of Camerino, who transformed a section of it for residential use. Recently restored, the building is once again occupied by monks, and can be visited every day, 9.30am–12.30pm, 3.30pm–6.30pm; Mon only afternoons (see plan below).

A classic example of Cistercian architecture, the church has a simple facade set with a portico having curved entrance steps. The grandiose aisled interior boasts remains of the early pictorial program; the frescoes in the square tribune date to 1473 (*Crucifixion with Sts. Benedict and Bernard*). Attached to the church, the monastery was built on a standard Cistercian plan around a *cloister* (15th cent.); from here one can enter the *Sala Capitolare* and the *Refectory*, whose vaulted roof rests on seven Roman columns salvaged from the ruins of the ancient colony of *Urbs Salvia*.

The abbey and its surrounding property lie within the "Abbadia di Fiastra" nature reserve,

Abbey of Chiaravalle di Fiastra

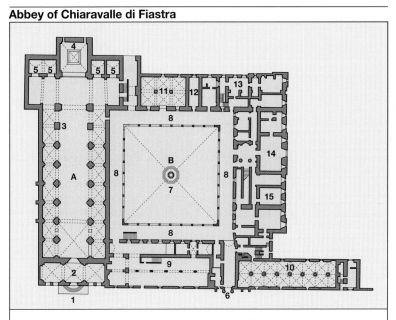

(A) the church
1 Entrance
2 Narthex
3 Fresco representing Virgin and Child
4 Frescoed apse
5 Chapels

(B) the monastery
6 Entrance
7 Cloister
8 Deambulatory
9 Cellarium
10 Refectory
11 Chapter hall
12 Auditorium
13 Scriptorium
14 Oil press room (exhibition)
15 Kitchen

The *carte* and the *selva*

The abbey complex of Santa Maria di Chiaravalle (see photo) is a rare example of cultural amalgamation. Set in the countryside, which over the years was reclaimed by the Cistercians, the architecture of the abbey has largely respected the original layout. Marble quarries nearby bear witness to the Roman *Urbs Salvia*. Over three thousand parchments ("Carte fiastrense," now in the Vatican) sanction the long-standing identity of the monastery and the history of the environs. A more concrete witness to the past is the Rancia castle, once the fortified granary for the monastery. In the southern section of the monastery is installed the Fondazione Giustiniani-Bandini, which continues its original activity as a center for the promotion of agrarian studies. While the interiors of this building are neoclassical in form, the facade is a wholly unusual application of "English" neo-Palladianism. Contact with the English stems from the supply of oak for boat-building.

on request, tel. 556058), with canvases and paintings removed from other churches in the vicinity.

Near the banks of the Ete Morto river, 4.5 km to the east, rises the *Crocifisso* (visits on request, tel. 556147), a Renaissance temple boasting a fresco dating from the 16th century.
Once back on the state road, at *Maestà* (elev. 213 m), the road reaches the small **church of the Maestà**, constructed at the beginning of the 15th century on the remains of a Roman building (see ruin along left flank); the interiors contain some interesting *votive frescoes* which once covered all the walls.

Urbisaglia

The defensive walls that still encircle most of the burgh were built over the ruins of the Roman colony of *Urbs Salvia*, an early,

where numerous species of animals and plants enjoy special protection; the park was set up in 1984 and covers an area of 1,800 hectares. Annexed to the reserve, in thick woodland covering over 100 hectares, is the *Museo Naturalistico* (visits on request, tel. 202942), which boasts an ornithological collection of 500 examples of native Italian birds. The *Museo della Civiltà Contadina*, a small museum of country customs and lifestyles, offers an exhibition of working equipment and tools relative to traditional agricultural techniques, testifying to the vital contribution of the monks in reclaiming this unyielding terrain.

Mogliano

A few remnants of old walls surround the town of Mogliano (elev. 313, pop. 4,761), including the ancient bulwarks of the original *rocca*, or fortress, can still be seen. The church of *Santa Maria Assunta* at the end of Via Roma contains an important work by Lorenzo Lotto, the *Our Lady of the Assumption with Saints**, signed and dated 1548. Beside the church stands a small *Museo Parrocchiale* (visits

powerful town that was laid waste by the Visigoth commander Alaric in 409–10. From its dominant position overlooking the Fiastra valley, Urbisaglia (elev. 310, pop. 2,665) has kept its imposing *rocca*, or fortress, built in the 14th–15th centuries. Nearby stands the collegiate church of *San Lorenzo*, erected at the end of the 18th century and restructured in 1925; inside is a fine *triptych* of 1507 by Stefano Folchetti. Along the main street rises the church of the *SS. Addolorata*, of 15th-century origin; recent restoration work inside the church has brought to light fragments of frescoes dating to the 15th and 16th centuries. Archaeological testaments to ancient *Urbs Salvia* are arranged in the *Museo Archeological Statale* (visits Fri–Sun 8am–2pm).

An important reminder of the Roman aqueduct that ran the crest of the hill is a huge *cistern* on the northern border of the town; the cistern comprises two long chambers and has a storage capacity of around 100 cubic meters.

The Archaeological Area of *Urbs Salvia*

More substantial vestiges of the ancient Roman settlement of *Urbs Salvia* are found in the archaeological site to the northeast of the present town (open Tue, Wed, & Thu 9am–1pm). In good condition is the *amphitheater*, built in the second half of the 2nd century; a little further on excavations have revealed a *cryptoporticus* dating to midway through the 1st century, with fragments in the 3rd Pompeiian style. Just before the crown of the hill, stands the Roman **theater***, built around the end of the 1st century, and considered to be the most significant archaeological monument of the entire region. Southeast of the theater is a brick building with five alcoves and arcading, which offered picturesque linkage between the various levels of the settlement.

Macchie (elev. 312 m) stands the church of Santa Maria delle Macchie (visits on request, tel. 663131), dating to before the 11th century and formerly belonging to a Benedictine abbey. A few remains of the Romanesque original can be seen, along with an interesting *crypt* on seven small aisles.

San Ginesio*

The Adriatic and Mt. Conero, the Sibillini mountains and the famous Gran Sasso: the view afforded by this burgh (elev. 680 m, pop. 3,912) perched on a hill to the left of Fenestrella valley. The town's layout is of medieval origin, enclosed in a broad ring of crenelated *defensive walls** (14th–15th cent.) and equipped with watch towers and bulwarks. Near the 14th-century *Porta Picena* stands the San Paolo hospital, built as a way station for the assistance of pilgrims bound for Rome or Loreto. This rustic building erected in the 13th century, boasts an arcaded front with low columns and a 15th-century loggia.

The Collegiate Church*. In the central square of San Ginesio rises the Collegiata, a Romanesque construction with a late Gothic facade of Germanic taste (1421). In the interior numerous worthy works of art can be admired: in the entrance wall an aedicule by Stefano Folchetti (*Madonna and Saints*, early 16th cent.) and a *Madonna and Child with Patron Saint* by the school of Perugino; along the right aisle are chapels hung with canvases by Federico Zuccari, Pomarancio, and Simone De Magistris; on the walls, a *Madonna del Popolo* by Pietro Alemanno (signed and dated 1485), and a *Madonna of the Rosary* by Si-

mone De Magistris. Embellishing the **crypt*** are frescoes by Lorenzo Salimbeni, signed and dated 1406.

Museo Civico "Scipione Gentili" (open Jul–Aug 11am–1pm, 4.30pm–6.30pm; Sun, and other months, on request, tel. 656072). Installed in the former temple of *San Sebastiano* (14th century), the public museum houses paintings spanning the 15th to 18th centuries, including two panels by Stefano Folchetti; a *Pietà* by Simone De Magistris; a *Madonna and Saints* by Vincenzo Pagani. The painting of *St. Andrew* (mid-15th cent.), known also as the *Battle between Sts. Genesius and Fermo* (1377), is particularly interesting for its links with the history of the town of San Ginesio.

A short distance from the central square rises the church of San Francesco, which has retained its original 13th-century portal and apse. Inside, reworked in Neoclassical style, one can see remnants of several 14th–15th-century *frescoes* of the Riminese-Marchigian school. The adjacent *convent*, now the seat of the municipal council, accommodates on its first floor a special section of the Museo Civico reserved for modern and contemporary works.

Caldarola

The name of this locality (elev. 314 m, pop. 1,608), the birthplace of the De Magistris family of artists, refers to ancient thermal sources that had already disappeared by the 16th century. In the *Palazzo Municipale*, a former patrician residence, is the *Stanza del Paradiso*, decorated by the De Magistris family (16th cent.); in the *collegiate church* next door are paintings and statues by the Marchigian school of the 15th and 16th centuries; and a 16th-century *Crucifix*. Via De Magistris leads to the *Castello Pallotta* (open Apr–Sep 10am–12.30pm, 3.30pm–6.30pm; Oct–Mar 10am–noon, 2.30pm–5.30pm); the building is mentioned in documents of 785. The most significant alterations date to the end of the 1500s, when the building was transformed from a military seat to an elegant summer residence. The rooms were frescoed throughout by the Caldarolese painters De Magistris.

Belforte del Chienti

With its steep, winding streets this ancient township (elev. 347 m, pop. 1,931) poised on the hill that overlooks the Chienti valley is still enclosed within its original 14th-century *defensive walls* (partially rebuilt in the 1700s); in the parish church of *Sant'Eustachio* hangs a magnificent **polyptych*** by Giovanni Boccati, dated 1468.

8 The Piceno and the Sibillini mountains

Profile of the area

From the banks of the Sibillini hills to the hillside formations of the sandstone and soft clay, cut through with deep, weathered gullies stretching as far as the terraces of sand and gravel along the coast itself. Hills and valleys were divided according to a system of sharecropping, with small tracts of farmland and scattered settlements on rustic estates bordered by clumps of trees; the woodland and historical forestry reached as far as the highland terrain. The landscape afforded by the province of Piceno is the fruit of a long cultural process: the *vici* and *paghi* of the high-

land Picenes were gradually amalgamated by the lowland Roman settlements, but the dispersion of the population in the early Middle Ages generated a spread of villages occupied by the Picene population. The lands was thus divided into *castra*, *plebes*, *cellae*, and *monasteria*. The feudal estates were represented by the abbey of Farfa, the bishops of Ascoli Piceno and Fermo, the Empire, and the nobility of Longobard and Frankish origin. With the onset of fortification, the feudal nobility moved

Fishing boats at San Benedetto del Tronto

to the towns: the towers that rise in Ascoli Piceno bear witness to the wealthy families vying for ascendancy within the city walls. The Age of Communes saw a reshuffle of power between the bishop, the non-religious *podestà*, the public magistrates, and the Captain of the People). The more important communes, armed against each other, continued to pursue a policy of expansion. The two main centers Ascoli Piceno and Fermo thwarted the others with their strong territorial role. In the 15th century, after the failure of Francesco Sforza's expansionist drive, the Papal States moved in, fortifying their possessions (16th–18th cent.). From the 16th to 19th centuries the papacy carried out planning works which fortunately left the town's basic layout untouched. In the 1900s, however, there was a population drift toward the coast, which soon represented the front line of demographic growth and productivity.

8.1 Ascoli Piceno and environs

Itinerary from Piazza Arringo *(see plan on pp. 142–143)*

Houses, palazzi, ancient towers, and churches, all built in warm travertine stone: the district capital with its close-knit medieval urban fabric offers the visitor a host of interesting features. In addition to the magnificence of the main square, there are also medieval streets, noble patrician palaces, and museums full of masterpieces of art. For the walking tour of the town, the itinerary takes a route that begins in Piazza Arringo and the nearby Pi-

azza del Popolo, an elegant *salotto* for the local inhabitants. After visiting the church of San Francesco, down Via Trivio the route leads off in the direction of the Tronto river as far as Piazza Ventidio Basso, and then continues down Via Solestà to the Roman bridge of the same name; from here the itinerary takes us as far as Piazza Cecco d'Ascoli near Porta Gemina, a city gate of Roman origin. We then continue up Corso Mazzini to climb the panoramic hill of the Annunziata. Once the city itself has been toured, there are several brief excursions to sights in the surrounding area. The first takes us to the church of Sant'Emidio alle Grotte, which is reached in around 30 minutes from the Ponte Nuovo. Recommended from the point of view of landscape beauty and the exceptional view over the district is the hill of San Marco, 11.5 km south of the city. The third outing involves a 6-km drive to the diminutive burgh of Castel Trosino, perched like a medieval castle on a rocky outcrop.

Ascoli Piceno**

Despite modern building programs, the historic center has conserved its long avenues and tight streets of distinctly medieval flavor that were built over the original Roman causeways. The warm hues of the travertine stone predominate throughout the historic center, cradled on a flattish terrace at the confluence of the Castellano and Tronto rivers. The site was chosen by the early Picenes for its strategic position. Various traces of the original Roman town, *Asculum Picenum*, are visible; these remnants are usually encased in medieval buildings, but it is the splendid Romanesque architecture that gives Ascoli Piceno (elev. 154 m, pop. 52,852) its distinctive character, together with its churches and powerful patrician towers, of which there were once around 200. For elegant Renaissance buildings, one of the chief architects was Cola dell'Amatrice, responsible for the facade of the cathedral.

Piazza Arringo* (B2-3). Built over the Roman forum, throughout the Middle Ages the square hosted public gatherings (the name comes from the "haranging" speeches made by the orators). It is bordered by historical buildings of varying periods and styles, including the cathedral (B3), dedicated to Emidius, a Christian martyr and patron saint of the city, whose relics are kept in a Roman sarcophagus in the crypt of the cathedral. Reconstructed at the end of the 15th century over an early medieval building, and having an unfinished 16th-century facade, the cathedral contains various important works of art. Over the altar of the chapel of the Holy Sacrament (right aisle) is a 14th-century altar frontal in silver, and a large **polyptych**** by Carlo Crivelli, signed and dated 1473, which is widely held to be one of the artist's finest works. To the left of the cathedral stands the **baptistery*** (12th

cent.), an octagonal building on a square plan, built over a Roman temple.

The longer side of the piazza is occupied by the Baroque facade of the **Palazzo Comunale**, a 17th–18th-century reworking of two buildings combined – the Palazzo del Comune and the Palazzo dell'Arengo (housing the Pinacoteca Civica, see below). The neighboring **Palazzo Vescovile** (B2-3) is a compilation of three buildings spanning the 15th to 18th centuries; this houses the *Museo Diocesano* (open Tue & Sat 10am–noon), containing a lavish collection of religious art, including frescoes and paintings of early masters (Pietro Alemanno, Cola dell'Amatrice, Ludovico Trasi), plus sculptures dating from the 14th to 17th centuries. On the opposite side of the square rises the unmistakable 17th-century facade of the *Palazzo Panichi*, now the home of the **Museo Archeologico Statale** (open 9am–7pm; Sun 9am–1pm; closed Mon), which boasts a collection of prehistoric finds and Roman remains.

Behind the baptistery runs Via dei Bonaparte, where at no. 24 stands the 16th-century **Palazzo Bonaparte** (B3), an interesting example of local Renaissance architecture. Alongside the building are two fascinating 15th-century *houses*.

Pinacoteca Civica*. Arranged on the *piano nobile* of the Palazzo Comunale (open Oct–May 9am–1pm; Jun & Sep 9am–1pm, 4pm–7.30pm), the museum was set up in 1861 upon the suppression of the religious orders, and was steadily enlarged with bequests and acquisitions. Among the early masters represented are Cola dell'Amatrice, Vincenzo Pagani, and Pietro Alemanno with *panels* and *polyptychs**. The picture gallery possesses three works by Carlo Crivelli: a panel with a **Madonna and Child***; a triptych featuring a *Madonna and Child with St. Lucy and Patrons*; another *triptych*, badly worn, with the image of St. James of the Marche, perhaps a true likeness of the Franciscan preacher, who died in 1476 and whom Crivelli knew personally. Other artists represented are Simone De Magistris, Carlo Allegretti, Luca Giordano, Titian (*St. Francis Receives the Stigmata**, 1561); Guido Reni (*Annunciation**); Sebastiano Conca, Orazio De Ferrari, Carlo Maratta, and Guercino. Of outstanding workmanship is the *Cope of Nicholas IV**, a 13th-century English work donated to the pope in the cathedral of Ascoli in 1288. The section dedicated to Italian painters and sculptors of the 1800s and 1900s includes works by Filippo Palizzi, Domenico

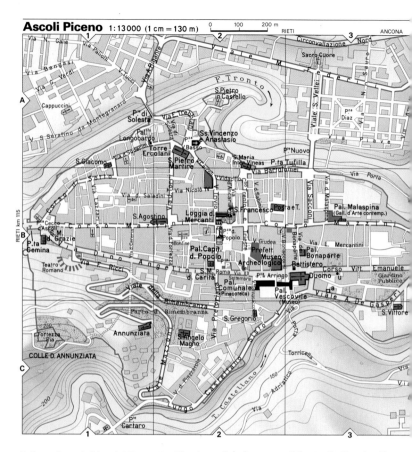

Induno, Antonio Mancini, Domenico Morelli, Giuseppe Pellizza, and Ettore Ximenes.

Other works by Italian painters of the 1800s and 1900s, particularly those of local extraction, are hung on the second floor of the building, where a collection of religious works gathered up from district churches has been organized (altarpieces, furnishings, and liturgical items). A special area has been set aside for the *Raccolta Pasqualini*, a collection of musical instruments and tools and equipment used by violin-makers.

Piazza del Popolo** (B2). With its enchanting arcaded buildings, the square provides a sort of public "living room" for the inhabitants. One of the longer sides is interrupted by the severe facade of the building raised for the **Captain of the People***, a fine 13th-century construction repeatedly modified over the centuries; the seat of the commune from 1400 to 1564, it still boasts the original tower and entrance portal of 1549; the arcaded and loggias of the courtyard is Renaissance. On the same side of the square stands the *Caffè Meletti*, a much-frequented meeting place in the

142

style known as Liberty (Italian Art Nouveau). At the northern end of the square rises San Francesco, alongside which stands the **Loggia dei Mercanti**, an elegant construction dating from 1513, with five arches; next to the loggia is the side *portal* of the church, surmounted by a *Monument to Pope Julius II* (1506).

In the basement of the captain's palace traces of Roman remains have revealed four successive phases of construction. Among the earliest constructions, from the Republican era, the structure of two dwellings are still discernible.

San Francesco* (B2). The church of San Francesco – which was begun in the Gothic style in the mid-13th century and only finished three centuries later – has a late-14th-century facade in the Abruzzo style; note the apse section, with its lively perspective effects. The *interiors*, restored to their original form in the 1800s, incude a crossing dome and seven beautifully ribbed apses.

Alongside the left flank of the church and preceded by a 14th-century porch is the Chiostro

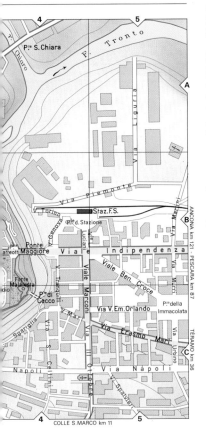

On the same street, opposite the main cloister is the Teatro Ventidio Basso, built to designs by Ireneo Aleandri in 184–46.

Santa Maria inter Vineas (A-B2). This Romanesque 13th-century church was partly rebuilt in 1954. The interior boasts *frescoes* dating from the 13th–14th centuries. On the entrance wall is a *funerary monument* of 1482, whose vault's figures may be the work of Pietro Alemanno, author of the *Virgin Annunciate* to the right of the entrance. On the high altar stands a wood 16th-century *Crucifix*. Close by, near the *Ponte Nuovo* (1911) over the Tronto river, stands the **Porta Tufilla** (A3), built in 1553.

SS. Vincenzo e Anastasio* (A2). This Romanesque church was erected in the 11th century and enlarged in 1389, with a facade* divided into sections that originally bore frescoes, and a portal dating to the early 15th century. The nave of the aisled *interior* belongs to the original structure; perpendicular to the main vessel is the *crypt*, an ancient underground cell dating to the 6th century. Converging on the square are various streets, Via Torri, Solestà, and Solderini (see below); here stands the church of **San Pietro Martire**, whose construction was begun in 1280 and completed only in the first half of the 14th century; the portal on the left flank (1523) is attributed to Cola dell'Amatrice.

Maggiore, or main cloister, built between 1565 and 1623 and now adapted for use as the market. Through an opening in the end wall one accesses the smaller of the cloisters (15th cent.), with its broad arcades and harmonious loggia.

Lined with towers and medieval houses remodeled in the 1500s is **Via Solestà*** which conspires with the neighboring streets to form an authentic medieval setting, and leads down

Bell-towers in the center of Ascoli Piceno

143

to the Roman bridge of the same name (A1), which dates to the first decades of the Empire, and is preceded by a 13th-century gateway and two medieval towers.

Via Solderini* (A1-2). One of the ancient town's main thoroughfares, this street is lined with medieval and Renaissance houses, some with Baroque floors built above, all of noble design. On the right rises the *Torre Ercolani* (11th–12th cent.), the best-conserved of the numerous patrician towers in Ascoli. Adjacent to this is the coeval *Palazzo Longobardo*, with a story of small two-light windows. Further on, in a small square, stands the church of *San Giacomo* (A1), erected in the 12th–14th centuries.

Piazza Cecco d'Ascoli (B1). The square is bordered by the **Porta Gemina** (1st cent. BC), the city gateway by which Via Salaria once led into the town. Alongside the gate one can still see a section of the old walls dating to the 3rd–2nd century BC. The church of *Santa Maria delle Grazie*, whose present conformation is the result of renovations carried out in 1780, is known as the *Santuario del SS. Crocifisso* owing to the venerated wood *Crucifix* dating to the second half of the 1500s.

In the nearby Via Ricci are the remains of the **Roman theater** (early Republican; B1), and was enlarged in the 1st century AD; only the radials of the cavea, or bleachers, are visible, however. Probably destroyed by the Longobards in 578, the construction was plundered for its material, which was reused for the construction of medieval buildings in the town.

Corso Mazzini (B1-3). At no. 39 of this long, straight avenue that crosses right through the town stands the *Museo di Storia Naturale*

Ascoli Piceno: the remains of the Roman theater

"Antonio Orsini" (open 9am–1pm; Tue & Thu also 3pm–6pm; Sat & Sun on request), which boasts an extensive collection of geological and naturalistic exhibits. Abutting the street is **Sant'Agostino** (B1-2), raised in

the 12th century and remodeled between 1317 and 1381, then enlarged in the mid-1400s; the 16th-century facade pays homage to the Romanesque style. Inside, on the right aisle, hangs a 14th-century panel featuring the *Madonna of Humility*; on the wall of the left aisle is a fragment of a fresco of *Christ Bearing the Cross* attributed to Cola dell'Amatrice.

Colle dell'Annunziata (C1-2). Lined with buildings dating from medieval times to the 1700s, the street leads from Piazza Roma along the characteristic *Via Pretoriana*; fronting the square is **Santa Maria della Carità**, B2, begun in 1532 to designs by Cola dell'Amatrice and completed around the end of the 17th century. Occupying a panoramic position on the hill is the former **convent of the Annunziata** (C1), once a hospital, upkept by the Observants Minors from 1482 to 1861. The complex comprises two *cloisters* (the larger of which is 14th century, the smaller from the following century) and the *church* itself, 1485–1505; in the refectory is a large fresco by Cola dell'Amatrice of the *Road to Calvary*, dated 1519. Just below the little square in front of the church are a series of important Roman remains known as the *Grotte dell'Annunziata*, thought to be the substructure of a colossal building. Along Via Barro our route climbs to the *Ospedale Civile*, which occupies the ancient convent complex, of which remains the church of Sant'Angelo Magno (C2), founded in 1292.

At the highest point of the hill, overshadowing the Castellano river, rises the Fortezza Pia (C1), built in 1540–43 on a site already fortified in Picene-Sabine times; the church was erected at the behest of Pius IV and to designs by Antonio da Sangallo the Younger. All that remains of the defensive complex are the walls on the north side and the eastern bulwarks.

San Gregorio (C2). A short distance from the Palazzo Comunale stands a small 13th-century Romanesque church which incorporates the remains of a Roman temple dating to the 1st century BC. The simple facade is graced with two Corinthian columns; vestiges of outer walls can be seen along the church's flanks. The interior, having traces of 14th-century *frescoes* in the small absidiole, comprises the original Roman *cella*.

The towns on stage

The "stage sets" provided by the intact architecture of Ascoli Piceno and Fermo are host to two yearly pageants: the Quintana jousting competition, and the Palio, or horse-race, in honor of the Madonna of the Assumption. The Quintana in Ascoli is a typical Renaissance contest in which the rider is associated with the Saracens of yore, in honor of St. Emidius, whose relics lie in the crypt of the cathedral. The saint reached Ascoli Piceno up the so-called Salaria way, perhaps built by the Picenes from Lazio; thence he continued up the *via publica*. On the feast-day of St. Emidius, celebrations are held for the origin of Ascoli Piceno, which was spared by Alaric because of its strategic position. But in the Middle Ages the town's various quarters developed, forever disputing the *palio*. The Cavalcata dell'Assunta, patron saint of Fermo, consists of a splendid procession from the church of Santa Lucia up to the hills, as far as Piazza Girfalco, which affords a glimpse of Fermo's *forma urbis*. The *palio* won by the horseman was supplied by the castle of Monterubbiano, as stipulated in peace agreements with Fermo, dating from 1182.

San Vittore (C3). Erected in the 12th or early 13th century, this church fronts Viale De Gasperi with its asymmetrical facade; inside are remains of important *frescoes* of the 13th and 14th centuries. At the end of Corso Vittorio Emanuele lies **Piazza Matteotti** (B4) in the vicinity of the reconstructed *Ponte Maggiore* over the Castellano river. From here one can make out the *Forte Malatesta* and the relics of a Roman bridge, traditionally called the *Ponte di Cecco* (C4) owing to a local tale by which Cecco d'Ascoli built the bridge in a single night with the help of the Devil. Cecco, a poet, physician, and astrologist, was tried for heresy and burnt at the stake in Florence in 1327.

Palazzo Malaspina* (B3). At the eastern end of Corso Mazzini, this palazzo is a 16th-century construction obtained by joining various 14th-century buildings, and has a striking loggia along the front articulated by a series of trunk-like columns. Today, the rooms on the *piano nobile* host the **Galleria d'Arte Contemporanea** (open 9am–1pom, 16 Jun–15 Sep also 4pm–7pm; closed Mon and winter, and Sat afternoon in summer); the gallery vaunts a collection of works that cover the artistic currents of the Italian Novecento, with a section devoted to the graphic works of contemporary Italian artists. Corso Mazzini, which leads into Piazza del Popolo, is lined with handsome 18th-century palazzi, most of which were built over earlier fabric.

Sant'Emidio alle Grotte
The church is built against the hill, a 30-minute walk from the Ponte Nuovo along Viale Federici. The site in which the church rises has historical ties to the early propagation of Christianity in Ascoli, because the grottoes of the church's title accommodated the burials of the Christians, and also the remains of St. Emidius, the town's first bishop, martyred in 309. Built in 1717–21 as a votive offering by those who survived the earthquake of 1703, the church is held to be the masterpiece of Giuseppe Giosafatti, who devised an elegant Baroque frontage in travertine on two orders, preceded by an elliptical vestibule; the interior (visits on request, tel. 257946) has been accommodated in a natural grotto or cave in the soft tufa rock face, whence the church's name, "alle Grotte."

The San Marco hill

The so-called hill of San Marco (elev. 694 m) is a plateau that looks out across the Piceno area like a balcony. Amid groves of fine chestnut trees, oaks, and conifers, the drive leads up gently to afford a broad view* of the Tronto valley. From the hilltop, with its excellent catering and sports facilities, the road continues up 6 km to San Giacomo (elev. 1,105 m), a small ski resort on the Marche-Abruzzo border.

Castel Trosino

In the valley of the Castellano river, some 6 km south of Ascoli, this little burgh (elev.

418 m) ensconced in oak and beech woods is a small medieval settlement bearing remains of the original defensive walls and access gates. At the center of town is a building of medieval construction, the *Palazzo di Re Manfrì*, so-called because local legend has it that this was the residence of Emperor Frederick II's son Manfred.

Not far from the town, at the end of the 19th century an important *Lombard burial ground* was brought to light, consisting of 209 tombs with rich funerary goods and personal items in gold, silver, and amber, most of which is now stored in the Museo Archeologico Statale in Ascoli, and the rest in the Museo dell'Alto Medioevo in Rome.

8.2 From the Tronto valley to the coast
Itinerary from Ascoli Piceno to San Benedetto del Tronto, 70 km

From the district capital to the long, welcoming beaches of the Adriatic Sea, this itinerary takes us away from the small industrial towns of the Tronto river valley, and climbs panoramic hills cultivated with vineyards for the production of well-known local wines. Few kilometers separate Offida, Acquaviva Picena, and Ripatransone from the sea; but in these highland coastal towns the atmosphere is quite different, with silent, medieval streets. The final goal of the itinerary is the seaside resort of San Benedetto del Tronto, one of the Marche's most renowned beaches.

Crossing through the new built-up areas of Ascoli, we leave the town for the Salaria road (SS4) which runs along the bed of the Tronto, for stretches duplicated by the Ascoli-Mare highway. Once past Villa Sant'Antonio (13 km), we take a left along the road that leads to Offida (11 km): from here the itinerary continues its path along the crest of the spur separating the Tesino and Tronto valleys. At Acquaviva Picena (13 km) and Ripatransone (10 km), the road descends scenically a further 13 km to Grottammare, straddling the A14 motorway. Rather like a long foreshore av-

8.2 From the Tronto valley to the coast

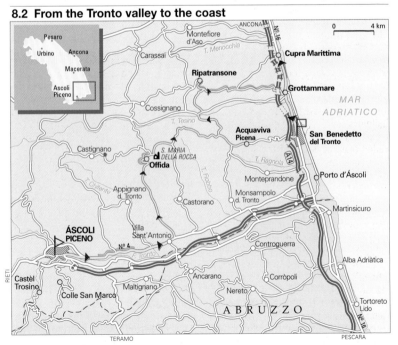

enue, the Adriatica state road reaches Cupramarittima (4 km), and, in the south, San Benedetto del Tronto (4.5 km), an elegant summer tourist resort and the "finishing line" of our itinerary.

Offida

The ancient tradition of pillow lace has long been the pride of the women of Offida, where for generations the art of casting and braiding with subtle fingers using the little wooden bobbins has been a specialty of the town. The crucial moment of the carnival held in Offida each

Lacemaking in Offida

year is the ox chase (actually, now a man dressed up, but until 1819 the animal was real!) which tears madly through the streets of the town. Offida (elev. 293, pop. 5,319) is an ancient burgh set in beautiful landscape of gentle hills between Tesino and Tronto, with small industries and wine-cellars producing DOC wines from vines grown on the Picene hillside.

The broad panorama that greets one at the entrance to Offida boasts the 15th-century **Rocca** (begun by Baccio Pontelli) at whose foot stands the *Monument to the Lacemakers*, fashioned in bronze in 1983. The social hub of the town is *Piazza Vittorio Emanuele II*, where the main public buildings stand. The finest of these is perhaps the **Palazzo Comunale***, with its arcaded main prospect of tall arcades on brick columns, an elegant loggia, and sturdy 14th-century tower. The building is home to the *Museo Archeologico "Guglielmo Allevi"* (open 9.30am–12.30pm, 3.30pm–7.30pm); the collection includes finds from the Paleolithic period, together with evidence of Picene and Roman culture; complementing this section is the small *Pinacoteca Civica*, which possesses a fine *St. Lucy* by Pietro Alemanno, and a signed work by Simone De Magistris (*The Three Kingdoms*, 1590). Inside the Palazzo Comunale is the **Teatro Serpente Aureo**, begun in 1820; also looking onto the central square is the *Collegiata Nuova*, built in

the 18th century to designs by Lazzaro Giosafatti. Via Cabattoni leads to the sanctuary of **Sant'Agostino**, an imposing brick structure of the 14th–15th centuries, largely rebuilt in the 1600s: within hangs a splendid 17th-century *Adoration of the Magi* by Carlo Allegretti (1st altar on right).

Just outside the built-up area stands the church of **Santa Maria della Rocca***, an imposing Romanesque-Gothic building with terracotta details (14th cent.) an unadorned facade, tall sides and lofty polygonal apses*; a 14th-century portal sculpted in travertine leads into the suggestive **crypt**, where *frescoes** of the 14th century can be admired, attributed to the Maestro di Offida, who was also responsible for the frescoes in the upper church.

Acquaviva Picena

Dominated by an imposing fort, Acquaviva (elev. 359, pop. 3,197) has conserved its medieval character, together with sections of the old defensive walls, ancient houses, and scattered towers. In the oldest part of town, the church of *San Rocco* has a Romanesque facade and flanks adorned with friezes. Well conserved is the **Rocca***, a fort begun in the 14th century and continued in the next by Baccio Pontelli; today the fort contains the *Museo delle Armi Antiche* (open Nov–Apr, Sat & Sun, 10.30am–12.30pm and 3.30pm–6pm; May–mid-June, and mid-Sep–Oct 4.20pm; mid-June to mid-Sep 10.30am–12.30pm and 4pm–8pm); the castle terraces offer a splendid view*.

Ripatransone*

The town's commanding position on the crest of a hill has earned it the title of the "belvedere" of the Piceno, Ripatransone (elev. 404 m, pop. 4,329) has managed to conserve its many medieval streets and houses from the 15th and 16th centuries. The **Cathedral**, raised in 1597, harbors art works from the 1600s, including a *St. Charles* attributed to Guercino. Also looking onto the square are the *Episcopio*, together with a 16th-century building with loggia, thought to have been the residence of Ascanio Condivi, the disciple and biographer of Michelangelo. The true heart of the town is Piazza XX Settembre, overlooked by the **Palazzo del Podestà**, which was raised in 1304 and enlarged in the 1800s (the building now hosts the *Teatro "Luigi Mercantini"*). Opposite rises the **Palazzo Comunale**, containing the *Archivio Comunale*, with manuscripts dating from as long ago as 1216, together with the early statutes of the commune; also here

147

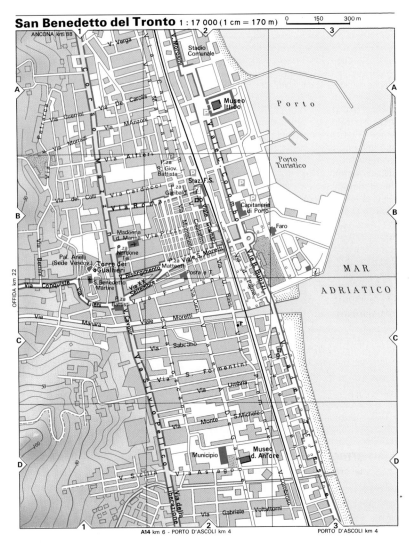

San Benedetto del Tronto 1 : 17 000 (1 cm = 170 m)

are the *Biblioteca Comunale* and the *Museo Archeologico* (open 9am–1pm and 3pm–7pm) housing archaeological finds from the Picene period, plus material of Hellenistic-Roman origin, and a collection of ceramics from Etruscan, Italiot, and Apulian sites. The 17th-century *Palazzo Bonomi-Gera* in the central Corso Vittorio Emanuele houses the **Gipsoteca "Uno Gera"** (open on request to the Museo Archeologico) featuring over a hundred casts by the Ripa-born artist Gera; here too is the **Pinacoteca Civica** (open 9am–1pm and 3pm–7pm; Sun 9.30am–12.30pm and 3pm–7pm), founded in 1877 and greatly expanded with the bequest of the entire collection of art works of the sculptor himself. Among the works on display are frescoes of the 15th century; a *Madonna* by Vittore

Crivelli; drawings, engravings by G. B. Piranesi, ceramics by the Della Robbia, and notable 17th-century majolica pieces.

Other works by Uno Gera can be seen in the monumental church of *San Filippo* (1680–1722) in Via Annibal Caro, where a lower room hosts the *Museo della Civiltà Contadina* (visits on request, tel. 99329).

Grottammare

This medieval town has narrow streets ranged with rural-looking houses. The palm-lined waterfront avenue is lined with hotels and tourist facilities which have transformed this once quiet burgh (elev. 4 m, pop. 13,455) into a busy seaside resort on the Picena riviera. In the older section of town, note the church of *Santa Lucia*, built in 1597 in memory of Pope Sixtus V (a

148

native of Grottammare), and vestiges of the *Castle* – of 14th-century origins, but heavy reworked over the centuries.

Cupra Marittima

The town comprises a section that extends along the waterfront, and a historic nucleus occupying the hill. The name of the town (elev. 4 m, pop. 4,757) is a reminder that here once stood an important religious center of the Picenes dedicated to the goddess Cupra, a deity of the Etrusco-Picene pantheon. Separated from the modern section of town, **Marano*** (elev. 12 m) is still encircled by the 15th-century walls; narrow streets lead up to the church of **Santa Maria in Castello**, of Romanesque origins, close to which one can admire the remains of the medieval *Rocca* or fortress. In the *Antiquarium Comunale* is an exhibition of archaeological finds from the territory of Cupra Marittima, and from the huge burial grounds dating from the early Iron Age in particular.

One of Cupra Marittima's principal attractions (in Via Adriatica 240) is the *Museo Malacologico Piceno* (open Jun 4pm–8.30pm; Jul & Aug 4pm–10.30pm; Apr–May & Sep: Mar, Thu, Sat & Sun 3pm–7pm), which boasts a collection of over 600,000 samples of shells from all over the world, and has a special section assigned to examples from the middle Adriatic.

San Benedetto del Tronto*

Palm trees, oleanders, and pines lend their shade to the waterfront promenade, which continues unbroken for over two kilometers. San Benedetto (elev. 6 m, pop. 44,621) is a coveted holiday resort owing to its long, clean beaches and excellent catering facilities. But it is also a very busy port with ship-building yards, and industries for the conservation of fish. The town (see street plan opposite) is composed of two distinct sections, the first built on higher ground, with the 14th-century *Torre dei Gualtieri* (B1), perhaps the remains of an ancient fortress; and the more extensive lower section with its tree-lined avenues where Liberty facade testify to the town's tradition as a tourist resort. In Viale De Gaspari stands the *Museo delle Anfore* (D2; open 9am–noon, and 3.30pm–6.30pm; closed Sun except in Jul and Aug) to receive the collection of amphoras of Phoenician, Italic, and Roman manufacture found in this stretch of the sea. In the port area, near the fish market, one can visit the *Museo Ittico "Augusto Caprotti"* (A2; open 9am–noon and 3.30pm–7pm; closed Sun).

Continuing along the Adriatic coastal road in a southerly direction, after 4 km the itinerary enters *Porto d'Ascoli* (elev. 4 m), a modern seaside resort at the mouth of the Tronto valley.

8.3 Fermo and environs

Circular itinerary of 110 km *(see map on p. 152)*

Seascapes, hills, and mountains, all within easy reach of each other, complemented by towns full of history and art, small burghs carefully restored, ancient traditions that are expressed in folklore, pageants, and colorful local festivals. A tour of the Fermo district seems to summarize much of the atmosphere of the entire region – from its fine sandy beaches to the "alpine" reaches of the Sibillini mountains, from the noble architecture of the city to the discrete charm of the many small towns and villages on the hilltops.
Once out of Fermo, the proposed itinerary leads seaward on the SS210 (Fermana Faleriense), which follows the valley bottom of the Tenna river. After 4 km it turns off to climb toward Sant'Elpidio a Mare and thence toward Porto Sant'Elpidio. It then coasts the Adriatic in a southward direction, passing through Lido di Fermo; a mere 2 km separate this place from Porto San Giorgio, another highly popular seaside re-

sort. At Pedaso, a key town of local fruit and vegetable production, we turn away from the coast to reach Montefiore dell'Aso, and Monterubbiano. After a quick visit to nearby Moresco a few kilometers east of our route, the road follows a panoramic drive down to the Ete Vivo river valley, before climbing the opposite bank to return to Fermo. The second branch of the itinerary climbs the Tenna river along the SS210 to Servigliano (30 km from Fermo). From the excavations of the Roman town of *Faleria*, 2.5 km before Servigliano, we propose a detour: the road that leads out of the bottom of the valley and after 4.5 km reaches Falerone; from here in 2.5 km the route arrives at Montegiorgio, and after another 6, Massa Fermana.

Fermo*

The busy central square of Fermo, one of the many splendid piazze of the Marchi-

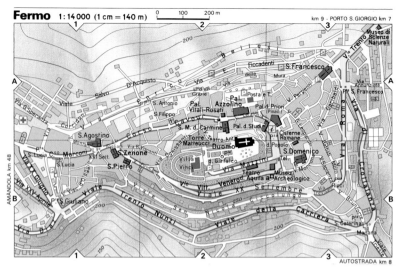

gian region, serves as both lobby and monumental "living room." The square mediates the relationship with the open "balcony" by which it is accessed, and channels visitors into the noble inner street network typical of the decadent nobility of the period. No wonder that the town's fulcrum is constituted by the peak of the hill, where the cathedral overlooks the open space and greenery, like the specter of an ancient castle. Denied a place in the administrative reorganization that followed the Unification of Italy, the role of provincial capital (elev. 319 m, pop. 35, 277; see plan above) has a strong "genetic makeup," so to speak. For every era of the past, from the proto-historic Villanovan and Picene cultures, the town bears evidence to its past importance, even when the reminders of the past are worn or have been extensively reworked. Every year, toward the middle of August, the town holds the Palio dell'Assunta, a lively pageant on horseback, with parades of costumed participants.

Piazza del Popolo* (A-B3). The center of the town from the very earliest settlement, this piazza is the *salotto* or central square, neatly defined by arcaded buildings constructed in 1569. One of the shorter sides is bordered by the *Palazzo Apostolico*, now the seat of the municipal authorities, built in 1532 as the residence of the town's governors and papal legates. Alongside stands the so-called **Loggia of San Rocco**, part of a destroyed convent of 1528. Closing the northern side of the square are the Palazzo dei Priori, and the Palazzo degli Studi, linked via a fine loggia over an archway.

Over the entrance portico of the 16th-century **Palazzo dei Priori** (A3) is the figure (1590) of *Pope Sixtus V*, bishop of Fermo from 1571 to 1577. The palace's rooms are host to the **Pinacoteca Civica** (open 9.30–12.30pm, 4.30pm–7.30pm; closed Mon). The gallery vaunts paintings from the Venetian and Marchigian schools, including the eight panels* of the *St. Lucy Polyptych* by Jacobello del Fiore (1410); a *polyptych* by Andrea da Bologna (1369); an *Adoration of the Shepherds** (1608), a youthful work by Rubens formerly in the church of San Filippo, from which a *Pentecost* by Giovanni Lanfranco was also transferred. Built between the 16th and 17th centuries, the **Palazzo degli Studi** (A2-3) carries a statue of *Our Lady of the Assumption* (1587) over its balconied entrance; the building also accommodates the *Biblioteca Comunale*, or public library, founded in 1866; of special interest is the *Sala del Globo Terracqueo*, for its huge *mappamondo** or globe, from the 18th century.

The Roman Cisterns (A-B3). Guided tours 9.30am–12.30pm and 4.30pm–7.30pm. A short distance from Piazza del Popolo, with its entrance in the steep *Via degli Aceti*, the Roman cisterns are a vast underground complex composed of 30 intercommunicating chambers. They were carved out in AD 40– 60 to collect the rain and spring waters that fed the public aqueduct. For Via Paccarone the route reaches the church of **San Domenico** (B3), begun in 1233 but transformed in the 18th–19th century; worth seeing inside are the fine *wooden choir stalls** of 1448.

Museo Archeologico (B3). The archaeological museum is installed in a construction dating from the first Imperial period under the Romans, at the time probably used as a warehouse (open 9.30pm–12.30pm and 4.30pm–7.30pm). The collection includes finds from the Villanovan burial grounds, relics of Picene culture (7th–5th cent. BC), and a section of sculptures and Roman inscriptions from the Republican and Imperial periods.

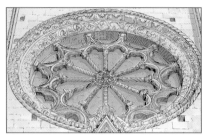

The rose window of Fermo Cathedral

Via Mazzini runs in a straight line from Piazza del Popolo up to the top of the hill, and is bordered by a prospect of Baroque architecture, interrupted by a niche bearing a statue of *St. Savinus* (1776), protector of the city. Along the street stands the **Teatro d'Aquila** (B2), built in 1780–90 to designs by Cosimo Morelli.

Piazzale del Girfalco* (A-B2). Formerly the site of Picene and Roman burial grounds, this large square with its oak trees and clusters of century-old cedars occupies the summit of the hill, where once rose a 13th-century fortress destroyed in the 15th century. Abutting the square is the **Duomo*** (A-B2), built over an early Christian basilica; of the original architecture (1277) time has spared the asymmetrical Romanesque-Gothic **facade**, the work of Comacini masters from the north: clad in Istrian stone, the facade is pierced by a *portal* decorated in relief and surmounted by a cusp bearing a bronze sculpture of *Our Lady of the Assumption with Angels* (1758). The **interiors** are the result of 18th-century remodeling under the supervision of Cosimo Morelli, but house important remnants of earlier date, such as the *Funerary Monument to Giovanni Visconti d'Oleggio* (1366) in the atrium; and on the 4th altar on the right, a Greco-Byzantine *icon** (11th cent.); in front of the presbytery restoration work has brought to light remains of the *floor mosaics** of the early Christian church (5th cent.); in the Cappella del Sacramento (left aisle) hangs a *Circumcision* by Andrea Boscoli; and a bronze *tabernacle* of 1571. In the 3rd-century **crypt**, the altar is composed of an early Christian *sarcophagus** of the 5th or 6th century; in the underground rooms of the church various remnants of early Christian and early medieval constructions have come to light.

Returning down Viale Vittorio Veneto, which affords a view right across to the Sibillini mountains, the itinerary continues in Via Lattanzio Firmiano (B1-2), flanking the *Monastery of Santa Chiara*, founded in 1503 but reworked in the 18th century; close by rises the square bell tower of *San Pietro* (B1), erected in 1251 but remodeled in 1490 and subsequently altered over the centuries. In Largo Fogliani, opposite the church of **San Zenone** (built in 1171) stands the 15th-century *Palazzo Fogliani*, having a fine Renaissance portal and Gothic windows in the Venetian style.

Sant'Agostino (A-B1). Built midway through the 13th century, this large

The main square at Fermo, Piazza del Popolo

151

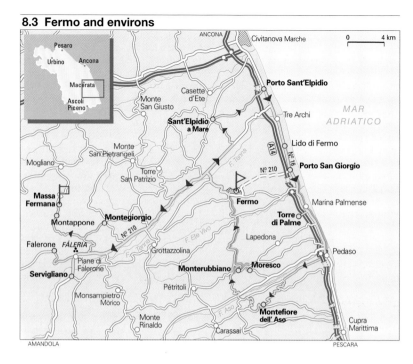

church with its plain facade was transformed in the ensuing century and then renovated once more in 1738. The interior, a product of 18th-century reworking, contains *frescoes* of the 13th–15th centuries on the walls and in the chapels. Attached to the right transept of the church is the **oratory of Santa Monica**, built in 1425 and transformed in 1623, which conceals a cycle of courtly Gothic frescoes (first half 15th cent.).

Corso Cavour (A1-2). Lined with patrician buildings, Corso Cavour climbs toward the center of town, reaching the 13th-century *Torre Mateucci*, which bears a 16th-century carved device on the facade. Alongside the church of *Santa Maria del Carmine* rises the facade of the **Palazzo del Monte di Pietà**, erected perhaps in the mid-14th century as the seat of the Misericordia hospital. Opposite stands the 16th-century *Palazzo Vitali-Rosati*, built to designs by Antonio da Sangallo the Younger. The powerful local family who commissioned the palazzo also commissioned Sangallo to built the **Palazzo Azzolino** (formerly Rosati; A2), a rare example of a thoughtfully scaled-down patrician palace.

San Francesco (A3). As was the custom with the Mendicant Orders, the church 152

of the Friars Minor was built on the fringes of the town, alongside the defensive walls. The church's flanks articulated with robust pillars and the lofty polygonal apse date to the Gothic construction (13th–15th cent.), while the plain facade dates to the 1700s. Inside are vestiges of *frescoes* of the Marchigian school of the 15th century. A large Gothic archway at the end of the right aisle marks the access to the chapel of the Holy Sacrament, in which stands the elaborate *Funerary Monument to Lodovico Effreducci**, sculpted in 1527 by Andrea Sansovino.

On the road to Porto San Giorgio, installed in the 18th-century *Villa Vitali* (A3), are the **Museo di Scienze Naturali**, and the **Museo Polare "Silvio Zavatti"** (open Mon, Thu, & Fri 9.30am–12.30pm; Tue, Wed, & Sat 9am–1pm and 4pm–7pm).

Sant'Elpidio a Mare
On the second Sunday of August each year a pageant of townsfolk in 15th-century costume recreates the so-called Contesa del Secchio. Despite its name, Elpidio "a Mare" is not actually at sea level (elev. 251, pop. 15,027). In the central Piazza Matteotti rises the church of **Maria SS. della Misericordia**, an example of late 16th-century architecture with a fine barrel vault frescoed by Pomarancio. At the side of the church stands the *Torre Gerosolimitana*, erected in the 14th cen-

tury. On the left is the **Collegiate church**, reconstructed in 1639 with remains of the original 14th-century building. Inside are paintings by Nicola Monti (*Our Lady of the Assumption with Saints*, on the high altar); Palma Giovane (*Crucifixion and Saints*, left transept), Pomarancio (*Madonna del Carmine*, 1st altar on left). In the presbytery lies a *Roman sarcophagus** of the 3rd century, with reliefs depicting a lion-hunt. Overlooking the main square is the *Palazzo Comunale*, with its classicizing 17th-century main prospect attributed to Pellegrino Tibaldi. The palazzo houses the public art gallery, with a polyptych* by Vittore Crivelli composed of 18 panels; and a *triptych* by Garofalo.

Porto Sant'Elpidio

The town (elev. 4 m, pop. 21,332) is an important center for shoe production.

Near the waterfront stands the 16th-century *Torre dell'Orologio*, built as a defense tower against the frequent incursions of pirates along the coast. The sea road reaches Lido di Fermo (elev. 3 m), a modern built-up area with long, sandy beaches.

Porto San Giorgio

In medieval times this town (elev. 4 m, pop. 16,009) provided an important coastal lookout station against marauding Turkish pirates. It rapidly developed its port facilities, becoming a thriving fishing center. The town's main business today is tourism, thanks to its beaches, an established catering tradition, and a pretty marina; despite this, fishing remains one of the principal local activities. Surrounded by greenery is the Rocca (B1), a fortified construction originating in 1267, with a tall keep, towers, and merlons, erected in

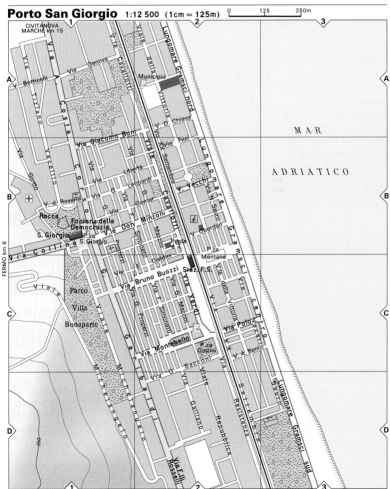

Porto San Giorgio 1:12 500 (1 cm = 125 m)

a phase of Fermo's intense economic and political expansion. Examples of Italian Art Nouveau can be seen in some of the villas along the waterfront and in the Fontana della Democrazia (1897), in front of the 19th-century church of *San Giorgio*; alongside the church stands the *Teatro Comunale*, built in 1817. Each summer in the month of July, the locals hold the traditional Festa del Pesce, which is cooked in a gigantic frying pan!

Torre di Palme
A small town on a hill with a superb view all round, Torre di Palma (elev. 104 m), Fermo but formed originally as an outpost for the ancient seaport of Palma, conserves glimpses of the medieval town. Along the main avenue stands the small church of *San Giovanni* (10th cent.?), in whose interior some fine Gothic frescoes (15th cent.) can be admired. Also of medieval origin is the *Palazzo Muncipale*. The town's most interesting building is **Santa Maria a Mare***, built in the 12th century, but subsequently modified; the interiors contain 14th-century *frescoes* of Byzantine taste. Opposite rises the Romanesque oratorio of *San Rocco* (12th cent.).

Montefiore dell'Aso
The glowing colors, the aristocratic female figures with their long tapering fingers, the exquisite Renaissance draperies of the saints: no one can remain indifferent to the glorious **polyptych**** by Carlo Crivelli, kept in the collegiate church of *Santa Lucia*. Next comes Montefiore all'Aso (elev. 412 m, pop. 2,275), perched on a high outcrop overlooking the Aso and Menocchio river valleys: the historic center has managed to conserve tracts of its original medieval defensive walls, and boasts several 17th–18th century residences. The 14th-century church of **San Francesco** contains in the upper part of the original apse a series of 14th-century *frescoes*. Exhibited in the *Sala "Adolfo De Carolis"* (open summer

The "Fountain of Democracy" at Porto San Giorgio

9am–noon and 3pm–8pm; other periods on request from the Municipio) is a collection of sketches and woodcuts by De Carolis.

Monterubbiano
A small *Museo Archeologico* (open 6pm–8.30pm, 9.30pm–11pm) installed in the 15th-century *Palazzo Comunale* contains reminders of the early Picene settlement which passed into the hands of the Romans, and was subsequently razed by the Goths in the 5th century. Monterubbiano (elev. 463 m, pop. 2,427) is the birthplace of the painter Vincenzo Pagani (1490–1568), whose work can be admired in the 19th-century collegiate church of **Santa Maria dei Letterati**. In Corso Italia stands *San Michele Arcangelo* (14th cent.) and *San Giovanni*, which boasts a superb portal from 1238 in the right prospect; in Via Piave rises the Romanesque *Badia di Sant'Angelo*, and in Via Roma, opposite the *Teatro Pagani* (1875), stands the church of *San Francesco*, founded in the year 1247, completed in the 1400s, and reworked several times over the centuries.

Moresco
Still enclosed within its walls, and having a characteristic main *piazza** designed like a courtyard, Moresco (elev. 405 m, pop. 618) boasts a typical fortified layout dominated by two ancient *towers*: the older of the two belonged to the since-destroyed castle (12th cent.); the other is the square-based *Torre dell'Orologio* designed by Vincenzo Pagani (16th cent.), which can be admired from the Gothic arcade in the main square.

Servigliano
It may appear strange to find, here in this land of medieval origins, a small burgh with such a distinctive, tidy 18th-century flavor, with neat little squares, gardens, and rows of terrace houses. The reason for its being so new in comparison is that Servigliano (elev. 215 m, pop. 2,306) – whose name is taken from the Roman settlement probably

Crivelli's polyptych in the church of Santa Lucia at Montefiore dell'Aso

inhabited by the *gens Servilia*, was completely rebuilt after the town was destroyed by a massive landslide in 1771.

Not far outside the town of Piane di Falerone lie the ruins of the ancient *Falerio Piceno*, the Roman town destroyed at an unknown date. A rough, uncovered road leads to the *Roman theater*, restored under Tiberius and decorated in the era of Antoninus; one call still recognize the vestige of the scaena and cavea. Archaeological fragments and Roman material from the excavation site are gathered in the *Museo Archeologico* of **Falerone** (elev. 432 m, pop. 3,266; visits on request, tel. 710115), whose principal square is graced with the 15th-century *Loggetta dei Mercanti* and the church of *San Fortunato*, begun in 1287.

Montegiorgio

The singular layout of the historic center of this town (elev. 411 m, pop. 6,702) is triangular, with narrow streets typical of a medieval burgh. The main building is the church of **San Francesco**, a fine example of Romanesque-Gothic, whose facade is punctuated by a superb 14th-century *por-tal*; inside, remodeled according to the going Neoclassical tastes, is the Gothic *Capella Farfense*, with some interesting vestiges of late Gothic *frescoes*.

Massa Fermana

Once past Montappone (elev. 370 m, pop. 1,802), with its Romanesque *Oratorio del Sacramento* and the *Museo del Cappello* (open winter, Sat & Sun 4pm–6pm; summer 5pm–8pm and 9.30pm–10.30pm; closed Mon) which has a display of traditional local trade and manufacturing activities; from here the route leads on to **Massa Fermana** (elev. 345 m, pop. 955); here the 14th-century *Porta di Sant'Antonio*, a gateway testifying to the existence of a castle dating from the 1300s. In the parish church of SS. Lorenzo, Silvestro e Rufino hangs a **polyptych**** by Carlo Crivelli; the small *Pinacoteca* (open 8am–2pm; closed Sun) installed in the Palazzo Comunale contains a *Nativity** panel by Vincenzo Pagani and a *Resurrection* (1542) by Giovanni Andrea De Magistris.

8.4 The Sibillini mountains of the Ascoli area

From Ascoli Piceno to Sarnano, 87 km (*see map on p. 156*)

Dense vegetation and woodlands, shady valleys, striking rock formations. The ancient legends of demons, sorcerers, and wood-nymphs seem to have found their perfect location in the landscape of the Sibillini, the "blue mountains" of which the local poet Giacomo Leopardi was so fond. It is said that a short distance away on the higher ground lies the cave inhabited by the sibyl, together with the "demonic" lake into which Pontius Pilate was supposedly dragged by oxen. The area

offers an unending trail of small, hidden villages, of places steeped in history, of little Romanesque churches adorned with frescoes – all unexpected witnesses to the past, but somehow happily coexisting with the demands of modern tourism and sport.

From Ascoli Piceno the route takes a south-west course on the SS4, which follows the Tronto river bed. After Acquasanta Terme (18.5 km), the valley narrows and passes through a picturesque gorge, emerging at

8.4 The Sibillini mountains of the Ascoli area

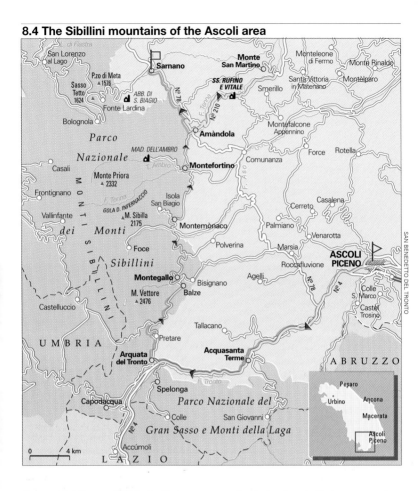

Arquata del Tronto (12.5 km), clinging to the densely wooded hillside. A panoramic road of 13 km leads northward to Montegallo, at the foot of Mt. Vettore, the highest point of the Sibillini (elev. 2,476 m). The itinerary then proceeds northward, reaching the town of Montemonaco in 1.65 km, whose position affords a panoramic view of the Aso river valley. Amid slopes and oak woods, the road continues for 9 km to Montefortino, and from here, after a mere 6 km, to Amandola. A detour along the SS210 that follows the bed of the Tenna river leads to the abbey of SS. Ruffina e Vitale (at 8 km), and to Monte San Martino (6 km). Back to Amandola and the route continues in a northwesterly direction along the SS78 (Picena) to reach Sarnano, and 11.8 km later, a tourist center and thermal spa in the province of Macerata.

Acquasanta Terme

The town's renowned springs of health-giving iodine-bromide waters were appreci-

ated as far back as the Roman times, when the site was known as **Vicus ad Aquas**. The town (elev. 392 m, pop. 3,647), which dominates the deep course of the Tronto river, boasts a 17th-century panel of the *Magdalene* in the church of *Santa Maria Maddalena*, together with frescoes dating from the 16th century.

Arquata del Tronto

Today the town is a thriving holiday resort and excursion departure point for treks up the Sibillini mountains. In Roman times it was an important *statio* or station on the Via Salaria. The name of the burgh (elev. 777 m, pop. 1,600), which lies on the border between the Marche, Umbria, Abruzzo, and Lazio derives from the imposing *Rocca* (in Roman *arx*) built in the 2nd century, crowning the hilltop. In the small Piazza Umberto I rises the *Torre Civica*, mounted with a 16th-century bell; the *parish church* contains a polychrome wood *Crucifix* of the 13th century.

The municipal territory of Arquata del Tronto covers a large area that lies between two national parks: to the north the Parco Nazionale dei Monti Sibillini; to the south the Gran Sasso d'Italia and the Monti della Laga. Evidence of the area's long history can be found in the villages: at **Capodacqua** (elev. 813 m) the church of the *Madonna del Sole*, a small temple built on a central plan in 1528 has some fine votive frescoes; in the *church* of **Spelonga** (elev. 946 m) hangs a Turkish war banner seized during the Battle of Lepanto in 1571; together with frescoes from the 15th and 16 centuries.

Montegallo

The beautiful excursions offered by Mt. Vettore have made this locality particularly appealing for summer tourists. The focus of the scattered villages is *Balzo* (elev. 886 m, pop. 748), whose 17th-century *parish church* boasts a fine decorated portal. Similarly, **Montemonaco** (elev. 988 m, pop. 748), one of the highest localities of the entire region, offers superb panoramic views of the mountains of Abruzzo. At the top of Montemonaco are two *churches* built against the remains of the castle walls: *San Biagio* dates from the end of the 15th century; *San Benedetto* boasts a handsome portal of 1546.

Among the many excursions of environmental interest is the climb up to the top of **Mt. Sibilla** itself (elev. 2,175), with its curious peak surrounded by a circle of gigantic pink rock: from the crest of the mountain, where legend has it the priestess of Apollo lived, the panorama* is breathtaking. Equally impressive is the landscape of the so-called **Gola dell'Infernaccio***, an impressive gorge carved for some 3.5 km and at places barely 2 meters wide by the Tenna river between Mt. Sibilla and Mt. Priora.

View of Arquata del Tronto

Montefortino

The town lies to the right of the Tenna river, and has conserved its atmospheric narrow streets between houses in stone and brick. In the higher section of town (elev. 612 m, pop. 1,365) rises the church of *Sant'Agostino*, built in the 14th century; at the crown of the hill is *San Francesco*, which contains a fine canvas of the *Madonna del Rosario* by Simone De Magistris, and a wooden sculptural group from the 1300s. Palazzo Leopardi is host to the **Pinacoteca Civica "Fortunato Duranti"** (open summer 10.30am–12.30pm and 5pm–7pm; open winter on request, tel. 859101): created in 1842, the gallery contains works from the 15th to 18th centuries, including a *Madonna Adoring the Child* by Francesco Botticini, plus three *panels** by Pietro Alemanno belonging to a dismembered polyptych.

A slightly declining route that runs the length of the Ambro river penetrates the heart of the Sibillini mountains, reaching after 6.5 km the sanctuary of the **Madonna dell'Ambro** (elev. 683 m), built in honor of the miraculous apparition of the Virgin, and now a much-frequented pilgrim site. The outer aspect of the building is 17th century, but the sanctuary itself was probably founded in the 11th century; the *Chapel of the Apparition*, behind the high altar, contains a polychrome statue in stone, a creation of the Umbro-Marchigian school (15th cent.).

Amandola

In the 14th–15th centuries, and particularly in the 1600s, Amandola enjoyed a flourishing reputation for its weaving industry and wool dying; today it is a prosperous seaside resort (elev. 500, pop. 4,051). From the central piazza a stairway descends to the 14th-century *Sant'Agostino* (visits on request, tel. 660164), enlarged in 1759 and remodeled in the early 1900s. Inside hang four 15th-century polyptychs, one by Carlo and Vittore Crivelli, one by Vittore alone, and two by Girolamo di Giovanni. The 18th-century interiors of **San Francesco**, founded in the 1200s but reconstructed during the following century and remodeled between 1660 and 1670, contain wooden *Crucifix* of Romanesque manufacture, and, in a chamber at the base of the bell tower, a cycle of *frescoes* (15th cent.). The former Franciscan convent, with a fine *cloister* from the 15th–16th century, is host to the *Museo della Civiltà Contadina* (open summer 10am–12.30pm and 4.30pm–6.30 pm; winter on request, tel. 84071, 848037), and the *Museo dei Fossili* (open summer 9.30am–1pm and 4pm–7.30pm).

The Abbey of SS. Rufino e Vitale

In the Trenna river valley, which is characterized by steep cliffs overlooking the Sibillini mountains, the abbey is 12th-century Romanesque, but was founded several centuries before (6th cent.). In the raised presbytery one can visit the 14th- and 15th-century *frescoes*; other frescoes from the 13th century bearing figures of *saints* can be visited in a room just off the *crypt*.

Monte San Martino

Monte San Martino (elev. 600 m, pop. 818) commands a panoramic position high above the Tenna valley. Tradition has it that the town was founded in the 9th century by the Franks. Hanging in the church of **San Martino** are a *polyptych** by Carlo and Vittore Crivelli; and a *triptych* by Vittore Crivelli; a further two 15th-century *polyptychs* can be admired in the church of *Santa Maria del Pozzo*. A few hundred yards from the town stands the church of *Santa Maria dell Grazie*, containing frescoes from 1590.

Sarnano*

The modern part of Sarnano lies on the plain, the antique core on the steep hillside. The town (elev. 539 m, pop. 3,414) is a very popular winter ski resort and a starting point for climbs up the Sibillini mountains. The **medieval burgh*** with its steep narrow streets culminates in a silent piazza. Dating from the 1200s is the church of **Santa Maria Assunta**, having a Gothic portal and a robust campanile (end 14th cent.). Inside can be seen 14th–16th-century *frescoes*; in the presbytery hangs a panel representing the *Madonna of Mercy* by Pietro Alemanno, signed and dated 1494, and a processional standard by Girolamo di Giovanni; on the back wall hangs a *polyptych* by Alunno. The *crypt* contains remnants of *frescoes* (1494) by Alemanno. Installed in the neighboring former *Franciscan convent* founded in the 13th century is the **Pinacoteca Civica** (open summer 5pm–8pm; winter 4pm–7pm), which vaunts a worthy collection of art works, including an *altarpiece* by Vittore Crivelli; a *Madonna and Child* attributed tentatively to Alunno, and various paintings by Vincenzo Pagani (16th cent.).

A road offering splendid views leads through oak woodlands toward the ski stations of Sassotetto-Maddalena (elev. 1,624–1,680 m), where visitors can take advantage of the numerous ski lifts up the mountain. The summer alternative is superb walks in the woods, which offer a truly magnificent view over the hills.

The Sibillini, nature and legend

The Sibillini mountains reach some 2,000 meters at their peak, with rocky cliffs, glacial moraines, depressions, and slopes cloaked with alpine flora. The carsic plateau of Castelluccio becomes particularly fascinating during the flowering of the lentil plants. Other important features include the lake of Pilato, the only Apennine lake that has glacial origins. In fact, the area does look as if it has been transported to this central-Italian setting. These mountains continue to have an air of magic and mystery about them, given that the legendary peak of the Sibilla, and its hidden cave, were part of ancient pagan cult worship. The geological structure of the mountain, with its crown cut into the rock, was seen as a symbol of the divine, perhaps the goddess Cybele, the *Magna Mater* which the Christians would later convert to the Virgin Mary. In the 15th and 16th centuries, the area was an unmissable stage of the esoteric "grand tour" of Europe: Antoine del La Sale, a leading Anjovin mounted soldier, was anxious to see the cave, and on 18 May 1420 climbed to Montemonaco. The experience prompted him to pen his *Le Paradis de la Reine Sybille*, a tale of a horseman exploring the Sibillan caves, known in Italy under the title of "Guerrin Meschino."

The lake of Pilato in the Sibillini mountains

Thematic excursions

Places of worship and pilgrimage

The Benedictine Order holds the primacy for the first monastery in the region, as early as the 6th century. The advent of the religious order involved mustering considerable human and material resources in order to guarantee this new system of organization, which was not only aimed at evangelizing through the district, but also at establishing an equitable and just administration, with programs for tilling uncultivated land, for water control, for reclaiming the marshes, and for cultivating land that had remained abandoned since the Turkish invasions. There was also work to do on the decayed Roman infrastructure. The monasteries and abbeys, which were independent and often fortified, became havens for the common folk, who, famished and terrified by the Barbarian invasions, gathered round, fleeing the crumbling towns, the horror and despair. Here in the monasteries the monks imparted fundamental knowledge on matters of science, art, and the literature of the classical world through the diligent work of the amanuenses, who copied out book after book, ensuring the continuity of the culture of the Eastern Empire. For this reason, a visit to the *scriptorium* of the hermitage of Fonte Avellana is well worth the time spent. As the population increased (10th–11th cent.), and donations of land came from the feudal landlords the abbey settlements continued to thrive. This was bolstered by the Benedictine and Cluniac reforms (particularly in the garrisoned centers), together with those being effected by the Cistercian and Camaldolese orders, which

Places of worship and pilgrimage

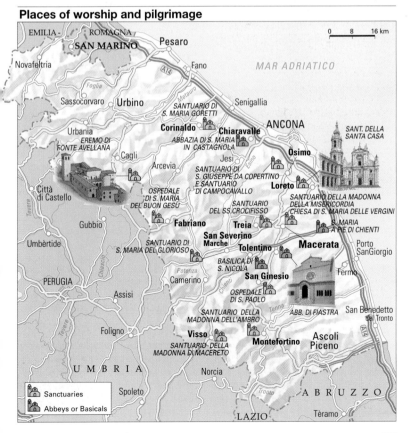

were particularly persuaded by the intense, lofty spirituality of such saints as Romuald and Peter Damian. The increase in physical safety enabled wayfarers to resume traveling along the old Roman ways (the Via Flaminia and Via Salaria and innumerable byways), and they could also follow the natural tracks along the riverbeds, multiplying and enriching the presence of abbeys until they reached a thousand in number (with particular concentration in the valleys of the Esino and Musone rivers). By contrast, hermitages and monasteries epitomized two ways – individual and collective – of experiencing the perfection of religious faith far from the civil life of the towns, which brought its doubts and uncertainties. Hermitages and caves became hospices for an ascetic breed of monk (Camaldolese, Romualdine, Sylvestrine, Capucine, and so on), whom many recognized as perfect examples of sanctity. These various monasteries provide a substantial part of the Romanesque legacy in the Marche, which has an estimated 200 monastic buildings.

On a wholly independent basis for centuries the area saw the proliferation of sanctuaries, sometimes with annexed hospitals for the pilgrims (San Ginesio, Fabriano, among others). Without going into the miraculous events surrounding the foundation of the sanctuaries that were built, the fact remains that they were the outcome of a genuine impulse toward the spiritual, as confirmed by the constant inflow of funds for their construction and maintenance through bequests and the voluntary labor of the local population. Starting with the extraordinary example of the sanctuary of the Holy House in Loreto, the region currently boasts an enviable number of over 160 active sanctuaries, well distributed through the four provinces of the region. Worth noting are the sanctuaries of San Nicola in Tolentino, San Giuseppe da Copertino, and San Giuseppe di Campocavallo at Osimo; Santa Maria in Castagnola in Chiaravalle, the Madonna della Misericordia, Santa Maria delle Vergini in Macerata, Santa Maria del Glorioso in San Severino Marche; the Madonna di Macereto near Visso, the SS. Crocifisso at Treia, the Madonna dell'Ambro near Montefortino, and Santa Maria Goretti at Corinaldo. Hieratic monuments that were not overlooked by the Cistercian reform include the abbeys of Chiaravalle at Fiastra, and Santa Maria in Castagnola a Chiaravalle. Lastly, worth visiting is the sanctuary of Santa Maria a Piè di Chienti near the town of Montecosaro – a rare example of the stock type of "pilgrim church" on two levels that dotted the medieval pilgrims' way down to the Gargano and thence to Jerusalem.

The Middle Ages along the coast: a tour amid 'castles' on the sea

Whoever believed the Marche coastline to be an uninterrupted series of bays forming a long, evenly distributed built-up area would be making a common mistake. Undoubtedly, the beaches and resorts are the first features that makes themselves present to the traveler (i.e., Gabicce Mare, Pesaro, Fano, Senigallia, Conero, Civitanova Marche, Porto San Giorgio, Grottammare, San Benedetto del Tronto), who immediately recognizes the typical features of the Adriatic resort. But on closer study, after excursions in the immediate hinterland, another face of the coast comes to light, namely, the historical face. And one immediately discovers the original historical settlements which witnessed the gradual encroachment of the share-cropping population toward the shore along a route which in certain cases has its roots in the great Picene (Numana, Cupra Marittima, Nolivara) and Roman civilizations, and in many others through the expansion of the communes during the Middle Ages.

Here the traveler will find unforgettable urban settings. This tour takes us through the upper towns of the coast which, in every sense, lead us back to the original nuclei of the coastal culture.

These towns on higher ground were once the *castra* of the Middle Ages, such as Gabicce Monte (then *Castellum Ligabitii*), or Fiorenzuola di Focara; castles of the Pesaro area such as Trebbiantico, Novilara, and Candelara, each one enclosed in its defensive enceinte. The tall eminence of Falconara Alta, the historical nucleus, the *castrum* of a large coastal town, Falconara Marittima. An example of the process of transformation of the classic marina from an original seaside burgh is Montemarciano. South of Ancona, Recanati, Sant'Elpidio a Mare, Potenza Picena – all once free communes, urban nuclei of a certain consistence and importance – lie at some distance from the sea itself. As a result, their ports and marinas, once no more than a moorage point, have since become full-fledged towns (Porto Recanati, Porto Sant'Elpidio, Porto Potenza Picena). An

Forts and castles

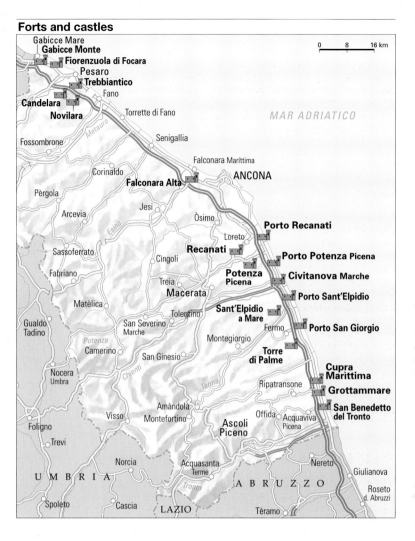

emblematic case of the relationship between an inland town and its port can be seen in Civitanova Marche; the roman *Cluana* reemerged from its ruins around the year 1000, fostering two separate settlements: Castel or Ripa Sancti Maroni, which coagulated around a *plebs* and a burgh perched on the hill; the other Civitanova Alta, the historic nucleus of the town we know today. Descending toward the south the itinerary comes to the *Navale Firmanorum*, namely, Porto San Giorgio, which has a part on higher ground (the Castello ward and the rocca of 1267) and, across the state road, the marina. Another case is Torre di Palme, consisting of a castle sprawled on a steep cliff overlooking the sea, and its placename indicates the site's role as a look-out station (the hilltop site took over from the earlier Roman *Palma Ve-*

tula). These three cases of "upper town," like the ancient heart of the marina, of the fishing villages that grew up from the demolished seaside settlemtns are Cupra Marittima with Marano; Grottammare with Grottammare Alta, San Benedetto del Tronto with the old settlement. In the vicinity of the Roman town of *Cupra Maritima* (albeit in a dominant position) toward the 11th century emerged the burgh of Marano, which crystallized around a Roman *plebs*. The toponym of Grottammare Alta was *Castrum Gruptarum ad Tisinum*. The "upper town" of San Benedetto del Tronto is basically a terrace overlooking the town, where stands the Torre dei Gualtieri, a noble family that settled in the castle in the 12th century; the castle itself stemmed from an earlier building, the *plebs Sancti Benedicti in Albula*.

Non-religious sites and events in the Marche

The summer calendars of the Macerata Opera Festival and the Rossini Opera Festival represent something that goes beyond the musical calendar. These two fundamental musical events are part of the Marche's long tradition of entertainment: in the distant past at Urbino (1513) the townsfolk were treated to a representation of the *Calandria*, with elaborate set-designs by the gifted Nicolò Sabbatini coupled with the superb stagecraft of the Giacomo Torelli. In the 18th and

Other cultural sites in the Marche

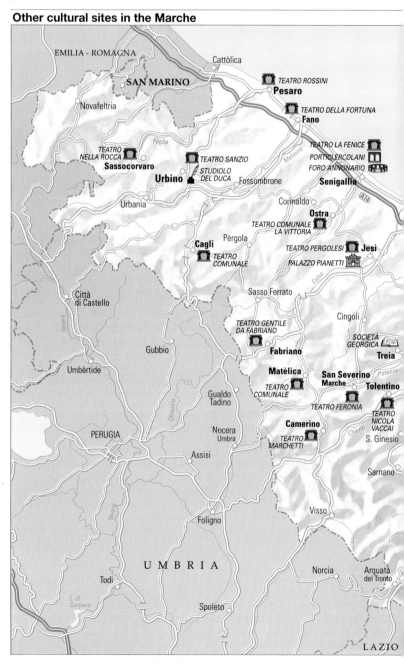

19th centuries stage design had reached its utmost splendor.

The theater-opera phenomenon is not peculiar to the larger towns, which obviously enjoy special facilities: special restoration campaigns for the renovation of the smaller theaters have been carried out all over the Marche, including Fermo, Jesi, Fano, Ascoli Piceno, Senigallia, Macerata, Urbino, Cagli, Ostra, to name a few. Some of the very small theaters have turned out to be strikingly beautiful, and, as can be expected, were designed in proportion to the number of local inhabitants; despite their size they are built with the same architectural format as their larger, more "noble" counterparts.

Generally speaking, one can say that the glamour of the full-fledged opera house or theater is in no way diminished by this cluster of smaller venues. Each one expresses the local bourgeois spirit, its architecture distinguishing markedly from the civic or religious architecture it shares space with. It is a critical aspect of the local character, that the Marchigians tend to avoid overstatement, preferring to express themselves with civic good sense rather than pomp.

The public ownership of the theaters, in many cases sponsored also by the municipal authorities, led to the creation of public gathering places that were independent from the institutions and marked a shift away from "feudal theocracy" toward a greater social mobility.

No wonder that while in the Marche there is a strong sense of "piazza" culture and one can turn a corner and enter a well-defined square, rarely are the public buildings and religious buildings raised on the same square.

In Palazzo Pianetti (18th cent.) in Jesi, in the pictorial decorations of the gallery the stylistic key is central-European Rococo; this is a unique case in Italy: the customary themes linked to the universe of agriculture and crop production are represented with technical and productive features (such as the inclusion of Australia among the continents; and detailed illustrations of farm equipment to designate the various seasons), which demonstrate to the townsfolk practical features which stray noticeably from the typical fresco imagery of mythological figures. In Urbino, three centuries earlier, the superstitious assembly of illustrious men on the walls of the duke's *studiolo* reveals the shift toward Humanism, and is much less literary than the arcane technologies inscribed in stone and bearing the tools of civil and military engineering.

There are other aspects by which the Marche are distinguished from other regions, such as the fortifications, which are nonetheless manifestations of technical and utilitarian activities; these are accompanied by many defensive works which, especially in the smaller

localities, seem more an expression of a spirit of civil unity than a defensive system as such.

But the buildings that perfectly match the civil or non-religious spirit are tied to more recent periods and have covered a wider range of uses. First and foremost is the Lazzaretto in Ancona, whose mixed functions are brilliantly encapsulated by the architecture of Luigi Vanvitelli. It was built in 1733–43 as part of the economic reorganization of the Papal States, though its design has allowed for the burgeoning commercial and production culture.

A example of the local spirit can be seen in the constitution in Treia of the Società Georgia (1775, having an elegant headquarters dating to later, 1823): originally the long-established Accademia Letteraria, the building was converted for studies in agronomy, with a regular technical bulletin published in-house.

A quite different spirit was followed by the Ercolani arcades in the town of Senigallia (second half 1700s): no less than six blocks of inner-city wards were merged for the celebrated trade fair, by which the town established its own monumental focus for trade (as in the Logge dei Mercanti of Ancona and of Macerata), becoming a city-within-the-city. In the same city, the Foro Annonario, nobly designed as a convergence point for the port activities, is currently being restored with the sponsorship of private investment. The Foro is architecturally in direct competition with the nearby Rocca built by the Della Rovere. But the most astonishing case of a "magnification" of contents can be seen in the Spheristerium (1820–29) in Macerata, whose main facade, inserted into a broad tract of the defensive walls, offers a noble and rational Neoclassical prospect replacing the 15th–16th century frontage. Such works are an open statement against the "gratuitous" cultural directives of the Restoration. The contribution of the private sponsors who financed the enterprise was immense, and the result is comparable in terms of size to the building of a new main church. In the case of the Spheristerium, of course, the activities to be held therein were originally sports for the general pleasure of the population. Small wonder that the rather caustic atheism of Giacomo Leopardi was inspired by the venue (see his poem of 1821 entitled "Per un vincitore nel Pallone"), and a certain player of *palla a bracciale*, for which the Sferisterio was originally built.

Nor does it seem a coincidence that, a century later, the building was remodeled as a theater venue, thereby linking it with the civil values for which it was designed.

Other places of interest: hotels, restaurants, events. Opening times and addresses

Town by town, the following list comprises the recommended hotels, restaurants, campsites, and holiday villages (besides a selection of hostels and farm-holiday centers); visitors are reminded that in Italy an official system of stars exists for classifying hotels and the like (Legge Quadro per il Turismo, 17 May 1983). The restaurants are instead graded with the TCI's system of "forks." This classification encompasses the price, comfort, general service and tone of the place in question. As for the price brackets, visitors can have an idea from the coding: ¶ less than 45.000 lire; ¶¶ from 45.000 to 65.000 lire; ¶¶¶ from 65.000 to 85.000 lire; ¶¶¶¶ from 85.000 to 105.000 lire; ¶¶¶¶¶ over 105.000 lire.

Some of the hotels, restaurants, and other faclities listed in this guide have made an agreement (renewed year by year) with the Touring Club of Italy, by which club members receive various discounts. Information regarding membership of the Touring Club of Italy may be obtained from the Member's Office (tel. 025359973).

The information contained here has been carefully cross-checked before going to press. We regret any discrepancies or variations. Visitors are advised to check in advance. All suggestions and corrections are most welcome.

Each location's code must also be used for local calls, indicated in the following list next to the symbol ☎. For those calling from abroad, the local code (including the 0) must be dialled after the international code for Italy, followed by the subscriber's number.

Acqualagna

✉ 61041 ☎ 0721

i *Municipio.* Tel. 798110, 798169.

Museums and cultural institutions

at Piobbico, 16 km ✉ 61046 ☎ 0722

Museo Geo-paleontologico, Naturalistico, Antropico e Ornitologico "Brancaleoni." Castello Brancaleoni, Via Brancaleoni, tel. 985418. *Visits on request to the Municipio, tel. 986225.*

at Apecchio, km 26.5 ✉ 61042 ☎ 0722

Museo dei Fossili Minerali del Monte Nerone. Via XX Settembre (Palazzo Ubaldini), tel. 99276, 99118, 99800. Visits by prior appointment, *winter 3pm–6pm, summer 10.30am–12.30pm.*

at Piobbico, 16 km

Castello Brancaleoni. tel. 985418. *Visits on request to the Municipio, tel. 986225.*

Festivals and entertainments

Fiera nazionale del Tartufo (Nov).

at Piobbico, 16 km

Incontro di Riappacificazione tra Brancaleoni e Ubaldini (end Aug).

Sport

at Piobbico, 16 km

Stazione sciistica of Monte Nerone.

Local guides and excursions

Cooperativa La Macina. Via Insorti Ungheresi 63, tel. 797240. Excursions and itineraries on mountain-bikes or on horseback on Mts.Catria, Nerone, and Petrano.

Acquasanta Terme

Page 156 ✉ 63041 ☎ 0736

i *Pro Loco.* tel. 801291.

Thermal resorts

Stabilimento SANTA. Via delle Terme, tel. 801268. Open May–Oct. Hydrosulfurous.

Museums and cultural institutions

Castello di Luco. tel. 802319.

Acquaviva Picena

Page 147 ✉ 63030 ☎ 0735

i *Ufficio Informazioni Turistiche.* Piazza S. Nicolò, tel. 765080.

Municipio. Via S. Rocco 9, tel. 764005.

Museums and cultural institutions

Museo delle Armi Antiche. In the medieval Rocca, tel. 764005, fax 765080. *Visits Nov–Apr, Sat & Sun 10.30am–12.30am; May mid-Jun and 2nd half of Sep–Oct 4pm–8pm; mid Jun–first half of Sep 10.30am–12.30pm, and 4pm–8pm.*

🏃 Festivals and entertainments

Acquaviva nei Fumetti (Jul). Tel. 764005.
National festival of humoristic graphics
and comic theater.
Sponsalia (Aug). Tel. 764077. Historical
reenactment of the wedding ceremonies
(123) of Forasteria, daughter of Duke Rinaldo of Acquaviva, and Brunforte, lord of Sarnano.

⚖️ Shops and crafts

Cantina dei Colli. Via Boreale 35/37, tel.
765033. Sponsored by the producers of
Rosso Piceno Superiore wines, and supplies information on itineraries of gastronomical interest in the area; mountain-
bikes for rent.
Forno Volpiani. Via Castello. Production
of traditional local desserts and sweets,
such as "pesche," *crostini, spumini, crostate,
ciambelloni.*

Amandola

Page 157 ✉ 63021 ☎ 0736

ℹ️ *Municipio.* Tel. 84071.

Pro Loco (summer months and holidays).
Piazza Risorgimento, tel. 847439.

Casa del Parco. Via Indipendenza 73, tel.
848598.

at Comunanza, 9 km ✉ 63044

Comunità Montana dei Sibillini. Piazza IV
Novembre 2, tel. 844379, 844253, fax
844526.

🏛️ Museums and cultural institutions

Museo della Civiltà Contadina. Cloister
of the church of San Francesco, tel. 84071,
848037. *Visits summer 10am–12.30pm and
4.30pm–6.30pm; winter on advance booking.*
Museo dei Fossili. Cloister of the church
of San Francesco, tel. 84071. *Visits, summer
9am–1pm and 4pm–7.30pm.*

at Montefortino, 6 km ✉ 63047

***Pinacoteca comunale "Fortunato Du-
ranti."*** Largo Duranti 5, tel. 859101. *Visits
summer 10.30am–12.30pm; winter on request.*
Raccolta dell'Avifauna delle Marche.
Piazza Umberto I, tel. 859101, 859122. *Visits on request.*

at Montefalcone Appennino, 18 km
✉ 63020

Museo Paleontologico. Via Roma 44, tel.
79136. *Visits 5.30pm–8pm and 8pm–9/10.30
pm.*

⛪ Churches

Abbazia dei SS. Vincenzo e Anastasio.
Visits on request, tel. 847142.

at Monte San Martino, 6 km

Church of San Martino. *Visits on request,
tel. 0733 660164.*

🏃 Festivals and entertainments

Festival Internazionale di Teatro (Sep). Tel.
847439. Avant-garde theater productions.

at Comunanza, 9 km

Presepe Vivente (26 Dec and 6 Jan).

⚖️ Shops and crafts

Cruciani Ariberto. Via Volta (industrial
ward). Creation and restoration of furniture.
Ebanarte. Via Fermi 5/7, tel. 847679. Creation and restoration of furniture.
Fabrizi Nello. Via Pignotto. Creation and
restoration of wooden articles.

at Force, 16.5 km ✉ 63045

Marino Malavisi. Via XX Settembre, tel.
373338. Articles in copper and wrought
iron.

🍽️ Sport

Rifugio Sibilla. Tel. 856422. Base for excursions with guide on Mt. Sibilla, the In-
fernaccio gorge, on Mt. Vettore.
Sci di fondo-escursionismo e telemark at
Campolungo and Piani Malattoni. Information c/o CAI, tel. 847353.

🚶 Local guides and excursions

Cooperativa Il Chirocefalo. Casa del Parco, tel. 848598. For simple or demanding excursions through the Parco Nazionale dei
Monti Sibillini.

at Montemonaco, 6 km ✉ 63048

Casa del Parco. Via Roma, tel. 856462.
Local guides to all the localities on the
Monti Sibillini.
Cittadella dei Monti Sibillini. Tel. 856361.
To tour on horseback in the area of the
Monti Sibillini.

Ancona

Page 32 ✉ 60100 ☎ 071

ℹ️ *APT.* Via Thaon de Revel 4, tel. 33249, fax
31966.

Informacultura. Piazza del Plebiscito, tel.
2225002.

🏨 Hotels, restaurants, and campsites

★✦★ ***Grand Hotel Palace.*** Lungomare Vanvitelli 24, tel. 201813, fax 2074832. 41 rooms.
Air conditioning, elevator; parking, bed
and breakfast (B2-3, **c**).

★✦★ ***Jolly Miramare.*** Rupi di Via XXIX Settembre 14, tel. 201171, fax 206823. 89
rooms. Air conditioning, elevator; parking, garden (C2, **a**).

★★★ ***City.*** Via Matteotti 112/114, tel. 2070949, fax
2070949. 39 rooms. Bed & breakfast. Wheelchair access. Elevator, garage (B-C3-4, **g**).

★★★ ***Fortuna.*** Piazza Rosselli 15, tel. 42663, fax
42662. 57 rooms. Bed & breakfast. Wheelchair access. Air conditioning, elevator;
parking (E1, **e**).

¶¶ **Corte.** Via della Loggia 5, tel. 200806. Closed Sun. Garden. Marchigian cuisine, specialty fish (B2-3, **x**).

¶ **Moretta.** Piazza Plebiscito 52, tel. 202317. Closed Sun, and part of Jan. Air conditioning, garden. Marchigian cuisine, specialty fish (B3, **u**).

at Portonovo, 12 km ⊠ 60020

★☆★ **Fortino Napoleonico.** Via Poggio 166, tel. 801450, fax 801454. 30 rooms. Wheelchair access. Air conditioning; parking, garden, swimming pool, tennis.

⬚ Cafés and pastry shops
Alla Tazza d'Oro. Corso Garibaldi 134, tel. 203368. One of the oldest cafés in the town.

🏛 Museums and cultural institutions
Biblioteca comunale Benincasa. Via Bernabei 32, tel. 2225021.
Biblioteca del Convento dei Frati minori Cappuccini. Via Fermo 14, tel. 82902.
Biblioteca dell'Istituto regionale per la Storia del Movimento di Liberazione delle Marche. Via Villafranca 1, tel. 202271.
Deputazione di Storia patria per le Marche. Piazza Stracca 3, tel. 203511.
ISTAO (Istituto Adriano Olivetti di Studi per la Gestione dell'Economia e delle Aziende). Via delle Grazie 77, tel. 85768.
Istituto marchigiano Accademia di Scienze, Lettere e Arti. Piazza Stracca 1, tel. 200051.
Istituto musicale G.B. Pergolesi. Via Zapata 1, tel. 52692.
Museo archeologico nazionale delle Marche. Via Ferretti 1, tel. 202602. *Visits 8.30pm–1.30pm.*
Museo diocesano. Piazza Duomo 9, tel. 2074703. *Visits Sab, and Sun afternoon (guided).*
Museo Omero. Via Bramante 7, tel. 52240. *Visits Tue & Thu 9.30am–12.30pm, Sat 9.30am–12.30pm, and 4pm–7pm.*
Pinacoteca civica "Francesco Podesti" e Galleria d'Arte moderna. Via Pizzecolli 17, tel. 2225045, 2225046. *Open Tue–Sat 10am–7pm; Sun & Mon 9am–1pm.*

🏃 Festivals and entertainments
Ancona Jazz (Nov). Tel. 2074239. The longest-running jazzfest in the Marche.
Premio Marche (Oct). Yearly festival of regional and national contemporary art.

at Polverigi, 17 km ⊠ 60020
Festival internazionale Inteatro (Jul). Tel. 200442. One of the most acclaimed theater events at European level.

⚖ Shops and crafts
Antichità Bugari. SS16, Aspio (industrial ward), tel. 8046355. An antiques dealer, mostly furniture of period design.
Azienda agricola Alessandro Moroder. Via Monteacuto 112, tel. 898232. Sale of Rosso Conero wine, extravirgin olive-oil and honey.

Bontà delle Marche. Corso Mazzini 96, tel. 53985. Wide range of local produce.
Casablanca. Corso Garibaldi 58, tel. 203721. Wine cellar.

〰 Sport
CAI. Via Cialdini 29, tel. 2070696.
Centro nautico. Via Enrico Mattei 16, tel. 206055.
Circolo ippico Le Torrette. Via Paterno 249, tel. 802227.
La Marina dorica (tourist marina). Via XXIX Settembre 2, tel. 54800.
Sef Stamura. Via Vanvitelli, tel. 207407. Sailing.

👫 Local guides and excursions
Blu Marlin. Via Grazie 40, tel. 891314. Excursions and trips by boat along the coast of Mt. Conero.

Apiro

⊠ 62012 ☎ 0733

ℹ *Municipio* (town hall) Tel. 611131, 611360.

🏛 Museums and cultural institutions
Raccolta della Collegiata di S. Urbano. Piazza Baldini 1, tel. 611118. *Open on request.*

🏃 Festivals and entertainments
Terranostra (Aug). International festival of folklore.

⚖ Shops and crafts
Colle verde. Contrada Cozzi 1, tel. 611755. Sale of wines, meat products, and olive oil.
Flores Salvatore. Contrada Piaggia 8, tel. 611517. Production and sale of excellent *pecorino* cheeses.

👫 Local guides and excursions
Comunità montana del San Vicino (zona G). Tel. 602823. For excursions and cross-country skiing on Mt. Elmo and San Vicino.

Arcevia

Page 54 ⊠ 60011 ☎ 0731

ℹ *Comune* (Ufficio Turismo). Tel. 97511.
Pro Loco (15 Jul–30 Sep). Corso Mazzini 22, tel. 9127.

🏛 Museums and cultural institutions
Museo archeologico statale. Corso Mazzini 67, tel. 9622. *Open 9am–1.30pm.*

⚖ Shops and crafts
at Avacelli, 10 km ⊠ 60040
Pieragostini Delfina. Via Fugiano 200, tel. 983028. Locally produced honey.

Arquata del Tronto

Page 156   ✉ 63043 ☎ 0736

ℹ️ *Municipio* (town hall). Tel. 809122.

Casa del Parco. Piazza Umberto I, tel. 809600.

🏛 Museums and cultural institutions
Rocca. Tel. 809122. *Open summer 10.30am–12.30pm and 4pm–6pm; winter 3pm–5pm.*

⛪ Churches
San Francesco. *Open by request to the Municipio.*

🎭 Festivals and entertainments
Alla Corte della Regina (19 Aug). Historical pageant in full medieval costume, with public banquet.
Reenactment of the Battle of Lepanto (Aug, every 3 years). This pageant involves all the local wards too.

at Pretare, 3 km
Discesa delle Fate (Aug, every 3 years).

⚖️ Shops and crafts

at Pretare, 3 km
Carlo Trenta. Tel. 804751. Craft work in wood.

🏆 Sport

at Forca di Presta, 12 km
Rifugio ANA. Tel. 809278.
Free flight with paragliding and hang-gliding; cross-country skiing.

at Forca Canapine, 16.5 km
Chair-lifts etc.
Rifugio Città di Ascoli. Tel. 808186.

🚶 Local guides and excursions
Cooperativa Cime azzurre. Casa del Parco, tel. 809600. For excursions and hiking in the Parchi Nazionali dei Monti Sibillini and the Monti della Laga.

Ascoli Piceno

Page 141   ✉ 63100 ☎ 0736

ℹ️ *APT.* Piazza del Popolo, tel. 255250.

Comunità montana del Tronto. Via Cartiera, tel. 251747.

Provincia di Ascoli Piceno. Assessorato ai Beni culturali. Corso Mazzini 39, tel. 277508, 277540; freephone 167019760.

🏨 Hotels, restaurants, and campsites

★☆★ **Gioli.** Viale De Gasperi 14, tel. 255550, fax 255550. 56 rooms. Bed & breakfast. Elevator; garage (B-C3, **a**).

★★★ **Pennile.** Via Spalvieri, tel. 41645, fax 342755. 28 rooms. Bed & breakfast. Parking, garden (C5, *off map*).

🍴 **Gallo d'Oro.** Corso Vittorio Emanuele 13, tel. 253520. Closed Christmas–New Year and for a period in Aug. Air conditioning. Marchigian cuisine (B3, **u**).

☕ Cafés and pastry shops
Caffè Meletti. Piazza del Popolo. A historical café which produces the celebrated Anisetta.
Da Sestili. Corso Mazzini. Characteristic interiors.

🏛 Museums and cultural institutions
Galleria d'Arte Contemporanea. Corso Mazzini 224, tel. and fax 250760. Closed Mon (winter) and Sat afternoon and Sat afternoon in summer. *Open winter weekdays 9am–1pm, holidays 9am–1pm; summer 9am–1pm, and 3pm–7pm.*
Museo archeologico statale. Piazza dell'Arengo, tel. 253520. Closed Mon. *Open 9am–7pm; Sun 9am–1pm.*
Museo diocesano. Piazza dell'Arengo, tel. 259901, 256528. *Open by request, Tue & Sat 10am–noon.*
Museo di Storia naturale "Antonio Orsini." Corso Mazzini 39, tel. 277538, 277539, 277540. *Open 9am–1pm; Tue and Thu open also 3pm–6pm, Sat and Sun on request.*
Palazzo dei Capitani del Popolo. Piazza del Popolo. *Visits on request to the Museo Archeologico Statale.*
Pinacoteca Civica. Piazza dell'Arengo, tel. 298213. *Open Jun–Sep 9am–1pm and 4pm–7.30pm; Oct–May 9am–1pm.*

⛪ Churches

S. Emidio alle Grotte. Borgo Solestà. *Visits on request, tel. 257946.*
S. Vittore. Viale De Gasperi. *Visits on request, tel. 257062.*

🎭 Festivals and entertainments

Teatro Ventidio Basso. Via del Trivio, tel. 298305, 298306, 298311.
Torneo cavalleresco della Quintana (First Sun in Aug). Tel. 298223, e 0735 261998. The most celebrated pageant held in the Marche.

⚖️ Shops and crafts

Enoteca Gastronomia Migliori. Piazza dell'Arengo 2, tel. 250042, fax 256611. An obligatory stop-over for all the typical local produce.
FAM. Via Amalfi 3, tel. 43123. Glass work.
Giancarlo Proietti. Via delle Torri 11, tel. 254628. Pottery specialist, with a large range of period furniture; also restoration work.
L'Acerba. Via Pretoriana 75, tel. 256454. Pottery center.
Luciano Cordivani. Rua Cappelli 1, tel. 254480. Art pottery.
Piera Vespa. Via Fortezza 10, tel. 258236. Notable range of antiques covering all periods.

at Folignano, 8 km   ✉ 63040
Sergio Baiocchi. Via Lungotronto Bar-

tolomei 17, tel. 491709. Carves and sculpts articles in travertine (masks, fireplaces).
Cesare Castelli. Via Lungotronto Bartolomei 7, tel. 252084, 259126. Violin makers of wide repute.

Borgo Pace

⊠ 61040 ☎ 0722

👥 Local guides and excursions

at Lamoli, 5 km

Centro di Educazione Ambientale. Tel. 80133. Bookings for excursions for stretches of the GEA (Grande Escursione Appenninica) and for the falls of Sasso.

Cagli

⊠ 61043 ☎ 0721

📋 *Pro Loco.* Tel. 787457.

Comunità montana del Catria e del Nerone. Via Alessandri 19, tel. & fax 787752.

Municipio. Piazza Matteotti, tel. 7911.

🏛 Cafés and pastry shops

at Cantiano, 6 km
⊠ 61044

Furiosi Robertino. Via IV Novembre. Specialized in the production of typical local delicacies.

🏛 Museums and cultural institutions

Centro di Scultura contemporanea. Torrione della Rocca. *Open on request, tel. 791232.*

Museo Archeologico e della Via Flaminia. Palazzo Comunale, tel. 7911, 791232. *Open Oct–May, Sat & Sun 10am–12noon; Jun–Sep 10am–12noon, and 4pm–7pm.*

Raccolta diocesana. Via Argotti 1, tel. 787288. Closed for alterations.

Teatro Comunale. Piazza Papa Nicolò IV. Scheduled to open in Autumn 1998.

Torrione della Rocca. *Open on request, tel. 791232.*

🎭 Festivals and entertainments

Palio dell'Oca (2nd Sun in Aug). Tel. 781511.

Teatro della Luna (summer). Avant-garde performances in Cagli and local towns.

at Cantiano, 6 km

La Turba (Good Friday). Reconstruction of the Passion performed since 1260.

⚖ Shops and crafts

Battistelli Armando. Via Venezia. Cabinetry, restoration of antique furniture.

Marzani Fernando. Via Bencivenne, tel. 782069. Cabinetry, restoration of antique furniture.

Sabine Alexandra Lindner. Località Smirra, tel. 709336. Pottery typical of local production.

Sordini Bruto. Via Tiranni, tel. 790043. Crafts production of pipes.

at Pianello, 13 km
⊠ 61040

Nicoletti Sandro. Producer of saddlepacks, saddles, and other accessories for horseriding.

⛷ Sport

Mountain-climbing, hang-gliding and paragliding, on Mts. Catria and Nerone.

🌲 Parks and natural reserves

at Cantiano, 6 km

Parco naturale Bosco di Tecchie. Information c/o Centro visite Balbano, tel. 789151.

Caldarola

⊠ 62010 ☎ 0733

📋 *Ufficio turistico.* Piazza Vittorio Emanuele, tel. 905529.

🏛 Museums and cultural institutions

Castello Pallotta. Tel. 905242. *Open Apr–Sep 10am–12, and 3pm–6pm; Oct–Mar 10am–12, and 2.30pm–5.30.*

Museo della Resistenza. Piazza Vittorio Emanuele 23, tel. 905529. *Open Thu, Sat & Sun 10am–12.30pm and 5pm–7pm.*

⛪ Churches

at Cessapalombo, 10 km
⊠ 62020

Abbey of S. Salvatore. Monastery locality. *Open on request, tel. 694387.*

🎭 Festivals and entertainments

La Giostra de la Castella (Aug). Tel. 905529.

⚖ Shops and crafts

Artigianferro di Cardinali Saulo. Viale Aldo Moro, tel. 905700. Craftswork in wrought iron.

Azienda agricola Alberto Quacquarini. Contrada Colli 1, tel. and fax 908180. Finest production of local wine (Vernaccia), plus a red wine accompanied by biscuits produced by the same company.

Farolegno. Via Buscalferri, tel. 905650. Custom-built furtniture.

Iridea. Via Moro, tel. 905863. Artistic glasswork.

🏊 Sport

Canottaggio e canoa on Lake Caccamo. Information, tel. 905529.

👥 Local guides and excursions

at Cessapalombo, 10 km

Casa del Parco. Tel. 967851
Cooperativa Il Balcone dei Sibillini. Tel. 694328.

Camerino

Page 111   ⊠ 62032 ☎ 0737

ℹ️ *Associazione turistica Pro Camerino.* Piazza Cavour 19, tel. 632534.

Comunità montana delle Alti Valli del Fiastrone, del Chienti e del Nera. Tel. 630424.

Comune di Camerino. Assessorato al Turismo. Tel. 636245.

🏛 Museums and cultural institutions

Biblioteca Valentiniana. Piazza Cavour, tel. 632394.

Museo Diocesano. Piazza Cavour, tel. 630400, 632611. *Visits on request.*

Museo di Scienze Naturali dell'Università. Former convent of S. Domenico. Scheduled opening, spring 1998.

Orto Botanico dell'Università. Viale Oberdan 2, tel. 633444. Closed Sun. *Visits 9am–1pm, 3pm–5pm, Sat 9am–1pm.*

Pinacoteca-Museo Civico. Former church S. Francesco. Will be transferred to the former convent of S. Domenico. Schedule opening, spring 1998.

Rocca dei Da Varano. Sfercia. *Visits on request to the Comune.*

Università degli Studi. Piazza Cavour (Palazzo Ducale), tel. 4011.

🏠 Churches

Convento dei Cappuccini e Museo storico cappuccino. Località Rena Cavata. *Visits on request, tel. 644480.*

🏃 Festivals and entertainments

Corsa alla Spada (Sun following 17 May). Tel. 630512.

Festival internazionale di Musica da Camera (Aug). Tel. 630193, 636245.

Premio nazionale biennale per la Drammaturgia, Scenografia e Interpretazione Ugo Betti (Dec). Tel. 636245.

⚒ Shops and crafts

Montanari. Via XX Settembre, tel. 632512. From cheese to "ciabuscolo."

Francucci. Via Conti di S. Maroto 17, tel. 636775. Production of fresh nougat.

Carpegna

Page 99   ⊠ 61021 ☎ 0722

ℹ️ *Pro Loco.* Piazza Conti, tel. 77153.

Comunità montana del Montefeltro. Tel. 77837, 77186, fax 77732.

🏛 Museums and cultural institutions

at Frontino, 6.5 km   ⊠ 61020

Museo Franco Assetto. Via Giovanni XXIII, tel. 71131. Closed Sun. *Open 4pm–6pm.*

Palazzo Carpegna. *Visits on request, tel. 77114.*

🏃 Festivals and entertainments

at Frontino, 6.5 km

Premio culturale letterario Montefeltro (Sep). Tel. 71131. Concentrates on the small-town aspects of Italy.

⚒ Shops and crafts

Allegretti Domenico. Via Roma, tel. 77228. Sale of Carpegna hams.

Moanni Gaetano. Via Carivaglia 8, tel. 77509. Fabrics decoration.

at Pietrarubbia, 7 km   ⊠ 61020

Tam (Trattamento artistico dei Metalli). Center founded by the contemporary sculptor Arnaldo Pomodoro, courses given; information tel. 75110.

〽 Sport

at Montecopiolo, 11.5 km   ⊠ 61014

Winter ski-lift service. Tel. 78130.

🌳 Parks and natural reserves

Parco regionale Monte Carpegna, e del Sasso Simone e Simoncello. Piazza Conti, tel. 770064.

at Montecopiolo, 11.5 km

Centro Educazione ambientale-Aula di Villagrande di Montecopiolo. Information and reservations c/o Cooperativa La Macina, Via Insorti Ungheresi 63, tel. 0721 797240, Acqualagna.

Castelfidardo

Page 61   ⊠ 60022 ☎ 071

ℹ️ *Pro Loco.* Piazza della Repubblica 6, tel. 7822987.

Ufficio Turismo. Piazza della Repubblica 8, tel. 7829342.

🏛 Museums and cultural institutions

Museo internazionale della Fisarmonica. Piazza della Repubblica 8, tel. 78291. *Visits 9.30am–noon and 3pm–6pm.*

Museo risorgimentale della Battaglia. Via Mazzini, tel. 7808152. Closed Tue (winter). *Open summer 10am–noon and 4pm–7pm, Fri 10am–noon, 5pm–midnight; summer 4pm–7pm, Fri 10am–noon and 5pm –midnight; winter 10am–noon and 4pm–7pm.*

🏃 Festivals and entertainments

Premio internazionale Astor Piazzolla (Nov).

Premio internazionale per Solisti e Complessi di Fisarmonica (Oct). Tel. 780014.

⚒ Shops and crafts

Baffetti Dino. Via Raffaello Sanzio 51, tel. 7822077. Handmade piano-accordions and other hand-operated organs.

Beniamino Bugiolacchi. Via Garibaldi 14, tel. 780091. Production of piano-accordion straps.

Cingoli

ℹ️ *ATC Pro Loco.* Via Ferri 17, tel. 602769.
IAT. Via Ferri 17, tel. 602444.

🏨 Hotels, restaurants, and campsites

*** **Miramonti.** Via dei Cerquatti 31, tel. 604027, fax 602239. 22 rooms. Parking, garden, tennis.

☕ Cafés and pastry shops

Balcone delle Marche. Via Balcone delle Marche 12, tel. 603371. Typical local cakes and sweets, with a view over the Marche countryside.

🏛 Museums and cultural institutions

Museo archeologico statale. Piazza Vittorio Emanuele II, tel. 602877, 603146. *Open 9am–1.30pm.*

Museo Castiglioni. Corso Garibaldi 85 (Palazzo Castiglioni). *Open on request, tel. 602531.*

Pinacoteca comunale "Donatello Stefanucci." Via Mazzini 10, tel. 602877, 603146. Closed Sun. *Open 10.30am–12.30pm.*

⛪ Churches

Abbey of SS. Quattro Coronati, or of S. Salvatore di Monte Bianco. *Open on request to the ATC Pro Loco or the IAT.*

S. Filippo. Via del Podestà. *Open on request, tel. 602416.*

S. Esuperanzio. Via S. Esuperanzio. *Open on request, tel. 602152.*

🏃 Festivals and entertainments

Cingoli 1848 (Aug). Tel. 603146. Historical pageant.

La Rosa d'Oro (Jun). Tel. 602823. National competition for flower arrangements.

⚒️ Shops and crafts

Guido Bravi. Via Molino Nuovo 2, tel. 616383. Production of flour from normal grain, maize, and wholemeal, ground with a water-powered mill built in the early 1800s.

Marchegiani Ivana. Corso Garibaldi 65, tel. 633441. Decoration on glass, fabrics, and production of *bomboniere.*

Rubens. Contrada Rangore, tel. 616142. Wrought iron work.

at Troviggiano, 7 km   ✉ 62010

Olio del Priore. Cooperativa Verdolio S.r.l. Via Occhiano 1/b, tel. 603615. Huge choice of purest oil pressed from olives grown in the area of Cingoli.

🚶 Local guides and excursions

Comunità montana del San Vicino (Zona G). Tel. 602823. Itineraries on mountainbike, horseback, and on foot to the Pian dell'Elmo, and the manganese mine at San Bonfiglio.

Civitanova Marche

ℹ️ *APT.* Via IV Novembre 20, tel. 813967.
Municipio. Tel. 8221.

🏨 Hotels, restaurants, and campsites

ᵢ **Miramare.** Viale Matteotti 1, tel. 811511, fax 810637. 79 rooms. Wheelchair access. Air conditioning, elevator; parking, garage, garden (C2, **a**).

*** **Tortuga.** Viale Vittorio Veneto 134, tel. 811087. 19 rooms. Bed & breakfast. Air conditioning, elevator; parking (D3, **b**).

🍴 **Gabbiano.** At Fontespina, Via IV Novembre 256, tel. 70113. Closed Mon, and for a spell in Nov. Marchigian menu, specialty fish. (A1, *f.p.*).

🏕 **Belvedere.** At Fontespina, Via Palazzaccio 19, tel. 70833. All year.

🏛 Museums and cultural institutions

at Civitanova Alta, 4.5 km   ✉ 62013

Civica Galleria d'Arte moderna "Marco Moretti." Piazza della Libertà, tel. 890160. Closed Sun. *Open 8am–1pm.*

🏃 Festivals and entertainments

Civitanova Danza (Jul–Aug). Tel. 812936. **Culinariarisinterra** (Jul–Aug). Tel. 812936. Gastro-humoristic festival!

⚒️ Shops and crafts

at Montecosaro, 9 km   ✉ 61010

La Luma. Via Bruscantini 1, tel. and fax 229701. Well-stocked wine cellar.

at Casette d'Ete, 10km ✉ 63011 ☎ 0734

Diego Della Valle. Tel. 871671. Sale to public of celebrated designer's footwear.

⛺ Sport

Circolo Tennis. Via dello Stadio 5, tel. 815398.

Solino Blu. Via Spontini 6, tel. 774431. School for obtaining boat licenses and permits for scuba diving.

at Civitanova Alta, 4.5 km

Circolo ippico Cluana. Contrada Le Grazie 12, tel. 890627. Riding school.

Corinaldo

ℹ️ *Associazione Pro Corinaldo.* Via del Velluto 20, tel. 679047.

Municipio. Via del Corso 9, tel. 67220 (Ufficio Cultura) and 679043 (Ufficio Turismo).

🏛 Museums and cultural institutions

Birthplace of St. Maria Goretti. Via Pregiagna, tel. 67123.

Civica Raccolta d'Arte "Claudio Ridolfi". Piazza del Cassero 15, tel. 67220,

679043. *Open Sat & Sun 10am–12.30pm, and 4pm–7.30pm; from mid-Jun to mid-Agu, and mid-Aug to mid-Set 10am–12.30pm and 4pm–730pm; mid-July to mid-Aug open also 9pm–11pm.*

Sala del Costume e delle Tradizioni popolari. Largo XVII Settembre 1860 5, tel. 679043. *Open Jun to 15 Sep 10am–12.30pm and 4pm–7.30pm; other months, Sat and holidays, 10am–12.30pm and 2.30pm–6pm.*

Villa Cesarini. Tel. 6790215. *Guided tour on request to the Ufficio Turismo at the Municipio.*

🏃 Festivals and entertainments

Festa del Pozzo della Polenta (3rd Sun of Jul). Recreation of the siege of 1517, *palio* of the Arcieri, charging of the quintaine of the Giarrettiera ward; info. c/o Associazione Pozzo della Polenta, Via Tarducci 20, tel. 679043.

⚖️ Shops and crafts

F.lli Maori. Via Nevola, tel. 679017. Permanent exhibition of antique furniture.

Lenci Arredamenti. Provincial road to Corinaldo, tel. 67069. Custom-built furniture, restoration work, and large display of antique furniture.

Corridonia

Page 126   ✉ 62014 ☎ 0733

ⓘ *Municipio.* Tel. 433067, 433235.

🏛 Museums and cultural institutions

Museo Filippo Corridoni. Piazza Corridoni, tel. 433067, 433235. *Open 7.30am–1.30pm.*

Pinacoteca parrocchiale. Via Cavour (church of Ss. Pietro e Paolo), tel. 431832. *Open on advance request.*

🏋 Sport

Impianto sportivo Sigismondo Martini. Tel. 434300, 433244. Horseriding lessons.

Cupra Marittima

Page 149   ✉ 63012 ☎ 0735

ⓘ *Laboratorio didattico di Ecologia del Quaternario.* Piazza Possenti, tel. 778622.

Municipio. Piazza della Libertà, tel. 777731.

🏨 Hotels, restaurants, and campsites

★★★ **Europa.** Via Gramsci 8, tel. 778034, fax 778033. 30 rooms. Wheelchair access. Elevator, parking, garage.

🏛 Museums and cultural institutions

Antiquarium comunale. Piazza della Libertà, tel. 777731. Undergoing renovations.

Museo malacologico piceno. Via Adriatica nord 240, tel. 777550. *Open Jun 4pm–8.30pm; Jul–Aug 4pm–10pm; Apr–May Sep, Tue, Thu, Sat & Sun 3pm–19pm.*

Parco archeologico di Cupra Marittima. Via Adriatica nord. *Open on request to the Laboratorio didattico di Ecologia del Quaternario, or to the Municipio.*

🏛 Churches

S. Maria in Castello. Via Castello. *Open on request, tel. 777120.*

Collegiate church of S. Basso. Via Roma. *Open on request, tel. 777118.*

⚖️ Shops and crafts

La Nova. Via Ciucci 47, tel. 778143. Artistic glasswork.

Cupra Montana

Page 53

ⓘ *Ufficio Informazioni turistiche.* Piazza Cavour 30, tel. 789746.

Pro Loco. Viale Vittoria 12, tel. 780660.

🏛 Museums and cultural institutions

Museo internazionale delle Etichette dei Vini. Corso Leopardi, tel. 780199. Closed Mon. *Open 10am–noon, and 5pm–7.30pm; summer 10am–noon, 5pm–7.30pm and 9pm–11pm.*

at Staffolo, 8.5 km   ✉ 60039

Museo del Vino. Via Marconi 28, tel. 779128. *Open summer on pre-holidays 7am–11pm, holidays 7am–1pm and 3pm–11pm; open winter by request.*

🏃 Festivals and entertainments

Festa dell'Uva (autumn). One of the oldest such festivals in Italy.

at Staffolo, 8.5 km

Verdicchio d'Oro (autumn). National wine-production fair.

⚖️ Shops and crafts

Azienda agricola Vallerosa Bonci & C. s.n.c. Via Torre 13, tel. 789129, fax 789808. Direct sale of local wines (Verdicchio, Rosso Piceno) and other typical gastronomical products.

Cherubini Manlio. Via Carpaneto, tel. 780562. Wine sellers.

Fabriano

Page 105   ✉ 60044 ☎ 0732

ⓘ *Ufficio turistico.* Piazza del Comune 41, tel. 5387.

APT Fabriano. Piazza Manin 11, tel. 625067, fax 629791.

🏨 Hotels, restaurants, and campsites

★☆★ **Janus Hotel Fabriano.** Piazzale Matteotti 45, tel. 4191, fax 5714. 75 rooms. Wheelchair access. Air conditioning, elevator; parking, garage (B3, **b**).

★★★ **Aristos.** Via Cavour 103, tel. 22308, fax 21459. 8 rooms. Bed & breakfast. Parking (B2, **a**).

¶¶¶ *Old Ranch.* A Piaggia d'Olmo, tel. 627610. Closed Tue, and in Jul. Parking, garden. Regional cuisine.

Museums and cultural institutions

Grande Museo. Loggiato XX Settembre, tel. 5726. *Open Sat & Sun 5pm– 7.30pm.*

Museo della Carta e della Filigrana. Largo Fratelli Spacca, tel. 709297. Closed Mon. *Open summer 9am–1.15pm and 3pm–7pm, Sun 9am–12.30pm and 3.30pm–7pm; winter 9am–1.15pm and 3pm–6pm, Sun 9am–12.30pm, and 3.30pm–6pm.*

Pinacoteca Civica "Bruno Molajoli." Via del Poio, tel. 709255. Closed Sun afternoon and all Mon. *Open 10am–noon and 3pm–6pm; Jun–Sep 10am–noon, and 3.30pm–6.30pm.*

Churches

S. Agostino. Via Ramelli. *Visits on request, tel. 23021.*

S. Benedetto. Piazza Altini. *Visits on request to the monastery of S. Silvestro, tel. 21631.*

S. Domenico (ex). Largo Fratelli Spacca. *Open on request, tel. 629403.*

Oratorio del Gonfalone. Via Damiano Chiesa. *Visits on request, tel. 709259.*

Festivals and entertainments

Palio di S. Giovanni Battista (24 June). Tel. 626848. Artistic events, concerts, and medieval pageants, costume parade of the Maglio.

Settembre Organistico Fabrianese. Tel. 7091. Organ playing in September.

Teatro Gentile. Piazza del Comune 1, tel. 709259, 4594. Calendar of prose reading and orchestral music.

Tibi Silentium Laus. Via Balbo 56, tel. 4506. Religious singing in the Romanesque abbeys in and around Fabriano.

at Precicchie, 26 km ✉ 60040

Palio dei Campanari (August). Tel. 74024, 74160.

Living nativity.

Shops and crafts

C. Bilei. Via Cialdini 7, tel. 3418. Historical shop selling typical products of local production, such as the celebrated salame from Fabriano.

Ecart. Via Cavallotti, tel. 5591. Production of paper with embossed watermarks.

Enzo Mecella. Via Dante 112, tel. 21680. Sale of locally produced wine.

La Cantina. Via Toti 18, tel. 24615. From wines to salami.

Maestri Cartai di Bartolini Mariano. Largo Bartolo da Sassoferrato, tel. 4022-21321. Handmade, watermarked paper.

at Campodiegoli, 9 km

Cooperativa agroittica fabrianese. Tel. 72003. Sale of smoked salmon trout, freshwater shrimps and other river fish (carp, sturgeon).

Local guides and excursions

Anello del Giano nell'Alta Valle dell'Esino. Tel. 624548. Mountain-bike excursions.

Monte Cucco-Poggio San Romualdo-Domo-Precicchie. Excursions on horseback, or bicycle; info c/o Centro Ippico Frinco, tel. 973202.

at Valleremita, 7 km

Laboratorio territoriale Aula verde di Valleremita. Info and bookings for guided tours c/o Cooperativa Ecologica L'Appennino, tel. 72328.

Falconara Marittima

Hotels, restaurants, and campsites

★★★ *Touring.* Via degli Spagnoli 18, tel. 9160005, fax 913000. 75 rooms. Wheelchair access. Elevator; parking, garage, garden, swimming pool.

¶¶ *Il Camino.* Via Tito Speri 2, tel. 9171647. Closed Sun and Mon, and a period of December. Air conditioning, parking. Regional cuisine.

Cafés and pastry shops

Caffè Pasticceria Bedetti. Via Flaminia 560, tel. 912940. Sweets, nougat, and ice-creams.

Museums and cultural institutions

Paese dei Bimbi. Via Castello di Barcaglione, tel. 911312. Closed Tue. *Open Apr–Sep 9am–8pm.*

Churches

at Chiaravalle, 8 km ✉ 60033

Abbey of S. Maria in Castagnola. Tel. 94350. *Open winter 6.30am–11am, and 5pm–6.30pm; summer 6.30am–11am, and 5pm–7pm.*

Sport

Aereo Club Ancona. Via Aereoporto, tel. 205978. Flying, deltaplaning, model aircraft club, parashuting; but also tourist flights.

Falerone

ℹ *Municipio.* Tel. 710115, 710472.

Museums and cultural institutions

Museo Archeologico Antiquarium. Piazza della Libertà 1, tel. 710115. *Open on request, summer, 9.30am–noon and 4pm–7pm.*

at Piane di Falerone, 2.5 km

Area Archeologica di "Faleria." Open on request, summer, 9.30am–noon, and 4pm–7pm.

🏃 Festivals and entertainments

Teatro Classico (Jul–Aug). Tel. 710115. Performed in the Roman theater of ancient *Faleria*.

at Servigliano, 5 km ✉ 63029

Torneo cavalleresco di Castel Clementino (3rd Sun of August). Tel. 750583.

Fano

Page 72 ✉ 61032 ☎ 0721

ℹ️ *IAT*. Via Battisti 10, tel. 803534.
Ufficio Cultura. Tel. 887412, 887413.
Ufficio Turismo. Tel. 887401, fax 825181.

🏨 Hotels, restaurants, and campsites

⋆✲⋆ **Elisabeth Due.** Piazzale Amendola 2, tel. 823146, fax 823147. 32 rooms. Air conditioning, elevator; parking, garage (A1, **b**).

⋆✲⋆ **Grand Hotel Elisabeth.** Viale Carducci 12, tel. 804241, fax 804242. 37 rooms. Air conditioning, elevator; garage, garden (A1, **a**).

⋆⋆⋆ **Angela.** Viale Adriatico 13, tel. 801239, fax 803102. 28 rooms. Wheelchair access. Air conditioning, elevator; parking, garden (B3, **c**).

⋆⋆⋆ **Corallo.** Via L. da Vinci 3, tel. 804200, fax 803637. 27 rooms. Air conditioning, elevator; garage (B3, **n**).

⛺ *⋆✲⋆* **Stella Maris.** At Torrette, Via Cappellini 5, tel. 884231, fax 884269. Seasonal opening.

♨️ Thermal resorts

at Carignano Terme, 10 km

Terme di Carignano. Tel. 885128. Season: Jun–Oct. Sulfur-rich, alkaline bicarbonate waters, with traces of magnesium-chlorate and iodine.

☕ Cafés and pastry shops

Bar Giuliano. Via Sauro 270, tel. 804579. Serves the *moretta* a typical Fano-style coffee.
Pasticceria Guerrino. Corso Matteotti 126, tel. 803440. Small, but with a fantastic reputation.

🏛️ Museums and cultural institutions

Biblioteca Federiciana. Via Castracane, tel. 805531.
Museo Civico e Pinacoteca. Palazzo Malatesta, tel. 828362. Closed Mon. *Open 8.30am–12.30pm, Sunday 8.30am–1pm.*
Museo del Mare. Via Adriatico 1, tel. 802689, 802736. *Open Sat 3pm–6pm, Sun 9am–noon.*

at Mombaroccio, 17.5 km ✉ 61024

Pinacoteca Conventuale "Beato Sante." Sanctuary of the Beato Sante. *Open on request, tel. 471122.*

⛪ Churches

S. Pietro ad Vallum. Via Nolfi. *Open on request to the Ufficio Cultura.*

🏃 Festivals and entertainments

Carnevale dell'Adriatico, perhaps the oldest carnival in Italy.
Fiera dell'Antiquariato (2nd Sat and Sun of the month). Tel. 887203.
Il Violino e la Selce (Jul). Tel. 830145. Contemporary music festival.
Jazz by the Sea (Jul). Tel. 807073. Jazzfest with groups and musicians of international standing.

⚖️ Shops and crafts

Azienda Agraria La Vigna delle Terrazze. Viale Romagna 47/b, tel. 823352. Selection of typical DOC wines of local production (Bianchello del Metauro, Colli Pesaresi Sangiovese).
Casa Mei. Via Fanella 13, tel. 802987. Sweets and cakes.
Mariposa. Corso Matteotti 21, tel. 827599. Decoration and production of pottery and porcelain.
Ricci. Via Cavour 67, tel. 803252. Highly characteristic wine store.
Romolo Eusebi. Piazza Costanzo 12, tel. 807919. Antiques dealer specialized in etchings, cartography, navigation maps, and antique books.

at Saltara, 15 km ✉ 61030

Berloni Rattan. Località Borgaccio, Via Furlo, tel. 894436. Rattan wickerwork.

at Montemaggiore al Metàuro, 16 km ✉ 61030

Fattorie Marchigiane. Tel. 895744. Production and sale of "caciotta d'Urbino," a typical cheese of the Metauro valley.

🏊 Sport

Porto turistico. Capitaneria di Porto, Largo della Lanterna 3, tel. 801329.

Fermo

Page 149 ✉ 63023 ☎ 0734

ℹ️ *IAT*. Piazza del Popolo, tel. 228738, 228329.

🏨 Hotels, restaurants, and campsites

⋆⋆⋆ **Astoria.** Viale Vittorio Veneto 8, tel. 22860, fax 228602. 49 rooms. Elevator; parking (B2-3, **a**).

⛺ *⋆✲⋆* **Spinnaker.** At Santa Maria a Mare, tel. 53413, fax 53412. Seasonal.

♨️ Thermal resorts

at Torre di Palme, 10 km ✉ 63010

Fonti di Palme. Tel. 30106. Season Jun–Sep. Cold-water springs (16°C) containing calcium and bicarbonate.

🏛️ Museums and cultural institutions

Associazione Marchigiana Rievocazioni storiche. Corso Cefalonia 69, tel. 225994.

Cisterne Romane. Piazza del Popolo (Palazzo dei Priori), tel. 284327, 226166. *Open on request 9.30am–12.30pm, 4.30pm–7.30pm.*

Museo Archeologico. Piazza del Popolo, tel. 284327. *Open 9.30am–12.30pm, 4.30pm–7.30pm.*

Museo Diocesano. Piazza del Girfalco (Curia arcivescovile), tel. 228729. Closed for alterations.

Museo Polare "Silvio Zavatti." Viale Trento, tel. 226166. *Open Tue–Sat 9.30am –12.30pm; Tue, Wed, Sat also 4pm–7pm.*

Museo di Scienze naturali "Tommaso Salvadori." Viale Trento, tel. 226166. *Open Tue–Sat 9.30am–12.30pm; Tue, Wed, and Sat also 4pm–7pm.*

Pinacoteca civica. Piazza del Popolo, tel. 284327. Closed Mon. *Open 9.30am–12.30am, 4.30pm–7.30pm.*

Churches

S. Marco alle Paludi. Tel. 640048. *Open Sun 8am–noon.*

Festivals and entertainments

Cavalcata dell'Assunta (15 Aug). Tel. 225924.

Fermo Festival (Jun–Jul). Tel. 284314.

Mercatino dell'Antiquariato e Artigianato (every Thu in Jul and Aug).

Teatro dell'Aquila. Via Mazzini, tel. 284281. Season of opera and theater.

Sport

Circolo Tennis Fermo. Viale Crollalanza, tel. 229676.

Fiastra

               ✉ 62033 ☎ 0737

i *Casa del Parco.* Via Umberto I, tel. 52598.

Museums and cultural institutions

at Pievebovigliana, 12 km   ✉ 62035

Museo "Raffaele Campelli." Piazza Vittorio Veneto 90 (Palazzo Comunale), tel. 44026. Closed Sun. *Open 9am–1pm.*

Churches

S. Lorenzo al Lago. *Open on request, tel. 52109.*

S. Paolo. Via S. Paolo. *Open on request, tel. 52109.*

at Acquacanina, 3 km   ✉ 62030

Abbey church of S. Maria di Rio Sacro. At Meriggio, tel. 52143. *Visits on request.*

at Pievebovigliana, 12 km

S. Giusto. Borough of San Maroto, tel. 633030. *Open Sun 8.30am–1pm, 3pm–7pm.*

Sport

at Acquacanina, 3 km

Sci di fondo on the slopes of the Ragnolo.

at Fiordimonte, 16 km   ✉ 62030

Valle di Fiordimonte. Hunting association.

Local guides and excursions

at Acquacanina, 3 km

Casa del Parco di Fiastra. Tel. 52598. For guided tours of the Fiastrone valley.

Filottrano

Page 126   ✉ 60024 ☎ 071

i Tourist office. Municipio, tel. 7220134.

  Pro Loco. Via dell'Industria 96, tel. 7222364.

Cafés and pastry shops

Bar Walli. Piazza Mazzini. On the old Porta Romana (demolished) since the late 1800s.

Museums and cultural institutions

Museo del Biroccio. Vicolo Beltrami 2, tel. 7221314, 33037. *Open Tue 3pm–6pm, Wed 9.30am–noon, 3pm–6pm; Fri 9.30am–noon.*

Museo dell'Esploratore Giacomo Beltrami. Vicolo Beltrami 2, tel. 7221314-33037. *Open Tue 3pm–6pm; Thu 9.30am–noon, 3pm–6pm; Fri 9.30am–noon.*

Churches

S. Francesco. Via Leopardi, tel. 7221560. *Open mornings on request.*

Festivals and entertainments

La Contesa dello Stivale (1st week of Aug). Tel. 7220968. Historical pageant in medieval dress recreating battles scenes between Filottrano and Osimo.

Fossombrone

Page 80   ✉ 61034 ☎ 0721

i *Comunità Montana del Metàuro.* Via Roma, tel. 740222.

  Pro Loco. Piazza Dante, tel. 740377.

Cafés and pastry shops

Pasticceria Rinci. Via Roma. One of the oldest in the town.

Museums and cultural institutions

Area Archeologica "Forum Sempronii." *Visits on request to the Pro Loco office.*

Corte Bassa. Via Battisti 59. *Open on request to the Pro Loco office.*

Museo Civico "Augusto Vernarecci." Corte Alta, tel. 714645, 723238. *Open Sat and Sun 3.30am–6.30pm.*

Pinacoteca Civica. Corte Alta, tel. 714645, 723238. Closed for alterations.

Quadreria Cesarini. Via Pergamino 23, tel. 714650. *Open Sat 9am–12.30pm, 1st and 3rd Sun of month, 3pm–630pm.*

Churches

S. Aldebrando. Rocca Malatestiana. *Visits on request to the Pro Loco office.*

Festivals and entertainments

Mostra Mercato del Tartufo Bianchetto (1st Sun of March).
Trionfo del Carnevale (2nd Sun of May). Tel. 723234. Historical pageant recreating the return of Cardinal Della Rovere in 1559.

Sport

FOCA Canoe Club. Val Metauro. Via Metauro 1, tel. 714549.
Deltaplane and hang-gliding in the Furlo valley.

Shops and crafts

at Sant'Ippolito, 7.5 km ⊠ 61040
Gasparucci Natalia. Viale Leopardi, tel. 728316. Artistic designs in stone.

Local guides and excursions

Bosco delle Cesane. Info c/o Comunità Montana del Metauro, Pro Loco.
I Monti e le Gole del Furlo. Guided visits by request c/o Cooperativa La Macina, Via Insorti Ungheresi 63, tel. 797240, Acqualagna.

Gabicce Mare

Page 71 ⊠ 61011 ☎ 0541
i *IAT.* Viale della Vittoria 41, tel. 954424, fax 953500.
Municipio. Via Battisti, tel. 953101.

Hotels, restaurants, and campsites

★₸★ Grand Hotel Michelacci. Piazza Giardini Unità d'Italia 1, tel. 954361, fax 954544. 60 rooms. Wheelchair access. Air conditioning, elevator; parking, garden, swimming pool (B2, **a**).
★★★ Marinella. Via Vittorio Veneto 127, tel. 954571, fax 950426. Seasonal. 60 rooms. Air conditioning, elevator; garage, garden (B2, **b**).
★★ Cavalluccio Marino. Via Vittorio Veneto 111, tel. 950053, fax 954402. Seasonal. 35 rooms. Elevator, parking, garden (B2, **c**).

Sport

Centro sportivo comunale. Tel. 953542. Tennis.
Porto turistico. Capitaneria di Porto, Via del Porto, tel. 967463.

at Casteldimezzo, 10 km ⊠ 61010
Hang gliding and paragliding over the sea.

Genga

Page 109 ⊠ 60040 ☎ 0732
i *Consorzio Grotte di Frasassi.* Largo Leone XII, tel. 973039-973001, freephone 167013828.

Thermal resorts

Spa of S. Vittore. Tel. 90012. Season Apr–Nov; sulfurous water.

Museums and cultural institutions

Museo dell'ex Chiesa di S. Clemente. Largo Leone XII, tel. 973039. *Open Sun 10am–1pm, 3pm–6pm; Jul–Aug noon–7pm.*

Churches

Abbey of S. Vittore delle Chiuse. *Open 9am–1pm, 3pm–7pm.*
Santuario di Frasassi. Freephone 167013828. Closed winter. *Open in summer, on request.*

Festivals and entertainments

Presepe Vivente (26 Dec, following Sun and 6 Jan). Tel. 973019. The costumes are based on the *Adoration of the Shepherds* by Gentile da Fabriano in the Uffizi, Florence.

Sport

River canoing from the Frasassi to the Rossa.

Local guides and excursions

at Camponocecchio, 9 km
CENF (Centro Escursionistico Naturalistico Frasassi). Tel. 973202. Mineralogy and archaeology excursions and discovery trails.

Parks and natural reserves

Grotte di Frasassi. Freephone 167013828. *Guided tours, Nov–Feb 11, 15, 16; Sun and Christmas period 9.30am, 11am, 12.30pm, 3pm, 4.30pm, 6pm; Mar–Jul and Sep–Octo 9.30am, 11am, 12.30pm, 3pm, 4.30pm, 6pm; Aug 8am–6.30pm; 19 Jul–24 Aug also 8pm–10.30pm.*
Oasi naturalistica WWF Bosco di Frasassi. Tel. 22937, 21296.
Parco regionale Gola della Rossa e Frasassi, Area naturale di Valle Scappuccia. Info c/o Comunità Montana Esino Frasassi, Via Dante 268, tel. 6951, Fabriano.

Gradara

Page 71 ⊠ 61012 ☎ 0541
i *Pro Loco.* Via Borgo Mancini, tel. 964115.
Municipio. Tel. 964123.

Hotels, restaurants, and campsites

¶¶ **Hosteria La Botte.** Piazza V Novembre 11, tel. 964404. Closed Wed (except in summer), mid-Nov to mid-Dec. Garden. Specialist local cuisine.

Museums and cultural institutions

Museo Storico. Piazza V Novembre 8/9, tel. 964154. *Open winter 9am–1.30pm, summer 9am–7pm.*
Pinacoteca Comunale. Via Umberto I 9, tel. 964123, 964126. Closed.

Rocca. Via Umberto I, tel. 964181, 964154. *Open winter 9am–13.30, summer 9am–7pm.*

🏃 Festivals and entertainments

Gradara Ludens Festival (from Apr to Sep). Tel. 964142. Games festival.
Seduzione al Castello (3rd weekend of Jul). Tel. 964115. Dancing, banquets, crafts display, medieval (and aphrodisiac) food to recreated the days of Paolo and Francesca.

⚖️ Shops and crafts

Bottega del Sapore Antico. Piazza V Novembre. Antiques, crafts objects, typical local food stuffs (cheese in black pepper preserved, truffle, truffle-flovoured and wild bear sousages).

at Tavullia, 7.5 km ✉ 61010

Bartolucci Francesco. Località Belvedere Fogliense, tel. 479351. Toys and items in wood.
Romolo Verdolini. Via Roma 48. Mosaics and pottery.

Grottammare

Pagina 148 ✉ 63013 ☎ 0735
ℹ️ *Ufficio Informazioni.* Piazza Fazzini, tel. 631087.

🏨 Hotels, restaurants, and campsites

★☆★ **Parco dei Principi.** Lungomare De Gasperi 70, tel. 735066, fax 735080. 54 rooms. Wheelchair access. Air conditioning; parking, garden, swimming pool, tennis.

★★★ **Paradiso.** Lungomare De Gasperi 134, tel. 581412, fax 581257. Seasonal. 50 rooms. Wheelchair access. Air conditioning, elevator; parking, garden, swimming pool, tennis.

🏛️ Churches

S. Lucia. *On request, tel. 631121, 631131.*
S. Martino. Via S. Martino. *On request, tel. 631121-631131.*

🏃 Festivals and entertainments

Sagra giubilare. Plenary indulgence since 1755, now only held at Santiago de Compostela.

Jesi

Pagina 49 ✉ 60035 ☎ 0731
ℹ️ *Ufficio turistico.* Piazza della Repubblica, tel. 59788.

🏨 Hotels, restaurants, and campsites

★☆★ **Federico II.** Via Ancona, tel. 211079, fax 57221. 76 rooms. Wheelchair access. Air conditioning, elevator; parking, garden, swimming pool (A3, *f.p.*).

★★★ **Mariani.** Via dell'Orfanotrofio 10, tel. 207286, fax 200011. 33 rooms. Bed & breakfast. Wheelchair access. Air conditioning; parking, garage (A-B2, **m**).

🍴 **Hostaria Santa Lucia.** Via Marche 2/B, tel. 64409. Closed Mon, holiday closure variable. Air conditioning. Classical cuisine, specialty fish (A3, *off map*).

☕ Cafés and pastry shops

Caffè Pasticceria Bardi. Corso Matteotti 27, tel. 4865. Distinguished café-pâtisserie; known also for its Easter pizzas.
Degustazione Caffè Saccaria. Corso Matteotti 24, tel. 58234. Sale to public of the locale's famous coffee.

🏛️ Museums and cultural institutions

Museo "Antonio Colocci." Piazza Colocci. *Open by request to the Pinacoteca Civica.*
Museo Civico. Piazza Colocci. *Open 9am–noon, 3pm–6pm, Sat 9am–noon.*
Museo Diocesano. Piazza Federico II, tel. 58443, 207007. *Open Mon, Tue, Thu, Fri 10am–noon.*
Pinacoteca Civica (Palazzo Pianetti). Via XV Settembre, tel. 538342. Closed Mon. *Open 9.30am–12.30pm, 5pm–8pm; Jul–Aug 9.30am–12.30pm, 5pm to midnight.*

🏛️ Churches

S. Marco. Via S. Marco. *Open on request, tel. 4334.*

🏃 Festivals and entertainments

Teatro G. B. Pergolesi. Piazza della Repubblica 9, tel. 538355. Opera season, with plays, concerts, and ballet.

⚖️ Shops and crafts

La Serva Padrona. Piazza Pergolesi 1, tel. 212550. Wine cellar.

Loreto

Page 61 ✉ 60025 ☎ 071
ℹ️ *IAT.* Via Solari 3, tel. 977139.

🏨 Hotels, restaurants, and campsites

★☆★ **Villa Tetlameya.** Via Villa Costantina 187, tel. 978863, fax 976639. 8 rooms Wheelchair access. Elevator, parking, garden (A3, *f.p.*).

★★ **Orlando.** Via Villa Costantina 89, tel. 978501, fax 978501. 22 rooms. Parking (A3, *off map*).

🍴 **Andreina.** Via Buffolareccia 14, tel. 970124. Closed Tue, holidays vary. Air conditioning, parking, garden. Regional cuisine (B3, *off map*).

🏛️ Museums and cultural institutions

Archivio Storico della Santa Casa. Piazza della Madonna (Palazzo Apostolico), tel. 970291.
Museo-Pinacoteca. Piazza della Madonna (Palazzo Apostolico), tel. 977759. Closed Mon in spring & summer. *Open spring and*

summer *9am–1pm, 4pm–7pm. Open Nov–Mar on request.*

🏃 Festivals and entertainments

La Venuta (9–10 Dec). Special festivities in honor of the arrival of the Holy House.
Rassegna Internazionale di Cappelle Musicali (Apr). Info c/o Ente Rassegne Musicali Loreto, Corso Boccalini 93, tel. 970648.

⚖️ Shops and crafts

Dante Ruffini. Via Brancondi 99, tel. 970774. Production of religious artifacts and decorated objects.
Lal di Luciano Moroni. Via Costabianca 43, tel. 978072. Production of religious articles.

Macerata

Page 120 ✉ 62100 ☎ 0733
ℹ️ *IAT.* Piazza della Libertà 12, tel. 234807.
Pro Loco. Via Costa 10, tel. 230860.

🏨 Hotels, restaurants, and campsites

★★★ Claudiani. Via Ulissi 8, tel. 261400, fax 261380. 38 rooms. Bed & breakfast. Air conditioning, elevator; garage (A2, **g**).
★★★ Della Piaggia. Via S. Maria della Porta 18, tel. 230387, fax 233660. 23 rooms. Bed & breakfast. Air conditioning, elevator; garage (A-B2, **b**).
🍴 *Osteria dei Fiori.* Via Lauro Rossi 61, tel. 260142. Closed Sun, New Year's and Epiphany, and for a period in Aug. Air conditioning. Regional cuisine (A3, **m**).

🏛️ Museums and cultural institutions

Archivio di Stato. Corso Cairoli 175, tel. 236521.
Biblioteca Comunale Mozzi Borgetti. Piazza Vittorio Veneto 2, tel. 2561, 256360.
Biblioteca Nazionale di Napoli (Macerata subsection). Via Garibaldi 20, tel. 232965, 232984.
Galleria d'Arte Contemporanea. Via Ricci 1, tel. 247400. *Open Tue and Thu 4pm–6pm, Sat 10am–noon.*
Museo della Carrozza. Piazza Vittorio Veneto 2, tel. 256361. Closed Sun and Mon morning. *Open 9am–1pm, 4pm–7pm.*
Museo Civico e Pinacoteca. Piazza Vittorio Veneto 2, tel. 256361. Closed Sun afternoon and Mon morning. *Open 9am–1pm, 4pm–7pm.*
Museo Marchigiano del Risorgimento e della Resistenza. Piazza Vittorio Veneto 2, tel. 256361. Closed for refurbishment.
Museo di Storia naturale. Via S. Maria della Porta 65, tel. 239717. *Open Mon–Sat 9am–noon.*
Sferisterio. Piazza Nazario Sauro, tel. 230735. *Open 10.30am–1pm, 5pm–8pm;* on public holidays, booking necessary.
Università degli Studi. Piazza dell'Università 2, tel. 2581.

at Montecassiano, 9 km ✉ 62010
Museo della Confraternita. Corso Dante Alighieri (church of S. Giacomo), tel. 598144. *Visits on request.*

at Morrovalle, 16 km ✉ 62010
Museo Internazionale del Presepe. Vicolo Buonarelli 4, tel. 221420. *Visits on request.*

at Villa Potenza, 3.5 km ✉ 62010
Area Archeologica di "Helvia Recina." *Visits by prior appointment to the Soprintendenza Archeologica in Ancona, tel. 071 2074829.*

⛪ Churches

Church of the Incoronata. Via dei Sibillini. *Open Mon–Wed, and Sat 10am–noon.*
S. Paolo. Piazza della Libertà. *Open on request to the Museo Civico e Pinacoteca.*

at Montecassiano, 9 km
Parish church of S. Maria Assunta. Open on request from the Municipio of Montecassiano, tel. 598135, 598275.

🏃 Festivals and entertainments

Macerata Opera Festival (Jul–Aug). Tel. 230735, 233508, fax 261499. Held in the Sferisterio, one of the world's best-known opera seasons.
Premio Rabelais (2nd Sun of Nov). Tel. 0523 326797. National competition of poems on the subject of wine.
Teatro Lauro Rossi. Piazza della Libertà, tel. 256306.

⚖️ Shops and crafts

Enoteca Simoncini. Galleria del Commercio, tel. 260576. Ample selection of typical regional and Italian wines.
La Tela. Vicolo Vecchio 6, tel. 232527. Weaving on traditional looms.

at Appignano, 9.5 km ✉ 62010
Fratelli Testa. Borgo S. Croce 33, tel. 57484. Vast production of decorated pottery from Macerata district's best-known potter's studio.

Macerata Feltria

Page 98 ✉ 61023 ☎ 0722
ℹ️ *Ufficio Turistico.* Via Antimi 10, tel. 74546, 74244.
Pro Loco, tel. 74546.

♨️ Thermal resorts

Terme Pitinum. Via Antimi 18, tel. 73245, 73246. Seasonal: Apr–Nov. Sulfurous spring waters.

at Montegrimano, 9 km ✉ 61010 ☎ 0541
Terme di Montegrimano. Via Martiri della Resistenza, tel. 971080. Seasonal: May–Oct.

🏛 **Museums and cultural institutions**

Museo Civico-Archeologico-Paleontologico. In the former Palazzo del Podestà and Maschio della Rocca, tel. 73231. *Open May–Sep 10am–noon, 3.30pm–7.30pm.*

Scavi di "Pitinum Pisaurense." S. Cassiano al Pitino. *Open on request from the Museo Civico-Archeologico-Paleontologico.*

⛪ Churches

Parish church of S. Cassiano al Pitino. *Open on request to the Museo Civico-Archeologico-Paleontologico.*

⚖ Shops and crafts

Alimentari Montefeltro. Via S. Maria Valcava. In-house production of cheeses seasoned in chestnut leaves.

Carlo Prisigotti. Via Saltersca. Production and sale of "porchetta" and other types of salami.

Lazzari Domenico. Via Apsa. Production and sale of "porchetta" and other types of salami.

Maiolati Spontini

Page 53 ✉ 60030 ☎ 0731

ℹ *Municipio.* Tel. 702972.

🏛 Museums and cultural institutions

Casa Natale di Gaspare Spontini. Via Nazario Sauro, tel. 702962. *Open on request.*

Centro Studi Gaspare Spontini. Via Erard 2, tel. 703303.

Museo Spontiniano. Via Spontini. *Open on request from the Municipio.*

at Castelbellino, 3.5 km

Museo civico. Piazza S. Marco 15, tel. 702429, 702682. *Visits by appointment, 8am–2pm.*

🏃 Festivals and entertainments

Spontini Classic. Tel. 701141, 702972. Promotion of the music of the local composer Gaspare Spontini, with events held at various moment of the year.

at Montecarotto, 18.5 km ✉ 60036

Verdicchio in Festa (Jul). Tel. 89131. Market of regional wine production.

⚖ Shops and crafts

Azienda Agricola Mancini Benito. Via S. Lucia, tel. 702975, fax 703364. Direct sale of typical local wines; excellent Verdicchio S. Lucia.

Cerioni Luciano. Via S. Andrea, tel. 701977. Typical country wine cellar where one can purchase excellent local wines.

at Pianello Vallesina, 7.5 km

Enea Ricci. Tel. 702626. A great craftsman working with wrought iron.

at Montecarotto, 18.5 km ✉ 60036

Cooperativa Terre Cortesi Moncaro S.r.l. Via Piandole 7/A, tel. 89245, fax 89237. Vast choice of typical local wines (Verdicchio, Rosso Conero), plus untreated (extra virgin) olive oil.

Massa Fermana

Page 155 ✉ 63020 ☎ 0734

ℹ *Municipio,* tel. 760258, 760127.

🏛 Museums and cultural institutions

Pinacoteca Civica. Piazza Garibaldi 60. Closed Sun. *Open 8am–2pm.*

at Montappone, 3 km

Museo del Cappello. Via 8 Marzo, tel. 760379. Closed Mon in summer. *Open Sat & Sun 4pm–6pm; summer 5pm–8pm, 9.30pm–10.30pm.*

⛪ Churches

SS. Lorenzo, Silvestro e Rufino. Via Guerrieri 28. *Guided tours on request in Jul–Aug to the Municipio.*

⚖ Shops and crafts

Ciccioli Paolo. Crafts district of Castellana, tel. 760201. Production of cloth hats.

Minicucci. Via Selava 8, tel. 760040. Production of woolen hats.

TS. Crafts districst, Castellana, tel. 760348. Production of straw hats.

Matelica

Page 114 ✉ 62024 ☎ 0737

ℹ *Ufficio Turistico Associazione Pro Matelica.* Piazza Mattei, tel. 85671.

🍵 Cafés and pastry shops

Al Teatro. Via Umberto I 7, tel. 83188. Café and wine bar.

🏛 Museums and cultural institutions

Museo Piersanti. Via Umberto I 11, tel. 84445. Closed Mon. *Open Sat and Sun 10am–noon, 4pm–6pm; other days on request; May–Sep 10am–noon, 5pm–7pm.*

🏃 Festivals and entertainments

Premio Nazionale Libero Bigiaretti per la Narrativa italiana (runs May–Jun every two years). Info c/o Biblioteca Comunale, tel. 787434.

Teatro Piermarini Città di Matèlica. Corso Umberto I, tel. 85088, 787434. Season of prose, and symphonic music.

⚖ Shops and crafts

Artelaio. Vicolo Cuoio, tel. 84445. Handcrafted fabrics.

Cantina Sociale Matelica e Cerreto d'Esi Belisario. Viale Merloni 12, tel. 787247, fax 787263. Direct sale of the local Verdicchio and other gastronomic items.

Rosa Anna Magnapane. Via Sainale, tel. 83632. Crafted wrought-iron products.

at Terricoli, 4 km

Salumificio Montano. Tel. 787360. Sale of typical products of the Macerata interior, the "ciabuscolo" salame.

Sport

Volo libero with a hang-glider or paragliding from Mt. Gemmo.

at Esanatoglia, 6.5 km ✉ 62023

Crossodromo. Info c/o Moto Club Esanatoglia, Via Battisti 1, tel. 89108. International competitions.

Local guides and excursions

Comunità Montana Alta Valle del Potenza (zone H). Via Salimbeni 6, tel. 0733 637245, 637246, San Severino Marche. Guided tours of the Canfaito plains, on Mt. San Vicino, to the sources of the Esino river, and on Mt. Gemmo.

Mercatello sul Metauro

Page 94 ✉ 61040 ☎ 0722

ℹ *Pro Loco.* Piazza Garibaldi (Municipio), tel. 89114.

Cafés and pastry shops

Caffè Rinaldi. Piazza Garibaldi, tel. 89579. Old-style café in the town center.
Pacio. Corso Garibaldi, tel. 89120. Famous cake shop which produces local specialties in season (i.e., the Easter "colomba" or dove-shaped cake).

Museums and cultural institutions

Museo della Collegiata. Piazza Garibaldi, tel. 89640. *Open on request.*

Shops and crafts

Taverna del Cacciatore. Via Mercato Sud, tel. 89147. Wild-pig sausages, truffles, mushrooms, cheeses.

Local guides and excursions

Gruppo escursionistico mercatellese. Tel. 89233. Information for walks to the Pieve castle.

Mogliano

Page 138 ✉ 62020 ☎ 0733

ℹ *Municipio.* Tel. 557788, 556014.
Pro Loco. Via Leopardi 2, tel. 556788.

Museums and cultural institutions

Museo Parrocchiale. Vicolo Boninfanti, tel. 556058. *Visits on request.*

Churches

Church of the Crocifisso. At Santa Croce. *Visits on request, tel. 556147.*

Shops and crafts

Nardi Claudio. San Pietro industrial precinct, tel. 556139. Production of items in wicker.
Parigiani Giuseppe. Contrada Trataiata 2, tel. 556872. Production and sale of complementary furniture items in cane.

Mondavio

Page 77 ✉ 61040 ☎ 0721

ℹ *Pro Loco.* Piazza Matteotti 11, tel. 97102.

Museums and cultural institutions

Museo Civico. Piazza Matteotti. *Open 9am–noon, 3pm–7pm.*
Museo di Rievocazione Storica e Armeria. Piazza della Rovere (Rocca), tel. 97102. *Open 9am–noon, 3pm–7pm.*
Rocca. Piazza della Rovere, tel. 97102. *Open 9am–noon, 3pm–7pm.*

Festivals and entertainments

Caccia al Cinghiale e Incendio della Rocca (15 Aug). Festival evening, involves a boar-hunt and a symbolic burning of the town's fort. Tel. 977331, 97102.

Shops and crafts

Della Rovere. Piazza della Rovere. Sale of minerals, fossils, semiprecious stones and pottery.

at Orciano di Pesaro, 2 km ✉ 61038

Azienda Agricola Fattoria della Ripa. Via Tre Ponti. Production and direct sale of fresh cheeses.

Montalto delle Marche

✉ 63034 ☎ 0736

ℹ *Municipio.* Piazza Umberto I, tel. 828015, 828507.

Museums and cultural institutions

Museo diocesano di Arte sacra. Piazza Sisto V, tel. 828750. Closed for alterations.
Museo e Pinacoteca. Piazza Umberto I, tel. 828015. *Open: winter 8am–2pm; summer 10am–noon and 4pm–6pm.*

at Monte Rinaldo, 16.5 km

✉ 63020 ☎ 0734

Area Archeologica. Cuma. Information from "Informagiovani," tel. 777121. *Open 9am–1pm and 3.30pm–7.30 pm.*

Churches

at Porchia, 5 km ✉ 63030

La Madonna della Pace. *Open on request, tel. 828042.*
S. Antonio. *Open on request, tel. 828042.*

Festivals and entertainments

Notte delle Streghe e dei Folletti (14–15 Aug).

Cantina Sociale Valdaso. Contrada Maglio 12, tel. 828033. Sale of DOC wines from Falerio and Rosso Piceno.
Marota. Via Cuprense 1. Production and sale of salami and other cured meats.

Montefiore dell'Aso

Page 154 ✉ 63010 ☎ 0734
ℹ *Municipio.* Tel. 938822.

🏛 Museums and cultural institutions

Sala De Carolis. Via Garibaldi 38. *Open sumer 9am–noon, 3pm–8pm; other months on request to the Municipio.*
Sala Domenico Cantatore. Largo De Vecchis. *Open summer 9am–noon, 3pm–8pm; other months on request to the Municipio.*

at Carassai, 8 km ✉ 63030
Museo Archeologico Comunale. Via Roma, tel. 930900. *Open on request.*

⚖ Shops and crafts

La Campana. Contrada Manocchia, tel. 938229. Typical local food products and various locally made items.

Monterubbiano

Page 154 ✉ 63026 ☎ 0734
ℹ *Municipio.* Tel. 259980.

🏛 Museums and cultural institutions

Museo Civico Archeologico. Piazza Calzecchi Onesti, tel. 259980, 59125. *Open 6pm–8.30pm, 9.30pm–11pm.*
Pinacoteca. Piazza Calzecchi Onesti, tel. 259980, 59125. *Open 6pm–8.30pm, 9.30pm–11pm.*

🏃 Festivals and entertainments

L'Armata di Pentecoste e Sciò La Pica (Pentecost Sunday). Tel. 59677.

⚖ Shops and crafts

Abruzzeti Silvio. Contrada Lago, tel. 59100. Oil-producers.
Roberti Eliseo. Tel. 59251. Hand-wrought copper work.
Speranza Giancarlo. Via Oberdan, tel. 59476. Hand-crafted goods in wood.

Monte San Giusto

Page127 ✉ 62015 ☎ 0733
ℹ *Municipio.* Piazza Aldo Moro, tel. 839006, 839011.

🏛 Museums and cultural institutions

Collezione di Disegni Alessandro Maggiori. Piazza Aldo Moro, tel. 839006, 839011. *Open 8am–1pm.*
Palazzo Bonafede. Piazza Aldo Moro, tel. 839006, 839011. Closed Sun. *Open 8am–2pm.*

Blackstone. Via Martin Luther King 10, tel. 539446. Production and direct sale of famous Blackstone footwear

at Villa San Filippo, 5 km

Fabi. Via Rossa, tel. 530044. Production and direct sale of footwear and leather goods.

Novafeltria

Page 101 ✉ 61017 ☎ 0541
ℹ *Comunità Montana Alta Val Marecchia* (zone A). Piazza Bramante, tel. 920442.

☕ Cafés and pastry shops

Caffè Grand'Italia. Piazza Vittorio Emanuele. Attractive art déco interiors.

🏛 Museums and cultural institutions

at Perticara, 7 km

Museo Storico Minerario. Tel. 927576. Closed Mon and Fri. *Open 10am–noon, 3pm–6.30pm.*

at Talamello, 2 km

Cella. At the cemetery. Frescoes from the late Gothic iperiod (15th cent.) *Visits on request to Municipio, tel. 920736.*

🏃 Festivals and entertainments

Mostra-scambio Minerali e Fossili (2nd Sun of Sep). Information c/o Pro Loco at Perticara, tel. 927576.

at Talamello, 2 km ✉ 61010
Fiera del Formaggio di Fossa (Nov).

Numana

Page 46 ✉ 60026 ☎ 071
ℹ *Summer APT office, Ancona.* Tel. 9330612.

🏨 Hotels, restaurants, and campsites

★★★ **Alessandra.** Via Risorgimento 13, tel. 9330739, fax 7360833. Seasonal. 20 rooms. Parking, garden, swimming pool.
★★★ **Sorriso.** Via del Golfo, tel. 9330645, fax 7360655. 38 rooms. Elevator; parking, garden.
🍴 **Il Saraghino.** At Marcelli, Via Litoranea, tel. 7391596. Closed Mon, Jan–Feb. Parking. Seafood specialties.
🏕 **Numana Blu.** At Marcelli, località Costa
★★★ Verde, tel. 7390993, fax 7360970. Seasonal.

🏛 Museums and cultural institutions

Antiquarium. Via della Fenice 4, tel. 9331162. *Open 9am–7pm.*

🏃 Festivals and entertainments

Numana Eventi (Aug). Tel. 200442.

Shops and crafts

Azienda Agricola Conte Leopardi. Via Marina II 26, tel. 7390116, fax 7391479. Besides a vast choice of high-quality wines, the firm produces extra-virgin olive oil, honey, and grappa.

Sport

Circolo Nautico Massaccesi. Via del Porto, tel. 9330566.

Circolo Sub Monteconero. Via Litoranea, tel. 9330279.

Circolo velico Dama Blu. Via Litoranea 220, tel. 73900350.

Porto turistico. Via del Golfo, tel. 9330847.

Sea Wolf. Via del Porto 22, tel. 9330392. School for scuba diving

Velo Club Numana. Via Flaminia, tel. 9331297. Cycling and information on bicycling routes in the interior.

Local guides and excursions

Cooperativa Traghettatori. Tel. 9391738. Boat excursions to the main beaches in the Conero area.

Offagna

Page 60   ✉ 60020 ☎ 071

ℹ *Municipio.* Tel. 7101005, fax 7107380.

Pro Loco. Piazza del Maniero 17, tel. 7107552, fax 7107578.

Museums and cultural institutions

Museo delle Armi. Rocca, tel. 7107552. *Open 25 Apr–30 Jun, Sat & Sun 9.30am–12.3pm; 4pm–7.30pm; 1st Jul–30 Sep 9.30am–noon and 4pm–8pm.*

Museo di Scienze Naturali "Luigi Paolucci." Via del Monastero, tel. 27107611, 27107612, 7107552, fax 7107578. Closed Mon. *Open Oct–May 9am–noon, Sun 10am–noon, 4pm–7pm; Jun & Sep 4.30pm–7.30pm; holidays 10am–noon, 4.30pm–730pm; Jul–Aug 10am–noon, 4.30pm–7.30pm.*

Rocca (fort). Tel. 7107552. *Open 25 Apr–30 Jun, Sat & Sun 9.30am–12.30pm, 4pm–7.30pm; 1st Jul–30 Sept 9.30am–12.30pm, 4pm–8pm.*

Festivals and entertainments

Feste Medievali-Contesa della Crescia (last week in July).

Offida

Page 147   ✉ 63035 ☎ 0736

ℹ *Ufficio turistico.* Corso Serpente Aureo 79, tel. 889381.

Pro Loco. Tel. 880526, 889992.

Museums and cultural institutions

Museo Archeologico "Guglielmo Allievi." Via Roma 17, tel. 889381. *Open 9.30am–12.30pm, 3.30pm–7.30pm.*

Museo del Merletto a Tombolo. Via Roma 17, tel. 889381. *Open 9.30am–12.30pm, 3.30pm–7.30pm.*

Museo delle Tradizioni Popolari. Via Roma 17, tel. 889381. *Open 9.30am–12.30pm and 3.30pm–7.30pm.*

Pinacoteca Civica. Via Roma 17, tel. 889381. *Open 9.30am–12.30pm, 3.30pm–7.30pm.*

Rocca di Offida. *Open on request to the Ufficio turistico.*

Churches

S. Maria della Rocca. Informazioni c/o Ufficio turistico e Pro Loco. *Open for guided tours in summer, Christmas, and Easter, 10am–noon, 4pm–7.30pm.*

Festivals and entertainments

Mostra del Merletto a Tombolo (Jul–Aug). Tel. 889381.

Lu Bov Fint ("The imitation ox"; carnival Friday).

Sfilata dei Vlurd (carnival Tue). Sheaves of burning cane sticks, with huge bonfire at the end of the day.

Shops and crafts

Azienda agricola Aleandri. Via Fratelli Cervi 34, tel. 889184. Extra-virgin olive oil produced by the consortium Marche Extravergine.

Azienda Agricola S. Giovanni di Silvano Di Lorenzo. Contrada Ciafone 41, tel. 0735 83784, fax 0735 780492. Excellent quality extra-virgin olive oil.

Cooperativa Artigiana Merlettaie. Via Roma 1, tel. 880229. Pincushion lace.

Enoteca regionale. Via Garibaldi 75. Quality DOC wines and various typical local products.

Gabriella Tassotti. Via Lava 161. Locally worked pincushion lace.

Il Gioiello. Corso Serpente Aureo 60. Boutique of pincushion lace.

Pandol. Via Ciabattoni 16. Baker producing typical local sweet cakes and breads.

Osimo

Page 58   ✉ 60027 ☎ 071

ℹ *Ufficio Informazioni turistiche.* Piazza Boccolino, tel. 7249247, 7249282.

Hotels, restaurants, and campsites

★★★ **La Fonte.** Via Fonte Magna 33, tel. 714767, fax 7133547. 36 rooms. Air conditioning (A2, **a**).

❙❙ **Cantinetta del Conero.** At Osimo station. Tel. 7108651. Closed Sat; holidays vary. Air conditioning, parking. Marchigian cuisine, specialty fish.

Cafés and pastry shops

Caffè del Corso. Piazza Gallo 2, tel. 714707. Also well-furnished wine cellar.

⌂ Museums and cultural institutions

Biblioteca comunale e Archivio storico comunale. Via Campana, tel. 714621.
Civica Raccolta d'Arte. Piazza Dante, tel. 714621. *Open on request to the Biblioteca comunale.*
Museo diocesano d'Arte sacra. Piazza Duomo 7, tel. 715396. Closed for alterations.
Museo S. Giuseppe da Copertino. Santuario di S. Giuseppe da Copertino, tel. 714523. *Open 7.30-noon and 3.30pm-7pm.*

⚡ Festivals and entertainments

Città di Osimo (July). Tel. 716222. International dance events.
Coppa Pianisti d'Italia (settembre). Tel. 716222. International piano competition.

⚖ Shops and crafts

at Osimo Stazione, 4 km   ✉ 60028

Azienda vinicola Umani Ronchi. Strada statale 16 km 310+400, tel. 7108019, fax 7108859. Red Conero wine and Verdicchio.

⚡ Local guides and excursions

MTB Avis Team. Tel. 204165. Mountain-bike excursions on Mt. Conero.

Ostra

Page 55   ✉ 60010 ☎ 071

ℹ *Ufficio turistico* (summer). Corso Mazzini, tel. 7980693.
Municipio. Tel. 7980606.

⚡ Cafés and pastry shops

Caffè del Teatro. Piazza dei Martiri, tel. 7980421. Cabaret and piano bar.

⌂ Museums and cultural institutions

Pinacoteca comunale. Via Gramsci 10, tel. 7980606. *Open Tue and Thu 3pm-7pm.*
Teatro comunale La Vittoria. Piazza dei Martiri 5.

at Belvedere Ostrense, 6 km
✉ 60030 ☎ 0731

Museo Internazionale dell'Immagine Postale. Via Vannini 7, tel. 62962. *Open Mon, Tue, Wed, Fri 4pm-7pm; other days upon request.*

at Morro d'Alba, 10 km ✉ 60030 ☎ 0731

Museo della Cultura Mezzadrile Utensilia. Piazza Romagnoli 6, tel. 63000. *Open Sat 16-18, Sun 10am-noon; 15 Jun-15 Sep 4pm-7pm, Sun 10am-noon, 4pm-7pm.*

⚡ Festivals and entertainments

Concorso Lirico Internazionale Angelica Catalani (Jul).
Mostra Regionale di Artigianato e Antiquariato (1st fortnight of Aug).

⚖ Shops and crafts

Bottega del Tarlo. Corso Mazzini 19. Antiques fair.
Falegnameria Verzolini. Via Riviera di Mezzogiorno, tel. 68085. Hand-crafted furniture manufacture.
Mobilificio Sellari. Via Aldo Moro 2, tel. 68018. Hand-crafted furniture.

at Morro d'Alba, km 10

Azienda agricola Stefano Mancinelli. Via Roma 62, tel. 63021, fax 63521. Vast production of typical local wines (including Lacrima di Morro d'Alba); also much appreciated are the local grappa, honey and extra-virgin olive oil.

Pennabilli

Page 99   ✉ 61016 ☎ 0541

ℹ *Pro Loco.* Piazza Garibaldi, tel. 928659.
Associazione Amici della Valmarecchia. Tel. 928578.

⚡ Cafés and pastry shops

Il Forno Panangeli. Via Cinzia Degli Olivieri 13, tel. 928434. Production of traditional cakes.

⌂ Museums and cultural institutions

I Luoghi dell'Anima. The poetical itineraries of Tonino Guerra. Info. tel. 928578.
Museo Diocesano "A. Bergamaschi." Vicolo Somina (Seminario Feretrano), tel. 918486, 928415. Temporarily closed.

at Pontemessa, 3 km   ✉ 61010

Museo di Informatica e Storia del Calcolo. Open on request, tel. 922172.

⌂ Churches

Pieve. Open on request at the Pro Loco.

⚡ Festivals and entertainments

Mostra Mercato Aazionale d'Antiquariato (Jul). Tel. 928578.

⚖ Shops and crafts

Giuliano Pula. Via Tre Genghe 30, tel. 928144. Honey produced on site.
Il Bosco dei Regali. Piazza Vittorio Emanuele II 17, tel. 928382. Typical crafts products of the Montefeltro district.

Pergola

Page 78   ✉ 61045 ☎ 0721

ℹ *Information office.* Corso Matteotti 53, tel. 736455.
Pro Loco. Corso Matteotti 63, tel. 736380.

⌂ Hotels, restaurants, and campsites

★★★ Silvi Palace. Piazza Brodolini 6, tel. 734724, fax 734724. 20 Rooms. Garage; garden.

📷 Museums and cultural institutions

Museo dei Fossili "Raffaele Piccinini". Open on request to the Biblioteca Comunale, tel. 734943, 778786.

⚖️ Shops and crafts

Azienda agricola Corrado Tonelli. Via Dante 66/a, tel. 734105. Visner (sour black cherry wine) and Fragolino.

Fattoria Villa Ligi di Francesco Tonelli. Via Zoccolanti 25/a, tel. 734351. Wines made from the local Vernaculo grape, *grappa* liqueur, honey.

Pesaro

Page 66   ✉ 61100 ☎ 0721

ℹ️ *APT.* Viale Trieste 164, tel. 69341, fax 30462.

🏨 Hotels, restaurants, and campsites

★✦ Bristol. Piazzale Libertà 7, tel. 30355, fax 33893. 27 rooms. Bed and breakfast. Air conditioning, elevator; garage (C3-4, **b**).

★✦ Vittoria. Piazzale Libertà 2, tel. 34343, fax 65204. 36 rooms. Air conditioning, elevator; garage, garden, swimming pool (C3, **g**).

★★★ Flying. Viale Verdi 129, tel. 69219, fax 67428. Seasonal. 33 rooms. Wheelchair access. Elevator; parking, garage (C4, **i**).

★★★ Mediterraneo Ricci. Viale Trieste 199, tel. 31556, fax 34148. 42 rooms. Elevator; garage, garden (C3-4, **c**).

🍴 *Scudiero.* Via Baldassini 2, tel. 64107, fax 34248. Closed Sunday, Jul, from New Year to Jan 6. Specialist Pesarese cuisine, fish (D3, **re**).

🍴 *Teresa.* Viale Trieste 180, tel. 30096, fax 31636. Closed Sun evening and Mon, Dec–Jan. Air conditioning, parking. Pesarese cuisine (C3, **ra**).

🏕️ *Panorama.* At Fiorenzuola di Focara, Panoramica highway, tel. 208145. Seasonal.

☕ Cafés and pastry shops

Casetta Vaccai. Via Mazzolari 22, tel. 69201. Café-pâtisserie housed in the town's oldest building.

📷 Museums and cultural institutions

Casa di Rossini. Via Rossini 34, tel. 387357. Closed Mon. Open Oct–Apr 8.30am–1.30pm, Sun 9am–1pm; May–Sep 9am–7pm, Sun 9am–1pm.

Musei Civici. Piazza Toschi Mosca 29, tel. 67815. Closed Mon. Open Oct–Apr 8.30am–1.30pm, Sun 9am–1pm; May–Sep 9am–7pm, Sun 9am–1pm.

Museo Archeologico Oliveriano. Via Mazza 97, tel. 33344. Open on request; weekdays 9.30am–noon.

Museo del Mare. Via Pola 9, tel. 387536. Closed Mon. Open Oct–Apr 8.30am–1.30pm, Sun 9am–1pm; May–Sep 9am–7pm, Sun 9am–1pm.

Museo Scientifico "Luigi Guidi." Via Cecconi 6 (Orti giuli), tel. 387293. Closed to public.

Tempietto Rossiniano. Piazza Olivieri 5, tel. 30053. Open on request to the Fondazione Rossini.

Villa Caprile. Strada di Caprile, tel. 21440. Open Jul–Aug 3pm–7pm.

Villa l'Imperiale. Strada S. Bartolo, tel. 23602. Guided tours only, apply to APT.

🏃 Festivals and entertainments

Festival internazionale "Eventosuono" (April). Tel. 35525. Music, and more music.

Mostra Internazionale del Nuovo Cinema (Jun).

ROF (Rossini Opera Festival; August). Tel. 30161, fax 30979. International appointment with the music of Rossini.

Sipario Ducale. Festival delle Terre di Pesaro e Urbino (summer months). Tel. 359312, fax 33320. Concerts, entertainment, stage works, dance, poetry in the historical centers of the duchy of Urbino.

⚖️ Shops and crafts

Bucci. Cattabrighe, on the Romagna road, tel. 27127. Hand-crafted pottery.

Franca Mancini. Via Mazzolari 20, tel. 65090. Contemporary art gallery with permanent exhibition of works by the Marchigian artists Arnaldo Pomodoro and Eliseo Mattiacci.

Ratti. Via Rossini 71, tel. 31031. Tailors of longstanding fame.

🏊 Sport

Centro Subacqueo Pesaro. Via della Sanità 24, tel. 31028, 25520.

Circolo The Boat House Club - La Rotonda Bruscoli. Calata Caio Duilio 92, tel. 400586. Sailing and windsurf.

Club Nautico. Tel. 25657.

Da Zorigo. Via Fontesecco 103, tel. 281313. Horseriding.

Federazione Italiana Pesca Sportiva Attività Subacquee. Follow the Adriatica 15, tel. 24682.

Poligono di Tiro e Tiro con l'Arco. Via Condotti 66, tel. 50811.

Porto Turistico. Capitaneria di Porto, Calata Caio Duilio 47, tel. 400016, 400017.

Sci Nautico. Bagni Giuseppe N. 30, Levante beach, tel. 25655, 22463.

Società Canottieri di Pesaro. Calata Caio Duilio 103, tel. 400010.

🌿 Parks and natural reserves

Parco Naturale Regionale Colle San Bartolo. Tel. 952610.

Piandimeleto

Page 97   ✉ 61026 ☎ 0722

ℹ️ *Municipio.* Via Matteotti, tel. 721121, 721124.

🏛 Museums and cultural institutions
Castello. Piazza Conti Oliva, tel. 721528. *Open 9am–12 and 3pm–19.*
Museo del Lavoro Contadino. Piazza Conti Oliva (Castello), tel. 721528, 721493. *Open 9am–noon and 3pm–7pm.*
Museo di Scienza della Terra. Piazza Conti Oliva (Castello), tel. 721528, 721493. *Open 9am–noon and 3pm–7pm.*
Raccolta d'Arte. Viale Dante, tel. 721808. *Open Mon 3pm–7pm, Wed 8.30am–7pm, Fri 8.30am–1pm.*

🏃 Local guides and excursions
Aula Verde di Piandimeleto. At San Sisto. Guided tours by request c/o Cooperativa La Macina, Via Insorti Ungheresi 63, tel. 0721 797240, Acqualagna.

Pioraco

Page 114   ✉ 62025 ☎ 0737

ℹ️ *Municipio.* Largo Leopardi 1, tel. 42142.

🏛 Museums and cultural institutions
Museo della Carta e della Filigrana. Former convent of S. Francesco, tel. 42485, 42142. Closed Sun. *Open 10am–12.30pm.*

Museo dei Funghi e dei Fossili. Largo Leopardi 1, tel. 42485, 42203, 42189. *Open Jul–Sep, weekdays 11am–12.30pm, holidays 11am–12.30pm and 5pm–7pm.*

🏛 Churches
San Francesco. Largo Leopardi. *Open on request, tel. 42117.*

🏐 Sport

at Fiuminata, 5 km   ✉ 62020
Hang-gliding and paragliding.

Pollenza

Page 124   ✉ 62010 ☎ 0733

ℹ️ *Municipio.* Piazza della Libertà 16, tel. 549981.
Pro Loco. Via Roma 32, tel. 549387.

🏛 Churches

at Rambona, 4 km
Abbey of S. Maria Assunta di Rambona. *Open on request, tel. 549346.*

🏃 Festivals and entertainments
Mostra dell'Antiquariato, del Restauro e dell'Artigianato Artistico (July): yearly festival of antiques and restoration.

🔩 Shops and crafts
Caterina Marinozzi. Via Leopardi 98, tel. 549439. Restoration and sale of furniture and other objects, from all eras.

Porto Recanati

Page 132   ✉ 62017 ☎ 071

ℹ️ *Ufficio Informazioni.* Corso Matteotti 111, tel. 9799084.
Pro Loco. Piazza Brancondi, tel. 9799151.

🏨 Hotels, restaurants, and campsites
★★ **Enzo.** Corso Matteotti 23, tel. 7590734, fax 9799029. 23 rooms. Bed & breakfast. Wheelchair access. Air conditioning, elevator; parking (A2, **a**).
★★★ **Mondial.** Viale Europa 2, tel. 9799169, fax 7590095. 44 rooms. Wheelchair access. Air conditioning, elevator; parking, garage (C3, *f.p.*).
🍴 **Fatatis.** At Scossicci, Via Vespucci 2, tel. 9799366. Closed Mon, and through Jan. Garden. Regional cuisine (A1, *f.p.*).
⛺ **Internazionale.** Viale Scarfiotti 47, tel. 9798567, fax 9798605. Seasonal.

🏛 Museums and cultural institutions
Area Archeologica di "Potentia." *Open on request, tel. 9799018, 2074829.*
Pinacoteca Comunale "Attilio Moroni." Piazza Brancondi (Castello Svevo), tel. 9799018, 7591283. *Open on request.*

🏃 Festivals and entertainments
Festival del Cinema Muto (August). Silent cinema festival. Tel. 200442.

Porto San Giorgio

Page 153   ✉ 63017 ☎ 0734

ℹ️ *Ufficio Informazioni.* Via Oberdan 2, tel. 678461.
Ufficio Turismo. Via Cairoli 2 (Municipio), tel. 680211; freephone 16721167.

🏨 Hotels, restaurants, and campsites
★★ **David Palace.** Lungomare Gramsci Sud 503, tel. 676848, fax 676468. 36 rooms. Wheelchair access. Air conditioning, elevator; parking, garage, swimming pool (D3, *f.p.*).
★★★ **Tritone.** Via S. Martino 36, tel. 677104, fax 677962. 36 rooms. Air conditioning, elevator; parking, garden, swimming pool (D3, *f.p.*).
🍴 **Cascina.** In S. Nicola 13, tel. 676926. Closed Mon, part of Nov and all Feb. Parking, garden. Classic cuisine (B-C1, *f.p.*).

🏃 Festivals and entertainments
Festival Internazionale di Scacchi (August). A chess-player's dream.
Regata del Doge (July). Historical recreation of the grand feast held in 1253 for the appointment of the doge of of the *podestà* of Fermo.

≋ Sport

Associazione Nautica Picena. Lungomare Gramsci nord, tel. 676200. Learn to sail.
Lega Navale Italiana. Lungomare Gramsci centro, tel. 678705.
Porto Turistico. Lungomare Gramsci sud, tel. 675263, 676304. With its 900 mooring points, this is the largest in the Adriatic.

🏃 Local guides and excursions

Il Trenino dell'Arte. Tel. 679938. Excursions to the interior and around the province of Ascoli Piceno.

Potenza Picena

Page 133 ✉ 62018 ☎ 0733
ℹ *Pro Loco.* Piazza Matteotti, tel. 671758.

🏛 Museums and cultural institutions

Pinacoteca e Museo Comunale. Tel. 6791. *Open Wed 4pm–7.30pm, Sab 5pm–7.30pm.*

Recanati

Page 129 ✉ 62019 ☎ 071
ℹ *Ufficio Informazioni.* Piazza Leopardi 31, tel. 981471.

Municipio. Piazza Leopardi 26, tel. 75871.

🏨 Hotels, restaurants, and campsites

★★★ **La Ginestra.** Via Calcagni 2, tel. 980355, fax 980594. 27 rooms (B3, **a**).

🏛 Museums and cultural institutions

Biblioteca e Casa Leopardi. Via Leopardi 14, tel. e fax 7573380. *Open winter 9am–noon; 3pm–5pm; spring and autumn 9am–noon, 3pm–6pm; summer 9am–noon, 3pm–19.*
Biblioteca del Centro Nazionale Studi Leopardiani & the Museo didattico-artistico Giacomo Leopardi. Via Monte Tabor 2, tel. 7570604. Closed Sat afternoon and Sun. *Open winter 9am–noon, and 4.30pm–6.30pm; summer 4.30pm–7.30pm.*
Museo Beniamino Gigli. Piazza Leopardi 26 (Palazzo Comunale), tel. 7587214, 75871. Closed Mon. *Open Apr–Sep 10am–1pm and 4pm–7pm; Oct–Mar 10am–1pm and 3pm–6pm.*
Museo Diocesano. Via Gregorio XII (Duomo), tel. 981122. *Open Jun–Sep 9.30am–noon and 3.30pm–7pm; Oct–Mar 9am–noon and 4.30pm–7.30pm.*
Pinacoteca Civica. Piazza Leopardi 26 (Palazzo Comunale), tel. 7587214, 75871. Closed Mon. *Open Apr–Sep 10am–1pm, and 4pm–7pm; Oct–Mar 10am–1pm and 3pm–6pm.*

🏃 Festivals and entertainments

Antica Fiera dell'Antiquariato e dell'Artigianato artistico di S. Vito (June and 1st Sat and Sun of the month).
Celebrazioni Commemorative della Nascita di Leopardi (Jun). Tel. 7570604.
Commemorazioni Gigliane (Jun), dedicated to the great Beniamino Gigli.
Premio Recanati per la Canzone d'Autore (May). Tel. 982772. One of the main appointments for singer-songwriters.

⚖ Shops and crafts

Luciano Lorenzetti. Via Giunta 51, tel. 98117. Handcrafted smoker's pipes.

Ripatransone

Page 147 ✉ 63038 ☎ 0735
ℹ *Assessorato al Turismo.* Piazza XX Settembre 1, tel. 97117.

Museo Civico Archeologico. Piazza XX Settembre 11, tel. 99329.

🍽 Cafés and pastry shops

Campanelli. Via Garibaldi 28, tel. 9384. Fresh breads and pâtisserie.

🏛 Museums and cultural institutions

Museo Civico Archeologico. Piazza XX Settembre 11, tel. 99329. *Open weekdays 9am–1pm and 3pm–7pm, holidays 9.30am–12.30pm and 3pm–7pm; Jul–Aug weekdays 9am–1pm, 3pm–7pm and 9pm–11pm, holidays 9.30am–12.30pm, 3pm–7pm and 9pm–11pm.*
Museo della Civiltà Contadina e Artigiana. Piazzale Fedeli, tel. 9378, 99329. *Open on request.*
Pinacoteca Civica - Gipsoteca "Uno Gera." Corso Vittorio Emanuele, tel. 99329. *Open weekdays 9am–1pm and 3pm–7pm, holidays 9.30am–12.30pm and 3pm–7pm; Jul–Aug weekdays 9am–1pm, 3pm–7pm and 9pm–11pm, holidays 9.30am–12.30pm, 3pm–7pm and 9pm–11pm.*
Raccolta Diocesana. Corso Vittorio Emanuele (Curia vescovile), tel. 9312. Temporarily closed.

at Cossignano, 10.5 km ✉ 63030
Antiquarium Comunale "Nicola Panzoni." Via Verdi, tel. 98130. *Open Easter and Christmas 5.30pm–8pm; other months on request.*

🏛 Churches

at Cossignano, 10.5 km
Santa Maria Assunta and church of the Annunciata. Via Verdi. *Open on request, tel. 98116.*

⚖ Shops and crafts

Amurri Egidio. Piazza Condivi, tel. 99009. Miniature pottery.

Cataldi Ines. Piazza Matteotti, tel. 99785. Sculpture in wood.

at San Savino, 9 km ☒ 63030
Azienda Vitivinicola Cocci Grifoni Guido. Contrada Messieri 12, tel. 90143, fax 90123. Production and sale of extra-virgin olive oil.

San Benedetto del Tronto

Page 149 ☒ 63039 ☎ 0735
🛈 *IAT.* Via delle Tamerici 5, tel. 582542.

Hotels, restaurants, and campsites

★☆★ *Regent.* Viale Gramsci 31, tel. 582720, fax 582805. 23 rooms. Bed & breakfast. Air conditioning, elevator; garage (B2, **b**).

★★★ *Arlecchino.* Viale Trieste 22, tel. 85635, fax 85682. 30 rooms. Air conditioning, elevator; garage (C3, **g**).

🍴 *Ristorantino da Vittorio.* Via Manara 102, tel. 583344. Closed Mon. Air conditioning, parking, garden. Regional cuisine, specialty fish (C2, **r**).

at Porto d'Ascoli, 4 km ☒ 63037
★☆★ *Excelsior.* Viale Rinascimento 137, tel. 753246, fax 655310. Seasonal. 126 rooms. Elevator; parking, garden, swimming pool.

★★★ *President.* Via S. Francesco 14, tel. 650838, fax 659441. Seasonal. 52 rooms. Air conditioning, elevator; parking, garage, garden, tennis.

🍴 *Pescatore.* Viale Trieste 27, tel. 83782. Closed Mon, Christmas to mid-Jan. Air conditioning. Regional cuisine.

Museums and cultural institutions

Museo delle Anfore. Viale De Gasperi, tel. 86855. Closed Sun except in July and August. *Open 9am–noon and 3.30pm–6.30pm.*
Museo Ittico "Augusto Capriotti." Viale Colombo 98, tel. 588850. Closed Sun. *Open 9am–noon and 3.30pm–7pm.*

Festivals and entertainments

Festival Ferrè (May–Sep). Tel. 892218. Only festival event in Italy devoted to the French singer Ferrè.
Incontro Nazionale dei Teatri Invisibili (Sep). Tel. 892218.
Rassegna Nazionale del Documentario Italiano and Premio Libero Bizzarri (July). Tel. 892218.

Sport

Circolo Nautico Sanbendettese. Via Marinai d'Italia, tel. 584255. Sailing lessons.
Porto Turistico. Capitaneria di Porto, Via Marinai d'Italia 14, tel. 592744.

San Ginesio

Page 139 ☒ 62026 ☎ 0733
🛈 *IAT* (summer). Piazza Gentili, tel. 656014.
Comunità Montana di Fiastra, Fiastrone, Tennacola, and Medio Chienti. Via Piave, tel. 656336, 656888, fax 656429. Get out of town and enjoy the hinterland.
Casa del Parco. Località San Liberato, tel. 694404.

Cafés and pastry shops

Caffè Centrale. Piazza Gentili. Great selection of ice-cream made on the premises.

Museums and cultural institutions

Museo Pinacoteca Comunale "Scipione Gentili" Ancient works: Via Merelli, tel. 656072, 656236; modern works: Via Capocastello (Municipio), tel. 656072, 656236. *Open 1st Jul–31 Aug, 11am–1pm and 4.30pm–6.30pm; Sun and other months by request.*

at Ripe San Ginesio, 10.5 km ☒ 62020
Pinacoteca Civica. Largo Repubblica 6, tel. 500102. *Open on request.*

Churches

at Macchie, 9 km ☒ 62020
Santa Maria delle Macchie. Open on request, tel. 663131.

Sport

at Pian di Pieca, 7 km ☒ 62020
Free-flight point for hang-gliding and paragliding. Tel. 658293.

Local guides and excursions

at Pian di Pieca, 7 km
Cooperativa Il Balcone dei Sibillini. Tel. 694328. For guided tours in the caves of the Fiastrone and the Frati grotto.

San Leo

Page 102 ☒ 61018 ☎ 0541
🛈 *Pro Loco.* Piazza Dante 14, tel. 916231.
Ufficio Turismo. Piazza Dante (Palazzo Mediceo), tel. and fax 916306.
Ufficio Cultura. Piazza Dante (Palazzo Della Rovere), tel. and fax 916184, 91621.

Hotels, restaurants, and campsites

🍴 *La Corte.* Via M. Rosa 72, tel. 916328. Closed Tuesdays and October. Romagnole and Tuscan cuisine.

Museums and cultural institutions

Forte. Via Leopardi, tel. 916242, fax 91616, e-mail: ProSanLeo@interbusiness.it. *Open winter 9am–noon and 2pm–5pm; summer 9am–noon and 2pm–6pm.*
Museo d'Arte Sacra. Piazza Dante (Palazzo Mediceo). *Open weekdays 9.30am–6.30pm; holidays 10am–7pm.*

Museo, Pinacoteca e Galleria d'Arte Contemporanea. Via Leopardi (Forte), tel. 916242, fax 91616, e-mail: ProSanLeo@interbusiness.it. *Open winter 9am–noon and 2pm–5pm; summer 9am–noon and 2pm–6pm.*

⌂ Churches

Convent of Sant'Igne. *Open on request, tel. 916277.*

🏹 Sport

Base for gliders, parachuting, hang-gliding and paragliding. Selection of departure points. Piega. Tel. 912227.

⚖ Shops and crafts

Carletti Cerliani Maria Luisa. Via Montefeltro 13, tel. 916216. Hand-painted pottery.
La Bottega di Mario. Via Montefeltro 28, tel. 916251. Sausages made from boar's meet. Cheeses seasoned in walnut leaves and ash.
Moretti Giorgio. Via Michele Rosa 77. Wrought iron work.
Panificio Giorgini Tommaso. Via Leopardi 17, tel. 916244. Typical local cakes.

San Lorenzo in Campo

Page 77 ✉ 61047 ☎ 0721
ℹ *Municipio.* Tel. 776847.

🏨 Hotels, restaurants, and campsites

★★★ **Giardino.** Via Mattei 4, tel. 776803, fax 735323. 20 rooms. Wheelchair access. Air conditioning; parking, garden, swimming pool.

🏛 Museums and cultural institutions

Musei Comunali Laurentini. Via Tiberini, tel. 776814. *Open on request.*

at Castelleone di Suasa, 7 km
✉ 60010 ☎ 071
Area archeologica di "Suasa". Tel. 966113. Closed to public.

⌂ Churches

San Lorenzo. Via S. Demetrio 2, tel. 776825. *Open on request.*

🏃 Festivals and entertainments

Premio Lirico Internazionale Mario Tiberini (August).

San Severino Marche

Page 115 ✉ 62047 ☎ 0733
ℹ *Ufficio Cultura del Comune.* Tel. 641296, 641252.

Comunità Montana alta Valle del Potenza (Zone H). Via Salimbeni 6, tel. 637245, 637246.
Pro Loco. Piazza del Popolo, tel. 638414.

🏛 Museums and cultural institutions

Area Archeologica di "Septempeda." *Open on request to the Museo Archeologico "Giuseppe Moretti."*
Galleria d'Arte Moderna. Piazza del Popolo 45. *Open on request, tel. 6411.*
Museo Archeologico "Giuseppe Moretti." Via Salimbeni 39, tel. 638095. Closed Mon. *Open 9am–1pm; Jul–Sep 9am–1pm and 4.30pm–6.30pm.*
Museo del Territorio. Viale Bigioli 126, tel. 638377. *Open on request.*
Pinacoteca Civica "Pietro Tacchi Venturi." Via Salimbeni 39, tel. 638095. Closed Mon. *Open 9am–1pm; Jul–Sep 9am–1pm and 4.30pm–6.30 pm.*
Teatro comunale Feronia. Piazza del Popolo 15. *Open on request, tel. 6411, 634369.*

at Pitino, 9 km ✉ 62027
Area Archeologica. *Guided tours on request; apply to the Museo Archeologico "Giuseppe Moretti" or the Pro Loco, in San Severino Marche.*

⌂ Churches

at Gagliole, 13 km ✉ 62020 ☎ 0737
Santa Maria della Pieve. *Open on request to the Municipio, tel. 641184.*

🏃 Festivals and entertainments

Palio dei Castelli (1st week of July). Tel. 638883.
Premio Internazionale Salimbeni per la Storia e la Critica d'Arte (Sep).
San Severino Blues (Aug).

⚖ Shops and crafts

Allegretto Galliano. Via Garibaldi, tel. 638618. The oldest bakery in San Severino Marche.
ATO. Via Salimbeni 56, tel. 634529, 637804. Sale of farm products and extra-virgin oil.
L'Idea e la Forma. Piazza del Popolo 95, tel. 634779. Laboratory of hand-crafted jewelry.

Sant'Agata Feltria

page 101 ✉ 61047 ☎ 0541
ℹ *Municipio - Pro Loco.* Salita Nastasini, tel. 929613, 929714.

🏛 Museums and cultural institutions

Mostra sull'Alchimia. Salita Fregoso (Rocca Fregoso), tel. 929714, 929111. *Open summer 9am–12.30pm and 3pm–6.30pm; winter, Sat and Sun 9.30am–noon and 3pm–6.30pm.*
Mostra sulla Sartoria. Salita Fregoso (Rocca Fregoso), tel. 929714, 929111. *Open summer 9am–12.30pm and 3pm–6.30pm; winter, Sat and Sun 9.30am–noon and 3pm–6.30pm.*

Rocca Fregoso. Salita Fregoso, tel. 929714, 929111. *Open summer 9am–12.30pm and 3pm–6.30pm; winter, Sat and Sun 9.30am–noon and 3pm–6.30pm.*

🏛 Churches

Convent of San Girolamo. *Open on request to the Municipio.*

🏃 Festivals and entertainments

Fiera del Tartufo bianco pregiato (Nov). Tel. 929314, 929613. Fair of choice white truffles.

⚖ Shops and crafts

Zanchini. Via Sassinate. Sale of local truffles.

Sant'Angelo in Vado

Page 93 ✉ 61048 ☎ 0722

ℹ *Municipio.* Piazza Umberto I, tel. 8498, 8232.

Pro Loco. Piazza Pio XII, tel. 88432.

🏛 Museums and cultural institutions

Museo dei Vecchi Mestieri. Corso Garibaldi. *Visits on request to the Municipio.*

🏛 Churches

Santa Maria dei Servi. Via Pratello S. Maria. *Open on request to the Municipio.*

🏃 Festivals and entertainments

Mostra Nazionale del Tartufo (Oct–Nov).

⚖ Shops and crafts

CAM (Cooperativa Agricola Metauro). Piazza Mercato Tartufo, tel. 8560. Sale of truffles.
Orciari Leandro. Via Gramsci 10, tel. 8569. Hand-crafted wrought-iron work.
Vin Italy. Piazza Giardini Pubblici, tel. 8478. Best local wines.

Sant'Elpidio a Mare

Page 152 ✉ 63019 ☎ 0734

ℹ *Municipio.* Piazza Matteotti 4, tel. 81961.
Pro Loco (summer). Corso Baccio 32, tel. 810008.

☕ Cafés and pastry shops

Bar Centrale. Piazza Matteotti. Famous pâtisserie.

🏛 Museums and cultural institutions

Raccolta Comunale. Piazza Matteotti 4, tel. 81961. Soon to open.

🏛 Churches

La Madonna dei Lumi. *Open on request to the Municipio.*
San Filippo. Corso Baccio. *Open on request to the Municipio.*
Santa Maria della Misericordia. Piazza Matteotti. *Open on request, tel. 810139.*
Oratorio dei Filippini. Corso Baccio. *Open on request to the Municipio.*

🏃 Festivals and entertainments

Città Medioevo (last week of July). Historical handicrafts in costume.
Contesa del Secchio (2nd Sunday in August). Tel. 858218. Recreation of the battle over possession of the water.
Festival Internazionale del Teatro per Ragazzi (July). Tel. 909278. Yearly festival of children's theater.

Sarnano

Page 158 ✉ 62028 ☎ 0733

ℹ *IAT.* Via Ricciardi, tel. 657144-657343.
Municipio. Via Leopardi 1, tel. 657160.

♨ Thermal resorts

Terme di Sarnano. Viale Baglioni, tel. 657274. Natural bicarbonate-sodium waters.

🏛 Museums and cultural institutions

Biblioteca e Pinacoteca Comunale. Via Leopardi 1, tel. 658126. *Open winter 4pm–7pm; summer 5pm–8pm.*
Museo delle Armi Antiche e Moderne. Via Leopardi. *Open on request to the Municipio.*
Museo d'Arte Contemporanea. Via Leopardi. Closed until further notice.
Museo dell'Avifauna delle Marche. Via Leopardi 1, tel. 657160. *Open on request.*
Teatro Della Vittoria-Mario Del Monaco. Piazza Alta, tel. 657487.

🏃 Festivals and entertainments

Mostra Mercato Nazionale dell'Antiquariato e dell'Artigianato (May and June).

⛳ Sport

Associazione Volo libero "I Sibillini." Tel. 658293.
Piste da sci in Sasso Tetto (tel. 651101) and the S. Maria Maddalena ski station (tel. 651103).
Cross-country skiing near the Ragnolo plains.

Sassocorvaro

Page 96 ✉ 61028 ☎ 0722

ℹ *Ufficio turistico.* Tel. 76148.

🏛 Museums and cultural institutions

Museo "L'Arca dell'Arte." Piazza Battelli (Rocca Ubaldinesca), tel. 76873. *Open Apr–Oct 9.30am–12.30pm, and 3pm–7pm; Nov–Mar Sat 2.30pm–6.30pm, Sun 9.30am–12.30pm and 2pm–6.30pm.*
Museo della Civiltà Contadina. Via Crescentini, tel. 76873. *Open Apr–Oct 9.30am–12.30pm and 3pm–7pm; Nov–Mar Sat 2.30pm–6.30pm, Sunday 9.30am–12.30pm and 2.30pm–6.30pm.*
Rocca Ubaldinesca. Piazza Battelli, tel. 76873. *Open Apr–Oct 9.30am–12.30pm and*

3pm–7pm; Nov-Mar Sat 2.30pm–6.30, Sunday 9.30am–12.30pm and 2.30pm–6.30pm.

at Casinina, 11.5 km   ⊠ 61020

Museo Storico della Linea Gotica. Via provinciale Casinina, tel. 362170. *Open 9am–noon and 3pm–7pm.*

🏃 Festivals and entertainments

Premio Pasquale Rotondi (June). Tel. 77186. Devoted to those who rescue art work at world, European, Italian, and regional level.

Sassoferrato

Page 108   ⊠ 60047 ☎ 0732

ⓘ *Ufficio turistico.* Piazza Matteotti 3, tel. 956231.

🏛 Museums and cultural institutions

Area Archeologica di "Sentinum." *Open on request, tel. 956231.*

Museo Civico. Piazza Matteotti. Closed Sunday. *Open 9am–1pm; for Easter, 25 Apr–25 May, August, Christmas 9am–1pm and 4pm–7pm.*

Museo delle Arti e delle Tradizioni Popolari. Via Don Minzoni (Palazzo Montanari). *Open on request to the tourist office.*

🏠 Churches

Abbey of Santa Croce. *Open on request, tel. 629450, 959030.*

San Francesco. Piazza S. Francesco. *Open on request, tel. 9354 e 0330 419223.*

Monastery of Santa Chiara. Via Bentivoglio. *Open on request to the tourist office.*

🏃 Festivals and entertainments

Rassegna Nazionale di Arte Contemporanea G. B. Salvi e Piccola Europa (July–August). Tel. 956230.

🚶 Local guides and excursions

CENF. Tel. 973202. Excursions on horseback or on a bicycle on the route Santa Croce - Costadella.

Senigallia

Page 55   ⊠ 60019 ☎ 071

ⓘ *IAT.* Piazzale Morandi 2, tel. 7922725.

🏨 Hotels, restaurants, and campsites

★☆★ **Duchi della Rovere.** Via Corridoni 3, tel. 7927623, fax 7927784. 51 rooms. Wheelchair access. Air conditioning, elevator; parking, garage, garden, swimming pool (A2, **f**).

★★★ **Cristallo.** Lungomare Alighieri 2, tel. 7925767, fax 7925768. Seasonal. 57 rooms. Wheelchair access. Air conditioning, elevator; parking, garden (A-B2, **b**).

★★★ **Senbhotel.** Viale Bonopera 32, tel. 7927500, fax 64814. 51 rooms. Wheelchair access. Air conditioning, elevator; garage (B2, **e**).

🍴 **Uliassi.** Banchina di Levante 6, tel. 65463. Seasonal, closed Monday except in July and August. Seafood and specialist cuisines (A2, **t**).

at Marzocca, 7 km   ⊠ 60017

🍴 **Madonnina del Pescatore.** Lungomare Italia 11, tel. 698267. Closed Mon and part of January. Air conditioning. Regional cuisine, specialty fish.

🏛 Museums and cultural institutions

Biblioteca Comunale Antonelliana. Via Portici Ercolani, tel. 6629302.

Museo d'Arte Contemporanea e dell'Informazione. Via Chiostergi 10, tel. 60424. *Open Tue–Fri 8.30am–12.30pm.*

Museo Pio IX. Via Mastai 14, tel. 60649. Closed Monday during winter. *Open 9am–noon 4pm–7pm.*

Museo di Storia della Mezzadria. At the church of Santa Maria delle Grazie, tel. 7923127. Closed Mon except 16 Jun–15 Sep. *Open 8.45am–12.15pm; 16 Jun–15 Sep 8.45am–12.15pm and 4pm,–7.15pm.*

Palazzetto Baviera. Piazza del Duca, tel. 6629266. Closed Thu afternoon, Sat and Sun (winter); Sat morning adn Sun (summer). *Open winter 8.30am–12.30pm and 3.30pm–6.30pm; summer 8.30am–12.30pm and 3.30pm–7pm.*

Pinacoteca Diocesana. Piazza Garibaldi 3, tel. 60498, 60094. Closed Sunday. *Open 10am–noon and 4pm–6pm; Jul-Aug 10am–noon and 5pm–7pm.*

Rocca Roveresca. Piazza del Duca, tel. 63258. *Open 9am–7pm; Jul–Aug 9am–1pm and 5pm–10pm; Sunday 9am–7pm.*

🏃 Festivals and entertainments

Concorso Pianistico Internazionale (Sep). International piano competition.

at Mondolfo, 13 km   ⊠ 61037 ☎ 0721

La Cacciata (last Sunday in July). Tel. 959677.

🏊 Sport

Porto turistico. All inquiries for port activities, apply to the Capitaneria di Porto, Banchina di Levante 4, tel. 64780.

⚖ Shops and crafts

at Roncitelli, 8 km   ⊠ 60010

Ciarloni Graziella. Tel. 7919954. Hand-worked items in copper.

Serra San Quìrico

Page 53   ⊠ 60048 ☎ 0731

ⓘ *Municipio.* Piazza della Libertà 1, tel. 8181, 86019.

🏛 Museums and cultural institutions

Cartoteca Storica Regionale. Via Marcellini, tel. 86019, 86024, 818207. *Open 9am–noon and 4pm–7pm.*

Museo dei Fossili. Via Aldo Moro 4, tel. 86030. *Open on request.*

Rassegna Internazionale del Teatro della Scuola (April-May). Tel. 86634.
Rassegna Nazionale di Canti Natalizi. Christmas carols.

Hang-gliding and paragliding from Mt. Muraro.

Serra Sant'Abbondio

☒ 61040 ☎ 0721

i   *Pro Loco.* Corso Dante Alighieri 26, tel. 787219.

at Frontone, 6 km   ☒ 61040

Castello di Frontone. *Open on request to the Municipio, tel. 786107.*

Monastery of Fonte Avellana. Tel. 730118. *Open weekdays 9am–11am and 3pm–5pm, holidays 3pm–5pm.*

Sirolo

Page 46   ☒ 60020 ☎ 071

i   *Ufficio turistico* (summer). Via Moricone, tel. 9330611.

★★★ **Conchiglia Verde.** Via Giovanni XXIII 12, tel. 9330018, fax 9330019. 27 rooms. Garage; garden, indoor swimming pool.

Ⓐ ★★ **Reno.** Via Moriconi 7, tel. 7360315. Open all year.

Abbey of San Pietro. *Open on request to the APT, Ancona.*

Alle Cave (July and August). Tel. 936102, 200442, freephone 167250147. Nationally renowned theater events.

Associazione Tennis Sirolo. Via Montefreddo, tel. 9331749.
CARMAS Squash Club. Via del Lavoro 11, tel. 7360016.
Circolo Sub Sirolo. Via San Remo 1, tel. 9332988.
Conero Golf Club. Via Betellico 6, tel. 7360613.
Il Ritorno. Via Piani d'Aspio, tel. 9331544. Riding classes.

Forestalp. Via Peschiera 30/a, tel. 9331879. For guided visits to the regional park of Mt. Conero.

Parco Regionale del Monte Conero. Via Vivaldi 1/3, tel. 9331161, fax 9330376.

Tolentino

Page 134   ☒ 62029 ☎ 0733

i   *IAT.* Piazza della Libertà, tel. 972937. *Municipio.* Tel. 901221.

★☆★ **Hotel 77.** Viale B. Buozzi 90, tel. 967400, fax 960147. 50 rooms. Wheelchair access. Air conditioning, elevator; parking, garage; garden (B-C1, *f.p.*).

Terme di Santa Lucia. Contrada Santa Lucia, tel. 968227. Season: April to December.

Bar Zazzaretta. Piazza della Libertà, tel. 968348. Bar in town center with long tradition.
La Mimosa. Viale Vittorio Veneto 69, tel. 969950. Pâtisserie with a menu of local cakes.

Biblioteca Egidiana. Piazza Silverj, tel. 969996.
Museo Civico Archeologico. Piazza Repubblica, tel. 901325, 901326, 969996. Soon to open.
Museo della Caricatura e dell'Umorismo nell'Arte. Via della Pace 3, tel. 969797. *Open Tue–Fri 4pm–7pm; Sat and Sun 9.30am–12.30pm and 4pm–7pm.*
Museo dell'Opera di S. Nicola. Piazza S. Nicola, tel. 969996. *Open 9.30am–noon and 4pm–7pm.*
Sale Napoleoniche. Via della Pace 3 (Palazzo Parisani Bezzi), tel. 969797. *Open on request.*
The Rancia Castle. Contrada La Rancia. *Open on request, tel. 973349.*

Biennale Internazionale dell'Umorismo nell'Arte (Sep and Oct on odd years). Tel. 901325.
Fiera Antiqua (each 4th Sat and Sun of the month). Tel. 974407. Antiques fair and sale of crafts work
Teatro Nicola Vaccai. Piazza Vaccai, tel. 968460. Plays, musical performances and theater for young people.

Ales Pelletterie. Via Sacharov. One of the best-known centers for leather goods.
Immobiliare S. Giorgio. Via S. Catervo 35. Furnishings in historical Marchigian style.

Laipe. Via Tobagi 2, tel. 971541. Handcrafted leather goods.

La Tre Mori. Via S. Lucia. Characteristic cake shop: malted cakes, Easter eggs, and nougat.

Multifirm. Viale della Repubblica 14, tel. 960800. Sale to public of products made by the company Nazareno Gabrielli.

Saipa Salumi. Contrada Pace, tel. 971560. Famous for its local salami and cheeses.

Tappezzeria Atom di Enrico Albani. Via Belluigi, tel. 974159. Produces for FRAU.

Treia

Page 124   ✉ 62010 ☎ 0733

ℹ️ *Pro Loco* (estate). Corso Italia 1, tel. 215919.

🏛 Museums and cultural institutions

Accademia Georgica. Piazza della Repubblica, tel. 215056, 215241.

Museo Civico Archeologico e Pinacoteca Comunale. Piazza della Repubblica (Municipio), tel. 215117. *Open on request, 10.30am–1pm.*

🏃 Festivals and entertainments

Disfida del Bracciale (1st Sunday of August). Tel. 215117, 219919. One of the most frequented historical pageants in the Marche.

Urbania

Page 91   ✉ 61049 ☎ 0722

ℹ️ *Pro Loco Casteldurante.* Corso Vittorio Emanuele, tel. 317211.

Ufficio Turismo. Municipio, tel. 318395.

Comunità Montana dell'Alto and Medio Metauro. Via Manzoni, tel. and fax 318052, 319783.

🍰 Cafés and pastry shops

Caffè Pasticceria Del Teatro. Piazza S. Cristoforo, tel. 318738. In-house production of cakes and sweets.

🏛 Museums and cultural institutions

Associazione Amici della Ceramica. Tel. 317644.

Biblioteca. Corso Vittorio Emanuele 23, tel. 319985, 317175.

Museo Civico. Corso Vittorio Emanuele 23, tel. 319985, 317175. Closed Mon. *Open 10am–noon and 3pm–6pm.*

Museo Diocesano. Via Urbano VIII, tel. 319643, 319463. *Open on request.*

⛪ Churches

Chiesa dei Morti. Via Ugolini, tel. 319866. *Open 10am–noon and 3pm–6pm.*

San Francesco. Via Ugolini. *Open on request at the Pro Loco.*

Oratorio del Corpus Domini. Via Garibaldi. *Open on request to the Pro Loco.*

🏃 Festivals and entertainments

at Fermignano, 12 km   ✉ 61033

Palio della Rana (1st Sunday after Easter). Tel. 330323.

🔧 Shops and crafts

L'Antica Casteldurante. Piazza Cavour 4, tel. 317573. Huge production of majolica.

Longhi Ravaldo. Corso Vittorio Emanuele 59, tel. 319459. Fresh and dried truffles.

Urbino

Page 82   ✉ 61029 ☎ 0722

ℹ️ *IAT.* Piazza Rinascimento 1, tel. 2613.

Ufficio Informazioni. Piazza Duca Federico 35, tel. 2441.

🏨 Hotels, restaurants, and campsites

★★ **Bonconte.** Via delle Mura 28, tel. 2463, fax 4782. 25 rooms. Air conditioning, elevator; garage, garden (B3, **a**).

★★ **Mamiani.** Via Bernini 6, tel. 322309, fax 327742. 72 rooms. Wheelchair access. Air conditioning, elevator; parking (A1, **f.p.**).

★★★ **Dei Duchi & Residence.** Via G. Dini 12, tel. 328226, fax 328009. 79 rooms. Wheelchair access. Air conditioning, elevator; parking, garage, garden (A1, **f.p.**).

🍴 **Il Cortegiano.** Via Puccinotti 13, tel. 320307. Closed Mon; mid-December to mid-January. Air conditioning, garden. Regional cuisine, specialty truffles (C2, **r**).

🍴 **Vecchia Urbino.** Via dei Vasari 3/5, tel. 4447. Closed Tue in winter. Regional cuisine, specialty truffles (B2, **m**).

🍰 Cafés and pastry shops

Caffè Pasticceria Cartolari. Via Raffaello 52, tel. 329590. A stone's throw from Casa Raffaello, an occasion to explore sweet and savory cooking.

🏛 Museums and cultural institutions

Casa di Raffaello. Via Raffaello 57, tel. 320105. *Open weekdays 9am–1pm e 3pm–7pm, holidays 10am–1pm.*

Museo Diocesano "Gianfrancesco Albani." Piazza Pascoli 1 (Duomo), tel. 2892. *Open 9am–noon and 2pm–6pm.*

Museo del Gabinetto di Fisica. Piazza della Repubblica (Collegio Raffaello), tel. 4146. Closed Sat and Sun. *Open 8am–2pm, Tue–Fri also 3pm–6pm.*

Orto botanico. Via Bramante 28, tel. 2428. Closed Thu e Sat afternoon. *Open 8-12.30pm e 3pm–17.30.*

Palazzo Ducale (Museo archeologico, Galleria nazionale delle Marche). Piazza Duca Federico, tel. 2760. *Open on request 9am–7pm, Sun and Mon 9am–2pm.*

Università degli Studi di Urbino. Via Saffi 2.

⌂ Churches

Oratorio di S. Croce. *Open su on advance request to the APT.*
Oratorio di S. Giovanni Battista. Via Barocci 31, tel. 320936, 53300. *Open weekdays 10am–12.30pm, and 3pm–17.30; holidays 10am–12.30pm.*
Oratorio di S. Giuseppe. Via Barocci 31, tel. 53300. *Open weekdays 10am–1.30pm and 3pm–17.30; holidays 10am–12.30pm.*

🏃 Festivals and entertainments

Concorso Internazionale di Flauto Dolce (July).
Festa del Duca (3rd Sun of August). Tel. 2626.
Festival Internazionale di Musica antica (July). Tel. 2788.
Teatro Raffaello Sanzio. Corso Garibaldi, tel. 2281.
Teatro Rinascimentale di Corte (July–August). Tel. 2281, 2788.

⚖ Shops and crafts

Casa del Formaggio. Via Mazzini 47, tel. 4035. Sale of typical local foodstuffs, including the famous "caciotta" cheeses.
Maiolica di Urbino. Via Puccinotti 27, tel. 2796. Wide choice of majolica pieces painted by hand in the local workshops.
Oggetti d'Arte E. Mari. Via Vittorio Veneto 38/40. Wide assortment of majolica and cups, ceremonial plates, etc.

🏇 Sport

Circolo ippico Le Cesane. Località Santa Maria delle Selve - Monte delle Cesane, tel. 340171.

Urbisaglia

Page 138 ✉ 62010 ☎ 0733
ℹ️   *Pro Loco.* Via Sacrario, tel. 506566.
Municipio. Corso Giannelli, tel. 506385.

🏛 Museums and cultural institutions

Area Archeologica di "Urbs Salvia." Località Maestà, tel. 506385. *Open Tue, Wed, and Thu 9am–1pm.*
Museo Archeologico Statale. Traversa Piccinini, tel. 50124. *Open Fri–Sun 8am–2pm.*
Museo delle Armi e delle Uniformi Militari. Via del Sacrario (church of San Biagio). *Open summer 10am–noon and 5pm–7.30pm; winter, Sat 3pm–5pm, Sun 10am–noon and 3pm–5pm.*
Rocca. *Open by request to the Municipio.*

at Abbadia di Fiastra, 4 km

Museo Naturalistico, Museo della Civiltà Contadina Abbazia di Fiastra, Raccolta Archeologica. *Open on request, tel. 202942.*

⌂ Churches

at Abbadia di Fiastra, 4 km

Abbey of Chiaravalle di Fiastra. Closed Monday morning. *Open 9.30am–12.30pm and 3.30pm–6.30pm.*

🏃 Festivals and entertainments

Rassegna di Teatro Classico (July–August) held in the Roman amphitheater of *Urbs Salvia*. Tel. 506385.

at Abbadia di Fiastra, 4 km

Fiera Mercato Nazionale dell'Antiquariato (week before Easter).

🌲 Parks and natural reserves

at Abbadia di Fiastra, 4 km

Centro di Educazione Ambientale della Riserva Naturale Abbadia di Fiastra. Local guides available by request, c/o Società La Meridiana, tel. and fax 202942, e-mail: pichin@mercurio.it. Services include a special nature walk for people with reduced vision.

Ussita

Page 118 ✉ 62030 ☎ 0737
ℹ️   *Pro Loco.* Piazza XI Febbraio 5, tel. 99124.
Casa del Parco. Villa Ruggieri, tel. 971000.

🏛 Museums and cultural institutions

at Castelsantangelo sul Nera, 11.5 km

Pinacoteca Comunale. Piazza S. Spirito. *Open on request, tel. 970063.*

⌂ Churches

at Capo Vallazza, 1 km

Sant'Antonio da Padova. *Open on request, tel. 99112.*

at Sorbo, 2 km

Santo Stefano. *Open on request, tel. 99112.*

at Vallestretta, 3 km

Santa Reparata. *Open on request, tel. 99112.*

at Castelsantangelo sul Nera, 11.5 km

San Martino. *Open on request, tel. 970063.*
San Sebastiano. Piazza del Ponte. *Open on request, tel. 970063.*
San Stefano. *Open on request, tel. 970063.*
Monastery church of San Liberatore. *Open on request, tel. 970063.*

⚖ Shops and crafts

Calvà Fabiana. Piazza Cavallari. Characteristic workshop for hand-made wooden articles.

at Castelsantangelo sul Nera, 11.5 km

La Bottega Artigiana. Via Roma, tel. 98309. Pork butcher's.

at Gualdo, 14 km

Fattoria Subrizzi Giocondo. Biological products (spelt, truffle oil).

🎿 Sport

at Frontignano, 9 km

Impianti di risalita (ski lifts). Tel. 90124.

at Castelsantangelo sul Nera, 11.5 km
> **Impianti di risalita (ski lifts)** for Mt. Prata.

🦅 Parks and natural reserves
> **Riserva Naturale Integrale Montagna di Torricchio.** Information c/o Università di Camerino, Via Pontoni 3, tel. 2527, 637211. *Open on request.*

Visso

Page 117   ✉ 62039 ☎ 0737

[*i*] *Casa del Parco.* Via Battisti 15, tel. 95262. *Ufficio Informazione Turistica* (summer). Piazza Martiri Vissani, tel. 9239.

🏛 Museums and cultural institutions
> **Museo - Pinacoteca Comunale.** Piazza Martiri Vissani (church of Sant' Agostino), tel. 95421. *Open on request, tel. 95200.*

🏠 Churches
at Pieve Torina, 20 km   ✉ 62036
> **San Giovanni - Pinacoteca Parrocchiale.** *Open on request, tel. 51308.*
> **Romitorio dei Santi.** *Visits on request, tel. 51308.*

⚖ Shops and crafts
> **Cappa Antonio.** Villa S. Antonio. Famous pork butcher's.
> **Ser Faustini Bernardo.** Via Castelsantangelo 5, Tel. 9261. Hand-crafted wooden items.
> **Troticoltura Cherubini.** Valle di Castelsantangelo, tel. 9292. Renowned center of production and sale of trout and salmon trout.
> **Vissana Salumi.** Via Battisti. Well-known production and sale of local salami and cold meats.

🦅 Parks and natural reserves
> **Ente Parco nazionale dei Monti Sibillini.** Via Antinori 1, tel. 95525, fax 95532.

Index of names

The index is ordered according to surname, or according to the byname or pseudonym of the individual in question, depending on which is better known. (Titian = Tiziano Vecellio). Where neither is indicated, the name followed by the figure's provenance. The page number after the biographical information denotes where the mention occurs in the book.

Abbreviations
arch., architect; *art.*, artist; *b.*, born; *card.*, cardinal; *d.* died; *doc.* documented; *fam.*, family; *gen.*, general; *geo.*, geographer; *engr.*, engraver; *eng.*, engineer; *milit. eng.,* military engineer; *med.*, medalist; *mos.*, mosaicist; *sc.*, sculptor; *stucc.*, stucco artist.

Index of places

The following index comprises place names mentioned in the itineraries and excursion, and from the "Other places of interest" section.

Photo p. 4: the Ancona coast at Sirolo.

Photos p. 5: Tolentino Cathedral Clock Tower, and a wooden notice board announcing medieval dances at Sant'Elpidio a Mare.

Picture credits:
Archivio fotografico Scala, pp. 21, 42, 88, 89, 155; *A.Buzzi/Marka*, p. 31; *Comune di Pesaro/Quattrone*, p. 24; *S.Malli/Marka*, p. 147; *Fabio Mariano*, pp. 13, 14, 15, 16, 18, 19, 40, 47 left, 52, 79, 81, 84, 87, 90, 99, 104, 109, 114, 125, 129, 131 bottom, 144, 157; *Pepi Merisio*, pp. 5 top, 11, 17, 20, 25, 26, 28, 29, 39, 45, 53, 54, 55, 57, 58, 59, 63, 78, 92, 93, 95, 101, 107, 115, 116, 117, 118 top, 126, 128, 131 top, 138, 140, 143, 145, 151; *P.Negri*, pp. 105, 108; *A.Novelli/Image Bank*, pp. 32, 33, 41, 43; *M.Pedone/Image Bank*, pp. 47 right, 60; *A.Pistolesi/Image Bank*, pp. 46, 75, 85, 121; *G.A.Rossi/Image Bank*, pp. 65, 102 bottom; *E.Salvatori*, p. 100; *M.A.Sereni*, pp. 77, 94, 158; *P.A.Tasman/Image Bank*, p. 82; *L.Tazzari*, pp. 4, 5 bottom; *Università degli Studi di Camerino*, p. 113.